Chasing Camels

From Yorkshire Pudding to Falafel

John Babicz

For my precious daughters
Larissa and Kimberley

CONTENTS

A NOTE FROM THE AUTHOR

In today's world with attractive technological gadgets taking over people's leisure time, and face-to-face communication becoming a rarity, it is easy to forget that there is a *real* world out there. Acquiring insight into the daily life of a Bedouin who lives in the Negev Desert; the various Druze cultures that inhabit the mountainous region between Israel and Syria; historical facts about Nabatean tribes that once wandered the Arabian deserts on incense-bearing camels; the price of a train ticket from Cairo to Aswan; where to eat in Istanbul; and the price of a basic room in an isolated Turkish village—all this information can be obtained at the touch of a button. However, real life experiences cannot be replaced electronically: To meet that Bedouin; to drink coffee with the chatty Druze; to ponder amongst desert ruins and try to imagine what life was like during the days of the nomadic traders; to be adventurous and not care too much about where to sleep the following night, and to simply embrace the unusual food that has just been placed before you. *This* is the real, ultimate pleasure.

The world is ever changing, and today it is different to the one I got to know while backpacking around the globe. But misconceptions persist. Israel is still misunderstood in the world; and Palestinians continue to be misunderstood by the Israelis; and Egypt is misunderstood by everyone—it has more to offer than pyramids and camels. This book is meant to entertain, but also to deflect any prejudices people may hold towards different cultures, lifestyles, and religious beliefs found in parts of the world most people have not seen. Once you venture into a foreign country with an open mind and accept all these differences, travel becomes intriguing. It is said that seeing the world is the best education one can have. I couldn't agree more. Those who have spent eons trotting the globe will surely understand. Those who have not traveled, with the dismal excuse that they don't have a fat bank account, should think again. More important than money, is the courage to simply "hit the road."

Exotic and isolated fishing villages, I was lucky to experience by the shores of the Red Sea and the Mediterranean, have now been turned into major tourist destinations. Prices have gone up—considerably. The Middle East has since become unstable, and nobody can guess what the future will bring to Israel where I spent many years working and traveling. Not everything is bad. Meanwhile, other countries have opened their doors to travelers who are in search of unique and memorable experiences.

Today, we are faced with the ever-increasing threat of terrorism: those dooming words that keep everyone on edge, but that is exactly what we are told, almost daily, embedding subconscious fear. It was the same while I was traveling in the mid-80's and 90's, when the media tried to poison people's minds with different kinds of terrorism and danger, especially in the Middle East. As hard as I tried, I never did experience any of it. Scaremongers will forever continue to haunt the news scene and to make sure the public remains afraid—afraid of the unknown. After spending many years traveling in such "dangerous" countries, I can honestly say that I had never felt threatened, but instead, met the most friendly and hospitable people one can only run into while on the road.

But beware! Traveling is an addiction—once started, it is difficult to stop. Getting started is the most difficult part—to cut oneself off from everything, to say goodbye to friends, quit your job, but maybe the deepest anxiety would be the realization that you don't know where you will be spending the next night. The rewards of travel, however, are vast, but be prepared—you will not come back the same person—if you ever come back at all. I didn't. The world is a wondrous place and will change you forever.

All places, events, and characters in my book are real, but the names of individuals have been changed in order to protect them (and myself). I have described places as they used to be, and may be very different to what they look like today.

Enjoy the adventure.

John Babicz

1
BREAKING AWAY

"The fighting between Lebanon and Israel rages on. Israeli planes bomb targets deep inside Lebanon. Scores of missiles are launched against the enemy. The southern part of Lebanon is a war zone with constant machine gun fire. Dozens are killed and wounded."

I had a knot in my stomach while fighting my backpack and watching the news that evening. The BBC reporter was on the war front giving a colorful description of the Israeli invasion of Lebanon. Israel was supposed to have started pulling out of Lebanon ten days previously, so were these the old reports or was the war still in progress? I didn't catch the beginning of the news, so I wasn't quite sure *what* was going on. My mind was in a whirl and not really focused, as I was too preoccupied with the realization that tomorrow I was flying to that part of the world. Such unnerving daily news reports did not motivate me one bit; invasion over or not, it didn't really matter anymore.

The eye-appealing photographs I had always seen of Israel were a complete contrast to what was being shown on the news every day, so what was the tangible truth? The war or the carefree life that was characterized in those alluring pictures? Those exotic depictions of paradise were *my* destination, but as my mind had been persistently poisoned by the media, doubt was creeping in, causing a sense of foreboding; even nausea, on my last day in England. It was too late to bail out now; not that I wanted to. My bulging backpack was stuffed like an oversized Christmas turkey—then there was the plane, probably my biggest cause of alarm, as I had never flown before; even worse, I had never left this country in my entire life. Despite the fear of the unknown, I was grateful to be leaving Leeds, Yorkshire, England, where life was just too dull for me. There was a big, enticing world out there, with promises of adventure, *and* it was awaiting my discovery. It may not be a perfect one, as one is constantly reminded by the vivid, dismal reports coming out of Ethiopia, a country that was being plagued by a severe famine. Indeed, certain parts of the world had their flaws, and so did Israel; not hunger, but it was unsettled by eternal conflicts.

My ticket and length of stay on a kibbutz was for ten weeks, after which, I was to return to England. The short stay didn't ruffle me, as I subconsciously knew that I would never be returning to live here. I had no plans what to do after the ten weeks were over... but what the hell! I had been told that it was possible to cash in the return part of the plane ticket. This would be the first thing I do, as the last connection to England—I would cut myself off completely and let fate take its course....

It all started many months ago when I had that nagging feeling that there must be more to life than the daily routine of work, eat, sleep—and that would continue until my retirement. This vivid compilation of my life scared the living daylights out of me, suddenly realizing this is what I was destined for, and I had to put a stop to it immediately. But how? Unquestionably, one needs to work for their pension! Wasn't that the general rule of life? I had not long ago finished school, and people were talking about retirement. Ridiculous! After retirement, comes death: quite normal. I spent many wakeful nights trying to decipher this enigma; this predicament I was in; whether that was *all* that life had to offer. "Surely, it couldn't be," I was thinking aloud, feeling fretful and confused. Was I in a midlife crisis? Already?

The revelation came to me one morning in autumn when I arrived at work; the answer hitting my head like a bullet and making me swoon. One man I was working with had recently returned from his holidays in Israel, having visited his relatives there. He was well past retirement age, but still worked part time to keep himself busy and for supplementing his pension, but officially enjoying his position as a retired upholsterer. Despite our vast age difference, our acquaintanceship evolved into periods of long and interesting conversations. He always emitted positive energy, compared to my other colleagues, who had long since turned into vegetables, and were also the main reason for my discontent; I perceived them as my destiny. This morning was his first day back and he brought in some pictures of his trip to show me. "Hi, Billy," I greeted, delighted to see him again. "How was Israel?"

"John, you don't know what you're missing," he grinned, then went on to show me the most exotic pictures I had ever seen; naming historical places and ancient ruins I had never heard of, and with names I could not comprehend or even pronounce. Jericho, Jerusalem, and Bethlehem were, of course, quite well-known; any first grade pupil will tell you they are names from the Bible. I knew *that* at least... and the Dead Sea? Yeah, I heard of it, but what *was* it exactly... and why was it dead? Mortified by my total ignorance, I managed to "oooh and aaah" embarrassingly, as Billy continued to mesmerize me. Were these places real? The pictures he showed me were far beyond what I had perceived Israel to look like. Palm trees dominated most photographs, and this alone had a strange pull on me, as I suddenly broke out in goosebumps. The only Israel I had known was the Israel constantly at war; reports seen on the news almost daily, and giving the distinct message that this is a "no-go" area. However, these photographs from Billy were of a different planet.

"*This*... is Israel?" I asked, totally spellbound.

"Yes, this is the *real* Israel... and not what you see on the ten o'clock news," he added, reading my mind.

"It's beautiful." I caressed the photographs as if expecting some magical infusion from them. Dumbfounded, I didn't know what else to say. Billy was observing my face, obviously paying attention to my reaction.

"I try to go every year, especially around this time when it's the most comfortable." It was October. "The summers are much too hot." He went on to enlighten me about the rich fauna and flora, the deserts, and the fact that one can sit and float inside the Dead Sea while reading a book. He told me about the all-pervading Crusader and Roman ruins, which are scattered throughout the Middle East. "You really should go there one day!"

It was that last remark that hit me—that short sentence was to change my life in the years to come, and I would never be the same again. Those seven little words penetrated deep inside my brain, and had I been a cartoon character, fireworks would have been shooting into space, launched from my head, and a chorus of angels would have been singing, "Alleluia!"

Once again, I had problems getting to sleep that night. All those images going around in my head—those incredible pictures Billy had shown me. *This* was the answer to my subconscious desires—to go to Israel—and travel to distant lands around the world. Now, I was traveling to those distant lands in my daydreams, imagining myself on a camel in a desert, still with that last sentence constantly repeating itself: "YOU REALLY SHOULD GO THERE ONE DAY!"

Next day at work, I asked Billy, "Did you see any camels?"

"In Israel? Nah! Never seen one."

"*Really?*" I was disappointed. Billy was still staring at me, still reading my mind.

"John, *why* are you wasting your life here? *This* is really not for you, this life you are leading. I'm sure you're destined for better things. You are young. Why don't you go and see the world before you settle down one day? Life is too short for you to waste it here. You can even go to Israel and stay on a kibbutz."

The words that came out of his mouth were those of a sage. His suggestions were sweet music to my ears, and he told me everything I wanted to hear. Years of yearning were about to disband, and the full perceptibility of that simple statement suddenly manifested itself. The more I conversed with Billy, the more I was overcome with wanderlust. "What's a kibbutz?" I asked, somewhat baffled.

He went on to explain this strange *kibbutz* to me: A kibbutz is a small community based on the purest form of socialism and Zionism. A kibbutz may have a few dozen members, or as much as over a thousand. People who live there don't own anything except their own personal belongings at home. The houses they live in and the cars they drive don't belong to them, but to all the members of the kibbutz. There is a main dining room, where everyone eats together; a laundry, where clothes are dropped off; a library; a kindergarten; schools; recreation areas; even a cinema, depending on the size and wealth of the kibbutz. Not every kibbutz has a school, but there will be one to serve several kibbutzim (plural) within a certain radius. Agriculture is the main source of income, but many kibbutzim now have factories, which bring in good money... and some have discovered tourism. All work is shared and rotated, but the people don't earn a salary for their input, as everything they need is provided—and it's free—even education. Sometimes, they don't have enough members to do all the work, so certain kibbutzim ask for help from other countries. This help comes in the form of volunteering. No money is necessary, as no money is used. Everything is provided for the volunteers: accommodation, food, entertainment, and even trips.

"So, I don't really need any money at all on the kibbutz?"

"Not *on* the kibbutz, but once you're outside, making trips or going to cities, you'd better take some. Israel is not cheap." That was it. I was going to Israel—but how to go about it?

I spent my days off going to the library and doing some research on Israel, but only old books with black and white photos were available. I even took out some videos I could find from my local video rental shop: movies, which portrayed the Middle East, thus giving me a better insight of the terrain, but ended up intensifying my yearning even more. But how do I get onto a kibbutz? I was perturbed by this dilemma. The library was useless for such information; it seemed that all the books were from the last century, and they even smelled musty. The search led me instead to a large bookshop in Leeds that was well known for its vast collection of books on every subject. Scanning the travel section, a particular book protruded from the shelf, not having been put away properly. The title caught my attention: *Work Your Way Around the World.* Seduced by the cover, I grabbed it excitedly and leafed through the pages. Diverse and exotic names of countries popped out, together with a compiled treasure trove of information on jobs that could be picked up around the globe. Detailed locations, and even specific addresses for making inquiries had been meticulously noted in the book. I flipped to the section which featured Israel, and there it was—the information I was seeking—an address in London, where potential kibbutz volunteers could apply. I clung to the book possessively, lest anyone should snatch it, and started drooling as if it was an extra elongated chocolate éclair.

Very eager to get home now and scrutinize this information I had found, I felt the adrenalin pumping through my veins, not even realizing yet that this book would become my bible for many years to come, guiding me to many parts of the world. That night, I wrote a letter of inquiry to the kibbutz office in London while watching the special news flash that had momentarily appeared on the screen: Prime Minister Indira Gandhi of India had just been assassinated.

I told Billy what I had done. He reacted jovially, patting me on the shoulder. "You're really gonna do it, I know it. I really envy you and admire you for this. You won't regret it."

I laughed. "How can you envy *and* admire me?"

"I wish I was young again and doing what you are about to do, but it makes me happy to see your stamina in this decision, which is going to influence your life... and for the better, too." He told me this with frank honesty.

Two weeks later, I got the reply from London—and an application form to fill out. There was the registration fee, the cost of the flight ticket, and the bad part—a series of vaccinations, which would turn my arms into pincushions. "Ouch!" I went about making appointments for my shots: cholera, typhoid, yellow fever (for Egypt in case I went there), and hepatitis. I could not get all of them at once, but had to return a couple of times to complete the full cycle. After being immunized against practically every nasty disease in the world, I was issued a nice *Certificate of Vaccination* (which I proudly included in my initial application) together with a form that also had to be filled out by the doctor. It specified that I was physically fit to work in a harsh climate *and* that I was of sound mind, which was a polite way of stating that I was not mentally deranged. My friends and family were convinced that I was, so I made do with the doctor's expert diagnosis.

There was not much to do now, but wait. My life was coming to an end here—this I could feel. I studied the book I had bought while listening to the new #1 release by *Band Aid: Do They Know it's Christmas?* All profits from the single would go towards famine relief in Ethiopia; the topic that was dominating world news. Ronald Reagan was also the headline maker: he had just gotten re-elected as the president of the United States.

Having submitted all the forms, a few weeks later, I received a letter inviting me to attend a group session in London and meet the other volunteers who would be joining me in Israel. Actually, it was not an invitation at all, but a mandatory briefing on dos and don'ts. I went to London as was required shortly after another tragedy had hit the headlines, also involving India: The worst industrial disaster in history instantly killed 8,000 people in Bhopal and injured 500,000. It seemed to me that nothing but disasters were occurring, or maybe I was paying closer attention to world events, and this was actually the norm.

Sitting in the slightly messy room of the kibbutz office, I was once again mesmerized by the slides depicting kibbutz life and popular historical sites that dotted the region. The enthralling landscape captions were like the pictures Billy had shown me, confirming the fact that I was not venturing into a war-torn country. The other group members, who will be accompanying me to the kibbutz, proved to be a pleasant and stimulating bunch, with an identical exposé of enthusiasm and excitement. The savvy lady giving the presentation addressed the subject with competence and alleviated any concerns we might have had. "And by the way…," she added, concluding the meeting with a final statement, "*don't* expect to see any camels in Tel Aviv." The group lingered a while longer and we got to know each other somewhat. Some were planning to stay for only ten weeks and then return home, but most intended to travel further. I was the greedy one —I wanted more—to see the world! We said goodbye for now, but would meet again at Gatwick Airport.

The meeting made me feel elated, appeased by the fact that this had been the right decision. While in London, I decided to see the famous Big Ben and the Houses of Parliament—places I had never seen before. The Tower of London was also on the "to see" list, but they picked a fine time to close it for restoration; however, a jaunt in Covent Garden presented an opportunity to browse through some amazing bookshops. This was my first time in the capital, but by spending only a few hours here, the feeling of being on the road ignited a spark that would soon transform my desire to travel into a burning zeal. Christmas was just around the corner, and the days were absolutely bone chilling. The dampness of the River Thames enveloped the city, which was quite colorless this time of year. People huddled in their warm winter coats and exhaled warm air, which shot out of their nostrils like steam from the spout of a boiling kettle. I took in the scene around me… and smiled to myself. My departure will be end of February, which meant enduring winter for another two months. Having been told that it is very mild in Israel this time of year, I could hardly wait for the departure.

Time was suddenly against me: I had two months left to quit my job, my apartment, my girlfriend, sell my motorbike, and get rid of my belongings. I transformed what I had into cash, which wasn't much. After Christmas, I handed in my notice, feeling relieved that this was finally happening. I had kept this a secret at work, only keeping Billy informed about the developments. The ensuing reactions were most discouraging:

"Are you crazy?" Boomed my overweight boss, his bulging eyes about to pop out.

"You'll get killed," commented several other work colleagues pitifully.

My friends were equally negative. "Well, it's been nice knowing you."

My girlfriend was in tears. "You'll probably run off with an Arabian beauty."

My sister was amused, dismissing my adventure as pure madness. "Oh, you'll be back in two weeks," she was convinced, putting me down as usual.

"You have to think about your pension and work towards it," was her husband's cynical comment. I was twenty years old at the time. "What will you do when you get back?" (I wasn't coming back.) "What about your job?" (To hell with it.)

"Israel?" My brother and his wife blurted out in unison. "What do you want *there?*"

I felt alone, not being able to share my excitement with anyone except Billy. Nobody encouraged me. I was enshrouded in scorn and pessimism, with the impression that there was some envy involved, as deep inside, others would have liked to simply get-the-hell-outa-here, but were lacking the courage to leave everything behind and face the unknown. I, on the other hand, had nothing to lose. At home, I sat alone in my room, thinking about the stir I was causing, and also about the warnings of "danger" from everyone, reminding me of recent hijackings that were also taking place. Even the weather was determined to make my life a misery in the last months as icy winter rains pelted the window panes with anger.

It had been almost three years since I started to work for this company —a large furniture store, which also specialized in bedrooms and kitchens. While there, I learned how to design kitchens, which was more fun than selling the furniture. It wasn't a bad job, but it just was not what I wanted to do. Of course, I was still a junior there, still learning, but also the youngest person. The others had been there for over twenty years, some even longer, and observing my colleagues—very boring—very lifeless—very grey, also instigated a fearful trigger in my mind, thus forming a mental picture of my life 20-30 years in the future. I would look like, and be like—them… if I stayed here. But there was no IF. Not this time!

It was still raining heavily outside while I stayed in my room the next day, thinking about all that had transpired in the last few months. The usual grey mist clung to the ground, and the probability of seeing the sun again in the coming weeks was very low. Yorkshire was cursed with eternal dampness. I was always sick—allergies. Every morning I woke up with puffy eyes and constant sneezing. Coughing spasms and phlegm seemed to be the norm for me, but the rest of the population of Leeds was coughing, too, so that shouldn't be unusual at all. My unhealthy-looking gray skin was always itching, exhibiting blemishes where I had scratched myself. I loathed this climate. Would I feel any different in Israel?

I was leafing through my passport; my brand new passport, which had arrived recently. I had never had one before—never needed one. It felt good with its black, hardback cover depicting the lion and the unicorn; very official looking, clean, crispy blank pages waiting for those exotic stamps—my entrance to the world. I could hardly wait to hear that sound: "Passport?"

That was the past. Now, back to the present, still trying to get everything rammed into my backpack. I tried it on and almost toppled over from the weight. There was absolutely no way I could carry all that—had to leave some stuff behind… and there was still the hand luggage. Did I really need that extra coat? Were four pairs of jeans too much? Maybe I was exaggerating with over a dozen T-shirts. It was over 20°Celsius in Israel right now, so what did I need all those sweatshirts for? It was only going to get warmer. I decided to redo the entire contents once more and leave half of my clothes behind (It was still too much). Anxiety took over rationality, and I kept rechecking whether I had my passport and flight ticket. I was advised to take Traveler's Checks instead of cash (which I kept inside a money belt) in denominations of twenty pounds. I managed to scrape a meager £280, which was what I had to face the world with—not much, but

I was confidently relying on my precious *Work Your Way Around the World* book, which would save me if I ran out of money. I would find work somewhere... somehow. On the kibbutz, I wouldn't need any.

I was staying at my brother's house those last couple of days, having sold or given up everything I had owned. There was one more thing left to do—to stop by for tea at Billy's house, as I promised not to leave the country without saying goodbye.

"So, this is goodbye then. In case you have any doubts, you will not regret this... believe me!" He then solemnly told me that he felt responsible for inspiring me to do this.

"Oh, I... I'll be back before you know it," I said hesitantly.

"No, you won't," he growled. "Maybe you don't know it, but I do. You won't be back!" Then he laughed. "Especially, when you meet those hot-blooded Israeli girls there." He turned serious again. "I don't expect you to write, but just promise me that you'll let me know how you're doing. That's all I ask."

I promised I would, and on that note, we embraced.

My other goodbyes were not as emotional: not with my friends, girlfriend, or family. Billy was a special person whom I was lucky to have known. He was the only one who understood my yearning.

My bus to Gatwick airport left at midnight. Panicking once again, I frantically rechecked everything, making sure I had my instructions handy in my money belt. I would meet the rest of my group at the airport. Upon arrival in Tel Aviv, we would be met by a kibbutz representative known as Ephraim, and then taken to a hostel in the city to await further instructions.

I said goodbye to my brother who came to the national coach station to see me off at this godforsaken hour. It was still damp and extremely chilly, spitting with icy raindrops on this last day of February. The heavy air made me cough. The red coach arrived punctually, and I was suddenly whisked away, but the trip would take until dawn, as the bus was stopping in all major cities on the way south. It was not scheduled to arrive till 8:00 A.M. For some reason, I was no longer as excited as before, but feeling rather miserable. Maybe it was the weather, maybe it was just me. It seemed that the entire country was covered by one giant cloud... ever present with its persistent precipitation. So gloomy. Total exhaustion finally took its toll from all the previous hectic excitement; I started to drift off....

There was no going back anymore, having gotten rid of everything—no more accommodation—no more job. My entire life in Leeds was about to become nullified—void—history. I wasn't sure whether I would ever see my friends again; or my girlfriend, who was still convinced that I would come back. The reality would dawn on her several months later, and I would start getting nasty letters. Now, all was being left behind, one day to become a vague, distant memory... I fell asleep.

"Sheffield!" announced the bus driver, letting in cold air as he picked up more passengers. I woke up briefly, but nodded off again as the bus continued.

"Manchester!" came the next announcement.

"Is that all?" I wondered. "Blimey, this is going to take forever. Can't even sleep!" Other stops went by in a blur; I was too drowsy to take much notice.

"Doncaster!" came the now familiar holler. I awoke with a start.

"*Doncaster?* Where the hell is *that?*" I mumbled to myself. It was dawn when the next announcement came. I didn't want to use the word sunrise, as this is such a seldom occurrence in England.

"Heathrow airport!" Several passengers now got off, and the coach became much emptier. "Next stop Gatwick." The magic word. I was suddenly very awake, feeling that knot in my stomach again. It began to rumble. I hadn't eaten since yesterday, being too nervous... and the sandwiches I had in my bag remained uneaten. "Gatwick airport—final stop!"

"Oh, my God," I said to myself. "This is it!"

So, where do I go now? I glanced at my printed instructions, which said to proceed directly to the Swissair check-in counter. I did as instructed and checked in, glad to be rid of the elephant on my back. The flight to Tel Aviv wasn't due for several more hours, so I hung around this beautiful airport—my first time in one. Finding my way around was easier than expected, and I was actually starting to enjoy myself by visiting the various shops and browsing through some books. I scanned *The Herald Tribune*, opening it up at the section where world temperatures were shown, and focused on Tel Aviv—sunny and 23°Celsius. Nice!

After having spent several hours in London in December to get to know the people I would be traveling with, it was easy to recognize two of the girls in my group—one of them looking quite "hot." They were coming from the opposite direction, also killing time.

"Hi!" we said to each other.

"How do you feel?" They asked.

"Nervous," I replied honestly. "How 'bout yourselves?"

"Also," they smiled apprehensively, then the three of us continued strolling around the airport. They were Sally and Judy... and shortly after, we were joined by Philip, who was also wandering like a lost soul. Kismet brought us together and we became good friends in the months to come. I no longer felt alone, but cheered up considerably, being with people who were sharing the same experience as I. My anxiety was diminishing, even when the Swissair passengers were called to proceed to their gate, but we still had to go through security.

The security officials were Israelis, and were giving everyone a good, thorough search. "WHY ARE YOU GOING TO ISRAEL?" One of them barked at me rapidly. I was dumbfounded by the question and pondered a reply.

"Why? Well, er... I'm going to a kibbutz."

"WHICH KIBBUTZ?" They fired back at me like a machine gun.

"Kibbutz Ha'ogen," I replied, still puzzled by this strange questioning.

"DO YOU KNOW ANYBODY IN ISRAEL?"

"No."

"HAS ANYONE GIVEN YOU ANYTHING TO GIVE SOMEONE IN ISRAEL?" They continued the interrogation in a cold-blooded, emotionless way.

"Er... what? Who?" I was confused.

"HAS... ANY PERSON... GIVEN YOU... A LETTER... OR... ANY OTHER OBJECT... TO GIVE... TO ANOTHER PERSON... IN... ISRAEL?" The interrogator repeated more slowly as if talking to an idiot.

"No... nobody... nothing," I replied, equally slowly.

"HAVE YOU EVER BEEN TO ISRAEL?"

"No."

"YOU MAY GO," said the woman with the dead fish eyes.

So... these were Israelis. I was wondering if they were all like that—grumpy and cold. Why were *they* doing the security checks and not the British? I met up with the other three again. "Wow, what did you think of that grilling?"

"Weird," they all agreed. After going through the metal detectors, body scanners, and bag searches, we were allowed to board the plane. Where *was* our plane anyway? I couldn't see it, but I was suddenly in it, and felt embarrassed for being so naïve. I had expected to walk along the runway, open the door to the plane, and look for a comfy seat. Well, it *was* my first time. Sadly, we four couldn't sit together: having checked in separately, we had been assigned different seats.

The plane started to move not long after being seated, then very quickly and suddenly, England was gone. It was all very swift, and I never even got the chance to think about plane crashes, hijackings, or explosions as it took off. Brushing such paranoia aside, the next thing I knew, there was a clear blue sky above, and the clouds that tormented England below, were left behind in the rumbling wake of the plane's engine. The seat belt sign went off and people started moving about. Food was being distributed, and my growling stomach made me realize that I hadn't eaten for over thirty-six hours, suddenly feeling extremely hungry. My appetite came back, and I felt surprisingly relaxed. Having new, chatty friends for company was the best antidote for anxiety attacks. The beverage cart came down the aisle, and some hours later, more food. This was great. I was ravishing it. It was the time of rebirth. A new life. A new beginning.

It was night when we arrived at Ben Gurion airport; the Tel Aviv city lights invitingly discernible from above, and not a cloud in sight. The landing was as smooth as the take-off, and shortly after coming to a stop, the plane was surrounded by soldiers with automatic weapons. Was this our welcoming party? We *did* actually disembark outside, and boarded a waiting airport bus that transported everyone to the arrivals section. I felt nervous with the military presence, but soon got used to such scenes, as it was to become a normal sight in Israel, in all cities and buses.

Unfortunately, my passport didn't get pounded; instead, they stamped a separate piece of document, which was clipped onto one of the pages.

This would be collected again upon departure of the country. This, I was told, was necessary if one wanted to visit a Muslim country in the future. An Israeli stamp in the passport would render it stained, and not allow the holder to enter an Arab country except Egypt, which had a peace treaty with Israel—thanks to Camp David. This was very considerate of the Israelis, who were actually friendlier here than in London, but maybe their hostility was due to their forced endurance of British weather.

The four of us retrieved our baggage and exited to the waiting hall to look for Ephraim, the kibbutz representative. There he was, holding a big sign with his name written on it. The unsmiling figure was standing like a statue. The statue spoke. "Good evening... or good night to some of you. I am Ephraim. Hope you had a good flight." He said this in a heavily accented monotonous voice without any expression. "Is everybody here?" He took out his list and checked it against our names. "Good, I will now take you to the Josef Hotel in Tel Aviv," said the robot.

Outside, it was amazingly warm, and I could see the silhouettes of palm trees in the parking lot. Ephraim had an oversized minibus where we all fit in comfortably with our luggage. Too bad it was dark outside. I was longing to see the landscape. It was a silent drive to Tel Aviv, everybody suffering from exhaustion and lack of sleep, but about an hour later, we were herded into the hostel. Dying for a bed, Ephrain didn't linger to chat, but left abruptly, which everyone was grateful for. "Goodnight, I will come back in the morning after breakfast and give you further instructions," said Ephraim sleepily.

I hit the sack immediately and didn't wake up until brilliant sunlight penetrated my eyelids in the dormitory. Such bright sunlight I had never seen, and as I looked out of the window, summer greeted me, but also the din of the traffic. Palm trees and luscious plants with enormous foliage of all shapes and varieties grew alongside cube-shaped concrete buildings that were painted mostly in white; almost all of them with a solar panel on the roof. I went downstairs and ventured outside, and most noticeable was the heat one only dreams about on a summer's day in Yorkshire. Something else was different: my eyes were not puffed up, neither was I coughing or sneezing. *What was wrong with me?* I felt like a million and exuberantly happy. Wondering what was for breakfast, I went back inside and found my friends also in high spirits. Amazing what a change in country does to a human being.

Breakfast was… umm… interesting: freshly-squeezed orange juice, tea, and strong Turkish coffee. I was suspicious of the coffee, as the granules remained in the cup, neither was I a tea lover (very un-English). Food consisted of natural yoghurt, short cucumbers, tomatoes, delicious bread, jam or chocolate spread, basic cereal, plastic-looking cheese (it was curiously shiny), and there was cottage cheese, too. That was way too healthy for the early morning, and the passageway to my stomach decided to close early as soon as my brain triggered the "do-not-eat-this" signal. I then realized with horror that the days of bacon, eggs and baked beans were over; more horrifying though, there was even a bowl full of olives on the table. FOR BREAKFAST? I hated olives. Forcing myself to eat something, I went for the bread and ate some cheese with it. The crusty bread was delicious, but the cheese tasted exactly as it looked—uncheesy. There was some consolation though—watching the others also struggling with such sustenance that had no place on a breakfast table.

Ephraim showed up as promised, walking into the breakfast room. "*Boqer'tov* everyone. That means good morning in Hebrew. I will now give you instructions how to get to your kibbutz," he went on in his toneless articulation. "I hope you had enough to eat. They have very good breakfast here." We glared at him incredulously. Mr. Robot gave us all a sheet of paper with a map, bus information, and directions to the kibbutz. "There is a *Bank Leumi* nearby, where you can change money if you don't have any shekels, and you can walk to the bus station. It is not far." He bid us farewell and wished us a nice time in Israel.

We went to the nearby bank where I changed the first of my twenty pounds, getting strange-looking money in return. Then, with a map in our hands, we proceeded to the bus station on foot, passing beautiful flowers everywhere. Trendy city people, wearing the latest European fashions, walked briskly through the clean and modern business district. My head was twisting in all directions, ogling at everything; especially the girls—all with blemish-free, glowing skin and beautiful long hair, looking as if they had stepped out of the *Vogue* magazine. No, I was *definitely* not returning to England. Billy was right—the girls *are* gorgeous here. That darned woman in London was also right: there *are* no camels in Tel Aviv. The sudden transformation from winter to summer induced a rapid change in *my* fashion—from coat and jeans to shorts and T-shirt, but I felt somewhat out of place with my gray skin amongst these healthy-looking Israelis.

As we approached the bus station, the buildings became more dilapidated, and food vendors started to appear. Loud, howling music was belching out within the bus terminal. Omnipresent soldiers swarmed the area—young men and women, all of whom had a weapon slung over their shoulders. They were waiting for buses; eating and chatting, like everyone else here. Just like at the airport, nobody took notice of them, except us, who stared in disbelief, being unaccustomed to such sights. I had never seen so many guns; in fact, I had never seen a gun.

Most people were eating something tasty-looking—better than that unappetizing breakfast. At the bus station, they were selling that tasty-looking-something. It was scrumptious-looking pita bread, stuffed with salad and meatballs, and covered in weird white sauce. I was hungry again (not surprising though, having had rabbit food for breakfast), and so, my friends and I got this "thing."

"You want falafel?" Asked the vendor in English.

"Falafel...? Oh, falafel. That's what you call it. Yes, one for me and three more." He put the unfamiliar meatballs inside the pita bread, handing it to me. He also noticed that I was a falafel novice, standing confused, with an almost empty pita bread in my hand. It certainly was a far cry from what the soldiers were eating.

"You fill the rest up with what you want and then you put tahina on top," he instructed. The counter had several containers filled with salads, pickles, and an assortment of sauces.

"Put *what* on top?" I asked, puzzled.

"Tahina—that white sauce." He pointed at it.

"Oh! Okay." I struggled with the strange currency, so he just leaned over impatiently, made a clicking "tut" sound, and helped himself to a note, snatched it, then thrust back the change. The snack was inexpensive. We stuffed our pita bread until it burst and the tahina sauce dripped down our arms.

The taste was out of this world, and the meatballs turned out not to be meatballs at all, but some vegetarian concoction deep-fried in oil. I found out later that they were made out of chickpeas. Oh, yes, I could surely eat this every day. Stuffing ourselves like everyone else here, we easily located the bus we had to take. It was already there, still with the engine turned off. Just to make double sure, I approached the driver. "Are you going to Kibbutz Ha'ogen?"

"SIT DOWN!" he bellowed.

"Yes, but do you go...?"

"SIT DOWN!" he barked again, glaring at us like a panther that is about to spring, daring me to say another word. We did as told, first paying the fare without even hearing a "please" or a "thank you." I didn't ask again, in case he pulled out his machine gun, which, I noticed, was on the floor next to his foot. A soldier on the bus called over as we walked down the aisle.

"Yes, yes, Kibbutz Ha'ogen."

"Why didn't that asshole bus driver simply tell us?" I muttered to myself. Next problem: How do we know when to get off? I asked the friendly soldier.

"The driver will let you know."

"WHAT? HIM?" I was doubtful.

I admired the rich green on both sides of the road once we left the city suburbs, noticing the orange balls hanging on the trees. We passed several signs written in Hebrew, Arabic, and English, pointing to Kibbutz so and so, all surrounded by orange groves—millions of them. After almost an hour on the bus, I *still* didn't notice any sign pointing to Kibbutz Ha'ogen, and the driver was *not* announcing *any* stops. We were getting fidgety while this continued, then the bus slowed down abruptly, and the driver bellowed loud and clearly, "KIBBUTZ HA'OGEN!"

2
ORANGES AND MONGOOSES

Our small group made its way along the straight road that led to Kibbutz Ha'ogen. Several flattened, long-tailed animals I couldn't identify lay on the ground. In England, I was used to seeing hedgehogs in this condition, but these were alien creatures. Everyone else in my group was equally perplexed as we speculated the classification of this anomalous species. On both sides of the road, the orchards were laden with ripening oranges. I made a mental note to dive into there once the opportunity arose. The sky was cloudless and the air was pure (except for the stench of rotting "strange animal" carcasses). A white van came our way and stopped. A woman with sunglasses leaned out of the window. "Are you the new volunteers?" She inquired cheerfully in a sing-song manner.

"Yes, we are."

"Come in. I'll take you to Gila. She's the volunteers' leader." We packed into the van and were driven the rest of the way inside the kibbutz compounds that resembled a tiny village. Luscious vegetation and exotic flowers grew everywhere. The kibbutz was exquisite and immaculately landscaped. Complacent-looking people wearing dark blue clothing were making their way towards a large building.

"What's that place?" We asked, pointing at the largest building.

"That's the dining room. You know what? I have a better idea. I'll drop you off here, then you can go inside and eat. It's lunch time now. I'll go and let Gila know that you're here. She will meet you in the dining room. Stay together at one table so she doesn't have to look for you. You can leave your bags in the van—I'll drop them off at the office. Enjoy the food."

We did as we were told, following the other people into the building. Nobody took notice of our arrival as we entered the huge dining hall, packed with people. Everybody wore the same dark blue apparel, reminding me of the folk in China I had once seen on TV. We stood by the self-service buffet that was set up at one end and observed how the system worked; still, nobody took notice of us—we were completely ignored. It was no different to the school canteen system I was used to, and equally noisy, but the food looked more appetizing than the English palate. I grabbed a tray, plate, bowl, and some cutlery, then followed the food line. Some kind of soup entered my bowl, and I piled up my plate with a chicken leg, salad, and something that resembled couscous, but much coarser. There was an assortment of dressings for the salad, and I chose the white sauce I recognized from my first falafel encounter—tahina. Dessert was a dream—halva. I used to buy that delicious sweet in delicatessen stores in England. The others didn't know what it was, so I coaxed them to try it. "It's very sweet... made out of sesame seeds." There was also a container filled with extremely fresh-looking oranges and grapefruit. The beverage section had *Wissotzky* brand teabags like in the hostel, and also that peculiar coffee again that didn't dissolve, but sank to the bottom. It was drunk black. There was also hot chocolate and milk, or just plain water from the siphon. I took the tea with a slice of lemon, which was piled up in a bowl next to the beverages. With our trays laden with food, we looked for an empty table where we could sit together as instructed.

The yellow soup was quite tasty with unfamiliar-shaped noodle things inside. The chicken was done to a turn and tasted much better than back on the island. The couscous wasn't couscous at all, but tiny, slightly firm balls of pasta—delicious with the chicken. Best of all was the orange. I had only known oranges that resisted all attempts at removing the skin; the end result was always broken fingernails, followed by a knife attack. The peel of this orange came off as easily as the skin of a banana, without even leaving any pith on the fruit, which was the sweetest, freshest, juiciest orange that had ever entered my mouth. It almost dissolved on the tongue. I was about to get up to grab another one when a woman approached our table. "Hi, everyone, I'm Gila," she sang cheerfully. "Else told me I would find you here. Welcome to the kibbutz. I see you've enjoyed the food."

"It's very good," I told her. "I'm not quite sure what I ate, but it was tasty."

"There is also a crate with oranges and grapefruit outside next to the dining room," she added. "You can take whatever you want to your rooms. I will take you there when you're ready. After you're done eating, we'll go to my office first to do the paperwork, and then give you a tour of the kibbutz so that you get to know where everything is. Take your time and eat more. I'll come back shortly."

We stood out from the rest of the people, not because we weren't wearing the blue work clothes, but our pale, gray skin was not unlike the English sky. To the eyes of kibbutzniks (kibbutz members), our unhealthy zombie-like appearance must have looked quite sickly. Everyone else sported a healthy tan. We took our empty dishes and placed them on a conveyor, which took them through a giant dishwasher that resembled a smaller version of a car wash center, where the doors close and the vehicle goes through different stages of cleaning, finally exiting sparkling clean, like these dishes. It was an ideal system to cater for the masses of people. Back at the table, Gila came to pick us up and we followed her to the kibbutz office. Our bags were waiting in front.

She first made sure that the people she had corresponded to the ones on her list. "It's better if you leave your passports, money, and flight tickets here in my office. I have a safe here and you can pick them up anytime— just let me know." She went on to explain the rules. "We want you to have good experience here and enjoy yourselves and make new friends, but all we ask is that you respect our life on the kibbutz and keep the noise level down in the evenings… and take it easy with alcohol… and absolutely no drugs. I know many volunteers will wish to stay longer than the ten weeks, but we have a strict policy not to extend your time beyond that. It is nothing personal, but we like to give as many people as possible a chance to experience kibbutz life. For those of you who wish to stay longer in Israel, and plan to go to another kibbutz afterward, the kibbutz office in Tel Aviv can place you on one. That will not be a problem."

"Will we be working with the oranges?" Somebody asked.

"Most likely not. You will probably work in the plastics factory or in the dining room. You only have to work six hours a day—from Sunday to Friday. Saturday is our Sabbath, so you don't work. There are also no buses that day, but it's easy to get a lift if you want to go to the beach in Netanya, which is not far from here."

The revelation that we would not be working outside was a slap in the face, as I had imagined myself working on the orange harvest. That task was performed by the kibbutzniks, we were told. I couldn't envisage having come all the way to Israel to end up working in a factory. Things were looking bad—no orange picking *and* no camels.

Gila gave us our bed sheets and blankets and allocated our rooms. "Oh, one more thing," she almost forgot to tell us, "there is a shop on the kibbutz if you need to buy some other things you may want, like chocolates or beer. We don't use cash on the kibbutz, only coupons. These you can buy here in the office, and you will also get pocket money every month, also in the form of coupons for you to use in the *kolbo*."

"In the what?" We asked.

"*Kolbo*. That's Hebrew for shop. You will learn many more words in time," she smiled. "At the end of your stay, the kibbutz will organize a 3-day trip to the Golan Heights and *Kinneret*."

"*Kinneret?*" I had never heard of it.

"You call it the Sea of Galilee. Any more questions?"

"What time do we start work?" Someone asked.

"It depends what shift you are on, but most of you will start at 6:00 A.M." There were gasps of disbelief. "You will start a day after tomorrow. First, I will show you around the kibbutz: where the laundry is, the games room, the entertainment room, volleyball and basketball courts, and of course, your rooms. We will go there now."

"I have one more question," I interrupted. "What are those flat long-tailed animals on the road?"

"They eat snakes," she told us, frowning slightly as she didn't know the English word. "Eat snakes" was not very enlightening, and we all looked puzzled. "Wait, let me look in the dictionary…. Is that what you call it?" She laughed, "…Mongoose?"

"Ah, mongoose." Of course, I had heard of mongooses, but had no idea what they looked like in one piece and 3-dimensional, *or* that they even ate snakes.

"You have snakes here?" One of the girls asked nervously.

"Oh yes, many. Just be careful if you go into the orchards, but most of them are harmless," she tried to reassure the girl who had just gulped, obviously not a snake fan. I noticed that Philip's face took on a look of terror.

Our rooms were very spartan and basic. There were always two volunteers to a room, two bedside cabinets, and a small table with two chairs. A wardrobe in the corner was divided into two. Stone tiles covered the floor, and an air-conditioner was built into a wall. My roommate was a Mexican volunteer called Pepe, whose English was rather bad, but that didn't deter his genuine friendliness, grasping my hand and shaking it vigorously. There were several other nationalities I was to meet: another Mexican, a guy from Chile, Switzerland, a couple from Columbia and Canada, there were Dutch, Swedes, Germans, Danes, three offensively loud and drunk cockneys, and some other English who seemed more civilized. It was a mixed bunch, but the English were dominant.

We threw our stuff onto the beds and followed Gila for a tour of the kibbutz, starting from the center—the dining room. She showed us the location of the crates containing the oranges and grapefruit. "There is an orange squeezer in the volunteers' kitchen if you want to drink juice—just help yourself." Next, was the laundry building. "This is where you bring all your clothes, but make sure you label them and put them into the laundry net I gave you." We were shown the post office and the *kolbo*, which was very small, but did have a good assortment of goodies. All were conveniently located around the dining room building. "Let me show you our plastics factory now." This was the ugly building at the other end of the kibbutz, which I didn't really care for, but had a feeling I would inevitably end up working there. She led us inside and gave us a tour of the factory. Actually, it wasn't as bad as I'd expected, and the people working there looked friendly enough. Most of them were just standing around and chatting. A grinning, sweaty guy with oil-stained overalls was stooped over one machine, banging with a spanner. Different shades of plastic sheets were produced on rolls, like carpets. "Most of you will work here sometime. There are four shifts of six hours each, starting at midnight," she reminded us. Gila also pointed out the clinic in case anyone should get sick, then proceeded to show us the kibbutz grounds.

The houses were all bungalow style—very quaint and very modern, set in the most picturesque gardens of lush greenery where different varieties of crooked palm trees dwarfed the houses below. Healthy, vigorous-growing willows trailed their limp, skinny branches to the ground. Giant cacti, several meters high, fanning out in all directions added the exotic touch. Gila stopped at one of the cacti to point out the fruit that was growing from it. "This, you can eat. We call it *sabra*—sweet on the inside, and tough and protective on the outside. A *Sabra* is also a name given to a native-born Israeli, whom we associate with the fruit," she educated us proudly, "but don't pick it with your hands, otherwise you'll never get the spikes out," we were warned. I had seen cactus fruit for sale a few times in England, but for a very hefty price. Here, it was growing wild and was plentiful.

The kibbutz also had a nursery and separate housing for the children. They did not live in the same house as their parents, but in shared rooms in their own building, thus affording them a sense of freedom and independence. This enabled their parents to get on with their own lives without having to worry about shopping or preparing dinner, and other errands that would encumber their work. All people of all ages were well catered for on the kibbutz, and the students also received an excellent education, but also *they* had various duties to perform. There was no crime, no boredom, and no loneliness. Cars were available for any members who wished to travel or go to the city when necessary. I did not encounter any people who appeared to be in distress or tormented by modern-day woes; even the elderly had an important role to play and were thus respected and actively engaged in kibbutz politics. Utopia was real!

After the tour, we went back to our rooms to make the beds and unpack our baggage. The volunteers had already finished work and were now in a state of relaxation. Some were reading, some were playing chess, some listening to music, but the English were still in their work clothes and guzzling beer. We soon made friends with the others and had hundreds of questions to ask about the work and the unusually placid life that dominated the scene.

"We never want to leave. It's just great!" The English drank to this.

"The food is excellent and you can eat as much as you want," the Swiss remarked.

"The work is so easy; it hardly seems like work and they have breaks every couple of hours," the Dutch pretended to complain.

"How's the factory?" I wondered.

"That's the best, especially if you get the midnight shift. All you do is eat and drink coffee all night. There's an Arab guy who comes in and always has a tray full of Arab sweets. It's really easy going," said the Danish.

"Also, if you end up working in the kitchen or dining room, they're *always* having breaks. You actually get tired from *not* working enough," laughed the English again. It was a nice mixture of people, and I felt most content in this magnificent kibbutz. England was far away, shrouded in gray clouds and drizzle, and I was on planet paradise, ravishing it. As soon as opportunity arose, I would go to Tel Aviv and sell my return ticket.

It was dinner time and we made our way to the dining room once more. Volunteers had their own tables where they preferred to congregate. Kibbutzniks kept mostly to themselves, but were friendly enough. Dinner was a major disappointment after the wonderful lunch: grated raw cabbage and carrots, that shiny plastic cheese again (probably manufactured in their plastics factory), three kinds of cottage cheese, avocados, peppers, oranges and grapefruit again, bread and olives—too healthy! There was also that soup I had earlier, which I took again, plus some rye bread, cottage cheese, and two oranges. This was going to be hard to get used to.

It was the first time I had met so many different nationalities in one group, and several languages were being spoken at the same time. The volunteers were talking about the crazy prices in Israel and how expensive food was here. "Make sure you don't have any shekels left," we, the newcomers, were warned. This was some bizarre advice coming from the Danes.

"What do you mean? But we need shekels!" We didn't understand what they were getting at.

"In that case, they'll be worth less tomorrow. Inflation is at about 200% and prices are doubling before your eyes." The other long-term volunteers confirmed this fact. "Change just enough money for what you will need that day," they advised.

"And don't change money in the bank. You get twice as much on the black market," the cockneys recommended.

"Where's the black market?" I asked.

"The Old City in Jerusalem is the best place to change. Almost all the Arab shops will give you a lot more for the dollar than banks… and they don't charge a fee, either."

"Thanks for the advice." We were grateful for this information. One of the girls had changed too much money when we arrived in Tel Aviv and was now concerned that her shekels were becoming worthless.

"Spend them as soon as you can," was the recommendation from the other volunteers.

There had been too much excitement in the last two days, and I felt my body giving out. I went straight to bed and slept like a log, despite the noisy volunteers outside who were enjoying the warm evening. Nothing could have kept me awake that night.

I awoke absolutely invigorated and ravenous. Our fresh-out-of-England group still had a day off before we began working. The others were already fulfilling their chores. I checked to see if my new friends were awake; they were also just getting up. I waited for them, then we made our way to the dining room. Horror stricken, we gaped at the food selection. It was like at the hostel, and like yesterday's dinner—very healthy! There were some boiled eggs though, which I sliced up on my bread with cottage cheese. I couldn't wait till lunch when they would serve real food.

Philip, Judy, Sally, and I spent the day exploring the new surroundings. For us, it was hot enough to wear shorts and a T-shirt, and we soon felt the effect of the Middle-Eastern sun on our gray skins. We ventured into the fields, where millions of gigantic sunflowers were in blossom. I guessed they were grown for oil. A plunge into the orchards was a must, and we were soon stuffing our faces with the sweetest oranges in existence. They were not as orange in color as one finds in shops in England, but were paler and without the sheen. Anyone who has eaten an orange straight off a tree will be hard pressed to ever eat a lesser fresh one from a supermarket.

We went back out of the kibbutz along "Flat Mongoose Road" to see what else was in vicinity—more oranges. However, there was a small shop on the main road selling ice cream, and luckily, we all had some shekels on us and were soon licking away. Judy brought a map with her, which we studied. "There's no work on Saturday, so why don't we hitchhike to the beach in Netanya? It's not far," she suggested. I liked the idea.

"Yeah, let's do that… can't be more than half an hour. Has anyone ever hitchhiked?" I asked. Nobody had.

"I wonder where we'll be working tomorrow?" Sally was keen to know.

"Let's go back and look at the work schedule. Gila said it would be hanging on the notice board by lunch time," I remembered.

It was. We all scrutinized it to see where we were scheduled. I was put in the dining room and Philip in the factory—6:00 A.M. start. Judy was in the laundry room (big disappointment there), and Sally's first day was in the kitchen. Our prior enthusiasm was soon eroded by such duties, but we realized that most of us would change every week—rotating jobs.

After the delicious lunch and my usual oranges, we sauntered back to the volunteers' quarters and mingled with the others. I took out the map of Israel and studied all the places I planned to visit. Biblical city names popped out and captured my awareness: Jerusalem, Jericho, Sea of Galilee, and Nazareth were not just haunting names of far-away, ancient, biblical places anymore, but were real and reachable within a few hours or less. The Dead Sea was a "must see" on my priority list, as well as the desert, where I hoped to see camels. There was so much to see in this country: thousands of years of history, hundreds of archaeological excavations, and ancient cities that had once thrived in the desert and were now excavated ruins inhabited by ghosts of the past. The map itself was seductive, and I was determined to see every part of Israel. I had time on my hands and no deadlines to meet. The world was mine; well, maybe one shouldn't be *too* greedy… let's say, Israel was mine—to explore… for now.

We were given the dark blue work clothes to wear, but they were not mandatory. They were just to protect our own clothes from grease and dirt. I decided to go to bed early again and be fresh enough for the dreaded six o'clock start. I wasn't. The alarm clock rudely woke me up at a godforsaken hour, giving me thirty minutes to spare before making a zombie-like appearance in the dining room, and there wasn't even any proper breakfast to look forward to. I could have killed for some bacon and scrambled eggs, or baked beans on toast, but I knew that only rabbit food and dairy products would be served. I was not the only volunteer in the dining room, but two other sleepwalkers made their appearance. Three friendly kibbutzniks were already there. "*Boqer tov*," they greeted. I guessed it was good morning, but at this time of day nothing was good, so I just grunted a reply. "I see it's your first day," one of them saw the obvious, "maybe you should have a coffee first?" She suggested.

"Good idea," I responded as she got me one, not realizing that it was *that* coffee I had been shunning all along. It seemed to be the only kind of coffee in existence. It was served in a glass, and the granules sank to the bottom. "Well, might as well try it," I murmured to myself as I took a swig of this strange muddy-looking brew. I was instantly awake as the brown liquid passed down my system, and I immediately forgot about my lethargy. That was the most extraordinary and unique coffee I had ever tried, and powerful enough to blow your brains out. "Wow, that is *so* good!" I exclaimed with a huge smile that spread across my entire face and made me look like a docile idiot.

"You like it?"

"Amazing," was my response. "What's that strange taste inside? It's nice, whatever it is."

"*Hell.*"

"Hell? Did you say hell? Do you mean it's as strong as hell?"

"No, no. It's *hell* inside," she stammered.

"What... in the dining room?" I was getting utterly confused by this weird lady. She yelled out to someone in Hebrew.

"Cardamom," I heard one of the other Israelis holler.

"Cardamom," she repeated. "Cardamom is *hell.*"

"Yes, I agree," I acknowledged politely. I didn't know what cardamom was, so it was all hell to me anyway. The coffee was so strong, I was well and truly awake and ready for work and still had no idea what the hell was inside the drink.

I started off by straightening the tables—hundreds of them. We then went around exchanging the sugar containers. After an hour of work, it was time for a break as if we had been physically laboring for the last six hours. I got myself another hellish coffee and downed it with as much enthusiasm as the last one, leaving the fine sediments to settle at the bottom of the glass. One of the Israelis brought out some tasty pastries from the kitchen, which I eagerly attacked. Twenty minutes of sitting, yawning, and chatting, and then it was time to wheel out the large metal food trolleys, put out the dishes and cutlery, and carry out the food from the kitchen, and the first arrivals for breakfast were on their way. That was the work so far. We could now sit down and join the other volunteers for breakfast. There was a long break at this point until work resumed after breakfast, then we started cleaning the tables and put the leftover food from the servers back into the kitchen. I became a little more audacious with my choice of food, adding a red pepper onto my tray and another glass of coffee.

After the serving trolleys were cleaned and the dining room put in order again, it was time to start bringing out lunch. Again, there was a pause and we sat down once more and had our food and my fourth coffee. The break was long, but as the dining room started to empty, our work continued; cleaning tables and returning unused food into the kitchen. That was my first work day, but the word "work" was an overstatement to describe the duties I had just performed.

My day was over, and for the rest of the time we exchanged stories about our assignments. "How was the factory?" I asked Philip.

"Quite funny, really. Didn't do much. The machine kept breaking down, so we had breaks most of the time."

"Did you try that coffee?" I wondered.

"Yeah, lethal stuff." Dinner time came and so did the health shock, but I was desperate for another dosage of coffee or two.

That night, I was wide awake, unable to sleep from tossing and turning. My heart was pounding heavily, threatening to jump out. I kept glancing at my illuminated watch: two o'clock... three o'clock... four o'clock. Damn that coffee!

Friday evening was the beginning of the Sabbath, and it also marked the end of the work week. People wore their neat clothes, and white was the dominant color. Special food was served that evening—turkey schnitzel and roast potatoes; meanwhile, my sensors picked up on an assortment of delicious desserts. It was five-star food of the highest quality. I made sure to steer clear of coffee in the evenings.

It was Saturday—the Sabbath, and that meant no work. It also meant no buses, as they stopped running Friday at sunset and would resume twenty-four hours later. Sabbath was taken seriously, and all shops would remain closed during that time. After breakfast, the four of us attempted to hitchhike to Netanya and see the beach. Everybody told us how easy it was to get a lift, and now we were to test that theory. During Sabbath, even the main road was practically deserted, and the cars that did go past would not stop. Angry faces simply glared at us as they zoomed by. We took turns sticking our thumbs out, and occasionally a car slowed down and made a rude gesture. Some honked as they whizzed past. We waited one hour. No luck. We waited two hours, and still no luck. "Easy to get a lift, huh?" Sally kicked the dirt angrily. Just then, a lone vehicle was slowly approaching from the kibbutz and stopped next to us.

"Want a ride to Netanya?"

"Desperately. We've been waiting for two hours," I complained.

"What! So long? That must be a record." The kibbutznik also mentioned how easy it was to get a lift. "Must be a bad day today."

He dropped us off at the beach and also showed us where the bus station was, in case we didn't get a ride back. "Maybe you're just unlucky," he laughed, then drove off. The beach was pleasant, but nothing to die for, and the coarse, pale yellow sand didn't look much different to a coastline in Northern England. But the sea was a different color; not the dirty gray of the North Sea I was used to. This was the Mediterranean—the gateway to ancient seaports of long ago; especially this part of the sea, which had seen Crusaders, Roman legions, Ottomans, and even the British fleets pass through, all leaving their marks upon this ancient land.

The beach was practically deserted, but not surprising, as it was only March. For Israelis it was winter; for us pale skins, it was summer with temperatures hitting the 24°Celsius mark. We splashed around in the water and sunned ourselves the rest of the day until late afternoon. Shops were starting to open up; Sabbath was coming to an end. Walking to the center, we came across a falafel stand where we had our late lunch. Tall, skinny palm trees with tufts of foliage sprouting from the top lined the main road in perfect symmetry. This was where all the shops and fast food places were located, but most of them remained closed. There was not much daylight left, so after the previous bad luck with hitchhiking, we opted for the easiest way of getting back—the bus. The ticket window clerk told us which bus we needed for the kibbutz, and we got on, apprehensive to ask the driver whether this was the right one, in case he decided to throw us off. After the

Tel Aviv experience, I wasn't asking anything.

At the kibbutz we dived into the orchards along the way, where I had my healthy nourishment. "Mind the snakes," I reminded everyone. It was Philip who had a snake phobia. He froze, expecting all the snakes on the kibbutz to come looking for him.

I was thoroughly enjoying myself, having succumbed to such an indefatigable state, which I was in at that moment. My allergies never came back, and tissues were a thing of the past. My eyes were clear, and after a week of Mediterranean sun, my skin was also starting to look healthier. All this had a positive psychological effect on me, boosting my energy and making me feel like a million. I had never realized that a change in environment would have such a noticeable impact, but here was proof.

"How was Netanya?" Asked Gila when we saw her that evening.

"Well, it wasn't exactly fun getting there. Nobody gave us a lift. Lucky that one of the kibbutzniks was going to town." We told her how difficult it was to hitchhike and only encountered unfriendly drivers. "We were standing there for two hours with our thumbs stuck out."

"You did what?" Gila asked with a shocked expression on her face, then she burst out laughing. "You know what you did?" She continued guffawing. "You stuck out your thumb?" She cackled again. We were then told that the thumb gesture in the Middle East is the equivalent of the middle finger in the West.

"Oh, no. No wonder the other drivers were so rude." We felt foolish. It would have been the same reaction in the West if we had been facing oncoming traffic and greeting every passing vehicle with the middle finger. ("Up yours... but please, please, please give us a lift.")

"How do we hitchhike then?" We wanted to know.

"You point to the ground with your index finger," Gila demonstrated, then went off to tell her friends, still sniggering. We, the Brits, were *not* amused.

I was in the dining room again the following week, but taking it easy on the coffee. Getting up so early was also becoming easier and I didn't mind the early starts anymore. Hearty, nutritious breakfasts, ubiquitous in this country, were still something I had to contend with, but in time, such foreign gastronomic intakes would also become easier.

Week three put me into the dishes where I had to compete with the conveyor, which, I was sure, was set at too high a speed. Dishes were split into two sections—big dishes and little dishes. Big dishes were the ones that did not fit on the conveyor and had to be done by hand. Little dishes were steaming, red hot, finger-scalding plates, bowls, and cutlery. I was wondering before why the "dishes people" were always dancing around in the kitchen with no music, but after my first taste of having my fingers singed, I also found myself yelping and performing bizarre acrobatics, at the same time attempting to clear the oncoming, ever-multiplying dishes, which might as well have been glowing pieces of coal. Some dishes did not make it to the rack, but ended up with a loud crash as they hit the stone floor, breaking into smithereens. This brought on some cheers from the younger generation. My shift didn't start until after seven and lasted until the end of the breakfast period. There was a long break until lunch when the work resumed, and my day was done by about two.

After another week, I was promoted to the big dishes, probably the worst job on the entire kibbutz. Here, I had to fight with giant cauldrons that needed a good scrubbing. Enormous metal forms, some burnt and greasy, were carted towards me, surrounding me on all sides in a metal heap as I made an attempt to scrub them clean. A very powerful hose hung suspended from the ceiling and was used to blast away the most stubborn foods, which had no chance against the powerful jet of water that shot out of the nozzle. For this job, rubber boots were worn, as well as a plastic apron. I was rather slow with this new task at first, sometimes not finishing until 4:00 P.M. when I once lost control of the powerful hose and ended up shooting a trolley full of dry, gleaming dishes and cutlery, which were on the other side of the room. They did not dry in time for dinner, and people had wet plates for their rabbit food, wondering if the heating element had broken down in the dishwasher. I, of course, knew nothing about it.

It was a wonderful first month on the kibbutz and I was feeling settled in. Temperatures were now in their upper twenties, what in England would be considered extreme heat. Nevertheless, it was time to go back to Tel Aviv and sell my return ticket at the Swissair office. I tried my luck hitchhiking again together with Sally, who also wanted to sell her ticket. "Here goes," I said, making sure to point to the ground with the index finger. Amazingly, after thirty seconds, the first car stopped.

"Wow," was all Sally could muster in utter amazement. "We're going to Tel Aviv," she told the driver.

"So am I," said a robot-like voice. "Come in." We did. The polite elderly man asked us if we were volunteers, and how long we had been in Israel. "So you have seen nothing yet," he stated. "Israel is a very, very beautiful and fascinating country. It is a small country, but you can spend all your life here and not see everything." We drove on, and the man continued to tell us about places we really *should* visit.

Tel Aviv came into view and the orchards came to an end. He dropped us off in the center at the main shopping precinct on Ben Yehuda Street, wishing us a pleasant time in Israel, and continued to his office. After several weeks on the kibbutz, I found the city to be too loud… and it looked enormous. The airline office was located nearby, so we walked there first to get that out of the way. Cashing in the return part of the tickets was straightforward, and we were given the refund in pound sterling. For a moment, I was afraid that they would give us our refund in shekels, which would have meant searching for the black market to change the money over into hard currency. The shekel was losing its buying power day by day; meanwhile, the pound and dollar were skyrocketing. As long as I kept my pounds, I was unaffected by the rampant inflation. Everything was priced in thousands, and even a cup of coffee with a pastry ran into several thousand shekels, but that was only about £1.

While in Tel Aviv, Sally and I decided to make a day of it, strolling through the busy shopping centers and a mall we had found. A most ridiculous fountain is located in the center—a large, bulky, round, and extremely colorful object which spins and plays music; simultaneously, water shoots out and dances to the melody, ever changing its form. I couldn't decide whether it was a work of art or a hideous eyesore. We also spent some time on the beach, which was lined with expensive-looking hotels and tall palm trees swaying in the warm sea breeze. My skin was already looking very healthy and quite tanned, and I no longer felt so self-conscious.

The city wasn't so big after all, and we slowly made our way to the bus station, which was located in the older and run down part of Tel Aviv. It was Friday again, which meant getting on that bus before sunset—the commencement of the Sabbath; otherwise, it would mean hitchhiking back to the kibbutz, or worse still, spending a night in the city until buses resumed the next day; on the other hand, spending a night with Sally wouldn't be so bad after all. Maybe we *should* miss the bus... hmmm. Before I could think of a devious plan to accomplish this, Sally cheerfully announced, "We're almost there, let's hurry."

The bus station was extra crowded today, and hundreds of soldiers with machine guns slung over their shoulders sat around on the ground and the metal bars, which divided the bus lanes, happily chatting and eating falafels while waiting for their buses, as if this scene was the norm. In Israel it was, but I still ended up gasping in disbelief at this bizarre sight. It looked as if the entire country was going to war, but the soldiers were actually going home to spend the Sabbath with their families. Our bus came and was immediately attacked by a pack of young soldiers, clambering to board it. Sally and I were too slow at this, having come from a country where forming a line was practically a religion. I hesitated with a sudden wicked thought. "How 'bout a falafel before we go? I'm really starving." I looked pleadingly at the mile-long falafel line.

"But... this is the last bus. Don't you know?"

"Oh, it is?" I answered innocently.

"Anyway, splendid cuisine awaits us on the kibbutz."

We did manage to squeeze on, but remained standing as the overloaded bus headed out of the station. We were so tightly packed that the muzzle of a machine gun was pressing against my ribs. One of the soldiers fell asleep while standing and let his heavy M16 slip off his shoulder, which landed on Sally's foot. She howled in pain as the soldier woke up with a start, picked up his gun, mumbled an unconvincing "sorry," and continued to doze while standing.

We still had some time to spare before the scrumptious Sabbath feast; enough time to take a shower and put on some fresh clothing. Other volunteers were playing cards and board games. I joined in, playing chess with the Dutch. "Is the new work schedule out?" I asked.

"Yes, it's hanging there," said Philip. "You're in the factory."

"No, really?"

"Midnight shift," he added.

"Damn!"

"All week."

"Shit!"

Friday nights were disco nights on the kibbutz, but mainly for the volunteers. Discos failed their appeal on me, and it was only through physical force that I was dragged over. Giving up the struggle, I joined my friends that night. It could have been pleasant, but the English volunteers were unable to socialize in a humane manner and had every intent to drink themselves into oblivion. A dozen empty beer bottles lay around, tossed haphazardly on the ground, and of course, there is always someone throwing up by the door. It was like being back in England. *Wham, Blondie, U2,* and *The Bangles* were playing their latest hits. At least the music was good, but there was no dancing or lively chatter; two of the rowdy cockneys staggered outside with a bottle of beer clasped firmly in their hands while attempting to light a cigarette. Judy was also far gone. Shame on her. I made a dash for the exit, with Philip and Sally on my heels, and went for a walk instead. We sauntered along the dark and now spooky "Flat Mongoose Road," hoping to see these creatures in one piece, but had no luck. The balmy night brought out shrill insects, which competed with the loud music. This was much more satisfying than that morbid disco.

I spent most of the Sabbath writing letters to England and playing chess. Keeping my promise, I first wrote to Billy to let him know how I was doing and how wonderful Israel was, but at the same time, I was also dreading the midnight start in the factory. What about sleep?

Didn't get any! Midnight came and I forced myself to idle my way towards the dreaded factory. "Good evening," came a cheery voice from within as I ventured inside. It was time to change over, and the 6:00 P.M. shift was happily looking forward to bed. The Mexican volunteer was working with me, too, but before starting work, we were encouraged to take a break first.

"A break?" I looked at the guy incredulously, not believing my ears. "Er... I'm the replacement for the previous shift. I just got here."

"Yes, yes, I know," said the kibbutznik impatiently, "but drink some coffee first."

"Fine with me," I mumbled. Thirty minutes passed, and then the factory worker showed us what we had to do. Plastic in various colors was produced here on a large scale, coming out in liquid form, and then solidifying in large sheets as it was spun around a tube. When the roll was full, it was ejected forward by the machine, and it was our job to stand at either end of the roll, pick it up, and carry it over to a pallet, which was collected by a forklift. The spinning was fast, taking about seven minutes per roll. We worked for forty minutes, and then Shlomo (who seemed to be the boss) came over and told us it was time for a break. "But we just *had* a break," I protested.

"We're changing grades now. We have to reset the machine for the next order. It takes time. Go to the kitchen… sit down… have a coffee… eat something… or sleep a little bit. I will call you when we begin."

I wasn't hungry, but checked out the kitchen anyway. The fridge contained yoghurts, some bread, and freshly-rolled plastic cheese—nothing exciting, but there was also a batch of halva that I grabbed for my coffee. Forty minutes passed until Shlomo strolled in with a half-smile. "We are ready to roll," he said casually.

It was almost 2:00 A.M. by the time the machine whirred back into action and the spinning started. There was a yell in Hebrew, which was obviously a "stop." The machine stopped for ten minutes, then came back to life. We could see the plastic sheets spinning onto the rolls, but at the same time, it was tearing. "STOP!" came the command, and the machine died once more. Shlomo came over with his arms out, shrugging his shoulders.

"We have to fix this problem before we start the machine again. The plastic keeps tearing. It may take some time. Go drink more coffee," he suggested.

Back to the kitchen we went to await the call to resume work. Thirty minutes went by—nothing! I was surprisingly wide awake and noticed the *Jerusalem Post* lying on the table, which I grabbed to read. I glanced at the world weather: London, 10°Celsius—rain. "Hah!"

Just then, some more people came into the kitchen; one of them carrying a large open box filled with strange-looking, small and sticky pastry things with green nuts inside them. "Baklava," one of the Israelis told me, noticing my quizzical gaze. "Here, eat!" he commanded, thrusting the box towards me. It was the most delicious object that ever made contact with my taste buds. I was in heaven.

"You like?" Asked the other Israeli, who, I learned later, was actually a Palestinian and had a full time job in this factory. Shlomo appeared with rolled up sleeves, a sign that he was still working on the machine, trying to fix it.

"This is Mohammed. He only works night shift and brings these cakes from his village. He's a great guy," and he whacked him on the back, then helped himself to a couple of cakes, which he rammed into his mouth.

"Back whacking" is a typical Israeli trait amongst the male population. They will whack each other on the back to show their affection, and the harder the whack, the more they like you. Mohammed got a painful-looking, spine-crippling one, a clear indication that he was well liked and respected amongst the Israelis. I made a mental note not to get too close to any of the Israeli guys. I wasn't sure how brittle my spine was.

Overall, the factory workers were all good-humored and very easy going. They were like family towards each other and everything was taken lightly, including the constant machine problems. "We should be ready soon," Shlomo promised and went back to his machine. The "ready soon" turned to another forty-five minutes and another half dozen Arabic cakes with a glass of coffee. We resumed work at 4:00 A.M.

Finally, the machine started rolling and the plastic rolls were intact. The remaining two hours passed quickly, and then the next shift came in; amongst them, two of the red-eyed English volunteers who looked as if they had spent the night on the binge. "How did the night go?" They asked.

"Oh, it was great," I answered honestly. I couldn't believe that I was saying this, but I thoroughly enjoyed working here, especially the graveyard shift. "Did you try the Arab cakes?" I asked them.

"No bloody chance! Not touching that foreign crap." They made a face.

"See you at midnight. Have a good sleep... and thank you," commented Shlomo. Despite the amounts of coffee I had consumed, I soon fell asleep and didn't wake up until the latter part of lunch. I leaped out of bed and rushed off to the dining room, hoping that the food trolleys were still there. They were, but the other volunteers weren't. I sat alone, gobbling up my lunch.

It was already the end of the work day for some volunteers who were now taking a siesta. Philip started his 12:00 P.M. factory shift. He had been assigned to the factory since we first arrived, not having experienced any other work, but he liked it there and didn't complain. Judy was also stuck in the laundry house all that time, which she also had gotten used to. But it didn't really make any difference where one was assigned because there was no stress anywhere (except big dishes, which I really disliked).

Several chess games were taking place amongst the volunteers. I joined in, playing with the hard-to-beat Canadian girl. We swapped partners, playing at different levels until the evening hours.

"Hey, why don't we form chess championships and compete against each other?" Someone suggested. "We can draw up a list of names to see who plays against whom, and the winners will go to the next round." So for the next few weeks, we battled it out on the chessboard, eliminating the losers. Our competition became so popular that several kibbutzniks even joined in, and we ended up playing for many long hours in the kibbutz dining room. This was also the last night for the Mexican volunteers. They were flying back home shortly, but would first make some trips to see the country's famous sights. We held a small farewell party for them.

At midnight I had to return to the factory. Shlomo greeted me with a smile and was as wide-awake as before. "We have problems with the machine, so have a coffee first. I will call you when we're ready." I did, also hoping that there were some of those delicious Arab cakes left. There weren't any, but there was some sausage in the fridge I helped myself to. We started an hour later, my partner for the night shift being one of the Dutch guys. Everything was going well for the next two hours until the now familiar Hebrew word for "stop" drowned out the noise of the machine. I could see that the plastic was tearing. Smiling Shlomo re-appeared. "It's a good time for a break."

"Coffee break or a break in plastic?" Asked the Dutch guy.

"Both. We have finished this batch and now have to change the grade again. It will take some time," Shlomo explained. "Mohammed should be here soon." Half an hour later, Mohammed did indeed show up, together with the same Israelis as yesterday. He also brought with him that beautiful box of goodies, which he placed on the table.

"Eat!" I needed no urging.

Almost ninety minutes passed until the machine was ready, and we continued lifting off the heavy rolls. After the fourth roll, it started to tear again, and the machine was shut down. Shlomo came over with a large spanner. Ten minutes of banging and adjusting the setting, then everything seemed in order. "Now *I* need a coffee break!" he grinned gleefully and disappeared into the kitchen. Shortly before six, our relief came and Shlomo bid us good night.

"Do you ever sleep?" I asked him. He seemed to be up twenty-four hours a day. He just laughed, dismissing my question with a wave of his hand. "Did I say something funny?" I wondered.

Factory work continued in the same way for a whole week; by that time, I was ready to go on a trip that I had planned together with Judy, Sally, and Philip. We wanted to visit Masada and the Dead Sea, but by public transport. There were too many of us to hitchhike. Gila, the volunteers' leader, made sure that we took enough food with us from the kibbutz for our 3-day desert trip. "Food is expensive in Israel. Try to take as much as you can," she told us. We also borrowed the necessary water containers. "Don't forget, it's very hot in the desert. You must drink all the time," she reminded us.

Getting around in Israel is very easy, and the public transport system is excellent. Netanya has a direct bus running to Jerusalem, but this ancient city required a "special" trip, so we didn't waste time with any sightseeing, and hastily changed buses to continue to Masada. Nevertheless, Jerusalem didn't feel as Jerusalem should have felt. I expected something biblical and exotic, but this was, after all, just a regular bus station. We jumped onto our third bus heading south to our destination.

From Jerusalem, the landscape started its rapid transformation from pine forests and limestone outcrops to the sudden encroaching beginnings of desert, as the bus made its downward descent eastwards. Evidence of Israel's ancient past began to emerge, where crumbled ruins blended with the tan shades of this jagged, primeval landscape. On parched, bare land, some Bedouins had put up a large black tent as a temporary abode. Their scabby goats chewed on the last remaining tufts of greenery. I kept my eyes open for camels, but there were none to be seen.

The desert came very suddenly. Not the stereotypical sandy type one imagines, but a barren, hilly, rocky landscape with small thorny bushes clinging to crevices that may still have retained some moisture.

The bus continued its sharp descent, causing the same effect on the body as an airplane landing. My ears started popping and temporary deafness subdued the sounds of voices and the bus. My head felt like a pressure cooker about to explode. I was not alone. The other three were going through the same ear-popping experience as we went down, down, down to the lowest point on earth—to the Dead Sea. All was silent on the bus; even the Israelis stopped talking for a while to take in one of the most breathtaking landscapes on the planet. A patch of misty, shimmering blue appeared in the distance, still very far down in the rift valley—the beginning of the Dead Sea. Low hills became threatening precipices with deep canyons and gorges, forcibly carved out by mighty forces of nature. At this point, not a blade of grass could be seen, nor any of those bushes we had passed earlier. There was no sign of life anywhere. The bus turned from its easterly direction towards the south, now following the coastline next to the turquoise-colored Dead Sea, which was as lifeless as its name suggested. Unusual, but persistent plants grew nearby as an act of defiance to this inhospitable terrain that was doing its best to eradicate all forms of life.

We were no longer descending as the bus continued south, but remained at sea level; well, Dead Sea level, that was actually about 400m below the real surface of the sea. A kibbutz came into view, surrounded by hundreds of palms growing in neat rows with clusters of dates suspended high up in the trees. Parched, towering brittle mountains served as the harsh background to the kibbutz, thus giving this oasis an even more luscious touch. But this was not our stop this time, somewhat later though.

Our arrival in Masada was like entering a furnace as we got off the air-conditioned bus into temperatures I had never imagined could exist on planet Earth. The eternal Dead Sea haze and the lack of air movement instigated a feeling of nausea, and my head decided to vacillate like a gyroscope. After downing a gush of water and stabilizing my equilibrium, I entered the dreamworld. Thousands of years of perpetual scorching by the vicious sun had left this landscape unchanged since the Israelites wandered in. Masada looked the same as 2,000 years ago, when residing Jewish families committed suicide, rather than be captured by the Roman armies. This had been the last Jewish stronghold on top of the mountain, now attracting armies of tourists who came from all over the world to witness a piece of this ancient, but bloody history.

Having done some research on Masada beforehand, we knew that there was a path, appropriately named Snake Path, that wound its way up to the summit. The name alone was enough to make Philip cringe. "Why couldn't they have named it something else, like... er... Camel Path?"

"Then it would get mixed up with the path going up Mt. Sinai," I retorted, having done a lot of research on this area, thus being familiar with names of places. I tried to make Philip even more nervous, jokingly informing him with: "Paths are named after the animals that use them the most." He paled, instantly losing the sun tan he had acquired. All kidding aside, we donned our bulky backpacks and proceeded towards the path. There was also an easier way of going up—the cable car. Cable cars cost money—a lot, and using leg power was free, so we had no alternative but the latter choice. This was also the most rewarding way up.

The Snake Path was clearly visible; the well-trodden rocks well defined and meandering 350m upwards, almost reaching sea level. This was the heart of the Judean Desert, and not a speck of anything green was to be seen. We topped up our water containers, which were already starting to get depleted, and we hadn't even begun the trekking yet. A fountain at the base of the mountain had been installed for this purpose alone. At first, it *was* just a walk, but once the gradient inclined slightly, the walk notched up a level to become a hike. It became steeper, and we were no longer walking upright, but bending forwards slightly to prevent the weight of our backpacks from toppling us backwards. Our pace became slower, and the strain could be felt in the biceps and thighs as the difficulty scale was cranked up two more notches. Looking back after a water rest, I could see the vast expanse of the Dead Sea and the high mountains of Jordan. We were the only fools attempting to reach the top on foot, but it was perfect, not to be a part of the crowd that was using the cable car. The silence was so intense, it suppressed our conversation. Such an arduous trek was not for the timid, as the path narrowed dangerously and a wrong footing would send a hiker plunging down to meet its creator. We were now bending over at a 90-degree angle, looking like hunch-backed primates from a distance with our dangling arms almost scraping the ground. The path took on an almost vertical route, so steep that steps and handrails had been installed as sheer exhaustion left no choice but to drag oneself up. The difficulty level was maxed out, reaching the bloody madness level, and our water supply was simply disappearing. If there was no water on top, we would have a severe problem.

The Judean Desert is a landscape that pops right out of the Bible. It still is very much a wilderness and has remained unaffected by Israeli modernization. The Romans would have admired the same kind of landscape as they dodged the boulders that had been rolled down towards the encroaching legions, and could still be seen at the base of Masada, just where they had stopped and have remained unmoved for 2,000 years.

Finally, with the few remaining steps, we entered the fortress, which would serve as our hotel for the night. A sign on top reminded tourists that it is forbidden to remain on top of Masada between sunset and sunrise. We took no heed of the warning, but looked at the sign and shrugged our shoulders in a "who cares" gesture—of course, we were spending the night there. I was looking forward to the sunset, which was only a couple of hours away, but it was time for lunch. We found some comfortable rocks, using them as tables and chairs, then began with a feast—chicken, bread, sliced up Lebanese cucumbers and tomatoes, followed by oranges, which we had a ton of. Israelis catered well for tourists, providing running water even at this elevation.

From the distance, this cliff looked as if the top had been sliced off, thus providing a most perfect location for building a fortress. In ancient times, it was also an ideal place to build a fire and signal other tribes who awaited other signals from afar, which announced the beginning of the month, and passing on this message to the next highest and visible point where fire signals could be seen. In such a way, this chain of beacons made it possible to pass on messages throughout the length of the country. For this reason, we did not build a fire when it got dark, announcing to the world that "we are here, come and arrest us!" The second reason was that there was nothing to burn.

The plateau was inundated with ruins. Signs written in Hebrew and English described what each one represented. There was an armory, storehouses for food and grain, and cisterns where rain water was collected. We entered an underground chamber that was probably one of the cisterns, and decided that this would serve well for the night. First of all, we fulfilled our tourist duty to witness the sunset together with a small crowd that had gathered to see this act of nature, but my attention was drawn to the

Jordanian mountains that had now turned a rich pink, and were changing to a deep rose color as the sun dipped below the horizon. With the show over, the tourists dissipated and made their way back down by cable car. *We* went the opposite direction and also disappeared, but like silent shadows… into the underground cistern; not daring to make any noise at first, in case we got discovered by the guards who were making sure that everyone had left. We waited until the last glow of daylight faded away and darkness enveloped the world outside. The guards were gone, too, and we had the mountain to ourselves. Alone, I would most certainly have freaked out with my imagination running wild and envisaging ghosts of Roman armies coming back to life. With the four of us, it was somewhat more bearable, but only slightly. The candlelight cast grotesque shadows on the walls of this ancient chamber—the small flame illuminating the place as if it was a 100-watt light bulb. We had a small gas cooker that we used for preparing some coffee, enjoying it with the kibbutz goodies. Our sleeping bags were spread out on the ground, but before turning in for the night, we ventured back outside to take a look at the sky. Trillions of stars dazzled so brightly, casting a faint glow upon the landscape. The moon was not out, but I would have loved to be up here during full moon when the desert is blanketed in silver light. Silence was total, without even a single insect disturbing the peace. For some unknown reason, we also whispered, nervous to speak normally as we trepidatiously clambered amongst the ruins in the middle of the night.

Back in our sleeping bags, we blew out the candle and there was a gasp from everyone as the darkest of darkness descended at the snap of a finger. The glowing wick continued to disperse the pitch darkness for a minute longer, but it lost the battle and we found ourselves in total blackout, so oppressing that even a ghost would have been spooked. We huddled closer to each other, making sure that nobody had disappeared into the black hole. Our voices were louder in the penetrating black pit, resonating against the chamber walls, so we continued to whisper, but even *that* sounded amplified and sinister like in a haunted house. It was better to hush up until sleep took over.

Bright daylight shone through the opening, forcing us to wake up. It was already eight o'clock, and soon the first tourists would be arriving. Maybe they were already here and about to discover four slumbering mummies inside a cistern. We hurriedly stuffed our things into the backpacks and gingerly climbed out from underground. A handful of early birds were *already* clambering amongst the ruins, but nobody took notice as we suddenly materialized out of nowhere. We sat down for a while, eating oranges for breakfast, transfixed by the encompassing view. The Dead Sea was barely visible, being just a haze, but I was enraptured by the stunningly beautiful, bleak desert; the barren, inhospitable canyons, which stretched far beyond the horizon. It was time to make our way back down. A guard stood by the entrance as we started the downward climb. "Did you sleep well?" He suddenly asked, eyeing us accusingly, but at the same time forcing himself not to smile. We were taken by surprise.

"Er... yes... umm, good morning," was our response as we briskly walked passed him.

"How did he know?" Hissed Sally.

Walking back down took less than forty minutes, but because of the loose stones, it was important to watch ones step. It would have been too easy to sprain an ankle. To my disappointment, but to Philip's relief, not a single snake crossed our path.

Feeling very dusty, we took the next bus further south to the southern end of the Dead Sea to Ein Bokek, an area that was famous for its mushroom-shaped salt crystals, which protruded out of the water. All seats were taken on the bus, and even the aisle was filled with compressed bodies, forcing us to edge our way to the end. Suddenly, there was a scream from the front as if someone was being murdered. I was already in the middle of the aisle when a woman on the front seat decided to start yelling in Hebrew towards my direction. I looked around, but everyone was staring at *me*. I shrugged my shoulders, not comprehending why and continued towards the end of the bus. The exacerbated woman screamed again, sounding like a constipated elephant, but this time I could see her rising from her seat. A long thread stretched from her pullover to the sharp earpiece of my glasses, which were half-tucked in inside the waistband of my shorts. Some laughter broke out amongst the passengers, but the front seat woman continued with her vehement hostility. Without realizing it, as I was trying to squeeze through the front blockage, I must have brushed passed her, and the earpiece of my sunglasses somehow hooked onto her thin pullover, and as I was walking up the aisle, the woman's pullover was rapidly ceasing to exist as I de-threaded her. She yanked on the thread, causing my sunglasses to drop out, reeling them in as if they were a fish. There was more laughter. Philip and the girls were in stitches; meanwhile, I was praying that the bus would stop and let me out. Someone caught the glasses, retrieving them for me. The livid de-threaded woman collected her mile-long yarn, still chastising me loudly. She had a huge hole in her side now. I could see the driver guffawing, too, but I sheepishly retreated as far away to the back of the bus as possible, looking for a place to hide. No amount of apology would have helped this now-hysterical woman who was committed to squeezing some blood out of me. Other passengers managed to calm her down eventually.

"If she's getting off in Ein Bokek, I'm staying on the bus," I warned my friends. Peace returned inside and people started dozing off again. We arrived in Ein Bokek and hurriedly shot out of the back door. I looked back apprehensively, expecting a crazy Israeli woman to pull out her M16 behind me, but we were the only ones getting off. I breathed a sigh of relief. "Why the hell was she wearing a pullover in the first place?" I wondered aloud. "It's bloody hot!"

Finally, we were at the Dead Sea, but I did not see any of those salt mushrooms that were featured in books. "Let's have some lunch first," Philip suggested. He was right. I was famished. We ate on the rocks, facing the famous salt lake. We still had some boiled eggs, bread, cucumbers, and schnitzels, which fared well despite the heat. The heaviest content of the backpacks were the oranges, but they were rapidly disappearing, thus making the bags lighter. We had left with about fifty oranges between us, and had about thirty left. As well as being a great hunger killer, they also quenched the thirst, which was endless. It was only April, but the temperatures were high enough to cause rapid dehydration.

Ever since getting off the bus in Masada, we were practically naked the whole time. Our bodies had acquired a rich brown tan, making us look like totally different people compared to the ones that had first met in London. That gray-skinned, coughing person, who had been prone to allergies, no longer existed, but was reborn. I was quite sure the others felt the same way.

We stealthily made our way into the Dead Sea, first feeling it with our fingers. It didn't feel like water at all, but more like thin oil. I licked my fingers ("Eugh!") and spat out the sharp, salty taste. The water was tepid as we cautiously and painfully walked barefoot on the sharp rocks that extended the entire coastline. The water was barely up to my knees when I felt a force trying to topple me over. I surrendered and found myself floating in a sitting position at a depth that couldn't have been more than 60cm. We were all astounded by this physical phenomenon, having seen photographs of people sitting afloat in the Dead Sea and reading a book, but to actually experience this oneself was something that could not be put into pictures. The only discomfort was the oily sensation of the water; otherwise, it felt like floating on a cloud.

"This is great!" hollered Judy. "Hey, can anyone swim in this?" We tried, but the movement was slow, like trying to swim in oil. In normal water, it would have been possible to propel oneself several meters after a good push, but in the Dead Sea, the best we could do was not even a meter.

Further down the beach, white rocks lay by the shore, but upon closer examination, they turned out to be rocks covered in salt. I broke off a piece and licked it—pure salt. I wish I had found it a couple of hours earlier for my hard-boiled egg. Continuing along the coast, I found what I was searching for—low, conical-shaped salt crystals that resembled mushrooms. They were by the shore in the very shallow parts of the water. The Dead Sea was constantly evaporating, thus leaving these awesome works of art created entirely by nature. Whatever object had contact with the water, had developed crystals, giving it a fantasy-induced, snow-like appearance like a fairy tale animation. We went back into the water once again to cool off. The oily sensation did not remain on the skin, but it soon evaporated once exposed to air and left a very thin layer of salt behind. We spent the entire day like this, in and out of the water, marveling at the salt crystals, basking in the sun, and fully absorbing ourselves in the total serenity of this region. A permanent halo remained suspended above the stretch of water, and a haze blanketed the entire valley, creating an enchanting atmosphere.

Leftover, partially-burned wood could be found scattered around the shore from previous visitors. We collected armloads and made a fire, getting ready for the evening. This would be our sleeping spot for the night, even though it was forbidden, so close to the Jordanian border. Once again, the mountains on the other side of the water turned pink as the sun went down in the west, and suddenly it was dark again. With the darkness came a more profound silence, and even the fire was unusually quiet until we threw orange peel into it and sent the flames soaring, causing them to crackle. I brewed a pot of Turkish coffee on the fire, and there were still plenty of snacks left over for a midnight feast.

Our private party was suddenly interrupted by an oncoming vehicle that had turned off the road and was heading straight towards us with a powerful searchlight aimed in our direction. We couldn't see what it was, as the blinding beam forced us to look away. Then it stopped beside our campfire and the light went off. A jeep with three armed soldiers and a large automatic weapon in the back pointing at us was enough to give anyone a fright at this time of night. "*Now* we're in trouble," winced Philip. The soldiers jumped out and the automatic weapon was redirected towards the sky, noticing that we were not a threat.

"*Ehrev tov*," (good evening) greeted one of the soldiers. "Ah, you are tourists, not terrorists," he said jokingly, making us relax after the military intrusion.

"Yes... er... we are... umm... camping," Judy answered meekly, but we were all expecting to get kicked off the beach.

"Do you get terrorists here?" I wondered.

"No, no. It's very safe. But we have to patrol the shores every night for security reasons," answered the other soldier while sniffing the air. "By the way, do you have some coffee left?"

"Yeah, lots. Wonna join us?" I offered. So all three soldiers made themselves comfortable by the fire, also sharing our oranges.

"You have a lot of oranges. Are you volunteers on a kibbutz?" One of them laughed. "Volunteers always travel with oranges."

"That's because they're so delicious here. We don't get oranges like these in England," Sally told him. The soldiers stayed for about twenty minutes, making smalltalk and recommended places to visit in Israel.

"Did you go up to Masada?" One of them asked.

"Yes, we slept there last night. Quite a walk up that path."

"Ach, it's nothing. Just a little walk." One soldier dismissed the fact that the hike up to Masada required extreme physical exertion. From the Israelis I have met so far, I didn't think anything could be regarded as physical strain for them. They reveled in substantial bodily torture and gloated over danger, unlike us softies from the West.

The soldiers downed their coffees and left as briskly as they had come. "Have a good night," was all they said, and sped off in their jeep to look for terrorists.

"They didn't kick us off!" Sally was surprised.

"I don't think they care. They were probably happy to meet some people and scrounge some coffee." Well, that was the impression I got. The rest of the night passed uneventfully, but the rocky protrusions in my back would not go away, no matter what position I chose. A couple of menacing mosquitoes tortured my other side, working on my exposed flesh all night. It was going to be a long one.

I must have dozed off just before dawn. Above the Jordanian mountains, the sun wouldn't allow me to make up on lost sleep as I started to cook inside the sleeping bag. At first light, mosquitoes disappear, only to be replaced by torturous flies that work the day shift and make life miserable for human beings. It wouldn't be so bad if they didn't bite, but in the desert everything seems to bite or is razor-sharp upon contact. The fact that flies land on all the food also didn't bother me, but the permanent buzzing over an extended period of time can drive one insane.

After devouring our final supplies and working on our last ten oranges, our backpacks were as light as a feather. We took a final dip in the Dead Sea, then made our way to the bus stop just outside the Solarium Hotel that was also a treatment center for people who suffered from skin ailments. A number of such health spas had been erected by the shores. Bromide and an abundance of other therapeutic minerals can be found in the Dead Sea, and are essential ingredients for treatments of the skin disorder psoriasis. Because of its low location, the area also has weakened ultraviolet radiation, making it possible to toast oneself without getting a sunburn.

The bus to Jerusalem was full of people returning from the Red Sea resort of Eilat. It had made a long journey, evident by the sleeping passengers. For some obscure reason, they nodded off as soon as the bus departed. Was it because of the smooth ride or the faint, hypnotizing, barely audible hum of the bus? I had no answer, but I *had* a good reason for feeling tired. I never slept last night and found it difficult to stay awake even though I was a standing passenger. I held onto the overhead metal bar, suspended from the ceiling, watching the same yellow/brown landscape whiz by, making me drowsy. It was like riding on smooth, gentle waves; up and down, up and down, up and... "AAAAAGHHH!" A piercing shriek woke me up as I found myself face down on top of a sitting woman passenger who was pushing me off her lap. I had fallen asleep and crashed down on top of her—she had also been sleeping. What a shock for her to wake up like that!

"Sorry, sorry, sorry," I kept repeating. "I fell asleep, so sorry." The rest of the passengers were suddenly awake, careening their heads over to see what the commotion was about. The bus driver hollered something in Hebrew through the loudspeaker and my victim answered, probably reassuring him that I wasn't trying to rape her. I felt myself turning a deep crimson color from embarrassment, still being apologetic.

"It's okay," she reassured me, but I did sense a little venom in that "okay" for such a rude awakening.

"John, what is it with you and buses? Do you always do these things?" Philip stared at me incredulously.

"It's *really* embarrassing traveling with you," Sally voiced her opinion, shaking her head in disbelief. Once again, I couldn't wait to get off the bus and was happy that the passengers slumbered off again, including the victim of sleep attack. I shuffled away from her slowly in case the incident should repeat itself, but I was wide-awake and fearful of closing my eyes. Sally kept prodding me in the ribs to make sure that I didn't doze off.

In Jerusalem the incident was forgotten after a very fine falafel, and I was happy to get a seat on the next bus where both Sally and I fell asleep on each other.

"How was the Dead Sea?" Was our greeting back on the kibbutz.

"Fantastic, but John kept attacking women on the bus," Philip told everyone.

"He did *what?*" The volunteers sounded shocked, and I had to explain several times what had *really* occurred. Philip's version was that I shredded a woman's pullover and attempted to rape another one, making me look like a monster.

"You have a new roommate," someone informed me, "from Africa." I went into my room to meet my new African roommate who turned out to be from Ghana.

"Hello, my name is Charles," he introduced himself with a handshake in perfect Queen's English. It was the first person and the only person I have ever met from Ghana and we became good friends in the days to come. Meeting someone from a different cultural background and to hear stories about their country was one of the pleasures of travel. New revelations about previously unknown parts of the world were an education I never got in school.

I was back in the factory for the next few days, then it was back to the little dishes. Chess championships were still taking place and I was still in the game. On the Sabbath, I hitchhiked to Netanya with Sally, where we spent a few hours on the beach and in cafés. The 10-week kibbutz limit was slowly coming to an end and we were trying to decide what to do next. I avoided buses like the plague for a while (for obvious reasons) and resorted to hitchhiking, which was, as I always had been told, very easy when done the "proper" way. Both Philip and Judy were returning to England after the kibbutz, but first they planned to travel around the country for a couple of weeks. Sally didn't want to go back for some reason, but to stay here for a year and try to see as much of Israel as possible. At the end of our stay, we would go to the kibbutz office in Tel Aviv to get a placement on another kibbutz that had no limitations on durations of stay.

I was back in the factory the following week, but starting at noon this time. Shlomo was there, too, bright-eyed and bushy-tailed. No surprise on that part as I had already decided that he wasn't human, but most probably an android of some sort—a prototype that the Israelis were experimenting with. How can he always be working? He greeted me with, "Have you had lunch?"

"No, not yet. Should I?"

"Go and eat first. We have a little machine problem. Will take a few minutes to fix." He grinned like a Cheshire cat as if he thrived on machine problems. I joined the other volunteers in the dining room, who were already nourishing themselves, and returned forty-five minutes later. "Ah, good timing. We are starting a new batch," said Shlomo as the machine whirred into action. "Now, I'm going to get some lunch," he rubbed his hands gleefully and left in his oil-stained overalls.

The machine was behaving for the next three hours until one of the workers switched it off. "Problems?" I asked.

"No, it's time for coffee. We'll continue after."

"Sounds good." The grade for a new batch was changed after the break, and that meant the "spanner job," which was performed by Shlomo. It was back to business as usual.

Chess continued in the evenings. There were just four of us left in the competition. Tonight's game decided which two will play against each other in the final game. However, the finals would have to wait until after the trip. Next day was the organized kibbutz excursion to the Golan Heights.

The kibbutz had hired a bus for the entire trip, taking all the volunteers along, as well as several of the kibbutzniks. Gila was joined by her 13-year-old son, David, who liked to hang out with the English volunteers for practicing his English. Four macho-looking men came along, too, bringing their M16's with them. "What are those for?" Someone asked.

"Security!" was the curt response.

As well as passengers, tons of food was loaded onto the bus: crates of cucumbers, tomatoes, peppers, onions, and oranges. We were going to continue living healthy. There were mounds of prepared schnitzels and other meats. Mountains of bread, sweet desserts, endless packs of coffee, and enough water containers to supply an army. With all that food and the four guards, it looked as if we were going to war.

We drove to the eastern side of the Sea of Galilee, where we would set up camp for the night. Dense clusters of banana trees with enormous foliage belonging to the local kibbutzim thrived in this area. This was also the lesser populated part, which was not frequented by tourists, and we had the entire beach to ourselves. Out came all the sleeping gear and the food, and cooking was soon in progress.

Despite the name, the Sea of Galilee is actually a freshwater lake fed by the melting snows of the Golan Heights and Mt. Hermon to the north. With heavy and sticky air, the lure of the lake was too tempting to put off until after lunch, and we soon ended up floating on large inflated inner tubes that had once belonged to monster-sized vehicles. With the intense sun bombarding us from above and wind velocity at zero, I was even sweating in the water. The humidity was so high it made us lethargic, and I was perspiring so much, it could have been considered a decent contribution to the lake.

"Food is ready everyone!" That sounded good, as I was famished. The endless supply of chicken and turkey in various forms would continue to dominate the food scene, as well as cucumbers and tomatoes; perfectly diced and so sweet that no dressing was necessary. Here, I also acquired a taste for avocados with lemon juice—a fruit I had never really cared for, but in Israel, everything tasted so much better, or maybe it was food more suited for this kind of climate—light and healthy. There were always baked goods and sweets in order to balance out the "health" scale, and after every meal, we had the usual Turkish coffee with cardamom for tipping the scale a little more to the unhealthy side.

Israelis were in their prime when dealing with outdoor life. Camping and hiking was something everybody participated in. They were experts at preparing food wherever they found themselves outdoors, always using fresh produce. I never saw any official campgrounds and neither any tents. The whole country was a campground—you simply choose any desirable spot, make a fire, and sleep under the stars. The only difference was that the Israelis slept with their machine guns, which I could not comprehend as I had so far never felt threatened and found the country even safer than England, but that was my point of view. The Israelis however, lived in constant political paranoia, expecting to be attacked at anytime… anywhere.

This was how the West portrayed this part of the world—a region in constant turmoil. The daily reports I had once seen on the Middle East conflicts and the missile exchanges between Israel and Lebanon, which the media latched onto, did not belong here. Why was the public not informed about the positive aspects of this country? My friends and family were still convinced that I was in grave danger, totally ignorant of the fact that I was in a much safer place than them, where they had to live with constant IRA (Irish Republic Army) threats, never knowing when and where an explosive device would be set off.

With the sun gone, the late evening moon appeared over the horizon, and as it continued to rise, the once placid lake became turbulent with waves pounding the shores. The Sea of Galilee was wild, but not wild enough to stop us from going back inside with inner tubes, where I was rocked from side to side. Silver moonlight reflected in the water and the air remained humid, sending carnivorous bloodsuckers to await my return to the shore. After some hours, the wild water subsided as suddenly as it had started, and a din of night insects and a chorus of frogs entertained us for the rest of the night. The Israelis built a large fire that helped repel most of the mosquitoes and gave me some respite for a while. We sat around the flames, snacking and enjoying the constant supply of coffee. The night was heavenly and there was much laughter, but it was time to look for a spot to roll out the sleeping bag as drowsiness took over. I sprawled out like a flat mongoose and watched the stars while the night creatures that inhabited the banana plantation serenaded the campers to sleep.

"*Boqer-tov*... breakfast," came Gila's cheery voice just as dawn was breaking. Israeli breakfast was still something I was not too enthusiastic about. How I now wished for sizzling bacon with scrambled eggs, and grilled cheese on toast. I had to make do with an avocado and boiled egg. There were, of course, oranges and grapefruit to eat, too.

Early rise and early start; we continued north to the Golan Heights, driving towards the Syrian border. The landscape changed dramatically as the bus started the noticeable ascent away from the basin area of the lake to the hilly region of Northern Israel. Lush palms gave way to deciduous trees as the undulating landscape took on a look of desolation. Because of the elevation, this was an ideal area for growing apples, pears, and plums—trees that needed the winter coldness. But in May, there was no hint of any coldness at all, being as humid as by the lake.

Our first stop was not the final resting point, but the beginning of a long and arduous macho hike not for the faint-hearted. The Israeli guides took us through rough, craggy terrain where no footpath even existed. We exerted our energy climbing steep, rocky basalt outcrops and back down the other side through pine forests. The ever-changing landscape was stunning, and we never knew what would come up next. If we had known, then the majority would have backed out—including myself! Our way came to an abrupt end as we stood above a waterfall. The grinning Israelis were ravishing our stunned and anxious expressions as it suddenly dawned on us that this was *not* the end of the trail, but the continuation was at the bottom of the waterfall. "It's no problem," announced the guide as he read our minds, still grinning malevolently.

"No bloody way," I heard a cockney accent. The loud-mouthed, beer-guzzling English volunteers suddenly became meek, whimpering victims of macho Israeli torture as we were lectured on how to jump down a waterfall.

"When you jump, try to spring out to the middle of the pool and avoid the sides as there are rocks near the edge *and* we don't wish to pick up pieces of you," instructed one of the guides. "I'll jump first and show you how." He sprang, fully clothed and without hesitation, ending up perfectly in the middle. "Oh, one more thing," he echoed from below, "the water's very cold."

We weren't given any time to discuss the safety issue of what we were about to do. The idea, I later realized, was to get us down that waterfall as quickly as possible before the reality of this insanity had a chance to sink in and feed off the subconscious fear. "Who's first?" Asked the other guide. Some brave soul volunteered and plunged into the unknown. We saw him disappear, then his head bobbed up. He was in one piece, but was screaming.

"Are you hurt?" The guide hollered, somewhat confused.

"No, it's bloody cold!"

"Next...," and we hopped in one by one. It was my turn. Legs trembling, I stood at the edge, not daring to look down to contemplate this jump. I simply took the plunge, and before I had a chance to think about the rocks and pieces of me strewn throughout, my body was immediately shocked by the frigid, deep water as I desperately swam upwards until my head reappeared. I crawled to the edge and immediately heaved myself out, shivering to death with nothing dry to change into. The hot sun never felt so good.

Four volunteers of our group were so panic-stricken that nothing in the world would make them attempt that jump. The Israelis were well prepared for such situations and had a climbing rope with them. The remaining four were tied up to the rope and carefully lifted down the steep precipice. From the bottom, it didn't look as high as from the top, but the waterfall and protruding rocks did not help that inherent fear; like jumping off the roof of a two-story building.

We made it, and the hike continued, this time wading in knee-deep water through a canyon, which later gave way to reveal lush, thick greenery. Wearing canvas hiking boots (borrowed from the kibbutz), which we were instructed not to take off even in the water, we walked and walked, or, I should say, waded and waded for what seemed like an eternity. We continued through the water, warming up again, but my feet were becoming wrinkled. The stream took on a different direction as we made an opposite turn and hiked through thick bamboo growth, which was infested with large and colorful insects. Some frogs hopped out of the way, disturbed by the rude intrusion. It became excruciatingly humid, making the bone-chilling rock pool water alluring once again. There were no paths anywhere in this area. We relied solely on the Israeli guides who obviously knew these hills like the back of their hands. I was convinced that this was one of the routes soldiers are taken on to bolster their fitness and endurance, but they would be outfitted with full combat gear and heavy backpacks. *We* had it easy.

There were no more fearsome surprises afterward, and the entire hike took eight hours to complete. It must have been the most exhausting thing I had ever done in my life, but also the most amazing and unforgettable hike one could imagine. Everybody was in high spirits after having survived the "nice walk," as the Israelis later referred to it. After arriving back on the bus, it was another 30-minute drive to a more level location where we set up camp for the night. A fire was soon made and meat was sizzling while the usual salad mixture was prepared.

I felt as if I would never walk again. My thighs were in agony, and I must have torn every single muscle in my legs. Taking my socks off was a mistake as my feet were favorite drilling spots for the mosquitoes. A nearby stream served as the wash area, and a place behind the bushes was designated the bathroom. "And make sure you bury everything," warned the Israelis.

We ate by the fire—the flames giving off enough light to illuminate our entire camp. There was loud, excited chatter about the suicidal hike, and the previous whimpering foursome were the loudest once more. We all helped with the cooking and cleaning chores, which speeded up the whole process. After everything was cleared and coffee was bubbling over the fire, conversations became more subdued until one by one we retired for the night. It was an early night for everyone and I was so grateful to finally get into the sleeping bag and not move anymore. If there were any insect sounds, they were drowned out by the loudest frog chorus in the Middle East. They were all around us, but I never did see one in the darkness.

There was no enthusiasm upon hearing the wake-up call next morning.

My body was in more pain than before. Something was terribly wrong with me though: when I tried to speak, only a strange sound came out and I couldn't find my tongue—it had disappeared. Panicking, I stuck my finger into my mouth and felt a thick, wet donut inside. That *was* my tongue, but it was swollen to the size of a potato, and as I prodded it, squeezed it, nipped it, I couldn't feel anything. I worked on my lips and noticed that they were also numb, thick, and crooked. Panicking, my attempt to speak to sleeping Sally beside me was a futile attempt. "Ahja ooh ngung eek," was all that came out of my hideous mouth. She woke with a start, then her eyes focused on my face and saw a monster. Her eyes shot open, suddenly (very) awake.

"Oh, my God! What happened to you?" She also panicked. "Are you sick?"

"Ahkahe eek." I tried to tell her that I couldn't speak, but my thick tongue did not move. It was totally paralyzed. What happened to me? Sally ran off to Gila to get help and came back running with her.

"John, what happened?" She was concerned, looking at my deformed jaw.

"Oohhhh," I moaned, pointing at my tongue. Caveman language was the only way I could communicate.

"Something bit you. Do you have pain?" She asked. I shook my head. "It's full of poison, but will wear off soon. Very sensitive spot to be bitten."

"Uuuhhh," I acknowledged with a nod and eyes wide with fear. She didn't seem too concerned, which made me feel better. I shot over to look at myself in the mirror on the bus, but could not recognize the crooked, thick-lipped monster that stared back at me. Only the hunched back was missing. I inspected my tongue, which really was swollen, but there were no visible puncture marks. "Damn!" I was thinking. "Definitely no good-morning kiss today."

Word soon got around about my lip and tongue deformation, and the curious came over to gawk, making me feel like the main character in a freak show. "John, you look gruesome." I growled in response, soon regretting it, as it made me appear even more grotesque.

"Your lips are all swollen."

"Why is your mouth crooked?"

"Don't think Sally will be kissing *you* anymore." I just glared menacingly at everyone, secretly hoping that the same thing would happen to them.

I stayed away from breakfast, not being able to swallow, but got some coffee, where I dipped my podgy tongue inside the hot liquid, hoping for some miracle. Sally was still concerned, with her arm around me, then I started to feel a tingling sensation on the tip of my tongue, and after several more minutes, the whole tongue was tingling. *Now* I was concerned. Maybe I had overcooked it, dipping it in the hot coffee for too long. My lips started to prickle as the venom dispersed, and within twenty minutes, blood circulation returned, and I could slightly move my tongue again as I attempted to drink something. It felt wonderful. The transformation from creature to human was almost instantaneous, and within the hour, I had almost made a full recovery and was able to talk again. The lips also straightened, the swelling disappeared, and in the second hour, my mouth was back to normal. "What the hell was that?" I wondered aloud, still slightly shaken by the ordeal. Sally was also relieved to see the human return.

"Are you okay now?"

"Yeah, seems to be normal again. I'm hungry." The worst thing was the fact that something had taken a midnight walk inside my mouth while I was sleeping. Someone suggested it might have been a spider. Gila thought a bunch of mosquitoes had held a drinking party inside my mouth.

"Maybe a poisonous frog hopped in?" Was another suggestion. The whole idea was repulsive, and I would never know what bit me that night. I shuddered at the thought. From that moment, I never again slept outside with my mouth open.

This was the last day of our trip, and we drove even further north to the Syrian border and made a stop to overlook the Syrian town of Quneitra, which was captured in the Six-Day War. Pounded to destruction, it now lies in the buffer zone and has become a ghost town ridden with bullet holes—the scars of battle were clearly visible on every wall. This region boasted an endless panoramic vista for miles around in all directions. The wind also picked up a bit at this elevation, dispersing the humidity. Another hike was on the agenda, but it promised not to be as murderous as yesterday's. This pleasant ramble led us through sparse coniferous vegetation where dormant volcanic cones had collapsed, and ancient volcanic lava flows provided excellent grip for clambering. Like yesterday, there were no defined trails, but we simply followed our guide, who never let go of his M16 while his partner trailed behind with *his* weapon. Gila also had a machine gun slung over her shoulder as casually as any tourist would carry a camera. Being directly on the Syrian border, the Israelis weren't taking any chances. The Golan Heights proved to be a hiker's paradise, but also a physical torture, as acknowledged by my shaky legs.

A letter from Billy was waiting for me when I returned. He was overjoyed to hear from me and asked about my further plans. He also wanted to know if I had found an Israeli girl. I wrote back immediately to let him know what had transpired in the last few weeks and about the Golan Heights trip, but omitted the "tongue" story. I had to disappoint him by letting him know that I ended up with a beautiful, long brown-haired English girl, rather than an Israeli one. I'm sure he'd understand after one look at her.

Only one week left on the kibbutz now, and I ended up back on the midnight shift in the factory. I started work immediately, very surprised that the machine was running normally. Nothing happened until almost three hours later when it was time to change the grade. "Call me when you're ready," I told Shlomo, familiar now with the routine. It was fast—only forty minutes, then the machine was rolling, but it was too good to be true.

"STOP!" Shlomo and spanner appeared. Some banging.... Action. Five minutes later, "STOP! STOP! STOP!" It was back to normal.... More banging.... No action. Shlomo reappeared with an entire tool kit, pausing for a moment.

"We have a *big*... problem," he acknowledged, shaking his head.

The chess games were over as I battled for many hours in the finals with the Canadian girl and reluctantly submitting. The ten weeks were also over, and it was time to move on. Gila had already phoned ahead to the kibbutz office in Tel Aviv to expect me and Sally, and she also gave us a nice letter of recommendation for the next kibbutz. The sad part was saying goodbye to all my other friends, but we all exchanged addresses and planned to meet at some point. Philip decided to go back to England and I couldn't fathom why—back to unemployment? There must have been too many reptiles and strange insects for his liking, and Judy wanted to do some more sightseeing before returning home.

Those ten weeks had been the most memorable in my life. I had never imagined that life had so much to offer once you get out of the usual menial routine. Meeting interesting people, making new friends, exploring the culinary culture, taking advantage of what nature had to offer—all that became the most important aspects of travel, and this was only the beginning. The members of Kibbutz Ha'ogen instigated a positive approach towards traveling in Israel and I will be forever grateful to them, also for their generosity by supplying us with advice, food, and everything we needed whenever we made a trip.

I left the kibbutz together with Sally, but before going to the kibbutz office, we decided to spend a week in Jerusalem first. It was a place that required at least a week to fully absorb, but time was irrelevant. We had all that!

3
GATES INTO THE ANCIENT PAST

Once again, I was forced to halve the contents of my backpack, making it more manageable, especially in the fierce heat that had now arrived and was here to stay. The coastal Mediterranean region is the most humid area, but as one starts to head inland to the hills of Jerusalem, the humidity disperses, and the clear air turns the sky into a deep shade of azure.

Sultry, oppressive heat denied us the pleasure of hitchhiking to our destination, but only the short distance to Netanya. Here, a direct air-conditioned bus to Jerusalem proved the most comfortable mode of transportation. It was mid-May, and summer was in full swing, which was not good news for those with fully-loaded backpacks. From the Jerusalem bus station it was, regrettably, a long (dripping with sweat) walk down Jaffa Road, leading us to the fabled Old City that drew hordes of pilgrims and tourists from all over the world to this wondrous place. Because of the sheer number of historical sites, we had planned our visit systematically by allocating certain areas for certain days, thus enabling us to see as much as possible instead of wandering aimlessly like lost souls. We had a week, but I knew that even with a whirlwind tour, what we would see and experience would only be the tip of an iceberg; therefore, our guidebook became our most important source of information, and for apportioning the best use of our time.

As we followed the map along the busy Jaffa Road, it still didn't feel like Jerusalem, but finally, the road came to a fork, and suddenly the imposing, impenetrable fortification of the Old City outer wall loomed over us, promising to fulfill ones' stereotypical fantasies of the East. Monumental castle-like stone entrances, known as "Gates," overpower any first-time visitor as they enter another world—a world seeped in ancient history. We were about to pass through Jaffa Gate, and as we followed the crowds of tourists inside, I felt as if we had just gone through a time warp that had taken us back hundreds of years, or even longer. All at once, I knew that *this* was the Jerusalem I had always dreamed about. There was a gasp from Sally as her jaw dropped upon the sight before us. I expected Ali Baba to suddenly come running around the corner with the forty thieves, or even Aladdin followed by his genie. "And for your first wish master...?" *My* first wish at the moment was to find accommodation and to get rid of these bulky backpacks, which were causing us a lot of distress in this heat, making us sweat more than necessary. Our wish was soon granted when a neatly dressed Arab gentleman in a modern suit approached us.

"Are you looking for a room?" He asked in excellent English.

"Yes. Do you know where there is a hostel?"

"I have rooms in my house." He beckoned that we follow him. "It's nearby... up these steps," and he pointed to a steep flight of steps leading to a dark passage. "Come, I show you and you tell me if you like to stay."

We hesitated for a moment, not quite sure whether we should follow this stranger into the dark passage, which looked as if it had been built well over a thousand years ago. "What the hell," I murmured to Sally, "let's just see what he has. I really want to get rid of this backpack, and he seems trustworthy."

At the end of the passage was a huge, impressive double door, which should have belonged in a fortress; intricately carved, it had visibly endured long-forgotten times. The man unlocked it with the largest key I have ever seen. Daylight instantly poured out as he ushered us into an airy stone courtyard, where luscious figs and oleanders grew out of clay pots. The floor was made up of elaborately-patterned oriental tiles, which must have been put down several centuries ago, as certain spots were completely worn out from countless treading of past generations. Against the whitewashed wall was an ornate bench that matched the rest of the courtyard.

"This, is my house," he pointed to the building in front, "and these are the rooms," and he showed us two rooms we could choose from; both containing six or seven beds, and both very basic. "You like?" he asked.

"We like," answered Sally. "It's beautiful," she added, and it was— not the rooms, but to be able to stay in such an ancient dwelling. The man told us the daily rate of the room, which was astonishingly cheap. We took it for the whole week. He disappeared for a few minutes while we collapsed upon the beds, exuberant to be rid of the weight off our backs. He came back shortly with a very small, stooped, shriveled up old woman with a hooked nose. She looked as old as the house and was carrying a small tray with two glasses of tea and a small bowl of Arabic sweets.

"This is my mother. She doesn't speak English… only Arabic." That was not a problem. The kind lady made us feel welcome and we felt at ease. He showed us the bathroom, which was another separate building in the courtyard, and was used by the family as well as the guests. It was basic and clean with a concrete floor, and also my first introduction to squat toilets. A pipe jutting out of the wall was the shower, but it was only cold water; never mind, it was sizzling hot outside, and a cool shower was a fine remedy. "I will leave the outside door unlocked, but will lock it in the evening. If it's locked, there is a doorbell you can press. There is always somebody in the house." We thanked them for the tea, changed out of our sweaty T-shirts, and went out to explore Jerusalem.

A kaleidoscope of vibrant colors greeted us as we blended in with the crowds pushing their way through very narrow alleys, where shopkeepers displayed and sold their goods; not only T-shirts and touristy junk, but a rich assortment of fruits, vegetables, and different varieties of sweets. There was halva covered in chocolate, and shops dedicated entirely to exotic spices, which were displayed outside in drum-like containers. Several vendors were selling shiny brass coffee sets and trays bearing the beautifully engraved Arabic script. I didn't have enough eyes to take everything in: apprehensive to look to one side in case I missed something worth seeing on the other. People of all nationalities and faiths mingled with equal fascination as several tourists haggled over souvenir items.

"Bargain for everything!" I was told before coming here.

The merchants attacked anyone who dared to display the slightest interest in an item, promising to give them the best price. However, the best price was always that which worked out best for the shopkeepers and *not* the customers. Sally flicked a tassel on a hanging checkered *kefiyeh*—the head scarves worn by Arabic men. The hawk-eyed shopkeeper detected Sally's scant interest and her momentary hesitation. But that was enough to distract one of his many eyes from what he was doing—immediately ditching the customer he was trying to coax into buying his other scarf; he pounced on Sally, snatching the *kefiyeh* she had touched, gave it a shake in the air, and spread it out in front of her eyes. "*Thiz* iz *all* hand made with zbecial markings and iz very, very beautiful work." Crap! Now we were in trouble.

"Let's go," I nudged Sally as we tried to glide away through the crowds, but the shopkeeper reacted with shock and horror that we didn't look to admire his so-called "zbecial" scarf.

"I make good brice forrr you." We ignored him. He persisted. "Do you zbeak Inglish?" We ignored him. "Barlez-vous Francais?" We ignored him. "Zbrechen Sie Deutsch?" We ignored him. "Habla Ezbañol?"

"My God!" Sally muttered annoyingly. "How many more languages does he speak?"

"Ruzki?" He made the last feeble attempt until another victim came his way—an elderly woman who wore a silly orange baseball cap with *Orange Tours* written on it.

"She must be American," I was thinking, because only Americans would wear such bizarre hats. She was, and the shopkeeper was all smiles.

"I love America. I have a brother who lives in..." We disappeared into the crowd before we could hear the rest of his nonsense.

Our shekel supply was critical; we urgently needed to change some money. That was not an issue here, where numerous money changers were more than happy to relieve foreigners of their valuable hard currencies. We had the hardest—the pound sterling, which delivered a considerable amount of shekels on the black market. It was simply a cash-only-and-no-receipt-transaction behind the counter of the Arab money-changers.

My second wish suddenly came true as we continued into the deep interior of the timeworn alleys. Huge, round metal trays, about a meter in diameter, containing the most seductive mouth-watering Arabic pastries suddenly materialized like a mirage in a desert. There must have been every variety that had ever been produced, and all were unique and dripping in honey. It was something I had fantasized about ever since first tasting such pastries in the factory on the kibbutz. I stopped and gawked at them, stupefied. "I guess we're stopping here," Sally laughed. She also found them delicious and had no qualms about sitting inside this café for a while to satisfy my gastronomic lust.

Inside were a few tables and chairs, dominated by snacking male Arabs. They paid no attention as we entered the café and claimed a table. The shopkeeper approached. "Welcome, you drink?"

"Yes, two coffees... and a lot of cakes." I had no idea what they were called because only Arabic squiggles was taped to the trays, so we got up and pointed out the best looking ones, which just about described every single variety. "Okay... I'll take this one here, hmmm... maybe that one, too. Oh, I like the look of that, ummm... yes, I'll try that also, and..."

"John, how many are you eating? You're gonna be sick!" Sally stared down at the laden plate, making me stop with three. She got only two for herself.

I almost howled in ecstasy as I wolfed down the scrumptious and still warm first bite of the most delicious thing on earth, saturating my desperate taste buds. One of the pastries contained apricots, cheese, and very green pistachio nuts. Although they were sweet, they were not sickly; the baker having used just the right amount of honey and sugar. The coffee I found to be even tastier than on the kibbutz. Sally savaged her pastries in an equally voracious manner, and we ended up making a daily stop here.

The problem here was that it was impossible *not* to get lost. Following the map of the Old City didn't help much, as only the wider alleys were shown. There were numerous narrow alleys that led to unknown destinations; some of them so narrow that daylight was completely cut off as the buildings above almost touched. We aimlessly wandered into one of those alleys, away from the tourist path and found ourselves in much quieter residential quarters where small Arab children played, their voices resonating against the walls. We had given up with the map, but continued to follow these ancient passages, curious to see where they would lead. It became narrower and even darker until there was an abrupt turn leading to another eerie alley: left, right, straight, we had no idea where to go—hopelessly lost inside a biblical city that had been destroyed and rebuilt many times in the several thousand years that have gone by; enough time for architects to design and re-design this nightmare maze. Crumbling, worn-out steps appeared, leading to another surprise—yes, another alley, but we were once again in a different world; no longer the Christian Quarter, we had ended up in the Jewish Quarter.

The buildings were in better condition in this part. Some of them even looked fairly new, but were actually restored. Pious ultra-Orthodox Jews with springy side curls walked briskly in their traditional black clothing. Lesser devout ones sported a *yarmulke* on their heads, but dressed "normally." We mingled with the religious folk and also the dawdling tourists, who casually window shopped. This part of the Old City was much quieter and there was no ferocious haggling. Expensive art galleries, where sculptures and paintings were exhibited, made up the bulk of the shops, whereas, some of the smaller retailers were selling Jewish religious relics. Compared to the Christian Quarter, this place might have been considered boring, but it was only after coming to a large opening at the end of the alley that I saw the most mesmerizing sight, making me stop and gawk in awe at the most sacred place in Judaism—the Wailing Wall.

So many times I had seen pictures of this, and I recalled the photographs Billy had shown me, but I was not prepared for the sheer size of this monumental edifice, nor the strange, haunting ambiance that was present within this compound. Wide steps lead down to the Wailing Wall below. Behind the wall is an even more dazzling sight—the gleaming, golden Dome of the Rock, which shimmered in architectural glory, also inside a separate compound known as Temple Mount, where Solomon's Temple had once stood. The outer wall of that temple is what remains, and is revered by the Jews. We were breathless when suddenly and unexpectedly confronted with this view and stayed rooted to our spot as if time had stopped. Driven by the compelling feeling to touch the Wall, we made our way down and joined the crowds who were either praying or taking pictures.

A box containing circles cut out of brown paper was placed at the entrance for all male visitors whose heads were exposed. It was required to don one on before nearing the Wailing Wall. Ultra-Orthodox Jews stood facing (almost kissing) the Holiest of Holies. With a shawl draped over their shoulders and a prayer book clasped firmly in their hands, they bobbed back and forth in religious fervor. We couldn't go up to the Wall together as it was segregated for males and females. The males had claim on the larger partition on the left, where there was also a separate cavernous room for praying—a synagogue. Inside, lower portions of the Wall had been excavated and illuminated to show the foundations that went back thousands of years to the beginnings of the Bible. It retained the overpowering atmosphere of an ancient civilization that had once presided. The eerie prayers being murmured by the pious, who were in a world of their own, reminded the onlookers of the sanctity of this holy place. Their sounds echoed within the grotto, coating my skin with a dimply layer of goosebumps despite the humidity inside. Within the crevices of the wall, pieces of paper with prayers written on them had been forcefully squeezed inside every crack and cranny. We stayed there for a long time and stared in silence at the spectacle in front of us, which still seemed more like a dream.

It was too late to visit the Dome of the Rock, but tomorrow was another day. Exploring the Old City was equally fascinating as we left the Jewish Quarter and ventured deep into the heart of the Muslim Quarter, and once again, we were surrounded by the hustle and bustle of vendors and shoppers. This claustrophobic sector was almost void of tourists for some reason, with hardly any tourist items for sale. It looked more like the general market for the locals, where varieties of Arabic foods could be found; mostly vegetables and wonderful-looking fruits, spices, and meats, which were actually skinned animal carcasses hanging upside down with slit throats and without refrigeration. Some of them were already changing color. All kinds of freshly-baked flat breads were strewn on old, wooden carts, and rings of white bread coated in sesame seeds piled up haphazardly. We bought one of those delicious rings, eating it while strolling along through crowds of Arabic shoppers. Traditionally dressed women lugged bulging baskets of fresh produce, but the men had the better part of life— they sat in cafés and smoked water pipes, and/or played backgammon while sipping glasses of tea. We also sat down there and had a coffee while absorbing the scene in front of us, which was not of this century. It was a scene out of *Arabian Nights*, but there were no exotic scents of the Orient. The dank and stale air was permeated with smells that have lingered here for over a thousand years. It was the smell of age and of past civilizations that had left their marks upon this city. Faint whiffs of urine, baked bread, roasting chickens, sweat, musty buildings, dirt; all combined with ancient odors, and I was sure there was also the smell of ghosts, which I was convinced there were plenty of. As there was no air movement inside, it never seemed to get replenished.

An elderly stooped Arab looking like Ali Baba himself, with grey bristles and dressed in a dirty *djellaba*, appeared in the alley. He was lugging a giant teapot on his back and shouting out, "SAHLEB! SAHLEB!" Some locals stopped to buy *sahleb* from him. It was a milky white liquid served from his gigantic teapot. We stopped in amazement. He came up to us. "*Sahleb?*" He asked. We nodded, feeling adventurous. The two previous women who had just downed their *sahleb* handed back the empty glasses, which he rinsed out with the water he was also carrying, and threw the contents onto the ground with a sharp thrust. He then crouched down to get into the right position and tipped the heavy-looking pot. With professional expertise, out of the long spout came the hot white liquid directly into the glass without spilling a drop. He must have been doing this since childhood. It was not finished. On top, he sprinkled cinnamon and crushed pistachio nuts. It was as delicious as it looked—sweet, aromatic, and tasted like nothing I had ever tried before. I found out later that it was made out of ground orchid bulbs.

The giant teapot man continued shouting out, "SAHLEB! SAHLEB!" while we took our time enjoying this delicious drink. One other person was waiting patiently for us to finish as there were only two glasses. "*Sahleb* good?" Asked the *sahleb* man as he paused briefly from his "*sahleb*" calls.

"*Sahleb* very good," I replied, and gave him the OK gesture with my thumb and finger. "Oops!" Should I have done that? Didn't someone tell me once that this gesture is a sign for "asshole" in the Middle East? Or was that in Greece? I didn't quite remember, but if I had just called Mr. Sahleb an asshole, he didn't seem to notice as he rinsed out Sally's glass…, but the other customer was frowning at me. I downed the last of my drink and nudged Sally to leave.

Sauntering and gazing at everything in awe, we ended up at a large opening where daylight and fresh air streamed in and another gate appeared. This was supposed to be the most impressive one—Damascus Gate. It *was* the most impressive one—and the biggest one. This was East Jerusalem, home to the Palestinian population, who made this part of the city *very* colorful. Arab vendors selling fresh produce piled up on carts were propped up around the gate—inside and out. We exited outside to escape the claustrophobic atmosphere and sat on the wall for a while, admiring the elaborate architecture of Damascus Gate, which was also a scene from ancient times. It looked as if it might have been connected by a drawbridge at one time, but now, everything was paved.

We started our way back to our room with no idea how we would ever find it again. It was only necessary to get to Jaffa Gate and then look for those steep steps near the entrance. Following the map proved useless once again, and the only way to get there was to ask people the way several times. Everybody knew the way, and by following their directions, we arrived at the familiar alley where *Orange Tour* groups were admiring camels carved out of olive wood, and the vendor was trying to coax them into buying a whole herd.

"You buy camel family. I give you very good brice. This olive wood, very, very difficult to carve," I heard him say.

I must admit, the olive wood carvings were *really* fine looking, as well as the chess sets with superbly made chess boards, crypts with religious figures, and crosses with Jesus. It was a truly magnificent shop, but looking meant buying, so I just walked past without lingering.

Our familiar stone stairway appeared, and on top, the door to the property was left open as promised as we walked into the courtyard. The old woman was attacking it with a broom with passionate energy, looking up as we entered and nodded a greeting. We dived onto our beds, sweaty and exhausted and ready for a nice cold shower. Ten minutes later, a shy, dusky young girl, about ten years of age (who must have been the woman's great-great-great granddaughter) came in with two glasses of tea on a tray with some more cakes. We were astounded by the generosity. "*Shokran,*" (thank-you) was all I could say in Arabic. She giggled and ran away.

Cold showers in Jerusalem are like liquid nitrogen compared to the warmer cold showers on the kibbutz, where the water didn't crystallize your bones with ice. The metal spout on the wall *was* nothing more than a metal spout on the wall, but at least it served the purpose and washed away the sweat. This toilet was another thing to get used to. Nothing more than a ceramic bowl with a hole on ground level, it was painful for thighs that were not used to this. A fresh unopened roll of toilet paper had been placed on the shelf, obviously for us Western bums, because in the East (I'd been told) it is quite natural to clean yourself with the left hand and water. Sure enough, there was a container of water placed alongside. I opened the fresh toilet roll.

Our room was extremely basic, with only beds placed haphazardly; so close that they were almost touching. We had the room to ourselves, so it didn't matter. There were no windows, but the door to the courtyard was left open for fresh air. Turquoise dominated the color scheme, and the dim light in the room made it appear dreary. There were no chairs or bedside cabinets—we simply strew our clothes over the other beds. But everything was clean and spotless, including the tiled floor; so clean, it was possible to walk barefoot and still go to bed with unsoiled feet. Another granddaughter came, an older one this time, and brought in more tea. She also had a plate of long, greasy-looking, black things.

"What are those?" We asked her. Her English was rather good.

"These are aubergines. My grandmother just made them, but she always cooks too much."

"Please thank your grandmother. What's your name?" We asked.

"Samira," she tweeted with a sweet smile. Samira suggested we eat at the table outside, otherwise we would get olive oil over the bed. She went back in to fetch us two rounds of pita bread for picking up the food with.

The absolute silence in the night was oppressive; broken by the sudden explosive sound of the muezzin that erupted while we were sleeping. "Aaaaaaalah-u-aqbar... " A pause. "Aaaaaaaalah-u-aqbar..., " then came the long recitals, calling the Muslims to prayer. The sound resonated deep inside our room despite the walls being thick. The praying went on and on, wailing, the imam sounding as if he was pinching his nostrils, or he must have had a bad cold. Nevertheless, I found the sound mystical, as well as eerie, but the performance was magnificent. We heard it several more times throughout the day, but in the still darkness it was clearer and more amplified. The praying ended as abruptly as it had started, and we dozed off back to sleep.

Because the door was closed, we had no idea when it was daylight, as a result, we ended up sleeping in longer than intended. Bright light infiltrated the room, making us squint as we opened the door into the courtyard. The old lady was there, cleaning as usual. She disappeared shortly and came back with two glasses of tea.

"*Shokran.*"

"Welcome," she answered; the only English word she knew.

Retracing our steps back to the Muslim Quarter was not an easy task, and after numerous wrong turns, we miraculously ended up where we wanted to be—near the entrance to the Dome of the Rock, which was accessible by a gate near the Western Wall. While entering the compound, we were once again speechless, as the most beautiful edifice I'd ever seen loomed up through an arched colonnade in its full majesty, overpowering all other man-made structures in vicinity. The shrine was immense; topped off with a golden dome. Blue, green, and turquoise mosaic tiles covered the entire exterior; Arabic inscriptions around the octagonal walls quoted Koranic verses. This, itself, was a piece of art. Scores of shoes marked the entrance to the shrine. We had to take them off, too. A scruffy, severe-looking man barred our entry, pointing at our feet, then to a nearby water fountain where people were cleansing them. We also had to stick our feet under the bliss of cool water, which felt so good that I wanted to stay there —only *then* were we permitted to enter.

Inside, it was equally striking. Aesthetic mosaics depicting exotic birds decorated the interior. Columns and arches had been constructed to encircle the sacred stone, which had a venerable position in the middle. This large rock (according to Muslim belief) is supposed to be the place from which the Prophet Muhammad jumped into heaven. The Jews believe it is the rock used by Abraham to sacrifice his son Isaac.

We left this vast and airy building and continued walking around Temple Mount, where there was no shade whatsoever. The extra bright sun reflected off all the historic buildings and bounced off the almost white limestone slabs that paved the entire compound, forcing me to squint, even with sunglasses. The fountain with its soothing cold water was the best place to be as we sat down on the red-hot steps and let the water trickle over our feet again. "Aaaah... bliss."

Also on Temple Mount is the very old and magnificent Al-Aqsa Mosque, which we were not allowed to enter, being non-Muslims. It was worship time then as the call to prayer was loudly blasted out of the speaker high up on the minaret while Muslims humbly shuffled their way in that direction. The powerful wailing continued and magnified in volume as the sound bombarded the entire compound, bouncing off walls and making sure it was even absorbed by the body, and infiltrated the eardrums of all Muslims as a reminder to fulfill their holy duties.

After taking in all the grandeur several dehydrating hours later, we retraced our footsteps to see the Wailing Wall once again. Numerous tour groups, including the now familiar *Orange Tours* baseball caps, had now congregated in this Jewish compound. Groups of Japanese arrived, but they didn't take any particular interest in the significance of where they were standing, but were happily taking snapshots of each other against the sacred background, then left again without giving it a second glance.

In the Muslim Quarter near Lions' Gate is the church of St. Anne, built on the site where the Virgin Mary's parents were said to have been born. We didn't go inside, but toured around the exterior on the way to see the Pool of Bethesda. The remains of this pool actually comprises of two separate baths: said to be the place where Jesus cured a cripple. Adjacent to this are the ruins of a Byzantine church. It didn't need a great mind to imagine the splendor of this city when Romans marched through Jerusalem's streets. Other tourists were wondering around with equal bewilderment and using the Bible as a guidebook, which I think was a marvelous idea, as this *was* the biblical city.

The gazillions of ruins, monuments, and places of worship were too overwhelming to absorb in such a short time. It was enough history for the day, and we went in search of some food. Still feeling gastronomically adventurous, we decided to eat something "weird" in the Muslim Quarter. We had long since established that all food is palatable, but still remained a miniscule cautious when it came to eating meat in this part of the Old City. The suspended, slightly green animal carcasses with slit throats from the day before still haunted my stomach thoughts. We ended up eating a vegetarian dish with creamy goat's cheese and salad. There was also an eggplant dish similar to what we had eaten the evening before. Making sure to leave some space for Arab cakes, we went in search of the same café as yesterday. I limited myself to two cakes this time, ordered coffee with cardamom, and grabbed one of the several backgammon sets, which were lying around. After walking and gawking all day, it was an ideal way to end it, and stayed in the café for two hours until chain-smoking local clientele took the place over with bubbling water pipes.

Getting around the Old City was already becoming easier, even though it was our second day here. But that was because we got lost so often the day before, and ended up going around in circles. Certain buildings, T-shirt shops, carpet shops, were already familiar landmarks. Back in the Christian Quarter, the olive-wood-camel vendor was still convincing customers to splurge out on these unique pieces.

"This very, very zbecial wood."

The *keffiyeh* salesman was the same. "Very beautiful scarrrf. Iz zilk. Iz hand made. Where iz madam from...? Oh, Canada. Canada is beautiful; I have an uncle who lives..."

It was an early night for us after such an eventful day and I welcomed the ice-cold shower. The usual tea and snacks appeared, too.

Next day meant more walking; this time to the Mount of Olives, which was located outside the Old City walls. The exit via Dung Gate was the beginning of a long and exhausting ascent up a steep hill. Thousands upon thousands of tombstones commanded the slopes overlooking the Old City. Here is the place where souls were first in line for judgment day at the end of all time, and there were thousands in line already. The kosher zombies would all gather on Temple Mount—creepy!

Tour groups didn't have the pleasure to experience this arduous hike. Lucky them! On the summit were the tour buses with refreshed-looking tourists casually admiring the awesome view of the Old City. Two perspiring, deeply tanned backpackers arrived, dripping with sweat, panting, slurping water, and too exhausted to enjoy the amazing panoramic vista that was spread out below us. I longed to be in that air-conditioned bus—I would even have worn an orange cap for the privilege. We found ourselves in front of the beautiful Greek Orthodox Church of St. Mary Magdalene we had admired from below. Its many golden domes jutted out like giant onions protruding against the dark blue cloudless sky. I wasn't sure if we were allowed inside as the door was closed. Others weren't going in either, but I was content just to tour the grounds of this imposing structure, looking up onto its magnificent onion domes, each one topped off with a cross. Down below, thousands of crumbling gravestones sprawled out in the valley.

Walking became easier as we headed back down the road to the bottom of the hill and found ourselves in front of the Church of All Nations with a beautiful mosaic façade depicting saints or maybe the Holy Family—I wasn't sure which. Orange baseball caps were just disembarking and regrouping in front of the church, waiting for their tour guide to speak. But we didn't linger here and continued to the adjacent Gardens of Gethsemane; famous for their ancient olive trees, which (according to my guide book) boasted to being so old that they might have witnessed the Crucifixion of Christ. These prehistoric-looking trees were so twisted and gnarled, and so old that their trunks had split into several pieces, and still continued to grow and widen. These were silent witnesses to all those past civilizations and battles that had taken place in the last 2,000 years. The grotesque trunks looked like deformed gargoyles, and the ominous side branches resembled sinuous limbs and arms with drooping, fragmenting tendrils, and black claws reaching out and ready to grab anyone who absconders off the path. I was grateful not to be here in the dark when my imagination would be running wild and picturing these deformed ogres coming to life. In daytime, it was a garden of serene, but eerie beauty. Across on the other side on Temple Mount, the howling of the muezzin was summoning believers to prayer.

Back on the road, we were facing the wall that surrounded Temple Mount, and in the middle was Golden Gate. This gate, although visible, has been sealed for hundreds of years. No one may ever enter this way. It is believed that the gate can only be opened by the Messiah, who will one day appear and make his way through the Golden Gate onto Temple Mount and start resurrecting the dead.

We ended up in the Kidron Valley and traversed amongst endless graves to the tombs we wanted to see. These towering carved stone structures were even older than the olive trees, dating back to the times when Romans marauded the holy city. One was known as Absalom's Pillar, which looked like a giant salt shaker, and the other one was Zachariah's Tomb with a pyramid-shaped roof. We sat on the steps by the one belonging to Zechariah, feeling totally exhausted *and* surrounded by death. Ancient tombs were a morbid fascination and attracted an endless influx of tourists. Here, there were no tourists; it was not the place for orange caps.

We sat alone, talking quietly and feeling like intruders in this valley of souls that have been abiding time for their resurrection for the last 2,000 years—and still waiting for the grand opening of Golden Gate and the ensuing wild party. Nevertheless, we were disrespectful as I took off my T-shirt, and we noisily devoured the last of our food and water, meanwhile, stretching out for a short siesta on the steps of the tomb.

Nearby is the Arabic village of Silwan. It was one place where we felt uneasy as we cautiously entered an area awash in poverty and derelict dwellings, most of them looking either half-built or half-destroyed—I couldn't tell the difference. Garbage was scattered everywhere, and ragged children screamed at us when they noticed our presence; not out of curiosity, but with venomous hatred. The commotion brought out the older youths, several of whom directed (in English) rude comments and gestures, particularly at Sally, who was too under-dressed for such neighborhoods where the exposure of female flesh sent the males into a frenzy. We turned around abruptly and rapidly retraced our steps away from this ghastly village with the most unfriendly people I had yet encountered. The youths followed and pestered us for a while, but kept a distance until they got bored and went back to whatever they were doing—being bored.

It was also a good time to call it a day, and with Silwan village well behind us, we re-entered the Old City via Lions' Gate and went in search of a falafel, which we were both longing for. Tomorrow, there won't be so much moving around. Our personal itinerary was to look at some churches within the Old City, and basically... just stroll around. Today was too exhausting, and I was convinced that we could have taken a shorter route to get to the onion-domed church.

History abounds in Jerusalem, and the guidebook is thick with proposed sites worth visiting. The guidebook doesn't mention though, the hundreds or thousands of other sites which are worth stopping at; and this is only on the surface. Excavations are everywhere; past and present, and new sites are still being discovered. It is unimaginable what lies under the surface. There are sections where previous excavations have been further excavated—even deeper into the earth, and goodness knows what else is buried below *that*. We had given ourselves a week to see Jerusalem, but *what* we saw was only a spit in the ocean. A lifetime wouldn't be enough to see it all.

We enjoyed our bed next morning, again not getting up until very late. Jerusalem was exhausting. There was no rushing this time, and we didn't leave till noon. Nearby is the Church of the Holy Sepulcher, where we spent several hours inside an endless church, which wasn't just one, but comprised of many chapels and churches belonging to several Christianity groups that included the Coptics and Greek Orthodox. This is the holiest shrine in Christianity, for this is the site of the crucifixion of Christ.

Inside the church, the many different exits, entrances, and hallways were most confusing. Holy representatives hovered everywhere, all wearing different robes to show which part of Christianity they represented: Franciscan monks, Greek Orthodox, Syrian and Ethiopian Coptics, Roman Catholics, and Armenians shared this holy site. Tour groups from around the world listened with boredom as their guides recited the full history of the church, none of which would stick an hour later. Pilgrims who had traveled from afar, wept over the Stone of Unction—the stone slab which marks the spot where the preparation of Jesus's body for burial had taken place. Water was trickling over the slab, and this water was collected by the pilgrims, who used tissues or cloth to absorb the water, and then squeeze it out into glass vessels or any other containers they had on them. Some of them would pour the water out again and repeat the process. I had no idea what this was about. Others would bring this water back to their homeland and claim to be in possession of the holiest of holy water.

Nearby is an ornate and intricately sculpted structure known as the Edicule, where the tomb of Christ was located. This tiny room was only big enough for a few people at a time, and a line had formed, waiting for this very personal and devout attestation of faith, which they would carry with them for the rest of their lives. We did likewise, but didn't encounter anything spiritual like the others seemed to. Other elderly pilgrims were in distress and sobbing incessantly. Nevertheless, it was a worthy experience to have witnessed this spectacle.

After some lunch, we strolled around the *souk*, flabbergasted by the amount of tourist junk that was being sold. It was even possible to buy canned holy air; in other words—a can of nothing! Some tourists were actually paying money for this—and it wasn't cheap. Baseball caps and T-shirts were the most popular items, and for the pilgrims; woe if they should return home without an olive-wood-carved crypt. Beautifully engraved, shiny coffee pots and trays were also something worth purchasing, and for those who really wanted to splurge out, there were hand-tufted carpets available for an arm and a leg. Some of them portrayed the image of the Dome of the Rock.

During the remainder of our time, we visited the Way of the Cross—more commonly known as Via Dolorosa. This part gets pretty crowded during Easter, when pilgrims from all over the world descend upon the Old City's narrow streets and try to duplicate Christ's suffering. This was undertaken by many insane individuals who lugged a heavy wooden cross along this famous route. Orthodox, Armenian, Copts, and Roman Catholics race towards the Church of the Holy Sepulcher, where the procession ends at a candle lighting ceremony. As there is not enough room inside for such crowds, arguments and bloody fights often break out as each party insists that they were there first.

Back in the Jewish Quarter the next day, we discovered what is known as the Cardo—the Main Street of Byzantine Jerusalem. It is possible to see these excavations close up or even walk down and try to imagine ancient Jerusalem's heydays when merchants and traders set up their stalls parallel to the perfect line of columns, which still line the street. Nowadays, parts of the Cardo have been reconstructed, and the stalls that once contained spices, silk, incense, and goods from the East, have been replaced by expensive gift shops, jewelry stores, and galleries—eradicating the mayhem of Byzantine Jerusalem and replacing it with order and tranquility—expensive tranquility. The prices in these stores were astronomical. We stayed here for the sheer beauty and went on to see the remains of Hurva Synagogue, where a single arch marks the spot where the famous and important synagogue had once stood before its destruction. We enjoyed the placid Jewish Quarter. There were no crowds in this part, no pushing, and no olive wood camels being thrust into ones' face. It was possible to look at something without being attacked.

However, the olive-wood-camel salesman was in heaven when we passed him on the way to our room. A Japanese tour group was crowded around his wood display. They were all handling the attractive carvings. "Where you from? (silly question) Jaban? Jaban very good… My brother he live in Jaban. He haz shop in Nagazagi. He very rich… zell garbets." That was his lie for the day.

"Nagasaki? Ohhhh… Nagasaki gooood," and the Japanese whispered and nodded amongst themselves, then… JACKPOT!

One of them bought a wooden camel, and the rest of the group decided that they wanted a camel to take back to Japan, too. The vendor was all smiles, especially as neither of them even attempted to bargain.

"I give you zbecial brice because my brother zay Jaban good beoble." They murmured and bowed with gratitude.

The nearby *keffiyeh* salesman looked upon with envy at the Japanese crowd, silently praying that one of them would buy a scarf from his shop. They would also be forced to listen to his *relative-in-Japan* fable.

Before leaving Jerusalem, we still wanted to see the famous landmark —the Tower of David. It was possible to take the staircase up to the tower, which is actually a Turkish minaret. On top, we were rewarded with a fantastic panoramic view of the Old City, where TV antennas spiked out of every house. Not too far is the golden dome on Temple Mount, and behind it, in the distance, the Mount of Olives, where we had swallowed a ton of dust a few days previously. The onion-domed church continued to shimmer in the perilous sun. It was a great place to have a picnic and nobody bothered us as we sat there for an eternity, happily chatting and devouring our recently bought barbecued chicken, and very much having the time of our lives.

While in Jerusalem, we only covered the most famous sights, and it would've been almost sinful to do a whirlwind tour—to simply go there, take some pictures, and move on to the next attraction. We spent many hours at each place to fully savor the historic significance. We could do that, and decide how much time to spend at each site. Tour groups that were pressed for time made flying visits, and for that they must have paid a considerable amount of money; especially for their stay in a fancy hotel inside modern Jerusalem. We were more than content with our simple accommodation in the heart of the Old City—to have experienced the hospitality of these people who continued to feed and to supply us with an endless amount of tea and Arabic snacks.

We went back to our favorite café on our last day where the owner had already gotten to know us and automatically brought the coffee and backgammon without being asked. He was in his sixties and spoke only a few words of English, but language issues didn't matter. He had the best

Arab pastries, and I was determined to try them all before leaving Jerusalem. I managed it after a week, but admittedly *did* feel a little sick after —just a little.

It was time to go back to Tel Aviv and to our next kibbutz. We thanked our host family for their gracious hospitality and slowly made our way to the bus station. Before that, we changed some more of our Traveler's Checks in one of the numerous shops that served as the black market. Because of the rampant inflation, we even ended up with more shekels than last week.

I left with a clean, dry T-shirt, but it wasn't long until it was soaked with sweat, especially on my back, which was covered by the heavy backpack.

In the following months, we returned to the Old City several more times and stayed in the same place, which, I couldn't understand why, was always void of other backpackers.

It was Friday, and people were doing their shopping for the upcoming Sabbath. The bakery on Jaffa Road filled the air with freshly-baked *challah* — a bread, which was commonly eaten on the holy day. We didn't stop to buy anything, but continued walking, wondering about the location of our new kibbutz. Buses stop running at sunset, so we had to get to our new kibbutz before that, wherever that may be. It was a mystery which part of the country we would end up in tonight. It could be anywhere. We wouldn't know until later.

4
COW MADNESS IN THE DESERT

Upon arrival in Tel Aviv, we went straight to the kibbutz office to find out where they were sending us. Inside, it didn't look any different to the office in London, with similar posters of famous sights and Israeli National Parks splattering the walls. "Shalom," greeted the woman in the office. She was expecting us. "Did you decide to travel a little first?"

"Yes, we wanted to spend some time in Jerusalem before the next kibbutz," we explained.

"That's good," she commented shortly, then added, "traveling is always good." She studied the map briefly and showed us a spot in the southern part of the country. "Kibbutz Shoval needs volunteers. That's where I'm sending you—to the Negev Desert. I had to make phone calls to several kibbutzim, but a lot of them don't take volunteers from England because of the drinking problem."

"But we don't drink!" We were shocked by the discrimination.

"I know, Gila told me. I did try to get you onto some other kibbutzim, but they've had so many problems with the British that many have completely banned volunteers from Great Britain. It is a big problem." I understood what she meant by the "drinking problem." Alcohol was cheap and easily available, but the Brits could not behave when confronted with it. Some of the volunteers I witnessed on our last kibbutz resorted to their prior barbaric ways: staggering and throwing up outside the disco. It was not surprising that many kibbutzim don't tolerate the English, as such disgraceful behavior is too disrespectful within their communities. Alcohol for kibbutzniks is something to be enjoyed in small amounts and not a product of total intoxication.

"Are there English volunteers on Kibbutz Shoval?" We asked.

"Yes, but also a mixture of other nationalities. If you don't like it, you can always come back and I will find you a place on another one. You should try it first. It's not too far from Be'er Sheva. Have you been there yet?"

"No, we haven't," we shook our heads. Be'er Sheva was also one of the places on my "to see" list. My guidebook mentioned that they had an early morning camel market there. "Okay, we'll give it a go," Sally and I both acknowledged. The woman made a quick phone call to the kibbutz to inform them of our arrival.

"You can take a bus directly to the kibbutz from here. It's easy." She wrote down the bus number we had to take, gave us some papers to hand over to the volunteers' leader, and we were ready to go. "Good luck," she wished us.

She was right. It was easy getting there. We ended up in the desert part of the country—the Negev. The Mediterranean greenery and the endless citrus orchards were gone. Field crops now dominated the scene, and where there was no irrigation, only parched, hard, and crusty earth was visible. There were still some orange plantations, but they became more sporadic.

We arrived in our new temporary home and headed straight to the largest building that was obviously the dining room. It was deserted. Lunch was over. There wasn't any sign of life anywhere, so we just started walking around aimlessly until a man on a bicycle came our way. "We are looking for the volunteers' leader," I said.

"I think she's sleeping, but I will let her know you're here. You can wait in the dining room," he told us, then rode off to find her. We went back to the empty dining room, located the beverage area, and helped ourselves to a coffee. The now familiar, ever-present *Wissotzky* tea bags were there, too. I never saw any other brands of tea anywhere.

"Where is everybody?" Sally asked.

"It's hot. They're probably *all* sleeping," I guessed. "I think that's what they do in hot climates—take a siesta."

An elderly, gray-haired and frail woman came in shortly after and introduced herself in a very British accent as Dvorah, the volunteers' leader. She *did* look as if she had just got woken up, and was not exactly in a cheerful mood.

"Come," she sighed. "I will first take you to your rooms, then we can do the rest later after dinner." I got the impression that she just wanted to get rid of us and go back to bed. "These... are the volunteers' houses," she pointed out, taking us to an area that was equally deserted. Only the noise of humming air-conditioners could be heard. "Are you a couple?" She asked abruptly, eyeing us. We nodded. "Good. Then I can put you into one room." She unlocked the door and told us she'd come and find us in the dining room after dinner.

Meanwhile, we unpacked and settled in. Our room was even more basic than on the previous kibbutz. The shapeless foam mattresses hadn't been used for a while and needed a good pounding outdoors. Fine, gritty sand covered everything. Other than that, the location was a dream. Rich, low palm trees with thick trunks looking like giant pineapples dominated the artistically landscaped gardens. Lawn sprinklers and infinite black irrigation pipes made sure that the soil never ran dry, thus creating a desert oasis. We heard voices outside. "He... llo!" A bronze couple with sun-scorched hair greeted us. "New volunteers?"

"Yes, where is everybody?" We asked.

"Over at the pool. They've just opened it today." That explained it.

"Don't recognize your accent. Where're you from?" I wondered.

"South Africa. There are two more blokes from down there, but most of the volunteers are from England." I was hoping for a broader international mixture.

Today was Friday, and we were looking forward to the promise of a tasty Sabbath meal that was sure to come in the evening. It was the perfect time to arrive on a kibbutz, and tomorrow will also be a day off. Other volunteers started to appear—all of them deeply tanned, but so were we after three months in this country. We met the other volunteers and the majority *were* English like we were told, but there were also a few other Europeans amongst us, as well as a Mexican and a very friendly married couple from Columbia. "What kind of work do they have here?" Sally asked.

"It's usually in the factory or the dining room; kitchen and dishes."

"What kind of factory?" I interrupted.

"Metal. They make parts. It's really easy: you just sit there, put a part into the machine, press a button, and the computer will do all the work, then you take the piece out again," one of the South Africans explained. "I think they're missile parts."

"The kitchen is the worst. There's a crazy bloke there who's always yelling at people and he's *really* obnoxious."

"I work with the cows," a large Dutch girl piped in. "I don't like it so much. The work is okay, but the people I work with don't really talk; just give orders. Anyway, I'm leaving in two weeks, so they will need a replacement. It's better than the other jobs though. I'm sick of smelling like a cow all the time." I didn't want to mention it, but she also *looked* like one.

We walked over to the dining room, which was now filled with neatly-dressed kibbutzniks. Like before on Kibbutz Ha'ogen, volunteers sat together around their regular tables and didn't mix with the kibbutzniks. There were others I had not yet met; one of them a black girl who seemed very reserved and didn't talk much. Sally asked where she was from.

"South Africa."

"South Africa? But the other couple told us that there were two more *blokes* here from South Africa," I sounded confused. "They didn't mention a girl."

"That's not surprising. None of the South Africans have anything to do with her because she's black. Weird bunch. They're full of that apartheid rubbish and can't understand how blacks and whites are treated as equals everywhere else." The English were especially confused with such racism. I decided to steer clear of the South Africans in case they said something I didn't like; meanwhile, Sally made friends with the South African girl (called Janet), who turned out to be quite an interesting person to talk to.

"Why do they travel in the first place with such warped mentality?" I wondered aloud.

Dvora came over, wide awake this time. "*Shabbat-Shalom*," she greeted. "When you are ready, let's go to the office and I will give you your bedding and everything else you will need." Sally and I got up and followed her. Like before, we got our coupons for the shop, dark blue work clothes, and brown canvas boots, which turned out to be the most ideal footwear for the desert. She also started handing out packs of cigarettes.

"We don't need those. We don't smoke," we told her in unison, pushing the cigarette boxes back. She shrugged her shoulders and put them away again. Our arms were loaded by now, so we carried everything over to our rooms and came back to the office to do the paperwork.

"Your visa is only good for another week," Dvorah told us, looking at our 90-day entry stamp. "You have to go to the office in Be'er Sheva to renew it as soon as possible." She fished out a form, which she stamped and signed. "Here, you have to hand in this form with your passport. It acknowledges that you are here as volunteers."

"Can we go next Thursday?" Asked Sally. "That's when they hold the camel market."

"Oh, yes. The famous Bedouin market," she corrected us. "Yes, you should see it, but you have to be there at dawn—it starts *very* early. I won't mark you down for work that day, so have a nice day out, but don't buy any camels except the wooden ones." She continued to tell us about the rules. "You were on a kibbutz before, so the rules are pretty much the same, but I don't think they concern you as you don't drink, which I find very unusual for English people. Enjoy your stay, and if there is anything you need, please don't come to my house, as I need to sleep in the afternoon, but observe the office hours, or you can find me in the dining room." We thanked her and left our money and passports in the safe. "By the way, we usually show a film in the dining room Friday evenings. It starts at nine."

The volunteers were back in their quarters and the English were already opening their first bottles of beer, sitting around a fire they had going. We decided to go and visit our new friend Janet who had a room to herself. She was also leaving in two weeks. "Are you going back home?" We asked.

"To South Africa? Never! I'm never going back. It took a long time just to get out. They didn't even want to issue me a passport." She said that with venom. "You can't imagine what it's like living under apartheid."

"We saw it on television. The whole world is against it. How did you get out?" I wanted to know. She just shrugged her shoulders.

"I knew some people." That was all the information she was willing to volunteer and we didn't press.

"Where will you go?"

"I'll stay in Israel for a while, but would like to go to America." She told us that she had an Israeli boyfriend she would stay with, and then they wanted to travel together. We had an interesting talk about how life was for a black person in South Africa; shocking for us to hear it directly from someone who had experienced it firsthand and was *still* being discriminated by the racist South Africans who didn't even acknowledge her existence. President Botha had done a great job in instigating hatred. After hanging out with her in the coming days, we were also ignored by them, but that was okay with us, as we didn't want to associate ourselves with them, either.

We walked over to the dining room, which had been converted to a movie theater, and wondered which film was being shown. It was a comedy, but in German... with Hebrew subtitles. The German and Dutch volunteers were most content with the film choice, but *I* had to use my imagination. "It's always a surprise film. We never know what language it's going to be in," a Belgian couple told us. They were the first Belgians that I met.

"How's life in Belgium?" I asked.

"It's the most boring country in the world," they informed us with complete frankness. "We have nothing there... not even mountains. We want to move to another country." They had already been traveling for two years and wanted to go to India next.

"Two years!" I gasped in disbelief. That was unimaginable for me. I had only been gone 3 months, and *that* seemed a lifetime.

"I spent six months in India," Hans, the German volunteer told us in his funny accent. "I got very sick, so decided to leave and then I traveled to Nepal." He was also a seasoned traveler, having spent three years on the road. He was also as thin as a rake, probably having left most of himself in Asian toilets. He told us horror stories about them. "No clean toilets anywhere—just holes in the ground with shit all around you. Flies crawl up your ass while you squat—and the cockroaches—everywhere."

"Eugh."

"See what I mean? Belgium is boring!" The Belgians interrupted, laughing.

Sally and I listened in awe to their fantastic stories of faraway places: alien cultures, scary toilets, corrupt officials, the awesome beauty, and acute poverty found in the darkest corners of the world. We were astounded by their adventures, and I felt the same way as I had done in England when I first saw pictures of Israel—that magnetic pull. I was starting to realize haw vast the world was and how little I knew of it. Israel was a place to meet novice travelers, adventure seekers, and backpackers alike, many of whom have been on the road for many years and were spending some months on a kibbutz to fatten up and recuperate: mostly from illnesses they had picked up in some third-world country.

Sunday was the first day of work. As before, I ended up in the dining room and Sally in the kitchen. The work was not different to the previous kibbutz, and I was not surprised when after ninety minutes it was time for a coffee break, joined by the kitchen staff this time. It was the same rabbit food for breakfast and the same plastic cheese. I was starting to eat red peppers, which I cut into strips and coated them with cottage cheese. Avocados, sprinkled with lemon juice, also became a daily intake, as well as tasty bread with unusual-looking and strange-tasting meat slices that looked as factory-made as the cheese. "How's the kitchen?" I asked Sally. She rolled her eyes.

"Tell you later." We met again over lunch and she told me about her kitchen experience. "They were right! There's a real nutcase working there. All he does is yell at everyone—and seems to hate volunteers. The others aren't too friendly, either; ignoring me most of the time."

A couple of days later in the dining room, the much talked about obnoxious person decided to have a go at the dining staff, rudely admonishing a volunteer for not filling up the sugar containers properly and spilling large quantities on the table in the process. I steered out of his way. Next day I was also working in the kitchen, where I had a mountain of peppers to wash, take out the stem and seeds, and cut them up. Mr. Obnoxious came over. "ARE YOU A MILLIONAIRE?" He roared into my face. I blinked quizzically, taken aback. I didn't know what I should answer to this pathetic question.

"Wish I was, but... no."

"Do you have money to throw away? You people have *so much* money, right?" He trembled with anger.

"No!" He picked up one of the pepper stems I had discarded and shoved it under my nose.

"This is waste! WASTE! WASTE!" he barked. "We do not throw food away here. You see this?" He snapped off a small piece of pepper I had left behind on the stem. It wasn't bigger than a centimeter. He put it together with the other chopped peppers. I was speechless as he grabbed my knife and rudely instructed me how to dissect a pepper, thus taking out the stem and seeds without disturbing any of the flesh. "All you people do is waste. You all have too much money." He continued to chastise me and I never found out what he meant by "you people."

I felt humiliated and continued with my peppers in silence. Looking around, I noticed other kibbutzniks, who were also silent and shaking their heads, either at me or at Mr. Obnoxious. I caught Sally with my glance and her eyes told me, "see what I mean?" Later, when he was gone, one of the kitchen women came up to me.

"Don't take him too seriously. It's nothing personal; he's always like that."

"What's his problem?" I wanted to know. The woman sighed.

"He was in a concentration camp—in Auschwitz. He was one of the survivors the Russian army found, almost dead from starvation. He hasn't been normal since, and goes crazy when he sees any food wasted. If you look at his arm, you can still see the numbers that were tattooed onto it. Just ignore him." She changed the subject and then attempted to make smalltalk. "You are new volunteers?" Sally also cheered up, also happy that the ice had been broken. We did ignore him as advised after that shocking revelation, and let him throw his tantrums. For us, it was unimaginable what he had gone through.

It was time to renew our visa in Be'er Sheva, the ancient city located in the Negev Desert. This city is also mentioned in the Bible as the site where Jacob and Isaac dug up numerous wells, and thus made it possible to establish a settlement in this very parched desert.

We got up at 5:00 A.M. and started hitchhiking the short distance to the city from the main road, but before we had a chance, a car from the kibbutz pulled up. A young guy leaned out. "Let me guess, you're going to buy a camel—no other reason to be on the road so early." We laughed. "Come, I'll take you there. I'm on my way to Eilat. Pity you're not going there, it would've been a great lift for you." This was a stroke of luck, getting a lift so quickly. We were told that everything is over by 9:00 A.M., and the actual camel market can only be seen very early.

Be'er Sheva today is a very nondescript, colorless, sprawling, dusty city; a far cry from it's ancient heydays when bobbing camels carrying spices, salt, and trading goods congregated upon this desert settlement from all directions. The camels of trade are long gone, now replaced by dust-churning motor vehicles. The driver took us directly to the market and continued to his destination.

We were suddenly in a different world: surrounded by colorfully wrapped-up Bedouin women with weathered faces selling all kinds of ware: ceramics, pots, and colorful garments. The dusty outdoor market was also a gathering place for the local Bedouin who lived in the desert. They came here to trade, but also to capture the attention of foreign tourists who swooped upon the market. I didn't see any men *or* camels. Where were they? Strange gargling noises caught our attention, coming from the direction of the numerous parked vehicles. There they were; long necks sticking out from behind the parking lot where there was a whole area of tethered camels and goats. Lots of goats. Lots of *noisy* goats. But I was overjoyed to see my first camels in Israel, even though the correct term for this one-humped variety was dromedary. Who cares? For me, they were camels, and I found them at last. "Yippee!"

Some were adorned in embroidered, richly decorated guise (camel regalia), looking very expensive and royal, others were naked and blended into the bleak landscape with their matted tufts of pitiful fur. Choosing a camel was no different to choosing a car. There were marked differences between them. It was like a choice between a polished Rolls-Royce with leather upholstery and a beaten up, unwashed Mini with stuffing coming out of its torn plastic seats. Camels had their different qualities, too, and I noticed that the royal-looking ones did indeed look snotty and didn't mingle with the scabby ones. We approached closer to be near the action. This was where the men were. They were taking care of the animal section, haggling with one another very loudly in guttural Arabic. The men wore the traditional Bedouin head scarves, but remained fully clothed despite the heat. We veered even closer to the camels to take a picture. One of the men suddenly snapped at us. "No bictures. No gamel bictures." I put away my camera again, disappointed. My first camels... and I couldn't even take a picture.

"A thousand curses upon you," I muttered. The Bedouin went back to his haggling, shooting us sideway glances in case we sneaked a photograph of his precious camels.

These romanticized desert beasts made the oddest noises: deep bass gurgling sounds came up from their cavernous interior, traveled up their ridiculously long necks, and emitted a most ugly sound, which sounded more like a spluttering tractor, or a cow trying to gargle. At the same time, their wet lips quivered and curled up to reveal crooked, bacteria-infested, yellow teeth, which were incessantly chewing even if there was nothing to chew, or maybe it was a cool thing to do for attracting the females. They also have enormous, elongated tongues, which probably go down the full length of their necks. One of them had a repulsive-looking, salivary, pink, fat one and was attempting to reach a bunch of flies that were bothering it around the eye, which was bulging out. It looked very stupid and docile. "So, how do you like camels?" I asked Sally.

"They stink." But the thousands of flies didn't mind, attracted to their camel *Eau de Cologne*. I wasn't sure whether it was their breath or body odor that overpowered all other smells, but the dream I once had in England of riding a camel across a desert, soon dissipated. The sight and smell of them made me weary of camels, but I did continue to admire the creatures (from a distance) as they blended in perfectly with the landscape and were a reminder of past civilizations that had relied entirely on such beasts of burden.

We strolled around the rest of the market, but decided there was nothing to buy. A plethora of tourist junk plied the disillusioned who expected to lay their hands on traditional, hand-made Bedouin antiques. Somewhat disappointed by the market, we left. It was, nevertheless, almost nine o'clock (closing time), and the animals were already being herded away onto trucks, and some of the sold and unsold creatures were led away back into the desert.

We walked over to the immigration office to have our visas renewed. Today was our last day to get an extension, so it was vital to get that done very quickly. Israel has strange opening hours and I didn't want to chance it. It was open. There were already bored-looking people waiting in line, but the receptionist sent us to a different department, which was empty. We handed over our passports and the paper from the kibbutz, filled out a form, and an uninterested, sluggish woman immediately stamped them without even looking up or saying a word. —My first stamp—I was proud of it. The whole process took less than ten minutes and we were good for another three months, when we would have to return for the next extension.

"Let's get a falafel, I'm starving," I suggested, as we never had anything to eat yet. We walked over to where most of the shops were concentrated and had our delicious breakfast. There were some shops selling beautiful postcards of the desert. I bought a bunch to send off to England. The ubiquitous wooden camels found their way to every shop, and plenty of Bedouin-fashioned, checkered head scarves were draped across tables. These were popular amongst tourists and cheaper than in Jerusalem. Sally bought one for herself. There was nothing really to see in this town unless one is a trained archaeologist and likes to ponder over ruins at the nearby *Tel Be'er Sheva*, but even that didn't compel me to stay any longer. The best place was a café with delicious fresh pastries displayed in the window. We sat down and I devoured two of them with my now favorite Turkish coffee. We decided to take the bus back.

"The passengers should be safe from you," joked Sally. "It's only thirty minutes, so you won't be collapsing on anyone."

I didn't attack anyone on the bus and we arrived back on the kibbutz when lunch was over, but we were more thirsty than hungry. It was 35°Celsius outside, and the air-conditioned dining room with the ice-cold water from the dispenser was the best place to be. We spent the rest of the day at the swimming pool, relaxing and reading the *Jerusalem Post* until supper was served.

Back in the kitchen next day, Sally befriended an incredibly vivacious Israeli schoolgirl called Navah. They worked side by side, which put Sally in high spirits, having someone cheerful to natter with. The rest of the kitchen staff were a subdued and quite a miserable lot, but maybe it was because of having to put up with bellowing Mr. Obnoxious. Navah took no notice of him at all, and actually did her best to flare him up. Again, there were peppers to clean and chop, but I had the exciting task of peeling a mountain of carrots, sitting alone on a short stool amongst sacks of long orange things. Sally and Navah were on the other side, giggling and playing with other vegetables. At least *they* were having fun.

Finally it was Friday, and I found it hard to believe that only a week had gone by since our arrival. Time came to almost a standstill and life went on in slow motion on the kibbutz. It seemed as if we had been here a couple of months. Each day was lively and unlike the other. I would get to know different characters, some of them quite unique, and often found myself engrossed in deep conversations about other countries, but I especially loved talking to the ones with crazy travel stories. In England, where daily routine was the norm, time whizzed by at a blink of an eye. Two weeks was like two days, and life had been meaningless and eventless for me. I wrote some postcards I had purchased to inform everyone of my new address. I already had some mail, redirected from the last kibbutz. From my family there was nothing, but a nasty letter from Paula, my ex, who was still convinced that she was not an ex, and that I was coming back home soon. I *did* make a point that I wasn't coming back from my previous letter. This time I wasn't going to reply. Sally was buzzing above the letter. "Ex," I said.

"Ex ex?" She raised her eyebrows.

"Very ex ex."

Today was another movie—a French one with Hebrew subtitles. None of the volunteers stayed this time. There were no French speakers amongst us except for the Belgians, and even they found the film too dreary. Some of the kibbutzniks walked out, too, mumbling to themselves and probably plotting to overthrow the film-choosing committee. The volunteers had a large fire going, and each of the Anglo-Saxons had a crate full of beer at their sides, determined to polish off the whole lot by daybreak. The cassette player was on full, blasting out *U2*, followed by *Bruce Springsteen*. The ones who already had reached their limits were vociferating nonsense. Making a scene didn't really appeal to me, so I retired to the room with the much more appealing Sally. The bellowing and raucous barbaric behavior continued all night, making it difficult to fall asleep. We were subjected to repetitions of *Bruce Springsteen's* "Born In The USA." It was a living nightmare… and the night was to be endless.

In the morning all was tranquil outside, but the area around the fire pit was littered with dozens of empty beer bottles, crates, and upturned chairs. It was disgusting. We closed the door again, not wishing to see the mess.

"What shall we do today?" I asked Sally. Before she could answer, there was an impatient pounding on the door. It was Navah.

"Hi-do-you-want-to-come-to-the-beach-some-of-us-are-going-to-Ashkelon-come-with-us," she rapidly fired at us in one sentence. "We-have-a-small-bus-that-will-take-us-there."

"Now?"

"After-breakfast-see-you-in-front-of-the-dining-room." She sped off again like a tornado without waiting for a response.

And so, we ended up spending the Sabbath with half a dozen high school students on a very nice Mediterranean beach. They brought along melons, more damn peppers, and piles of chicken. We sat together on bamboo mats by the shore, eating and frolicking around. Despite their age, they were much more mature than most of the volunteers I had met, and all had their own strong political opinions based on the constant turmoil in the Middle East. It was a perfect day and we had a wonderful time with them. Their English was flawless, so they didn't need any practice, but attempted to give us some Hebrew lessons on useful-bad-words-everyone-should-know. The heat was intense, but several refreshing dips in the blue Mediterranean averted a meltdown. Israeli girls worshiped the sun as much as the Europeans did, determined to turn themselves into dark chocolate bars. Navah had the darkest tan all over, and looked as if she already *had* fallen into a cauldron of melted chocolate. She was an extreme bundle of fun, and the *jois-de-vivre* she emitted was infectious.

We arrived back on the kibbutz as the sun was setting, now a red fireball on the desert horizon. This serene beauty was shattered upon arrival at the volunteers' area, only to be greeted by "BORN IN THE USA" turned up full blast. The drinkers from the night before looked as if they had just gotten up, looking extremely groggy with an apparent hangover. The night will be a restless one for them: insomnia. They will feel even more rotten tomorrow morning when they finally doze off, and some minutes later, the dreaded alarm clock. I went to check the work schedule.

"I'm in the factory and you're in the kitchen again," I told Sally.

"Oh, good! It's fun with Navah."

I didn't mind going to the factory anymore; in fact, I didn't care where they put me to work. Nothing was strenuous and I looked forward to meeting different people all the time. I hardly saw Sally that week as my shift started when hers finished. She spent some time with Navah meanwhile.

It turned out that I *did* mind the factory. It was downright tedious. I sat on a stool in front of a lathe. On my right were piles of hand-sized cylindrical metal pieces. I placed one onto the lathe, pressed a button, and a bunch of pronged, metal claws grabbed it and slotted the piece into a compartment where different sized drills bored intricate holes into the sides. Another metal claw appeared and ejected the finished product. This is where I took it out and placed it on the pile on my left. The whole process took about four minutes and was as exciting as a French film with Hebrew subtitles. There were no machine breakdowns, no Arab cakes, and the workers were as surly as the kitchen staff. It was, nevertheless, easy going, and there was (thank God) also a kitchen stocked with other tasty snacks and coffee, and I *could* take a break whenever I wanted. I needed one after the first forty minutes. After two hours I was ready to call it a day, but had four more mind-numbing hours to go. So far, I was not exactly enjoying this kibbutz. If it hadn't been for Navah, we would've already left. Maybe we *should* go back to Tel Aviv and ask for a different one.

The change came two days later when I looked at my schedule and saw that I had been assigned to the cows. The Dutch girl had left and she did mention that they would need a replacement.

"COWS?" Sally shrieked… laughing. I groaned. I wondered what I had to do there.

"You have to bring the cows in for milking," hissed the cow boss—a humorless, thin-lipped woman with a face like a storm cloud, who never even introduced herself or greeted me. I was there at 4:00 P.M., the beginning of my shift, and the stench in this heat was overpowering. Outside, the cows waddled in their pies for moisture, as there was a lack of mud in these scorching temperatures. The vicious sun baked everything to oven crispness. Even the day-old cow pies were bone-dry and hard; they could be picked up and used as a frisbee. The cows were separated into different enclosures, but I was never told why, whether it was by age or stock. There were nine enclosures altogether, and my job was to start with the first one, open the gate, herd them into the dairy for milking, prepare the next herd, bring the previous group back, then bring in the second group.

Easy.

Actually, not: The gates were a problem, and the opening and closing of specific gates defined which enclosures the cows would return to, so it was absolutely crucial that the correct gates were opened or closed when certain herds came through, otherwise they would get mixed up.

On my first day of work, I simply strutted behind the pissed-off-looking cow boss as she taught me the-way-of-the-gates. She never made conversation, never smiled, and never said more than she had to. A walking corpse would have made more pleasant company. "Make sure you first close this gate before you open that one and make sure that gate is open when the third group comes out, but that other one must be closed and this one is never to be opened. Those are the sick cows." My gate lessons went on like this for over four hours until all the cows were milked, but my mind was spinning and trying to decipher which gates should be opened in what order. This was madness, and I had the impression that she tried to make sure that I was well and truly confused. It worked, and I concluded that she was the most despicable person I have ever met. The work was done for the day. "You can go," she hissed again. I made a beeline for the dining room as supper was now being served.

Sally was there, nice and clean, sitting together with sparkling Navah. They mooed me a greeting. "Was it fun?" Before I had a chance to answer, "John, you stink like a cow. You can't sit here."

"I didn't have time to shower, sorry." No excuse. I was forced to sit alone at the adjacent table. Gobbling up my food, I dived into the shower right after.

Next day at the cow amusement park was no different—no greeting, no conversation, and further gate training. That was bad. If I was being trained, that meant only one thing—a permanent cow position. Why would they train me otherwise? The day ended again with a "you-can-go" hiss. I made sure to shower first this time before supper. I had no desire to sit alone again.

Cow day number three arrived, and this time it was my turn to do the gates. Cow boss followed me like a shadow, ready to murder me in case I got my gates mixed up. "No, you cannot open this gate if that one is still open." The drained herd was on the way back. "And where do the cows go *now*? *You* have closed *all* the gates." She was right. Even the cows looked stunned for a moment, giving me a "what-the-hell-are-you-doing" look. All rights of passage were blocked. "OPEN THE GATE!" She snarled. "NO, NOT THAT ONE! This is the sixth group, not the seventh." She sighed, shaking her head. "You are doing this alone tomorrow, so pay attention: I don't have time to hold your hand all the time. I have to help with the milking so that we can get out of here earlier." That was the most she had spoken so far.

"Alone?" I gulped.

I tried my best to memorize the sequence of the gates, losing some sleep that night because of it. I felt I was ready.

I arrived next day well before four o'clock, and cow boss was already there with two other milkers getting the machines ready. The other two who worked there (Ilana and Danny) greeted me nicely with a smile, but frowning cow boss didn't even look at me, but simply ordered, "Bring the first group." That's the easy one, the first group. The cows knew it was milking time and they were already there waiting in front of the gate. I opened it and they slowly plodded into the dairy without any pushing. As the milked cows wandered back, it was time to block them with another gate and release the second group, immediately shutting the gate behind them. I then unblocked the first group and they wandered into their enclosure, where the gate remained open. I was proud of myself. It went well. I also had to keep running to the building to make sure that the cows were consistently shuffling forward. They were constantly moved along by a metal rod that emitted a slight electric spark when touched. This was moved horizontally in a circular motion at the height of a cow's body. It was also my job to press that button to keep electrocuting them. "Bring in the next group," ordered cow boss. I went to fetch group three. So far, so good. Group two was coming out, but... OH, NO! I forgot to open up the gate again to the second enclosure, utterly confused... *and* they weren't blocked, either... Too late! Group two went towards group three, but as they couldn't move in either direction, group three turned back to their enclosure and group two followed. Now I had both groups in the third enclosure. It was a bovine mess. I tried to separate them, but they all looked the same. Cow boss hollered, "John, where are the cows?"

"Cows?" My attempt at faking surprise was somewhat too obvious.

"Oh…! The cows… umm… (gulp), I lost them. Actually, they're… er… everywhere…. " I WAS DEAD! I knew it. Cow boss will kill me. All three of them came running out. Ilana burst out laughing when she saw what had happened. Danny was grinning. Cow boss scowled and glared at me murderously, her lips quivering with rage. Danny broke the ice.

"It happens to me sometime, too. No problem. We bring them all to the building together and separate them as they leave, then start again." Cow boss stalked off back into the building and never said a word to me for a whole week. Danny stayed and helped me out with the cow separation. He carried a constant grin on his face, a total opposite to cow boss, who preferred to glower. The remainder of the groups went smoothly and I was glad to finish for the day. Cow boss didn't even look at me and I sensed that she was contemplating my execution, but couldn't decide which weapon would inflict the most pain.

Two dogs came at me on the way to the dining room, but both stopped abruptly, sniffing my legs in utter confusion and reminding me that I should first head into the shower. Tails wagging, they darted off again, satisfied that it was only an escaped cow.

We decided to take a couple of days off and travel to a different part of the country—to Acco. This ancient city dates back to the time of the Pharaohs and has been invaded by armies for several thousand years. It used to be a Crusader port and also an important trading hub. Located north of today's modern port of Haifa, goods used to be delivered and traded in this ancient seaport, which served as the gateway to Asia… or Europe; whichever side of the compass you wanted to look at it from.

Because of the time and distance involved getting there, taking the bus made more sense, but we thumbed (fingered) a lift to Tel Aviv for the first leg of the journey. Less than five minutes was all it took until a large, fancy-looking car stopped. An immaculately-dressed man with balding white hair rolled down the window. "If you are going to Tel Aviv, I can take you there," he stated in perfect English and in a deep voice. We climbed in with our backpacks. The interior was spacious with leather seats. "Volunteers?" He asked. "Are you enjoying the country?"

"Very much. It's incredible. Beautiful. There is a lot to see even if it *is* small."

He nodded. "Better to see as much of the country while you still can —it will get even smaller." I looked at him, not quite comprehending. "One day, we will have to give back the Palestinians the West Bank and the Gaza Strip, if we are to achieve peace, just like we returned the Sinai. It will happen."

We hit the early morning congestion to Tel Aviv. I looked at the man again. He looked familiar. Where from? Television? I tried to dig into my deepest subconsciousness, but wasn't able to come up with a name. Yes, now it's coming. He's, he's... in the government. Yes, that's who he is. No, wait! He *is* the government... I think. He never did introduce himself and neither did I ask his name, getting the impression that he preferred to remain anonymous. We talked about the Middle East and were given a history lesson on the events that led to the Six-Day War, and how Israel had acquired all the territories. He felt no animosity towards the Arabic people and spoke of them with respect. "Are you sorry for giving up the Sinai?" I asked.

"Sorry? No. We have peace with Egypt now. That is *more* important. You must visit Egypt, too, if you haven't done so yet. There is much to see there." With that last statement, we arrived in Tel Aviv. He shook our hands with a firm grip and wished us a good time.

"Do you know who that was?" I asked Sally. "I'm sure he's from the government."

"He seemed a bit familiar, but his name... I just can't remember. You're right though, definitely government, especially with a car like that." We took the bus to Haifa, happy to have gotten a seat, as it was one of those slumbering bus rides. The standing passengers did fall asleep, but have acquired a way of remaining upright from years of practice. From Haifa it was a short distance to Acco.

Acco has its own intrinsic charm; more compact than, and not as overwhelming as Jerusalem. It also comprises of an old city, which is occupied by the Arab population that has made its home amongst these ancient labyrinth alleys that enchant the visitor with the magic of the Orient. Stores selling spices displayed an amazing array of colors, tempting every eye and nose in vicinity. Coffee and cake shops were *my* weak spot and acted like a barrier, not allowing me to pass by without sampling some deliciousness. Despite the haunting, ancient beauty of this place, centuries and centuries of habitation have caused the Old City to acquire the pungent aroma of age, urine, and rotting garbage, but that could also be due to the ancient sewers... or the lack of them. However, the smell didn't bother me anymore.

While lounging and watching the world go by at one of the cafés, a donkey carrying a load was being ushered along. A bulging mountain of hay was placed on its back, piled so high that the donkey was barely visible. An Arab boy was slowly leading the beast of burden, and another boy was behind, prodding the animal along every time its pace slowed. The alley was so narrow that people had to dart out of the way to let the beast through. There was a lot of shouting; I don't know whether towards the donkey or its owner for attempting to carry the entire contents of a field on the animal's back. We did see other donkeys within the city walls, as no other mode of transportation would have been possible—they were also used for garbage removal. This is how it's been done for thousands of years and nothing has changed.

Before getting distracted again, we checked into a basic hostel, which was practically void of other guests. It was run by Arabs, which I liked, as their hostels always carried an air of mystery about them. This place was also smack in the middle of the old city and gave us a full blast of calls to prayer coming out of the loudspeakers from the nearby minaret. It was almost like being back in Jerusalem. We were lucky to have the room to ourselves, so we just dropped off our backpacks and went out again.

We admired the beautiful architecture of the mosques, citadels, and churches and took a walk by the marina, which boasted more cafés and restaurants. We scrambled amongst the ruins that dotted the shores and tried to imagine what Acco looked like during the times when traders were bringing in their merchandise along the spice and incense routes, which handled the Eastern trade. It was not hard to imagine: take out the modern vehicles, raze the modern buildings, churn up the roads and "*Voila*" —the port city is back in its original state.

On this site, deep down, excavations have revealed Acco as it went through various stages of transformation since the days when Pharaohs were the regional power, and ships sailed from the Egyptian port of Alexandria to Acco. Over many centuries, the city had flourished several times, and several times it had been razed by invading armies as empires clashed. New sections had been added on the debris of previous sites, making the city look like a cross section of a lasagna dish. Below our feet, remains of a subterranean Crusader city still exists, keeping teams of archaeologists active for the next several decades. But the splendor and historical value of this city was not a hidden secret, and was accessible for all visitors to appreciate.

We went back inside the colorful oriental markets, where we were careful not to show too much interest in the goods or make any eye contact with the vendors. I failed. A beautiful coffee pot captivated my attention and I hesitated for a moment, pointing it out to Sally. Like a genie, a merchant appeared out of nowhere, grabbed the pot, and started the game. "Misterrr, you like? I make you a zbecial brice."

"No, no it's okay," I politely declined and continued walking. Too late. He blocked the passage, still clenching the coffee pot. With his dark, piercing eyes and a grin that revealed teeth not unlike those of the camels in Be'er Sheva, he became persistent.

"How much you bay?"

"Nothing. I don't want it." I tried to escape. No chance.

"For you... feefty dollars. It is antique," he lied.

"No, it's not. I don't want it. It's too big."

"No broblem. Give me thirty dollars."

"It's *still* too big... and too expensive." I picked up a smaller, simpler coffee pot—a good size for traveling. I knew it would be impossible to leave without making a purchase; after all, it was something that I wanted to buy. "How much?"

"Ten dollars." I put it back and started to walk away. Again, he blocked our way. "What you give?"

"Two dollars." He laughed. I laughed. I left. He grabbed me.

"Only for you because you my friend. Five dollars."

"Three dollars. Not more." I wanted that coffee pot. I walked away again. He grabbed me again. This time he had a newspaper in his hand and was wrapping up the coffee pot.

"Four dollars," he insisted. He won. After the transaction was over, he hollered something to a bored-looking young boy resting on a chair (probably his son). In a flash, he was gone, but reappeared almost instantaneously with a tray holding three glasses of tea. The merchant handed both of us a glass and took one for himself. "Where you from?"

"England."

"You are welcome my friends." He meant it. After some smalltalk, he shook our hands with sincerity and we continued with our browsing.

"Don't point at anything," Sally warned me. I was proud of my purchase. This coffee pot would accompany me around the world for years to come.

After a deal is sealed, it is not unusual for the Arab merchant to offer tea or coffee to "drink" to the transaction. This has always been done throughout the ages and continues in modern times. No matter how far down you bargain, you will always be respected and made welcome. Sometimes, I enjoyed the game, but when I just merely wanted to look at something, it was most annoying to get attacked in such a way. But this *is* the Middle East and this *is* the way of life here.

A restaurant overlooking the port was the perfect place to eat. The food was fabulous and as fresh as can be. After taking free food on the kibbutz for granted, paying for it didn't seem right. It was getting dark, a good time to retire for the night, but the trading and intense bargaining continued. Haunting calls to prayer stirred us out of our sleep that night and reminded us where we were. The soothing wailing continued for a while, but I soon returned to my dreams.

Another early morning prayer call was our wake-up alarm, but we did want to get up early and continue sightseeing. The sesame-coated bread we bought last night together with some goat's cheese was our breakfast, and to make the breakfast complete, a pause at one of the cafés for a Turkish coffee was a must. We studied our map to see how far Caesarea was—the next destination. But distance was irrelevant in Israel; such a small country, nothing was too far. It was located nearby our old kibbutz. "Let's try and hitchhike to see how far we get," I suggested.

A nice long walk brought us to the intersection of the road going south. A group of soldiers had already taken over the best spot, so we had to wait until they were gone. Soldiers always got priority, and before long, they were lugging their burdensome luggage and weapons into several vehicles that had stopped for them. The group of eight were suddenly whisked away and we tried our luck, too. After less than five minutes, we were also picked up, by a woman who was driving to Tel Aviv. "Yes,

Caesarea is on my way. It's a nice place to visit, but a day trip is enough." I was fearful that we would get stuck in Haifa, but this lady was a godsend: she was driving right through.

We were dropped off at the intersection and hitched another lift the few remaining kilometers to the old part of Caesarea where the Roman amphitheater was located. This used to be the largest harbor in the Mediterranean, and like Acco, was also the trading center between the Romans, Greeks, and empires of the Far East. After King Herod had built all the structures that are typically associated with Roman cities, Caesarea became the capital of Judea. Not much is left today except for a few columns and walls. Many of the structures have been long claimed by the water gods—Neptune and Poseidon. The amphitheater remains intact and is still used today for concerts.

The place was practically deserted, with only a handful of tourists clambering amongst the ruins. We did likewise and tried to visualize the city in its Roman splendor when Herod's temple once stood and commanded the sea; now only parts of it remaining. We walked along the beach where Herod also built an aqueduct and where we sat down to have lunch. The lady who gave us a lift was right—a day trip *is* enough. In fact, a few hours are quite sufficient. After Acco, Caesarea seemed quite dead, like the ruins, and lacked the mystery and Middle-Eastern flair. Even the cafés and restaurants on the quay were lifeless. The gentle Mediterranean breeze gave some respite from the suffocating heat. There was no shade anywhere. Scurrying lizards delightfully roasted in the sun and were now the sole inhabitants of the once prestigious Roman pride. It was too hot to stay more than a few hours here. We slowly made our way back to the kibbutz, arriving just in time for supper.

"FOUR A.M. START?" I blurted out while glaring at the cow schedule. "Must be a mistake." It wasn't. My alarm went off at 3:30 A.M. Not a pleasant buzz from a clock-radio with a *snooze* button for those extra minutes, but a cruel, shrill, "get-up-or-else" ringing that couldn't be switched off without hurting the fingers while fumbling behind the clock. That *off* switch would always, strangely disappear while it was ringing. The end result was always the violent temptation to throw the clock against the wall, but by the time that happened, the alarm would stop.

I didn't wash myself, nor brush my teeth, but miserably hobbled towards the dairy. It was still dark outside, but the heat was on and so was the faint hum of the milking machines. "We can start," was the good morning greeting I got from cow boss. By that time, I had gotten used to the gates and no longer feared a cow mix-up. The 4:00 A.M start should not be different to the afternoon shift. In fact, it was more pleasant, as the (cow muck) stink was not as intense as when the scorching sun was baking the pies. The cows, on the other hand, were as groggy as I was… and the majority of them refused to get up.

I opened the first enclosure, but only a few of them made their own way to the building with swollen udders swaying from side to side. Cow boss came out and hollered impatiently. "John, what are you doing? Where are the cows?"

"Still in bed." I heard her snort at my reply, then she came out with a stick, which I assumed was for whacking the cows with, but as she was a cow herself, it would not have surprised me if she had started walloping *me* with it. She stomped into the enclosure and started yelling at the lazy bovines. They must have been afraid of her, too, as they suddenly snapped out of their bovine dreams once they sensed her fiery aura. She whacked the stubborn ones: their response to this rude awakening was an explosive fart followed by a noisy emptying of their bowels as they sluggishly rose from their slumber.

"Now bring the cows!" She left me the stick and marched off into the building. The docile animals were covered in excretions as they continued farting and urinating on their way. I had already gotten to know the "good cows" and the "bad cows." The good ones were those that needed no urging to move. The bad ones were the stubborn variety and refused to budge unless they got a good whacking. Cow number 166 was one I had long since decided to despise. It was always the last cow out of the enclosure, and no amount of yelling or whacking would make it move: it simply stayed put; it would go when it decided to, which was well after the others had already gone in. Number 166 at 4:00 A.M was even worse than number 166 at 4:00 P.M., and I was quite sure this obstinate creation knew what it was doing to me. I hated it. I planned to electrocute the miserable creature once I herded it inside the building.

I released the second group that was equally lazy, and also *they* greeted me with farts and squirting diarrhea. In the darkness, the sounds of "plop, plop, plop" piled up on the fields, and as I had to trudge inside the enclosures now to rouse the cows, my foot very often ended up in the still warm, stinky and gooey cow crap that the cows had attentively prepared for my arrival. "Eugh." I made my way into the dairy to move the cows along as the last of the first group were lining up for their milking. Number 166 was not lined up yet, refusing to budge a single centimeter. Great! Now was my chance. I moved the metal bar along until it was touching its rump, but it would still not move along. With an evil grin and malicious intentions, I switched the electricity on. Instantly, the loudest "moo" I've ever heard reverberated throughout the milking compound and number 166 shot forward like a katyusha rocket, rudely shoving the other bovines aside.

"John, what are you doing with the cows?" Cow boss shouted over.

"Me?... Nothing. One of them panicked and then slipped on the floor," I responded innocently. With this sadistic satisfaction, I happily went on with the rest of my cow gathering.

It was 7:30 A.M. and my work was done for the day. I was in a great mood and planned to do some writing after my shower and breakfast. The other volunteers had begun their day, so I had a nice quiet volunteers' quarters all to myself, without *Bruce Springsteen* or *U2* blasting away. It also gave me a chance to observe the local birds known as hoopoes that abound in this area. They have a long, skinny beak and a crown of feathers on their heads, which make them so attractive, it is not possible to simply ignore them. Other colorful birds made their home here, but the hoopoe was my favorite. I joined my friends for breakfast, went back to relax, then came back for an early lunch. There was no sign of any other volunteer yet, and I had the table to myself this time. I gobbled up my food, grabbed my book, and spent the next few hours at the swimming pool, but feeling suddenly tired after my ridiculously early start, I fell asleep until a cold, wet, dripping Sally on top of me startled me awake.

"Hey, you lazy cow," she teased.

"Hmmm?"

Walking distance from the kibbutz is Rahat—a Bedouin settlement established by the Israeli government. Sally and I strolled over to this settlement out of curiosity one Sabbath morning while the plastered volunteers still slept and made a sobering recovery. We went right after an early breakfast, determined to beat the ferocious heat that was already starting.

On the way we encountered "whistles and whoops" as beaten-up cars crammed with Bedouin youths slowed down to gawk at us on their way. Walking seemed to be a rare sight—especially walking Westerners. "There's nothing there to see," one of the kibbutzniks told us yesterday. He was right. Strewn garbage welcomed us into town as we walked past the Rahat sign, written in English, Arabic, and Hebrew, like every sign in Israel. The contrast between the kibbutz and Rahat was like comparing planet Earth to the moon. It was desolate and littered with plastic containers, rusting cans, left over building material, and even car batteries, which were simply tossed with the rest of the garbage. There were no beautiful flowers or bushes or lush palm trees. Even birds avoided this place, preferring the green paradise of Kibbutz Shoval. Only wild trees grew here, planted by nature, but looked miserable in their surroundings.

The ugly, half-finished concrete blocks that served as houses were constructed in order to settle the Bedouins, but the problem here was that Bedouins are, and always have been desert wanderers, and cannot be settled. What should they do with a house? Even *they* had no idea how to cope with this development. Many of the houses remained empty, while at the front or back, the typical black Bedouin tents had been erected, and they continued to live in their own traditional ways, using some of the buildings to house goats and sheep instead. We also passed a couple of houses that had been gutted by fire. I read about a recent blaze here in the newspaper. It was mentioned that a family had built a fire on the floor inside one of the houses in order to cook their food. The result was evident.

Hardly any signs of life stirred within the settlement. The thousands of goats and sheep, with the occasional shepherds keeping an eye on them, seemed to be the exclusive inhabitants. They lifted their arm up in a greeting gesture. (The shepherds—not the sheep.) We did come across some old men later, sitting on the ground in the shade of a scraggly tree. They barely battered an eyelid as we walked by a few meters from their gathering. They were all wearing the traditional head cover, lounging with stretched-out callous feet protruding from their worn-out sandals. This was the age group that would never adapt to such modern lifestyles. The young generation though, would slowly leave their traditional pasts behind and settle down. They would never live in a tent or even know how to put one up. Desert wanderings, camel markets, traditional clothing, would become a thing of the past. The settlement of Rahat was the beginning of doom for these people. I hoped I was wrong.

But there really was nothing here. We walked back to the green oasis of the kibbutz, desperate for the soothing water of the swimming pool.

My early starts continued for the next couple of weeks. Getting up so early didn't become easier, but I could now do the gates with my eyes closed, and they *were* for the first hour. Cow 166 continued to slow me down and I continued giving it a spark on its rump, projecting it into a missile. It never seemed to learn.

I was now shown the ropes of the milking process and how to attach the machines onto the udders. I was to become one of the team. When I wasn't herding the cows, I would be doing the milking with the other three. Cow boss was as friendly as before, but it didn't bother me anymore; it was just the way she was. As the cows lined up at an angle, I had to hose down their udders with a spray gun so that none of their excretions were sucked up by the machines. The four nozzles were then attached onto their udders in a particular order and stayed on by the suction and pumping method. Milk then flowed into glass containers, filling up rapidly. Some of the cows had small udders and the machine could not grasp them properly as there was hardly anything to suck on. The suction nozzles often fell to the ground.

Some cows that had no chance to relieve themselves in the fields did so inside the dairy; not a pleasant sight with all the rear ends facing me. They took turns emptying their bowels, the pies splattering noisily onto the concrete floor. The urinating was the worst. It came out like a waterfall, splashing on all sides, and you had to move fast to dive out of the way. This job required eyes all around and fast reflexes. The place was constantly being hosed down, but more splats kept coming. I was running around to re-insert the fallen suction pads, and at the same time dashing out of the way when a waterfall gushed out from above, only to be threatened by a bombardment of falling pies on the adjacent row. The outdoors were much safer.

Another annoying cow (not number 166) had such small udders that the machine had to be hand-held during the whole milking process. My hands were free, so I had the honor of milking it. The cows were parked on a raised platform above to facilitate the machine insertion from below, but it was necessary to lean over when having problems with the udders. I leaned over quite far, holding the suction machine with both hands as it was getting heavy. At that time, the nasty, ungrateful cow decided to piss on me, showering me with very warm, yellow liquid. It was a good time to scream. "Aaaaagh." I dropped the machine to the ground, startling everyone. Cow boss took one look at the dripping figure and cracked up, almost choking with laughter. The others joined in, unable to continue with their work. I stood there, the center of their amusement, but *I* was *not* amused. I hated cows! It was the first time I had seen cow boss laugh, and she wasn't able to suppress it. Tears were running down her cheeks while cow piss was running down *my* cheeks. She found her voice at last.

"John, you must go and shower now." More laughter. "No problem, we can manage." More laughter. "Don't forget to change." More laughter. "If you want, you can come back afterward." Endless laughter. The cows were also laughing at me; I was sure of that as their heads swung to the side to see what the commotion was about, their eyes bulging with a triumphant expression.

This was war! "Tomorrow, I will electrocute them all," I muttered to myself.

It was just starting to get light outside as I headed towards my room, already peeling off my soaked shirt while walking. A volunteer on the way to the factory noticed me shirtless and my disheveled look. "Hey, what happened to *you?*"

"A cow pissed on me." More laughter. That made his day. I undressed outside before entering my room. My shoes, thank God, were dry. Sally was just leaving for her kitchen duties and caught me outside in just my underwear. She stared at me goggle-eyed.

"John, *what* are you *doing?*"

"A cow pissed on me. I'm soaked. Need a shower," I mumbled, in a bad mood.

"What...! How... how can a cow piss on you? What were you doing under the cow anyway?" I briefly went over the nasty cow incident. Sally's reaction did not help. She cracked up like cow boss, also unable to suppress her laughter.

I took a nice long shower, making sure all cow aromas was eradicated, shampooing my hair several times. Ready for battle, I put on some fresh work clothes and went back to those horrible creatures. The radio was on when I arrived, tuned into the famous pirate station—The Voice of Peace. It advertised itself as being broadcast from *somewhere* in the Mediterranean. It was in English and always played the latest chart hits—popular amongst volunteers and young Israelis alike. Cow boss was humming to a tune and was in a fantastic mood.

Cow boss noticed my arrival. "Ah, John, you look much better," she guffawed. The others were still grinning, but I was still pissed. "We're almost done. Just one group left." It was the first time she was speaking to me like a human being, and from that moment, I was accepted as a fully-fledged member of this group. Today was my day of initiation and I seemed to have passed the test. Cow boss acquired her real name—Idit, and always greeted and thanked me for my help ever after. Even in the dining room she would ask, "Hi, John, how are you?" While milking, she also made conversation, telling me about some attractions I should visit in the Negev Desert. "There are some ruins of ancient Nabatean cities in the Negev you should see. There are three: Shivta, Mamshit and Avdat," she told me one afternoon.

"Never heard of them. Where are they?" My ears pricked up when she mentioned "ancient cities."

"Not so well known to tourists. Guidebooks don't really point them out." She showed me on the map where they were located—middle of nowhere—in the heart of the Negev Desert. The location alone sent shivers down my spine. I wanted to see them. "Might be a little difficult to get to. Make sure you take plenty of water when you go. We still need you for the cows." Great. She had a sense of humor, even if she did visualize my shriveling up and gasping for a drop of water in the middle of the Negev.

My guidebook briefly mentioned those three places as if they were insignificant, but also confirming the fact that they were difficult to reach. I went to Be'er Sheva to find a more detailed map of the Negev Desert and also managed to find some beautiful postcards showing an aerial view of Avdat. It looked as barren as Masada and promised an equally fascinating adventure.

"You're going where?" Asked one of the English volunteers. "Avdat."

"Never heard of it," was his comment; not from ignorance, but it proved the fact that this place was an insider tip rather than a tourist hot-spot, and it was too much off the beaten track. Those who had not really done any thorough research on this region would miss the most spectacular places, but not everyone had time on their hands.

The volunteers' leader arranged foods to take with us on our desert trip, and also three containers of water, which we would schlep the entire time. Keith (one of the English volunteers) joined us on this adventure. He was one of the quiet ones when drunk, and normally just passed out when a certain alcohol level was attained in his body. He also happened to be good company even though he continued to wear his dark blue kibbutz work clothes.

The easiest way to get there was to hitch a lift to Be'er Sheva, then take a bus to Sde Boqer. In this heat, hitchhiking in the desert is not something I recommend, but the short distance to the city was bearable. I couldn't wait to get onto the air-conditioned bus. Getting out of it was the worst part when the doors to the furnace opened and we had to step outside into temperatures so hot, it felt as if flames were engulfing me. A gentle breeze caressed the body, but that also felt like a hairdryer set on high. Breathing in the hot air made me nauseous and I immediately started slurping on my water container.

We were at Kibbutz Sde Boqer, the former home of Israel's first Prime Minister Ben Gurion. This is where he spent his last years after his retirement. But we didn't stop here, continuing to the hill in the distance; the location of Avdat. A car from the kibbutz stopped and a very friendly driver offered to take us to the site, which was only about fifteen minutes from the kibbutz. "If you run out of water, you can fill up the containers there. They have a water fountain." He noticed our sleeping bags. "Are you planning to sleep on top?"

"Yes."

"Be careful of scorpions. They like to hide beneath rocks." We thanked him as he dropped us off in the middle of nowhere. Literally. I have never seen middle-of-nowhere as such. It was more desolate than Masada, which had *some* life below. Here, there was nothing. Nothing! Nothing! Desert, in its purest form engulfed us puny humans from all directions. There was no sound—no life—no traffic; wait, there were two cars parked below the hill, but no sign of any people.

Avdat used to be a flourishing Nabatean city, serving as a seasonal campground for caravans traveling along the Incense Route from the East. Those were the times when deserts belonged to the camels, when spices and incense were being transported across vast expanses of wasteland. Romans and Byzantines also had a go at shaping this lonely desert outpost, but in the seventh century, a powerful earthquake destroyed the city. Still, impressive ruins remain today; so impressive in fact, that in 1973 it was chosen as the setting for the filming of *Jesus Christ Superstar.*

The climb was steep, but not as steep as Masada. The sprawling ruins were located on top of the hill, thus commanding such a view that it was possible to see the arrival of your guests the following day. Camels would have blended into the landscape perfectly with their tan color, so maybe it wouldn't have been possible to see them from afar after all. We saw nothing—no animals and no people. Dust devils, appearing out of nowhere were the only inhabitants, twisting sporadically and stirring up loose sand in the distance while they waltzed across the desert. We three took a swig of water and rested amongst the endless ruins. This place was huge. I remembered the scorpion warning and was mindful of where I sat.

Despite the endless sprawl of ruins, the attraction for me was the vast expanse of never-ending desert, carved up by past torrents of destructive flash-floods. I could sit here for hours and gaze upon the hills and canyons, pondering life several thousand years ago, imagining all those thousands of traders who had passed along this path en-route from Arabia to the ports in Gaza. The heat shimmered in the distance, distorting the view, causing rocks to blend in with the different shades and transform themselves into a procession of traders. The image dispersed when Sally interrupted my musing. "Ready to eat?"

"Always. That chicken must be roasting inside the backpacks." It was. Meat would not keep until tomorrow, so we ate our entire chicken supply before it spoiled in the heat, tearing off pieces of bread to absorb some of the grease. "Mmmm, nice and warm." We located the water and filled up our containers for brewing up some coffee.

Remains of previous fires were scattered upon the hill, and the leftover sticks and wood were there for the take. I was overjoyed to be using my recently bought coffee pot from Acco, which brewed enough coffee for two. Being *very* English, Keith never did acquire a taste for Turkish coffee, so he ended up stewing *Wissotzky* teabags in a small cooking pot. "Did you bring milk for your tea?" I asked him. Keith proudly pulled out a small bottle he had filled up with fresh milk that morning. As he attempted to pour some into his tea… *plop;* a large piece of milk fell into his cup, followed by an even larger plop.

"My milk!" His jaw dropped in shock. It had curdled in the intense heat.

"Want some coffee?" I offered.

"I'll drink it black," he murmured miserably, grimacing when he tasted his milkless tea. "Eugh!" An Englishman without "proper" tea can become somewhat grumpy, but Brian coped well with the catastrophe. "Got some beer though," he grinned, producing four bottles from his bag.

As well as the ruins, several trails indented the landscape as they led towards shimmering horizons, and were (I was told) relatively easy to follow; some of them entered deep canyons. I wondered which one was the Incense Route—as used by caravans of long ago. It would have been a fantastic route to retrace, but August is not a time for hiking in this region. I barely made it to the ruins and could not imagine going on any hike. There was no shade anywhere, so for anyone who developed sunstroke, it was tough luck. Neither of us did. Soaking our T-shirts in water, we wrapped them around our heads, looking like nomadic traders. Only our camels were missing.

As dusk approached, we noticed that those two cars were still at the bottom of the hill. "They probably went on a hike," suggested Keith. We made ourselves as comfortable as possible and restarted a leftover campfire for the night. The stars came out in full splendor… and so did my coffee pot. Keith produced his four bottles of beer, but had forgotten the bottle opener, whereas he almost stabbed himself in the chest attempting to get the caps off with a knife. We had some packs of cookies from the kibbutz and some dates to chew on.

The flickering flames cast scary-looking shadows on the walls, and for no reason at all, we ended up whispering as we had done on Masada, even though there was nobody else here. I wouldn't say "not a soul," as there probably were a *number* of souls around. The stones that absorbed the sun's rays during the day now radiated heat, cooking us at night. It was bloody hot.

Spending the night amongst the ruins of Avdat was the highlight of our little excursion, but after a fine breakfast of sugar-sweet melons, still warm from the day before, we made our way back down the hill. It was barely ten in the morning and already we were being scorched. The two cars were still parked in the same spot. Shortly after, another car arrived and parked next to the other two. An Israeli couple got out and waved to us. "*Shalom...* did you spend the night here?" We must have looked as if we had —stubby chins, disheveled hair, unwashed faces.

"Yes, now we have to find a way of getting back."

"We're only staying here about an hour. If we see you on the road, we'll pick you up. Make sure you have enough water." Then they both started their climb with amazing energy and giant strides as if they had a time schedule to keep.

"*Israelis,*" Sally winced, watching them practically run up the steep incline. "How do they do it?"

"They're superhuman," I remarked.

It wouldn't have made sense to wait on this lonely desert road for a car that wouldn't come, so we started walking towards Sde Boqer... and a very long walk. Hardly five minutes went by when we heard the hum of an approaching vehicle; two vehicles in fact—the same two cars that had been parked all night. They both stopped. In each car were two middle-aged men who looked worse than us. "We can take you to Be'er Sheva if you like," one of the men offered politely.

"Couldn't be better." Sally and I filled up one car, but Keith had to squeeze into the other one, which was also stuffed with camping gear. "You're camping too?" I asked. They told us that they had spent two nights in the desert, but not on top of the hill.

"There are other ruins here, too, not only on top of the hill," they informed us. "If you're lucky, you can still find some coins," and he showed us five coins dating back to the Roman period that they had found the last two days. They were hard to make out after being covered up for 2,000 years, and each one had an irregular round-ish shape, an indication that these metal pieces were cut out by hand. I could barely make out the head on the coins. "Julius Caesar," acknowledged one of the coin hunters. I gasped in disbelief.

"They must be valuable," I presumed.

"Not really. These are the most common coins to be found. If they were gold, *then* they would be valuable." They told us that the four of them got together whenever possible and traversed the whole country in search of coins, camping out for several days at a time in historical places such as this. "The whole country is a treasure trove wherever you dig, especially in the desert regions where the dry heat preserves coins for an eternity."

"How do you find them?" I wondered.

"Metal detectors. Very good for coins, but very illegal. That's why we do it at night," they laughed. "If we get caught, we're in trouble, but it's our hobby."

The other guy interrupted. "Not just Israel, but the entire region stretching from Egypt to Persia and all the way north to Turkey—it is full of treasures. History is a fascinating subject, and when you find a piece of history, it makes it more special."

The friendly treasure hunters kindly dropped us off in the city where Sally and I headed to the immigration office to renew our visas once again. Three more months were almost up. It was also a good spot to satisfy our insatiable passion for falafel.

The cows were waiting for me back on the kibbutz. It was a 4:00 A.M. start again, but it had now become routine and fun. Since I started milking cows I have never drunk a glass of milk ever again. After witnessing what goes inside those jars, it was enough to put me off for life. Despite spraying the udders, it wasn't always possible to avoid getting those chocolate pieces into the milk. Some of the cows had internal bleeding, thus producing strawberry milk. It all came together and was pasteurized, then the milk attained its brilliant white color.

Some weeks later, a devastating earthquake struck Mexico City, and thousands of deaths were reported. One of the volunteers was from Mexico City and he was not able to get through to his family there despite trying to call for many days. Phones were not working in Mexico City and he had no way of knowing whether his family was affected. Panic stricken, he left a few days later to fly back home. We all felt sorry for him. After the body count many weeks later, estimated deaths were 10,000.

Life on the kibbutz continued as a routine, and so did the drinking parties Friday nights, which Sally and I never participated in. Fridays was a time for us to dig into the map of Israel and search for new destinations. "We have to see Jericho," Sally announced. I agreed entirely and we made plans to take a couple of days off again.

"Traveling again?" Idit's (cow boss) eyebrows shot up.

We approached Jericho the same way we had gone to the Dead Sea many months ago, but instead of continuing east, the bus made a sharp turn north at an intersection, and before long, ancient sunburned adobes started to appear. In the shimmering distance, tops of minarets sprouted from the haze. There were goats and sheep on both sides of the road, attempting to nibble anything green and edible, but the merciless sun extracted every bit of moisture that might have been left in the plants, leaving only frazzled brush behind.

This area is abundant in springs: subterranean water sources, which have turned Jericho into an oasis, thus allowing plants with long roots to develop and flourish. A sign boasting that Jericho is the oldest city on earth and that it is 10,000 years old, welcomes every visitor. We got off in the center, and most noticeable were the rich, exotic trees and bushes filled with gorgeous flowers that released sweet perfume into the air. Banana and papaya trees grew in many of the gardens.

Jericho was packed with tourists and bus tours. Roadside restaurants with scores of seats and tables were thriving, satisfying the gastronomic needs of tourists. We were also hungry, but opted to sit at a quieter and smaller restaurant that looked as if it catered more for the locals. The prices in such places are usually lower, too. I had recently acquired a taste for hummus—a dip made out of chickpeas and sesame. The hummus I ordered here was the best one I have ever tasted, and the quality would never be surpassed. It was served with a dollop of fiery-hot paste in the middle and drowned in delicious local olive oil. Freshly-made pita bread baked on a hot stone accompanied the meal. A salad with chopped cucumbers and tomatoes came in an extra dish. The taste was amazing.

We continued our stroll. "Look, a camel!" He was crouched by the roadside, looking like a prince; adorned in exotic riding gear and waiting for tourists to ride him. The owner stood by its side, also dressed up, but in a spotless white gown with a red and white *kefiyeh* over his head. "Want to ride a camel?" I asked Sally.

"No way! Looks expensive anyway." It did. Compared to some of the scabby camels in the Negev, this one was royalty. We went up to the crouching creature to admire it. It was beautiful and didn't even smell. "Must've had a bubble bath this morning," Sally whispered. At that moment, it made one of its deep-from-the-stomach-camel-gargles and curled its lips, thus destroying any proud majestic image it had momentarily possessed. It was, after all, just another camel.

"You like ride camel?" asked the owner. The camel gawked at us stupidly with its tongue out, showing us its teeth, which badly needed a dentist. We shook our heads and walked on to browse around the colorful roadside stores where vendors sold all kinds of delicious fruits. We bought some local papaya to snack on later. With only some hours to spare in this town, we located a quiet road to see what lay beyond, following its steep ascent towards the barren hills. No tourists absconded so far from the center, but neither did the locals, preferring to mingle with the tourists with the hope of extracting some business from them. From this vantage point, the whole of Jericho was visible, swallowed up in a haze of humidity and dust. I tried to make out where the famous Walls of Jericho had once stood and were razed after those famous trumpets blew. If there were any walls, they would have been mixed up with countless other ruins which overwhelmed the entire area.

Ten thousand years of history were being excavated, keeping archaeologists occupied for the rest of their lives. In and around Jericho, areas had been cordoned off and divided into small squares, where archaeologists with their teams of students and volunteers brushed away loose dirt, looking for shards of pottery or remains of some long-forgotten temple. Some of these volunteers came for a short time, then returned to their studies abroad after the season.

We walked all the way to the top of the hill, passing black Bedouin tents on the way, but saw no inhabitants. They were either sleeping or sensibly sipping tea in a café. Our water supply was diminishing rapidly in temperatures over 40°Celsius—and that was in the shade. We *had* no shade, so we sizzled like the desert brush and blended into the landscape, brown as we were. We reached an area where water flowed along an aqueduct, still in use after 2,000 years. I read that natural spring water bubbles up from the ground and is channeled and re-routed around the whole area—and it is potable. We tried it. It was refreshingly cool and tasted pure. We filled up our canteens, dipping them inside the flowing water.

Walking back into town was slow going. The iridescent heat caused movements to appear in slow motion. Large black lizards basked on sides of buildings—the only creatures that were thoroughly enjoying the sun. We were suffering, looking for even the slightest shade and guzzling our water supply. It didn't help anymore. Back in the bustling center, we waited for the heavenly air-conditioned bus to take us back to Jerusalem. Last time we were in Jerusalem, we slept in a private hostel in the Old City. It was the same place we headed to again.

There was commotion in Israel. Israeli air force planes flew to Tunisia and bombed the PLO headquarters in Tunis. Their mission to blow the Palestinian leader Yassir Arafat to "kingdom come" failed, but there was uproar in the Arab world. Palestinians in Israel strongly protested the attack. A week later, Palestinian terrorists hijacked the famous Italian cruise ship *Achille Lauro* off the coast of Egypt, and now the West was in uproar.

It was time to move on: we have both had enough of kibbutz life, *Bruce Springsteen, U2,* and now, *The Bangles* and *Madonna.* It was always the same cassettes. I came to Israel hoping to work outdoors, but that never happened. The only possibility would be to go to a moshav. A moshav, we were told, is quite different to a kibbutz. There, we would also have a volunteer status, but get paid for our work. We would have to buy our own food and prepare it ourselves, as there is no communal dining room. All farmers do share farm machinery with other members, but each one is responsible for their own crops and their own volunteers. The volunteers work directly for their assigned family and only in the fields that belong to that family. It's supposed to be physically challenging compared to kibbutz life, but it will also put a few hundred dollars a month into my pocket. My cash supply was slowly drying up, making it necessary to replenish the wallet. I enjoyed trying out different things and this was a good opportunity.

Idit was unhappy to see me leave and let me know how much she appreciated my work. "Wow!" I even ended up patting cow number 166 on the head on my last day. A new volunteer was taking over the next day, and he or she would have to be trained from scratch. I didn't envy them, but couldn't help wondering how long it would take until *they* got "initiated."

"Give 'em hell," I whispered into 166's ear.

5
WHO'S AFRAID OF THE BIG BAD WOLF?

Although Jerusalem is the capital, Tel Aviv seemed to be the main business district with all main offices located there, and that included the moshav office. Dvora had given us a nice letter of recommendation to hand over to the family we were to work for. She had called the office in advance to expect us, and when we arrived, the woman in charge already had the address of our destination. It was the same procedure as with the kibbutz. "Moshav Faran." She handed us a map and circled the location. Her pencil trailed all the way to the south of the country.

"It's not far from Eilat!" we both exclaimed. "Perfect." That would put us near the Red Sea resort, we had not yet seen. In fact, we hadn't been so far south at all yet, and now the moshav office was sending us all the way down to the tip. It was the most ideal location and we were excited about the prospect of living within such close proximity to Egypt.

I noticed some unusual, but beautiful posters hanging inside the moshav office—pictures of ruins that seemed out of ordinary, and eerie landscapes that could have served as the perfect backdrop to science-fiction movies. "Where's that?" I asked the woman, assuming it was another hidden and unknown part of Israel, but her answer surprised me.

"Turkey! When you're done with Israel, consider going to Turkey.

Now, *that's* an adventure. You'll love it. The people are very friendly *and* it's dotted with mindboggling wonders. Most importantly, it's cheap."

"Hmmm… Turkey… " I pondered for a moment, looking at Sally. She also honed in on my thoughts. It had never crossed my mind going there, but why not? We looked at each other, both on the same wavelength. "Yeah, let's travel to Turkey afterward," I blurted out.

"Let's see how much we can save up on the moshav and then… " she suggested, trailing off in thought. It sounded like a plan, and we now had a purpose. The office lady wished us a lot of fun on the moshav and phoned the family we were to work for to let them know about our arrival.

It was to be a very long bus ride from Tel Aviv: back south, back to the enchanting Negev Desert, then onto the smooth and endless main road, which would take us to an arid region squeezed between Egypt and Jordan. This was the Eilat bus, and it was packed with Israeli and foreign tourists alike. Without a seat, I wouldn't have survived this trip, but we were one of the first ones on the bus, having ferociously fought for one and prevented others from boarding by blocking the doors with our bulging backpacks while paying. We were learning. Muttering aggressors tried to squeeze in between us. "*Reggah!*" I admonished their impatience. The door to the luggage compartment at the side of the bus was locked. A frowning Israeli couple with oversized baggage impatiently banged on the driver's window to unlock the latch.

"REGGAH! REGGAH! REGGAH!" He barked back with a threatening gesture.

The Fine Art of Waiting… *or telling people how to wait: When asking an Israeli for something, they will most certainly not give you the satisfaction of an immediate response. They will tell you to wait, but there are different forms of such a command in Israel. The general Hebrew word for "just a minute" is "reggah" as translated in any dictionary, and with a clear pronunciation of the letter "R." This short, 2-syllable word may have the humble meaning of, "Oh, just give me a second," or it may give you the clear venomous message, "WHY THE FUCK ARE YOU BOTHERING ME? CAN'T YOU SEE I'M BUSY?" It is therefore, of utmost importance to be able to define the meaning of this innocent little word, which is used with various body gestures.*

Now the hand comes into play: it can be either; left or right. The thumb, index finger, and middle finger are put together to form a point facing upwards, and the leftover two fingers remain clenched. This gesture is used with an up and down shaking of the wrist action as if there was an imaginary piece of string coming down from the sky above and it is being pulled between the first three fingers. This alone is a gesture for making you wait. It may be used without uttering a sound, and upon seeing this, you will only have to wait a moment. There are several combinations in force:

1. When the hand gesture is used together with the command (reggah), the meaning behind this is nothing more than a firm "WAIT!"

2. By using the hand gesture and repeating "reggah" three times, is already an indication that there is some impatience there. You may come across this in shops or restaurants when asking for, say, "Can I have some more pita bread for my hummus?"

3. Beware, when you see just a sharp flick of the wrist action and a glaring look, as this indicates, "You are bothering me!" If you see a slight rise of the chin, it's better not to ask again, but just simply wait.

4. Now comes the more threatening part when the lower jaw and the eyes get into the game. The "reggah" word is roared out loud, and the hand gesture is no longer pulling a fine piece of imaginary string, as it now becomes your imaginary neck being squeezed and your head wrenched off by an extremely sharp tug; no longer with the wrist action, but by the use of the entire arm. At the same time, the lower jaw will protrude and the eyes will pop out. This is a threatening situation and extremely life endangering if the lower teeth are shown. Retreat, is the best action in this case. One consolation is that you will not get this kind of response when asking for extra pita bread for your hummus..., but on buses, maybe.

The landscape changed and became more rugged and unforgiving as the bus hummed its way through a different kind of desert where low thorny trees and bushes made their home. Hours went by, and the bus still plowed forward, but stopping at a few settlements along the way and even at a falafel shop where we all gorged ourselves on these delicious snacks. Again, the landscape transformed itself as the desert became flatter and attained a lighter tan color. Flash floods that had occurred in the past had left behind dramatically eroded gullies where plants struggled to survive. Where torrents of water had once gushed, bone-dry cracked surfaces now gaped, waiting for the next rainfall. I never knew that a desert had so many faces. In school I had learned a desert to be a hot and dry place with sand dunes where nothing grew, but what I was witnessing was contrary to my former education.

"Faran," announced the bus driver. We arrived an hour before sunset, glad to be off the bus, and the only foolish passengers getting off in what looked like a lonely desert outpost while the rest continued to the populous Red Sea resort. Such desolation had its own intrinsic beauty, with the clearly discernible mountains of Jordan trapping the valley to the east and adding a twinge of pink to the desert palette as it caught the sun's rays. Shimmering heat and total stillness enshrouded us as the bus pulled away. Not far from here (as the crow flies) on the other side is Egypt; so near, but yet so far, separated by the Wilderness of Paran, hence the name where the moshav derived its name from. It truly was a wilderness: a *cruel* wilderness without any mercy for the foolish.

But I was hoping that the farmer wasn't cruel. Will we be forced to work all day long? We had heard horror stories of farmers who treated their workers like slaves all hours of the day.

We followed the sign pointing to the moshav and made our way towards the settlement, our voices seemingly out of place in this oppressing silence. The sound of a tractor in the distance also disturbed the eternal stillness as it approached in a cloud of dust. The passing farmer stopped to pick us up, looking a bit like a ferocious walrus with his blonde mustache and a thickset, stocky build with hands as large as shovels. "New volunteers?" He growled. We told him the name of the family that was expecting us. "Come, I take you to them," and we hopped onto the back of the trailer, and by the time we arrived, our bodies were covered in fine sand.

The layout of the moshav was not so different to a kibbutz, but the large imposing dining room was missing. There was a different kind of center—with a shop, but no laundry building. Families did their own laundry here and they were also supposed to do ours. Impressive palm trees were growing everywhere, but yet again, different to the ones in the northern part of the Negev.

The walrus pulled to a stop outside a house and simply barged in roaring, "YIGAL!"

"*Reggah!*" came the reply.

Yigal was to be our boss. One problem: Yigal didn't speak any English; his wife Ronit did. We shook hands, and Mr. and Mrs. Farmer took us to our own little house equipped with a kitchen, bathroom, and the one room which was a bedroom/living room combined. It was very spartan inside: a bad sign, as that probably indicated that we didn't *really* need any accommodation, and the farmer was planning to keep us in the fields the entire day. He was explaining some things in Hebrew, whereas we just stared blankly and shrugged our shoulders. "*Reggah*," he indicated with a flick of wrist and went to get his wife who was picking up some litter outside. Yigal shrugged, grinned sheepishly, and said slowly, "Me... no English speak. Ronit speak you."

Ronit spoke. "You will have to teach him English, but he's very lazy to learn," she shook her head disappointingly. "Our last volunteers were from Argentina; also a couple, but their English was very bad and neither of us speaks Spanish. But we managed and had a lot of fun. We hope you enjoy yourselves here and stay a long time. If you need anything, anything at all, just knock on our door, or just come in." Ronit offered to do all our laundry and told us to help ourselves to anything they grew in the fields, which was a lot. "I will also bring you fruits or vegetables from time to time. Other farmers grow different things, so we share."

"What do you grow?" I asked.

"Peppers." I groaned. More darned peppers. I was getting sick of them. "And various kinds of melons," she added. Ah, that's better. I could eat melons all day. Israel has the sweetest melons I have ever tasted.

They left while we took the foam mattresses outdoors to give them a good walloping. They looked as if they'd been used for sleeping on in the desert. Part of that desert was also on the floor, which we swept out, but the wind would blow it back in through the gap some hours later, so it was pointless.

Ronit showed up again with the bedding, left, and returned with some food for us to prepare in our kitchen. "The shop's already closed, but you can go there tomorrow morning." She also brought us a melon, and... peppers. A pack of my favorite coffee appeared, too. "You like coffee with *hell*?" She asked, frowning as she couldn't remember the English word for *hell*.

"I love hell." I thanked her.

"Oh, I must tell you. We get a lot of scorpions here, so always check your shoes before you put them on, also your beds before you climb in."

I noticed lizards scurrying around on my way to the house. "Are there snakes here?" I asked.

"Many. You'll see them in the mornings out in the fields. They're harmless, so don't worry. We live and work with nature and don't have problems. Just be careful of the scorpions," she told us cheerfully and left.

We were both grinning, thinking the same thing, imagining our friend Philip from kibbutz Ha'ogen working here. He would already be running for the return bus.

The temperatures increased in this part of Israel, and I couldn't believe that they could go any higher. It was already dark outside and we were starving. I checked out the food Ronit had brought us: chicken, potatoes, and salad ingredients. The red peppers were amazingly sweet and I often ended up eating them freshly picked in the fields.

With the night came the tranquility we were not used to. On the kibbutz, music or voices of other volunteers could often be heard. We sat on the doorstep of the house and listened to the wonderful silence. Not quite silent though: there were the sounds of insects. This was, after all, the wilderness.

First thing in the morning, we checked out the shop. After being pampered on the kibbutz, it was the first time that we paid any attention to food prices. They were astronomical. Fresh meat was so expensive we quickly decided to become vegetarians; well, at least partially. For some obscure reason, the shop was also selling peppers. Was that a joke? Obviously not, as a price tag was attached to the box. Our tenderfoot stance caught the attention of other volunteers, giving us fleeting looks. The English were easy to spot. *Their* shopping baskets contained more beer than food. Thankfully, the most important item (Swiss chocolate) was reasonably priced. We bought some fresh bread, goat's cheese, and pricey meat slices. Eggs were cheap and were good for breakfast. Rice and pasta were quite affordable, as well as tomatoes and cucumbers.

We went to pay. "Why are you wasting your money buying these?" The cashier looked horrified as he took our tomatoes and cucumbers out of the basket. "Just take them from the fields. It's cheaper."

"Well... er... okay." I didn't buy them. Why sell them in the first place? "Can I... buy... the onions?" I asked the cashier cautiously.

"Onions. Yes. WE DON'T GROW ONIONS!" He said this with utmost dismay, perturbed by the fact that the whole world was clueless regarding the agriculture of Moshav Faran. We also treated ourselves to some ice cream to put into the freezer compartment. Walrus came past just then, recognizing us and growled a *shalom*.

The moshav was full of agricultural activity. This time of morning, everyone was in their scruffy work clothes. People looked different than on the kibbutz, which was a lot tamer than a moshav. Moshavniks looked gruffer, and many faces retained the weathered leathery complexion, which was probably typical for pioneers in the desert wilderness. Sally and I were chocolate brown and grateful for the fact that we didn't stick out amongst the Israelis or volunteers who also had been burnt to a crisp. We knew that work would now be physically demanding and the lazy kibbutz days were over. But the cremated volunteers looked content and neither of them gave the slightest inclination that they were suffering from over-exertion. Maybe work won't be as bad as the rumors made out. We shall see tomorrow.

Tomorrow came too soon as the 5:00 A.M. alarm aggressively introduced the new day. It was too early to eat anything, and we would have no dining room to come back to after a few hours of work. Forty-five minutes later we heard the tractor outside our door, and then a knock. Dawn was breaking, but the mornings were still pleasantly warm. It was end of October, and shorts and T-shirt sufficed. We climbed into the tractor and sat on top of the wheel guard, holding on to a metal bar while Yigal drove us to his field—only fifteen minutes away. Rows and rows of crops had transformed the dry desert into a rich fertile region. All that was needed to accomplish this was water, and that was delivered via endless irrigation pipes that were responsible for the taming of the desert and for survival in this inhospitable region of thorns and scorpions.

Yigal drove past the green area and took us further out to a field where countless rows had been invaded by giant weeds—a lot of them over a meter high. In the middle of the rows, small green plants were struggling to compete for space and water with the tall invaders. It was obvious what we had to do, and Yigal required no English to explain. He did, however, speak in Hebrew and showed us how to weed anyway. As the plants were so tall, it was not necessary to go down on the knees and do the arduous weeding one is used to in temperate climates, where they don't grow into monstrous triffids. Pulling out monsters was much simpler and more enjoyable, as they came out very easily from the light sandy soils. Yigal left us to it and drove off, probably to a different field.

After the tractor left, utmost silence descended upon us, and so did the heat, which started an hour after our arrival in the field. I peeled off my T-shirt, but it was a bad idea as the sand flew into the air and coated my body when I tugged on the plants. An impressive weed, almost two meters tall, dominated one row. This was going to be fun to pull out, but required a little more force. Tugging sharply, I could feel the roots loosening in the sand, not able to hang on anymore, and suddenly with a heave, a burst of sand went flying in all directions and the plant shot out, but together with a yellow scorpion, which also flew into the air. We both yelped in horror, darting out of the way in case the nasty insect should land on us. It was a ghostly, pale yellow one, with a protruding stinger on its back, and it was very angry as it landed on the ground and rapidly scurried away in fear. In movies, they always crawled very slowly towards a sleeping victim, so I was amazed to see how fast they actually did move; so fast, I didn't have a chance to kill it. I used to think that spiders were the ugliest insects in existence, but scorpions beat the ugliness contest by a long chalk. They are the most grotesque insects I have ever seen. They even *look* poisonous. I was told that the larger black ones are not as venomous, but just give you a nasty sting, enough to deliver pain and cause sickness. These pale yellow ones were the deadly variety, and I definitely did not want one of those in my bed.

The scorpion discovery instigated a more cautious approach: where we placed our hands in the future, and to make sure to wear gloves at all times. Fighting with the weeds turned out to be fun, especially with the pioneering notion of participating in the reclamation of the desert. When we paused for a while to admire the view, we were rewarded with a vista of ever-changing shades of yellows, tans, and browns, as the colors altered with the position of the sun. They were most vivid just before sunset, when the sun caused elongated, dramatic shadows to appear, and the earth became a deep shade of ocher.

Sometime around nine o'clock, we heard an approaching tractor. It was Yigal. He brought a fresh container of ice-cold water, melons, and red peppers. He also brewed up some coffee and joined us for breakfast. "You eat," he commanded, slicing up the juiciest melons in the world. He tried to make conversation in his very limited English vocabulary, but noticed our blank expressions, which clearly indicated, *I-don't-know-what-the-hell-you-are-talking-about,* so he decided to switch to Hebrew. At least he felt more confident communicating in his language, and if we didn't understand him, that was our problem. I managed so far to acquire the basic questions in Hebrew, and I knew all the numbers; therefore, my Hebrew vocabulary was as rich as his English. Asking how many rows we had to do was easy. "*Arba-eem.*" Well, thirty seven left.

Yigal went off again and we continued murdering giant weeds—without scorpions this time. I forgot to ask him how long we were supposed to be working; for all I knew, it could be till dusk. It wasn't so long. He came back at noon to pick us up and we hopped onto the tractor. "Was that our work for the day?" I tried to ask, but that was too complicated. The answer was a blank stare. He dropped us off at home and we started cooking after a blissful soaking in the shower. There was sand on the floor again and also in the shower now. My hair was tangled and full of sandy grit. Sally was in worse condition, as she had long hair, which held enough sand for growing a cactus. Ronit came over shortly after with a couple of melons and to relay the information that Yigal will be picking us up at four. Again, we would have to shower.

This time we drove to a different field, but it was free of weeds; in fact, it was free of everything, and where plants should have been growing, were wet patches where water from irrigation pipes trickled in droplets. Ronit also joined us that afternoon, coming separately in her car, bringing with her several trays of tiny plants that she took out and looked for some shade to put them into. There wasn't any, so they went under the tractor, which provided a little respite from the fierce heat. "Peppers," she smiled. "We have to get them in before dark." There were about twenty rows to plant, but with the four of us working, it should go fast. Yigal showed us how to plant the peppers. There was nothing to it: with the three middle fingers make a hole, stick the plant in, and squeeze the hole shut. Easy. To make it go faster, one of us placed the individual plants on the wet patches, and the other three did the planting. It went remarkably fast until Sally reached a row which hadn't been irrigated. Well, part of it was, where water was streaming out and causing a large puddle to develop. A segment of the irrigation tube looked as if it got chewed up. "Wolves chewed it up," Ronit told us matter of factly.

"There are wolves here?" We gasped in disbelief.

"Wolves, jackals, wild dogs… all the same. They chew the irrigation pipes to get at the water," she laughed. "They are clever. They know where to find a drink. Every day they get thirsty and look for a source, and every day we have to walk down all the rows to make sure no pipe has been broken. Sometimes you can see a whole row where the plants have died after not receiving water for a few hours." She translated to her husband what she had told us; he also had something to translate. "John, go to Yigal. He wants to show you how to fix the pipes. He will give you a knife and connectors so that you can fix them yourself if you see that the wolves damaged them."

Yigal grasped a razor-sharp knife, slit the pipe easily into two while getting wet, discarded the chewed up piece, and applied a connector, which snapped on from both ends. It was repaired, and had taken only a couple of minutes. Immediately, droplets of water started to darken the entire parched row, but there was not enough soil saturation for planting yet. We would save this row until last.

The work was enjoyable and all the peppers got planted. As the red fireball rapidly dipped below the horizon, shadows became more elongated as dusk descended upon the wilderness. We were back on the tractor heading home with warm wind blowing through our hair. The landscape had taken on a different look, and I imagined seeing packs of wolves and jackals coming out to roam the fields in search of tasty irrigation pipes; it was only moving shadows. It was a satisfying day, and we both knew that moshav life was going to be fun. Physical work brought out the hunger, but the heavenly kibbutz dining room was missing to make our stay perfect. Preparing our own food was to become routine. I was already starting to miss the conveyor for placing the dirty dishes onto. It was all hand-washing from now. An 8-hour workday with a 4-hour afternoon break seemed to be the norm here, and while doing the cooking and shopping, there wouldn't be much time left for recreation.

In the evenings, volunteers had an opportunity to get together and we did get a chance to meet several of them. They were all Europeans, all with their funny accents and intonations, and most of them have been here forever... and they *did* look it with their sandy hair and very lean bodies that have had to put up with thousands of peppers and melons in their system. I was wondering how many I would devour by the time our departure was due, but that day was far away. We had no idea how long we would be staying: schedules, time, watches—all became redundant in the timeless desert.

The following morning, Yigal dropped us off again by the giant weeds. The imminent hunger pangs would strike within two hours, but we were prepared this time, armed with a stack of sandwiches for combating the forthcoming craving for breakfast. Scorpions stayed away this time, but not the heat, which ignored the fact that November was approaching, but there was no sign of temperatures abating: it was still 36°Celsius in the shade. Yigal showed up later with more breakfast (melons and peppers) and to check our progress. While sitting down, I noticed a movement in the distance. Some kind of animal was pacing back and forth. A dog. What was a dog doing out there? It was middle of nowhere and quite a distance from the moshav. We told Ronit about the lost dog later that morning. She came to pick us up in her car and not Yigal.

"That was a wolf. It was probably waiting for you to leave so it can get some water." She also told us that we weren't going back out to the fields until Sunday. Today was Friday, and they were preparing for *Shabbat*. "The shop is closed tomorrow, so you'd better get what you need today." She dropped us off in the center where other volunteers were already doing their shopping.

The special bread, *Challah,* was for sale today. I had eaten this bread before: platted, slightly sweet, and very light yellow texture. It is delicious eaten plain with butter, especially when it's fresh. In this shop they *were* fresh, and so, we bought two. While standing outside and chatting with other volunteers, we asked what there was to do here on the Sabbath. "Get pissed," was the expected response from the English we had just met. "There's a club house with music and beer." That sounded boring.

The Germans and Swedes were more creative. "We usually make a fire and barbecue."

"Behind your house?" I assumed.

"Oh, no. We go out into the desert. *Ja*, it is much fun. You want come we go together," spoke the German volunteer in a strong accent. That did sound like fun. "And bring some beer," he reminded us. So we went back to the shop to buy some beer, but the sweet, dark malt non-alcoholic variety, which was very popular amongst the Israelis, and which I found delicious and refreshing when drunk ice cold. It was the perfect beverage for hot desert evenings.

As soon as daylight bid farewell, there was a knock on our door. It was Thorsten, the German volunteer. "Ready to go?" He was carrying some bottles of beer and sausages for the barbecue. We did likewise and followed him to the spot where the barbecue was taking place. A good twenty-minute walk out of the moshav brought us to a clearing enclosed by two hills on either side. A low, wide thorny tree marked the spot where the fire had already been started and people were already barbecuing. It was pretty crowded. Two more couples were there: from Sweden and The Netherlands; an Israeli girl; a girl from Finland; a very talkative Italian guy with about six arms flapping around in the air, and two more guys from Germany made up the crowd. We all sat around the fire despite the night being warm, but it felt nevertheless cozier having the warmth of the flames caress the body. We used rocks for sitting on, but found it more comfortable to sprawl out on the ground. The almost full moon cast a silvery streak across the entire desert, making it possible to walk and hunt for more fuel to keep the fire going. There was plenty of dry wood and brush to be found—brought down by heavy rains and flash floods in the past. We took turns gathering it.

We were down to the bare basics in life—food, drink, and fire. Nothing else was necessary. Together with a bunch of people who were sharing the same pursuit in life as Sally and I, we were living a dream which could never be bought. Out here in the rugged wilderness of Paran, the volunteers/workers/travelers attained a mutual respect for one another, and nobody was judged or prejudiced. It made no difference who was from where and what kind of background they came from. In England, these questions inevitably came up as a prerequisite for judging a person and slotting them into a social class.

Not long ago, these people had been strangers, but even without introducing themselves, Sally and I were treated like old friends and we talked as if we had just left off a conversation a few days previously and were now resuming. The Finnish girl spoke. "You know, this landscape looks exactly like in Africa," she told us. "If you forget for one moment that we are in Israel, this could definitely be East Africa. All that's missing are some elephants," she reminisced.

"Have you been to Africa?" I asked.

"I was in Tanzania and traveled overland to Egypt, then crossed the border to Israel. That was eight months ago."

"Isn't there a civil war in Sudan?" Someone queried.

"Yes, but it's not constant. When they're not shooting, it's possible to travel… and the people are really nice." She said that with confidence. "Had a problem crossing into Egypt though," she added. I was thinking of the news reports I had seen in England about the famine that had devastated Ethiopia. She must have crossed that country, too. I asked her about it. "Yes, it's true. It's worse than what you see on TV, and what's even worse is that there is nothing you can do about it. Millions and millions of people are starving to death and you are powerless to help them. There are too many. It's the same in Sudan." She told us about other horrific experiences she had encountered. Nobody asked her whether it was dangerous. Nobody suggested that she was foolish traveling to such regions. Nobody ridiculed her. In England, she would have been scorned and assigned to the lunatic asylum for traversing such "dangerous" countries, especially alone.

"What's wrong with Mallorca?" They would have quizzed.

We stayed by the fire most of the night until some people got a little tipsy and decided to spend the night here instead, as the ground they were standing on became too soft to walk on—beer and wine didn't mix. But tomorrow there was no work, so it didn't matter. Sally and I walked back to the house, also a little giddy from the wine we had been offered. I still had a phobia against strange insects crawling into my mouth after the Golan Heights experience, and had no desire to sleep out in the desert without my sleeping bag.

On our day off next morning, we got together with our new friends and went for a hike along one of the numerous bone-dry wadis. It was so tranquil on this day: no tractors starting up, and no activity around the shop. The moshav was dead, and going for a walk was the only form of entertainment, but that suited me just fine. I loved it here.

Sunday morning was the familiar time-to-go-to-the-fields sound of the tractor. We were dropped off at the same weed field and heard the recognizable sound of water streaming out of a chewed up pipe. Yigal didn't seem at all surprised, and quickly set about repairing it, but hesitated and called me over, handing it to me. I guess he wanted me to have a go fixing it. I cut off a section like shown, attached the connectors, and the job was done. Yigal seemed satisfied. *"Tov,"* (good) he nodded, and went back to wherever he goes back to. We took a break after two rows and noticed that dog/wolf watching us from a long distance, probably planning another water disruption.

"Big bad wolf!" Sally waved a tall weed towards the animal. The big bad wolf sat down and observed us while we continued with our weeding. It was too far away to be seen clearly, but I think it saw *us* very well.

We worked quickly now, determined to get as much done as possible; not because we were fine workers, but every time we came to a standstill, flies would attack. While moving and throwing sand into the air, it kept them away. I didn't even care about scorpions anymore; it was these ferocious flies that were causing much more discomfort. Yigal was very satisfied with our progress when he came to collect us for lunch. He was also covered in sand and sweat, so he couldn't have been having a siesta as previously suspected. Weeding recommenced in the late afternoon, but Mr. Wolf was gone.

The pipes were still in order the next day, but one of them decided it didn't want to stay there anymore and slithered away to the next row. Was I hallucinating or did a part of irrigation pipe just get up and leave? I looked again, shaking my head to re-focus, but it was still there, and a long, black snake was rapidly disappearing towards a dry riverbed. "SNAKE!" I yelled the obvious. Sally chased after it, but the snake was faster and found a crevice to slither into. "I thought it was an irrigation pipe," I laughed.

"Oh, yeah… an irrigation pipe trying to escape. *That's* a good one." Sally eyed me as if I'd had too much sun.

After breakfast the wolf reappeared in the distance, sat down, and observed our prancing around for the rest of the morning. I was sure it had edged somewhat nearer, as its outline was now clearly defined. Yigal came over a little earlier than usual, said something I didn't understand, and took us back to the moshav. Sally was dropped off at the shop, but he beckoned that I stay. He stopped the tractor, got up from the drivers seat, and sat me down in his place.

"Er... w-w-what?" I stammered.

"You... tractor...," he trailed off, lacking the vocabulary, but the meaning was clear. He wanted *me* to drive.

"Oh, no... I can't. I don't drive." I shrugged my shoulders and made the international I-don't-know-how-to gesture. I had never driven a car, and now he wanted *me* to drive a tractor? Insane. I protested.

"No problem, you... tractor." He was insistent. I gulped.

"Can't be so hard," I was thinking. After all, twelve-year-olds were driving around on them all the time. "Okay," I nodded glumly.

He nudged me to the side again, sat down, and went through the motions, explaining the clutch, brakes, accelerator, and gears. It was all gibberish as my twenty-minute tractor-driving lesson was in Hebrew and I didn't understand a word he was saying, but tried to comprehend what he was doing with the pedals and gear stick. Now it was my turn. I started the ignition and the tractor roared to life, then I had to get it into gear. It worked until I released the pedal too quickly and the tractor lurched forward and stalled. Yigal sighed. I tried again and got the thing moving, then had to change gears. It stalled again and Yigal impatiently took over and tried to explain to me what I was doing wrong. Still gibberish, but I tried again until I could change gears without stalling it. Yigal seemed satisfied and gestured that I take him home. I made it and got off, my legs still trembling with shock.

"*Reggah*," gestured Yigal. "Ronit come." Ronit came and explained to me what was going on.

"Yigal has to go to the army for a week, so you have to take the tractor to your house and go to the field alone every morning." She also explained that I should take it now and they will both come out to meet us in the field later this afternoon. "Is that okay?" She asked.

"Yes, that's okay," I nodded, knowing that nothing was okay. "But I've never driven a tractor *or* a car before." I tried to explain that this was my first time.

"Ach, it's easy!" Ronit dismissed my dismal excuse with the wave of her hand. "See you later," and they both went in and left me standing there with no choice but to get on that green monster and drive it away. It started, and I slowly chugged along towards my house, determined not to stall it again. Sally shot out of the house open-mouthed when she saw me pulling up.

"Why are you driving the tractor?" I explained to her what was going on and that we had to make our own way to the fields from now on. "But you can't drive!" She looked nervous.

"Yes, I can. Didn't you see me?" She wasn't convinced, and neither was I. It was a long way to the fields, but the worst thing that could happen was that I stall the tractor. Controlling it was very easy, and from the seat I commanded a good view, and the chances of crashing into anything were zero. Maybe I will manage after all. Other volunteers were driving themselves to the fields, too, so this was not unusual.

We went back out at the usual time of 4:00 P.M.—me driving, and Sally sitting on the metal wheel guard beside me and holding on to dear life. We nervously chugged along to our weeds, amazingly arriving there without mishaps. Sally was impressed, and admittedly, so was I.

It now became routine to scan the horizon for our wolf friend, but he wasn't there. We continued the fight with the weeds for twenty minutes. Subsequently, the wolf appeared, sitting in his usual position, but closer to the field than yesterday. I could now make out his panting tongue. He just sat there, observing us the entire time. Mr. and Mrs. Boss arrived shortly after.

"Tractor good?" Asked Yigal, gesturing towards the green John Deere.

"Tractor good," I acknowledged, whereas he came and whacked me on the back with such force that I almost toppled over into the peppers.

Ronit translated what we had to do for the next few days: to finish weeding the field and then to check the irrigation pipes for "wolf damage." Some pipes had become clogged, thus starving large sections of plants that had long died, leaving them crispy and shriveled up. Others had been completely suffocated to death by invading weeds that greedily fought for water and overtook precious growing space. We were to replace connectors and replant the empty spots in the late afternoon when the sun wasn't so strong. "I'll show you where to get the plants from," said Ronit. Yigal also instructed us to walk through all his other fields to check on the pipes. We pointed out the wolf to them, but he was gone again; probably too many people here for his liking.

"Yes, we see them here often. Sometimes when you drive back in the dark with full beam, you can spot several in the fields—their eyes illuminated. They are cowards; they run away as soon as you get near them." The farmers said goodbye and returned to the moshav in their car. Yigal was already in his army uniform, meaning that he was leaving immediately. We stayed until sunset and also drove back as the night creatures came to life.

Life and work on the moshav became routine, and I gained confidence in using the tractor. The lone wolf also became our curious daily visitor, keeping an eye on us from afar. While checking one of the fields one day, we came across another damaged pipe that had been ravaged. A quick fix put it right. We encountered more snakes, almost every day, and always in the same position. They liked to snake out in the rows where water dripped out and the ground was moist, camouflaging themselves amongst the black irrigation pipes. We often surprised their snaking around and prodded them with a stick. In the mornings, they were sluggish, not fully charged by solar energy yet, and slowly slithered towards a less disruptive spot. As the sun picked up heat, so did the snakes, and to prod them in the late morning made them take off with unbelievable lightning speed, almost leaving their skin behind with fright.

The time had finally come to see the Red Sea resort in Eilat, which surprisingly, was still 100km away. It was a straight road all the way down to the southern tip, where the resort was squeezed in between two borders—Jordan and Egypt. No bus was necessary for getting there. We were on the main road (the only road) and hitchhiking was easy. A few minutes wait was all that it took, and with a speed-happy driver, we were soon deposited near the bus depot in Eilat in less than an hour.

The town itself is probably one of the least impressive ones in Israel. It was missing the Middle-Eastern flair and old architecture. Around the bus station are nondescript shops selling souvenirs, postcards, and fast food. Fast food in the form of falafel was fully acceptable, and that was where we headed. It had been a while since we had one and it was high time. Looking around, it was obvious that this was purely a tourist resort, evident by all the hotels that made up this disappointing town that everybody raved about. However, we were not here for the architectural wonders, but to visit the underwater observatory, which had been recommended by our friends. Eilat was also the gateway to the Sinai Desert in Egypt, but we had no plans to go there just yet. There was no hurry.

A short walk down to the shore brought us to the entrance of the underwater world, which charged a nominal entry fee. Set some distance from the shore, a narrow wooden bridge spans the short stretch, connecting it to the observatory. Inside, we descended down to below sea level and suddenly found ourselves beneath the Red Sea with a panoramic view of marine life. This was not an artificial aquarium, but a scope of the real, ever-changing world beneath the sea, and it wasn't even necessary to get wet. It was like being inside a fish documentary. We stayed there for over two hours, staring at the most beautiful array of moving shapes and colors that nature could boast. Living coral swayed with the movements of the waves, and spiky sea urchins dotted the seabed, and all this was happening a stone's throw away from the beach.

Viewing marine life from a glass-bottomed boat is another possibility, but according to my guidebook, it wasn't worth the money. The glass is so badly scratched that it's hard to see anything at all. The best recommendation was to rent a snorkel and view the sea life close-up. We took the advice and sidetracked back to the center to the diving shop. Walking back to the shore to find a place for trying them out was easier said than done. The whole coastline is overrun with hotels, which block access to the beach; so unless one is a guest, the possibility of stumbling upon an attractive stretch of shoreline seemed unfeasible. Common sense and the hideous build-up of hotels persuaded us to keep walking; and walk we did, quite far towards the Egyptian border. So far, this area was not fulfilling my exotic expectations of what a Red Sea resort should look like.

We continued on foot for almost an hour until a very extensive and attractive beach came into view. It wasn't occupied by any hotels, either. Wrong: there was one—The Hilton—directly on the border, but it didn't command the entire beach like the others. This was Taba, the border crossing into Egypt. Taba beach was fairly empty, and (I must admit) quite gorgeous. But instead of admiring the encompassing beauty, we were keen to try out snorkeling, which neither of us had any experience in. Coral is supposed to be razor sharp, and it was advised that footwear be worn *while* snorkeling: sharp, broken pieces cover the shoreline. This was where I had to sacrifice my only pair of sneakers. It was either them or have my feet sliced up. The Red Sea was a favorite hangout for sharks, and I didn't want to attract any with my blood.

The deep blue color of the Red Sea and the tan colors of the desert that meet the water spur the human imagination and give the impression that the sea is bathtub warm. Surprisingly, it wasn't. The Mediterranean was warmer. At first, it felt somewhat cool, but as the body acclimatized, it didn't feel so bad after all. Donning my mask on, I got another cold shock on my head as it went below the surface of the water, but the sudden transformation of the world below me was enough to forget about the temperature, and my body quickly warmed up.

The fish were close enough to be touched, but any attempt to prod them was impossible: they simultaneously darted away when my hand reached out. Further out, the water became deeper and darker, and the coral retained its beautiful unbroken form. Also here, the black, spiky sea urchins were scattered on the sea bed, and it was crucial not to step on their poisonous spikes. They can even pierce through a pair of sneakers. Steering clear of spiky things, we warily observed them from the top while staying afloat in a horizontal position and letting the sun toast our backs. We spent the whole afternoon in the water until the sun made its dip behind the Sinai and splattered the mountains in Jordan in a rich pink light. Yes, Eilat *was* beautiful, but rather the location than the town itself.

Fish watching would make anyone hungry, but fortunately, we brought with us food we had prepared the day before. Of course, there were peppers and the usual melons. Since giving up meat a while ago (being too expensive), we didn't really miss it, especially Sally, who could almost live off fruit alone. Israel is a fine country to become a vegetarian, as both Israelis and Arabs perform amazing culinary wonders with non-meat products by using appropriate spices and seasonings.

We made a small fire on the beach out of other leftover firewood and brewed some cardamom coffee over the glowing embers as dusk descended abruptly like a blanket. Our sleeping bags were rolled out by the fire. Cozy and carefree, we lay on top, still in our swimwear, caressed by the warm air, which produced hardly a breeze or a ripple upon the sea. Across the water on the other side, the lights from Aqaba in Jordan sparkled; meanwhile, the Egyptian side was enshrouded in total darkness. I noticed earlier the untouched pristine deserted beaches along the Egyptian coastline with no resort in sight. Christmas was not far away, and as we lay there by the fire, we realized that it had been a year since that first meeting in the London office: the mandatory briefing all volunteers had to attend.

"Do you remember the weather that day...? And how cold it was?" I chuckled, recollecting the bone-chilling damp conditions.

"And how nervous we all were at the airport?"

Now we could laugh about the past as we lay there amidst paradise and total freedom. The dim glow of the Taba border crossing could be seen, and obviously, *they* could see our fire, too, but after my experience with Israeli soldiers, I wasn't concerned whether a fire was allowed or not, or whether camping on this beach was even permitted. They were used to foreign backpackers traveling on a shoestring, and didn't seem to give a hoot who was camping where. Such excursions were also popular amongst Israelis, who also slept under the stars and built campfires. This was the best way to experience this part of the world. We were alone on this beach, but felt very safe like everywhere else in Israel.

As the night progressed, the howling started—wolves—a whole pack of them serenading the night away. The howling came from the desert hills on the other side of the road where there was nothing but wilderness. Their calls were answered by their Egyptian counterparts from across the border, and together, the ethereal canine choir sent goosebumps down my spine, more as a consequence of delicate beauty than fear. Nevertheless, Sally tightened her arms around me. The howling may also have been the sound of jackals: I was no canine expert, but it sounded very wolfy to me, and I was glad we had a fire going; otherwise, four-legged uninvited guests might have come sniffing around for food.

Zipping up the sleeping bag was too warm, but leaving ourselves totally exposed was also not appealing, especially with howling animals around. Our backpacks were covered with a towel, thus transforming them to pillows. The soft sand made sleeping comfortable and we soon drifted off to sleep while the wolves held a song contest.

We woke up together with the sun and felt amazingly refreshed. After a quick breakfast of some sandwiches we had put together, which were now quite flat after accidentally sleeping on them, we went back into the water. I was still in my swimming trunks and Sally in her bikini. Staying on the beach required no change of clothing. Other people decided to invade our private beach, most of them coming out of the nearby Hilton that straddled the border. Several bodies were now lying horizontally in the sea and ravishing the beauty of marine life. I was quite sure the hotel guests never heard the wolves last night, but only the hum of their air conditioners. Our accommodation was quite unique.

I was, however, grateful for the hotel being within such close proximity, where we took advantage of the facilities. They also had a water fountain outside, which was perfect for filling up our container. The friendly hotel staff didn't seem to mind.

When the rest of the Sinai was handed back to Egypt in 1982, Taba remained on the Israeli side, as Israel insisted that Taba belonged to them. This was still a disputed area, and the Israeli and Egyptian governments had not yet come to an agreement where the actual border should be.

After another day of snorkeling, we walked back to town and returned the snorkels and masks, had some lunch, and took the bus back to the moshav, arriving in the late afternoon. We returned to Eilat several more times in the course of our stay on Moshav Faran; every time to the same beach.

The work in the fields continued, and the rows that we had previously weeded were now filled with beautiful and healthy-looking pepper plants. While those were growing, we set up the drip irrigation in other fields and prepared them for new seedlings. Other times we picked peppers, and I also happily ate them freshly-picked in spite of having consumed hundreds of them. The wolf continued to visit, but kept its distance, and as we attempted to get much closer, he took off with terror, only to return again later.

Christmas was quite uneventful, as it is not celebrated in Israel, but a bunch of volunteers decided to get drunk. Sally got a parcel from England with goodies and decent European shampoo. The Israeli shampoo must be the worst in the world. Upon washing, it immediately transforms one's hair into dry straw. It's the same with the soap and other care products in this country. The locally produced ones are the cheapest and of the most inferior quality, resulting in whimpers and yelps, as it did horrible things to the hair and body. European products were for sale everywhere, but were unaffordable as if they contained liquid gold instead of just shampoo. Washing-up liquid also didn't seem to exist, and there was only one product for sale: a container of thick, yellow paste. This was applied to dishes with a scouring pad, while washing them under a running faucet: like the Israeli shampoo and soap products, it didn't foam.

The year was at an end, and the new year began with a drop in temperatures and cooler mornings, forcing us to wear a coat on the way to the fields, but after a few days, the temperatures shot up again and it stayed hot for another couple of weeks. That was during the day, but the mornings became cooler and cooler. It remained dry, but sometimes the wind picked up and we watched the spinning dust devils waltzing aimlessly across the fields. When they came towards us, we had to duck with our heads down until they passed, throwing more sand into our hair.

It had been a while since we had a Friday night barbecue. For some strange reason, every time it was Friday, the wind picked up, blowing the sand around. It was too breezy to build a fire and too sandy to stay outside. We stayed in the house most of the time after work and usually hitchhiked to Eilat on Saturdays, but only made day trips. Eilat is a winter resort, and many European tourists who had escaped the cold in their countries, could be found sunning themselves on deck chairs by the hotel pools. The thermometer was struggling to hit the 24°Celsius mark, but for the pale-skinned tourists, it was sizzling heat. We spent our usual time on Taba beach and visited our now regular falafel shop and café.

Our time in Israel was coming to an end, and as always, our plans were made over coffee and pastries. Strangely, the combination of the two always set my brain working, and good ideas came flowing. Our plan was to take the ferry from Haifa to Limassol in Cyprus, travel around the island, and then go to Greece. From Greece, there was a boat to Turkey, to the mysterious and seldom traveled country I couldn't wait to see.

The people we had gotten to know on the moshav had already left, and we couldn't really be bothered getting to know the newcomers. We both felt that it was time to move on to seek out new adventures and do some extensive traveling. Our savings would enable us to travel comfortably for the next few months.

We were sad to leave the moshav, not because of the work, but I would miss the desert, our Friday night fires, Eilat, even the wolves and the snakes. The scorpions I could do without though. The family we worked for were grateful and thanked us for our hard work, letting us know that we were welcome to come back after our trip to Turkey.

The endless bus ride to Tel Aviv was a killer, then another one to Haifa—to the port where the ferry was waiting. Here, we were interrogated by security officials while they leafed through the passports. They wanted to know where we had been and where we were going. In fact, they were similar questions that were barked at us in London. Keeping our cool and giving the right answers allowed us to proceed towards the waiting ferry after an exit stamp.

It was a Greek ferry. This was also the first time for me—to travel on the sea. We bought the cheapest tickets known as "deck class," which meant exactly what they said. The more expensive tickets would have gotten us a shared cabin, but we were content with unrolling our sleeping bags on the deck, which would serve as our bed for the night. We were not alone. Dozens of backpackers were traveling deck class, too, and very soon, international groups started forming.

At dusk, the deafening noise of the chain being wound up indicated that the ferry was ready to go. Israeli pilot boats nudged the huge ship into position; we were on our way to Cyprus. Instead of feeling sad to be leaving Israel, I was now looking forward to the unknown. There was still so much to see in the Holy Land; so much, that it would require another visit or two. I will definitely be back, as Egypt was still very much on the agenda, but first, I wanted a break from the desert, no matter how much I loved it.

6
GOING SLOW IN THE LAND OF APHRODITE

The distant city lights in Haifa were the final farewell from Israel, slowly being snuffed out by the Earth's curvature, and then darkness swallowed up the last remaining twinkles. The Mediterranean crossing to Limassol takes ten hours, and that meant an extremely early arrival in Cyprus. A cozy corner on the deck was an ideal and windproof spot to roll out our mats and sleeping bags. The small gas cooker we used for making coffee came along with me, and together with some sandwiches and fruits, we banged up a nice meal. Hours went by, and the chatter of fellow "deck campers" became subdued as they drifted off to sleep. Benches became beds; candles became reading lamps; someone was strumming a guitar, as several backpackers sat around candlelight. The deck consisted of travelers with fantastic tales of faraway, exotic places they had seen, and now we were all in the same boat, where each one of us were seeking out a new destination: each one with their own definition of paradise.

This will not go down as one of my most comfortable nights—not because of the metal floor, but the ship's sustained vibrations gave us a free all-night, full-body massage, as we juddered in pulsating rhythm to the sounds of the engine. I tried to put as much soft padding as possible on my backpack, which doubled up as a pillow. This softened the vibrations somewhat, but with the ear close to the floor, it was even louder, sounding more like a roar. The sandman did manage to pay a visit despite the din, only to wake up a few hours later to the deafening sound of the horn announcing our arrival. It was dawn, and I was a trembling wreck as I groggily put away the sleeping bag, ready to disembark.

Dawn turned into bright sunlight, and the island of Cyprus loomed up like a friendly giant sea monster with outstretched arms and welcomed us to the safety of the harbor. Ships and boats with bizarre names painted on them sailed from all directions, and so did the swooping seagulls, hoping for a morsel from passing fishing vessels. An overpowering noise, sounding like a passing freight train, thundered throughout the ship, but it was only the dropping anchor. Suddenly, we were in Limassol. As the hatch was lowered to the ground, cars started rolling off the ferry, eager to hit the road. There was no hurry, as the ferry would stay docked for several hours until it departed again later in the morning.

We slowly made our way off the ship into the harbor and to the immigration office where the friendly officer stamped our passports without even examining them or asking any questions: quite unlike the Israeli immigration. The displayed exchange rates at the *Bureau de Change* were depressing—and a shock to discover that the Cypriot pound was actually valued higher than the British pound. Instead of the pound sterling being worth thousands of shekels, it was now reduced to a meager eighty cents.

"Sixteen pounds?" I spluttered in disbelief after having just changed £20 and receiving only three worthless-looking notes in exchange.

"I hope Cyprus is not so expensive," worried Sally as she visualized our hard-earned cash suddenly diminishing to a few pieces of paper.

There was a lanky German backpacker exchanging his beloved Deutschmarks, and we also heard him gasp in horror as he was forced to part with many more notes in exchange for two. He bumped into us, shaking his head in disbelief. "Cyprus is expensive, yes?"

"Looks like it," I replied.

"You go to Old City? We go together, yes?" The friendly German teemed up with us as we looked for some mode of transportation to the older quarter of Limassol.

There was an empty, beaten-up bus standing by the port, and an old man with a gray, bristly chin was leaning against it, enjoying his cigarette. He beckoned us over. "You going to Limassol?" He asked in excellent English. We nodded, then he gestured that we should board the bus. "Slowly, slowly. We have time. It is still very early and everything is still closed. Welcome to Cyprus. Everything is slowly, slowly here. No hurry." He continued puffing on his cigarette.

There were no other bus passengers besides us three: there was also no bus stop or timetable. Finally, he sauntered in behind the wheel and started the engine. "We go, but slowly, slowly." Such an ancient bus I had not seen before. Once he started the engine, it sounded more like a truck, and then started to tremble. I had just gotten over *my* trembling from the vibrating ferry, and now it was to start all over again. The bus had no door either, allowing passengers to hop on or off, like with the old buses in England. But this one was a scaled-down version and built like a tank, and could very well have been a model from the fifty's. Slowly he drove, so slowly, that jogging would have been faster. The engine heaved as the bus reached about 20kph and the driver had to change gears. A little faster, and the engine sounded as if it was grinding metal. We continued at this pace for about fifteen minutes until the driver saw two elderly men sitting by the roadside who started waving to him as he came to a stop. They were sitting at a café. "We go slowly, slowly... no hurry," the driver repeated to us. "First we drink some coffee, then we go... slowly, slowly." We looked at each other, amused: such a contrast to the speed-happy and aggressive Israeli drivers. Coffee sounded good, so we joined the bus driver and his friends. We had no choice.

The waiter seemed to know him, too, as they shook hands and started chatting in Greek. We sat at the other table and waited to order our coffee, but the waiter disappeared again. He came back shortly afterward with strong Cypriot coffee for the driver *and* for us.

We chatted amongst ourselves and got to know the German, known as Thorsten. He had also spent time on a kibbutz in Israel, but in the northern part near the Lebanese border. "It was funny, yes. Many times goes the alarm and we must go into shelter," he told us excitedly.

"Did a missile land on the kibbutz?" I asked.

"Oh, no. Lebanon shoot missiles, but they miss. Ha ha. They just shoot anywhere. Is crazy, but was fun. Yes."

We stayed there for at least thirty minutes until the driver started to get up slowly. The waiter came to collect the empty glasses and we were about to pay, but were told that the driver had already taken care of the bill. We thanked him. He dismissed the gratitude with a wave of his hand. "Welcome to Cyprus," he simply answered, but with that simple statement it was obvious that he was trying to make a point: that the Cypriots are very generous and friendly people. He was right. "We go slowly, slowly."

Slowly, the bus crawled and grinded along until we arrived in the old part of the city. After paying the bus driver, he handed us the bus tickets, which weren't necessary anymore. It cost peanuts for the trip, and even though we didn't pay for the coffee, I noticed that it cost a mere fifteen cents. Maybe Cyprus wasn't so expensive after all!

The guidebook recommended cheap, but clean accommodation in this quarter. The quaint surroundings were beautified with flowering bushes; grapevines crawled up trellises; old buildings had doors and shutters painted in rich colors, mostly blues and whites—the colors of Greece. There were plenty of *pensions* (small private hotels) in this area, and we chose a fine-looking one with a cozy courtyard, but did they have vacancies?

"We have lots of rooms," the friendly owner informed us. "It is low season now."

Sally and I ended up in a spacious room with a desk, small table, and chairs. The furniture was old and basic, but the view from our second floor balcony was breathtaking as we looked down upon the Old City. Below us was the courtyard with a breakfast area under a canopy of foliage. Best of all, the room was reasonably priced. I needed a shower, a shave, and a change of clothes before venturing back outside. The bed felt good and I was tempted to use it immediately.

Thorsten was waiting for us in the courtyard when we came down. He was pawing through his guidebook, looking for places to eat. Neither of us wanted to splurge out on restaurants on our first day, so we decided to walk around the markets and see what foods were for sale—a profusion of gastronomic wealth. I recognized the sesame-coated rings of bread, which looked like the ones in Jerusalem. "Yes, we'll take two of those." Very cheap, too! An array of cheeses caught my eye; much better than the varieties in Israel (sorry, but Israel didn't have cheese varieties). We bought some *Laughing Cow* cheese spread and a piece of what seemed to be Cypriot cheese, known as *halloumi*. Salamis and other sausages were in rich supply and finally affordable. In Israel they were valued in carats. We bought baklava and mandarins, which were for sale everywhere. The measurement of weight in Cyprus was not in kilos, but in "okes." We had no idea what an oke was, so we simply bought an oke of mandarins, which turned out to be a heavy bag full—it was more than a kilo. Now we had all these mandarins to lug around. Shopkeepers were friendly, the food was good, fresh, and reasonably priced—we were happy. Very happy.

We brought our purchases back to the courtyard and started to prepare breakfast, sharing everything between the three of us, especially the oke of mandarins. "Mmmm, *haloumi* is good, yes?" Thorsten had found something that sent his taste buds wild.

I dived into the baklava. "Mmmm, it's so fresh." We still had enough food left over for the rest of the day, and even for the next morning.

Limassol Old City is very attractive with its narrow streets and numerous shops. Souvenirs were for sale everywhere, and considering this was low tourist season, there were quite a few shoppers around. Shops that were selling postcards and T-shirts were also selling sea sponges and starfish. Wine was in plentiful supply; locally produced wine, which I made a mental note to sample one evening. English was widely spoken, but that was due to the British influence on the island with its vast army bases. We passed several fish and chips shops, also a reminder of the Britishness of this island.

Despite the historic beauty and enchanting architecture in this city, it wasn't worth staying more than a couple of nights. Limassol served its purpose as a point of arrival and a great place to get the first taste of Cyprus. We found a very informative tourist information office where they showered us with literature and gave us an excellent map of the whole island.

Just a short distance from the city is the Kolossi Castle, which we visited the same day. I had seen enough castles in England, and this one didn't really impress me, but it was nice nevertheless.

In the darkness, the Old City develops a different kind of charm: *Tavernas* (small, family-owned restaurants that serve local cuisine) open up, and Greek music can be heard as a pleasant accompaniment to a meal. We passed one small local eating spot where an old woman was sizzling meat on skewers on top of charcoals. When done, the meat pieces were inserted inside large oval-shaped pita bread, and the rest of the hollow was filled with salad, sprinkled with lemon juice and freshly chopped parsley. The three of us could not resist the alluring sizzling pork, and sat down to devour one each. As I promised myself, I also ordered a jug of wine to give the evening an extra boost of pleasure. The delicious combination of the food and wine was enhanced by Greek music that supplemented that extra perfection as we sat under a sprawling, ancient and gnarled vine that served as the roof.

We spent a couple more nights in Limassol, as there were some interesting ruins to see; both of them easily accessible by local buses that were replicas of the first one we had taken. They also chugged along as if they had all the time in the world—slowly, slowly. Apollo's temple in Amathus was one place worth visiting. All that remained were crumbling, once splendid, intricately adorned columns that had formerly stood with majestic pride to fulfill the desires of the god of sun and healing.

Cyprus was obsessed with gods, especially Aphrodite—the goddess of love and beauty. The whole island seems to be dedicated to her. But that was the southern part of the island; the northern part being off limits since 1974 when war broke out between the Greeks and Turks. The island has been divided since, and the border to the northern half is securely sealed.

Also nearby is Kourion, where we spent most of the day amongst the Roman ruins that included a very well-preserved amphitheater, which looked as if it was still in use. Beautiful mosaics had been excavated and were now protected under a large canopy that spanned the site. With the Mediterranean Sea in the background, this place didn't look much different to Ceasaria in Israel. There were also remains of an early Christian Basilica. Not too far from this site is the Sanctuary of Apollo, which I especially found impressive. It is where offerings had once been made to the god.

It was time to hit the road the following morning. Thorsten wanted to linger in Limassol a little longer. He was enthralled by the easygoing lifestyle of the island, and especially the endless supply of *halloumi* cheeses he was going through. "Life is much more complicated in a German city and not so slow," he pointed out to us. We shook hands with the jolly German and walked out of the city onto a main road that would take us west. I would imagine that such a friendly country would be a hitchhiker's paradise.

It was. A car stopped without us even attempting to hitchhike yet. Just as well! We were trying to figure out whether a thumb or the index finger was used in this country. An elderly man leaned out of the window. "Where would you like to go?" He asked.

"Pissouri."

"I'm driving to Pathos. Pissouri is on the way." He invited us to join him and opened up the trunk for our bulky backpacks. "Are you looking for Aphrodite?" We told him that we had just arrived and wanted to spend some time on the beaches. "You must go to Pathos after and see the catacombs. They are most unique. Pathos is smaller than Limassol and not as hectic."

"Hectic?" I repeated. If Limassol is hectic, then Pathos must move in slow motion

"You should also visit Troodos Mountains. There are some very beautiful villages up there, which I'm sure you'll enjoy. Some people still live there like a hundred years ago." He was keen that we see mainland Cyprus; not merely concentrate on the coastal regions.

I was still amazed how fluent everybody was in English; no matter what their age. Like is Israel, the people who gave us a lift were very informative about their country and were the best source of information. Now we had a good reason to visit Pathos, too.

"There's your Aphrodite," the driver pointed towards the ocean where he dropped us off near the village of Pissouri.

The location turned out to harbor an enticingly beautiful beach, and far enough away from the city to give it a secluded setting. A handful of sunbathing tourists were also enjoying the serene beauty of this place, which really was a perfect location for the goddess of love and beauty. This area was, after all, the birthplace of Aphrodite, and her splendor we would continue to see along the entire coastline to Pathos and beyond. There was no rush in our itinerary, and we heeded the advice to do things *slowly, slowly.* Sitting on a rock, stress-free and at ease with the world, we mulled over the places we should visit in Cyprus, amidst the nonchalant sounds of crashing waves upon the rock formations that protruded into the sea. A huge stack jutted out of the water, and according to my guidebook, it was supposed to be Aphrodite's rock, but another information pamphlet I had from the tourist office mentioned that the Rock of Aphrodite was in Pathos. Whatever! Whoever the rock belonged to, it made a statement. There were simply too many Aphrodites here to keep track of.

This was a fine place to spend the night, even though the beach was all stony and grainy, but at least we wouldn't have that problem with fine sand finding its way in everywhere. Before leaving the city, we had stocked up on some groceries in case we did end up sleeping on the beach. Unfortunately, unlike Israel, there was no wood anywhere and no evidence of campfires. Is beach camping even permitted in Cyprus? Who cares! As we watched the sun disappear into the west, the few remaining tourists dissipated and we were left alone. In the darkness, the waves sounded much louder as they pounded upon the rocks. It was almost full moon this night and we watched the silver waves dance towards the shores, almost expecting a goddess to reappear inside them, as she had once, and rolled ashore inside a giant shell. As the moon rose higher, the entire beach became illuminated, and the silhouette of the endless coastline sparkled like a jewel. Indeed, this was a *very* fine place to spend a night with my own Aphrodite.

The disadvantage of sleeping outdoors is that one is awake at first light; there is no nice bathroom to go to, and neither the luxury of a sink or shower. But how else can one appreciate nature's beauty? The *other* nature was calling on my part, and the nearest bathrooms were in the village, which was still very much in slumberland. We always carried toilet paper around for such emergencies, and in a secluded spot, dug up a hole like a cat, and covered it up again. The sea was our bathroom for now, where we washed ourselves and used water from our container for brushing our teeth. We slumbered and lazied a little longer in our sleeping bags, then made breakfast, and soon afterward, wandered over to the village, which was a good walk from the beach.

It was a village postcards are made of, with its attractive narrow streets and potted plants placed around each doorstep. Homely, small *tavernas* situated around village life, made this the ideal place to escape to for several days. The few tourists mingled with the local inhabitants without distracting their daily lives. The village was spotless and still being scrubbed, as we noticed some elderly women brushing their doorsteps and sidewalks clean with a broom and soapy water. Gourds were suspended on strings in many places, especially at the *tavernas*. I could really stay here for a long time, and *that* is exactly what we did, seduced by Aphrodite's lingering spirit.

We found a small, simple *pension* in the village and decided to rent a room for several days, to enjoy the village and beach without lugging our backpacks around constantly. Daytime is beach time, but as soon as the sun sets, *tavernas* start filling up and the village springs to life to the sounds of sizzling kebabs and Greek music. We limited ourselves to eating in the *tavernas* only in the evenings, whereas during the day, we made our own food with what we bought in the local grocery stores; usually unfamiliar Cypriot foods, which we knew would taste good, as everything was so fresh.

Kouklia village was our next stop, as another friendly driver dropped us off at the village center. The coastline along this sandy shore was equally gorgeous, and we immediately decided to spend a night here. But first, we wanted to see Palaepathos, the Sanctuary of Aphrodite, where the temple had once stood—the main reason for our coming here. After seeing pictures of it on postcards, we could not simply bypass this place. Some people we met at the *taverna* yesterday told us that Kouklia also had several old churches that are worth seeing. We saw them, but only admired their architecture from outside.

After another wonderful night on the beach in Kouklia, we hitched a ride to Pathos, which I took an immediate liking to. It really was more relaxing than Limassol, and a lone Pelican stood like a statue on a jetty as if to prove how relaxing it actually was. Also on the water was the old Turkish fort, looking quite menacing as it commanded the sea front.

The ubiquitous cafés and *tavernas* in Cyprus were not only places to eat, but created as homely an atmosphere as possible where guests would feel so relaxed, they would stay there all evening, eating and chatting while lively Greek music and plenty of wine kept everyone in high spirits. Most of these guests in Pathos were English expatriates. These were the English who had long since decided to make this sunny island their home, having bid their final farewells to the infamous British weather. Pathos seemed to be a popular destination for them. We spoke to several of these expatriates while in the city, and they proved to be as relaxed and friendly as the Cypriots.

The alluring aroma of fish and chips by the water was hard to resist, drawing us inside like a magnet. The take-away had the familiar salt and vinegar on the counter. We sat down eating our very English lunch on the jetty while the pelican came to life and focused its beady eye on our food, hoping for a chunk of fish. We threw him a chip, as the fish was too delicious to share with greedy, large-beaked birds.

Pathos was rich in Roman history and ruins, but I was beginning to get tired of them. After a while, they all start looking the same to someone who only sees broken columns and crumbled walls. Fascinating as they are, and the historical significance that they portray, I wanted to see something different… more ruins—tombs this time, known as the Tombs of the Kings.

We arrived there in the late afternoon just as the last tourists were leaving. There was a small group still lingering inside what looked like an underground courtyard, where high, cylindrical, well-preserved columns had been erected. Some steps led the way down to the entrance of the tombs, which covered a vast area, and parts of it were still being excavated. The columns were outdoors, but built below the surface, and as soon as we entered the chamber, spooky darkness enveloped us. Continuing our way through the dank passages, daylight became harder to make out. There were tombs everywhere, carved out from rock and varying in size—some single, some double. I was staring at the double one. "Great place to spend a night," I suggested to Sally.

"What? Here?" She looked at me incredulously.

"It's perfect. It's *very* private. After all, it would be quite an experience to sleep in the tombs… " I tried to talk her into it, "and we have candles…," I reminded, "and food."

"Yeah, I guess it could be quite cozy. What about the former residents?" She worried.

"Oh, they're quite dead," I assured her. "They died 2,000 years ago. Anyway, I haven't seen any mummies or skeletons, have you?" I was wondering what had happened to all the bodies.

The last visitors had left as we made our way back to the tombs after our search for any previous remaining occupants. There was nothing, just empty, gaping, coffin-sized spaces that were now void of corpses. We had supper outside by the columns where we could sit on the ruins and use them as a table… or was that table a tomb? Daylight was quickly disappearing underground as we were finishing our *dolmades* (stuffed vine

147

leaves) with our side dish of feta cheese and sesame-coated bread. "We should've brought a bottle of wine along," I mentioned.

"What? And hallucinate even more? I'm *already* seeing ghosts." She sounded nervous.

We had already reserved our double tomb: the nearest one to the exit, so that we could escape… just in case. As we entered the chambers with our flickering candles just before it became pitch black outside, it was then that I realized this had not been such a good idea after all. But it was too late and too dark to backtrack to Pathos. For some reason, it felt much colder this time, and we swiftly clambered into our hole and rolled out the mats and sleeping bags. We intended to keep the candle lit throughout the night to keep unwelcome spiritual guests at bay.

It reminded me a little bit of sleeping inside the Masada ruins in Israel, where we also had to contend with such darkness. But they were not tombs. I became a little restless on the hard stone surface, scrutinizing the chamber where we lay, shoulder height from the ground, and inside a sheer stone wall. "What are you looking for?" Sally was getting irritated.

"You know, this is where the bodies were placed… exactly this spot. I'm just making sure there are no pieces of skeleton that might've come detached when they were removed. I don't want to sleep with a leftover finger or a foot near me."

"Eugh!" Sally uttered in disgust… and also started going over the stone tomb with the candle.

Sleep was something that would not come easily. It was too silent and unusually cold. I imagined skeletons clambering out of their tombs and trying to evict us. I suggested that we blow out the candle, as it made matters worse when shadows began to dance in flickering candlelight that illuminated other entrances to adjacent tombs. We blew it out and attempted to sleep. Never again will I sleep inside a tomb. The darkness seemed eternal, and we were waiting for the slightest sounds from the underworld that would make us scarper to the exit. There was no sound. The tombs were as dead as they should have been, and sleep eventually took over.

It was an uneventful night (thank goodness), and friendly daylight shone through the entrance. The tombs no longer looked so sinister, and we made a beeline for the exit in case the first tourists should discover two bodies emerging from the tomb and scaring the hell out of them. This, we wanted to avoid.

We headed back into Pathos looking quite disheveled and feeling like the walking dead. *Tavernas* were open for breakfast and some were serving English cuisine. I settled for a coffee, some buttered toast, and an egg. A prim and proper woman sat at the nearby table—English, of course. She was reading the *Herald Tribune* and stretched her neck as our English accents drifted across, but that was nothing unusual in Cyprus. Noticing our backpacks: "Are you backpacking around the island?" She tried to strike up a conversation.

"Yes, we started in Limassol. That's where the ferry arrived from Israel."

"You were in Israel?" She was suddenly interested.

"Almost a year," we told her.

"But that is so wonderful," the woman acknowledged. "I love it when young people travel. I traveled a lot, too, when I was younger. There is so much to see. Where are you staying?"

"Nowhere at the moment. We spent the night in the tombs."

"You slept *there*?" She laughed.

"It was quite an experience," we admitted, "but never again."

"I have a spare guest room in my house. You are welcome to use it for a few days if you want. I live alone now, so there is plenty of space. When I was traveling, strangers very often offered me a place in their homes, and I would like to return the favor."

"That's very nice… thank you." We couldn't believe our luck. After breakfast, we followed the woman to her house, which was a short walking distance from the *taverna*. Her home was typical Cypriot architecture—an old stone house with blue shutters and potted plants on the doorstep. Inside, terracotta-colored tiles covered the entire floor with a few small rugs thrown on top, and all the walls were painted a brilliant white with pictures of old Greek houses and churches… and she liked pine furniture, which was in every room. It was very modern, very bright, and cheerful. The guest room looked the same.

"Hope you like it. I'll make some tea and you can tell me about your adventures." The woman's name was Dorothy, and she seemed quite happy to have some guests in her house and someone to make tea for. She lived alone, but from the way she acted, it was obvious she was not lonely. "In Cyprus, one can never be lonely, not like in England," she told us while serving tea. I knew exactly what she meant.

We educated her on kibbutz and moshav life in Israel, and filled her in on our adventures there. Dorothy listened with deep interest. "You've convinced me. I will definitely travel to Israel this year," she beamed with enthusiasm. In return, she told us about East Africa and India, when they were still part of the British colony, and she had traveled there with her husband. "Wonderful people—the Indians. I feel ashamed how we, the British treated them... and the Africans, too... always friendly, always smiling.... " She lapsed into silence for a moment, reminiscing the past.

With our hands free, we set off to see the attractions of Pathos. The town had a lot to offer, but the most pleasant part was the town itself. I understood why Dorothy had chosen to live here. We walked back down to the harbor and went inside the imposing Byzantine castle with its sheer walls that stood out in the water and emitted a warning to any potential invaders.

The most impressive and best preserved mosaics can be found in the House of Dionysus. They attracted quite a crowd as we all craned our necks to see how the Romans decorated their floors; much better than they did today, with people wanting everything to be plain. Romans had a great sense for art, and even the construction of a floor was not a simple endeavor.

Putting the Romans and Byzantines aside for a while, it gave us great pleasure just to stroll around the harbor and watch fishing boats bobbing in the water. The Pathos pelican was still in the area, hoping for a sample of the latest catch from the local fishermen.

As we were saving money on accommodation, which was always the most expensive part of traveling, we did splurge a little on Cypriot pastries, which were not unlike the Arabic ones. Nevertheless, we looked forward to the evenings when the *tavernas* filled up and the mild air smelled of sizzling meats. Our favorite *taverna* was the one where bulbous, bottle-shaped gourds were suspended from the entire ceiling, and enormous vases and statues of Greek gods defined the property line. As the evening progressed, the *Bouzouki* music became louder, or maybe it was the marvelous wine that clarified the hearing senses.

We dawdled back to Dorothy's house. She had told us that in case she wasn't home, the door would be left unlocked. "This is not England. We don't have to lock our doors here." Dorothy *was* home—reading and listening to classical music. "Would you care for some tea?"

"Sounds like a splendid idea," we both chirped. After a slight possibility of having drunk a teensy, weensy bit too much wine, a cup of tea was the perfect antidote; however, not to drink a jug of wine with a meal would almost be considered a crime.

"Wine is good in Cyprus, isn't it?" Smiled Dorothy.

"Fantastic!"

It was a mistake sleeping at Dorothy's house. We had long ago bid farewell to the comforts of a real bed. In Israel there were only foam mattresses to sleep on, and this here was a *real* bed that consisted of a *real* mattress. It was like sleeping on a cloud, and we never wanted to spend a night anywhere else again. We were in heaven, and when the bright sun's rays filtered through the thin curtains the next morning, we were forced to leave our cloud and continue sightseeing. There was a knock on the door as Dorothy heard our voices. "I've made some breakfast and tea when you're ready," she called cheerfully. The lady was an angel.

Also in the Pathos area, there is an old monastery attracting a fair number of visitors. We weren't modestly dressed for holy places, and not wanting to offend, didn't attempt to go inside, preferring to tour the grounds instead while observing monks chatting to visitors in the courtyard. They were dressed in their traditional black Greek Orthodox robes and oversized silver crosses that hung loosely across their chests under their beards. One of the younger monks noticed our strolling around and beckoned us over. "Would you like to look inside?" He asked in perfect English.

"It would be nice, but… we are not wearing… umm…, " I trailed off. The monk laughed.

"We don't live in the Middle Ages. The outer body is unimportant; it is one's heart and thoughts that matter. Come inside, I'll show you around." We followed him into the monastery behind thick stone walls. The temperature instantly changed and goosebumps broke out on our bodies. The monk noticed the temperature shock on our skin and laughed again. "Now you know why we wear black robes. You are English?" Without waiting for a response, "Let us drink some tea," and he went to a samovar that was standing on a simple table and filled up three glasses. He also offered us some powder-covered misshaped sweets. "You like *leukomi*?"

"*Leukomi*? What's that?"

"I think in England you call it Turkish Delight. This is Cypriot Delight —very sweet," he explained. "Very sweet" sounded good, and we took a piece. I was very familiar with Turkish Delight, and at one time in England, I was actually hooked on the chocolate-covered *Fry's Turkish Delights*, which were sold everywhere. *Leukomi* was even better.

"Mmmm, this is gooood," I acknowledged. The Cypriot Delights were absolutely delightful, and while I was sucking on my *leukomi* inside the monastery, I made a holy vow to purchase a sickly amount.

"You will notice that people sell them by the roadside as you leave Pathos. Those are the freshest ones," the monk informed us. After we downed our tea, he briefly showed us the chapel where they prayed, and the hall where they ate. It was very spartan inside with only the basic necessities, and not much light anywhere, but enough to illuminate the numerous icons that depicted saints. They took up a lot of wall space and watched over the monks in case they should sinfully over-indulge in *leukomi*. The monk was genuinely interested in our travels and was happy to learn that we had been to Jerusalem. "I was there two years ago," he told us. "It is a special place." We agreed. "Where will you go after Cyprus?" He asked.

"We'll take the ferry to Greece, then cross over to Turkey." Turkey was a sore point with the Cypriots, and I didn't want to elaborate. The monk, however, liked our plan and had no qualms with the enemy. We thanked him for showing us around and went back outside where the warmth of the sun smoothed down our goosebumps.

We came across a launderette in town yesterday, which was a reminder that it was high time for some fresh clothing. After another tasty portion of fish and chips at the harbor, we went back to the house to pick up our dirty clothes. It was unlocked and Dorothy was out. Stuffing one backpack, we trudged into the most boring place in the world and prepared ourselves for the excitement of watching clothes being spun around. There wasn't even any Greek music inside for entertainment. To fight boredom though, we brought our guidebook along to plan our next move: to the Troodos Mountains that promised quaint isolated villages. We also wanted to see

Lefkara, which was famous for its hand-made lace, not that I was interested in it, but the village itself was mentioned as "not to be missed."

Another wonderfully comfortable night, and the next day was to be our last one in Pathos. Nearby are the Agia Solomoni Catacombs, which had been carved out of rock and date back thousands of years. This area consists of several such caves and chambers, which had once been in use. Many chambers had holes in the roof, and this allowed natural daylight to pour in. Not only catacombs are found here, but a very ancient underground church had actually been established inside one. Carved out of bare limestone, the church is a wonder, and still a place of worship today. Outside, at the entrance to the church, is a holy tree whose branches are covered in cloth. It is believed that when people hang offerings upon it, they will be cured of illnesses. I didn't have anything to hang, neither did I suffer from any illnesses, so I just bypassed the tree.

For the remainder of the day we lolled on the beach until the sun started its descent upon the horizon and it was time to return to our favorite *taverna*. That evening, we had a major feast, but took it easy on the wine. Dorothy was back and started brewing tea when we appeared at the house. We told her about our plans to go to the Troodos Mountains tomorrow, and then to catch the ferry to Rhodes the following Monday. "Rhodes is ghastly," she screwed up her nose. "They have lost all their culture. It's all touristy. We have tourists in Pathos, too, but it hasn't been ruined." She was right. There were quite a few tourists here, but they somehow seemed invisible. Pathos was riddled with historical sites; so much in fact, that the whole area had been designated a World Heritage Site, and the tourists who came here failed to change the town for the worse. "I think you'll be running off to Turkey on the next boat once you see Rhodes," she was convinced.

We packed our backpacks and bid Dorothy goodnight. "I will really miss this bed," I mumbled to Sally, as we lay upon the cloud for the last time.

"I wonder where we'll be sleeping tomorrow?" She mused.

"Wherever we end up, it's going to be way more uncomfortable, unless some kind person offers us a room in a five-star hotel."

Sleep came too soon, and so did the morning, and then the final parting of the bed. Dorothy the early bird was already chirping around in the kitchen preparing breakfast. "Are you going to hitchhike to the mountains?" She asked.

"No, we'll take the bus. It looks a little tricky getting there. Too many twists and turns. It might take all day."

"Believe me, it'll take all day by bus, too. The buses are so old and slow," Dorothy warned. She gave us a huge hug as we parted company and told us that we should see as much of the world as we can. We gave her a box of assorted *leukomi* we picked up from the gift store. "Oh, you shouldn't have, but thank you. They taste so good with tea, you know."

We were on the Troodos bus. The word "bus" did not seem appropriate for this vehicle—an ancient Bedford "thing" that had gone dreadfully wrong at the manufacturing plants in Great Britain and condemned to a lifetime of exile—far away from the British Isles. It was smaller than the one from Limassol harbor, and I didn't think it possible, but older, too. Black fumes shot out from the exhaust when the driver stepped on the accelerator, which produced the now familiar grinding noise, but no increase in speed. Dorothy was right: this *will* take all day. Better to relax and enjoy the view. Relaxation was to be another problem. The hard, uncomfortable seats had a worn out, shiny, plastic cover, which made us slide around every time the bus turned. The driver was another friendly man who also stuck to the "slowly, slowly" rhythm. While leaving Pathos, roadside vendors started to appear, and after a quick visual scan of their merchandise, I saw that it was *leukomi*. "Oh, look! They're selling *leukomi*," I exclaimed a little too loud that the driver heard me.

"You want I stop? You can buy *leukomi*. We have time. We have all day. No problem." We jumped off the bus and bought several boxes of Cypriot Delights, which would last all the way to Turkey. The driver also got off to enjoy a cigarette while the other three local passengers took no particular interest in this sudden break. They were probably accustomed to such bus journeys with unusual, sporadic stops. Sally and I were the only foreigners on the bus: the other three consisted of two men and a woman who all looked to be in their eighties. The men had coarse-looking skin and bristly chins; old, but still seemed energetic and had probably spent their days farming. The woman was on the large side with shovel-sized hands that looked as if they had spent decades kneading dough in the kitchen. She looked like a good cook, and the evidence was beside her—the fresh produce overflowing from half a dozen shopping bags. All three of them were engrossed in deep conversation. The driver would occasionally join in.

For a while, the bus followed the coastline towards Limassol, and then it made a sharp turn northwards. We passed farmland: rich and green after the winter rains put an end to the summer drought. Citrus groves and banana trees resembled the coastal regions of Israel. As the bus started to climb further inland, the elevation increased, and the lush vegetation of the coast was replaced by olive trees and endless vineyards. Small villages started to appear, surrounded by the most fantastic landscape that deserved a few pages in the *National Geographic* magazine.

We made our first stop at one of these villages which time forgot, and from the modern lifestyle along the coast, we went back a couple of hundred years. The few, almost vintage cars that parked on the streets were a reminder that this was indeed the twentieth century. As I was hoping, the bus stopped at a café where grizzled old men in worn-out gray jackets sat outside and gazed upon the leafless vineyards below. Small, square tables, time-worn and chipped after many decades of use and repainted several times, blended in appropriately with the surroundings. The equally simple chairs were all mismatched and had also suffered years of scuff marks and outdoor elements of nature. The indented seats were worn away to a perfect sheen, like on the bus.

"How long are we staying here?" I asked the driver. He shrugged his shoulders.

"However long it takes. We have time. No problem. You eat. You drink. We go slowly, slowly." Sally and I grinned at each other. This driver must be related to that Limassol bloke.

We all sat down in the café, which only seemed to serve coffee. There was no menu, so I assumed there was no food. One of the sitting men turned out to be the owner as he shot off to the kitchen after shaking hands with the bus driver. Friends? Relatives? I had no idea. But this seemed to be a regular stop for the driver, and shortly after, the owner brought him a plate of food. The other three passengers each ordered some pastry, which was the size of a plate and looked temptingly good. How did they know what to order? There was no menu. The owner/waiter came to us. "Coffee please… and that!" I pointed at the pastry. "What is it?" He told us what it was, but the Greek name was too complicated to remember for more than a few seconds.

"It is cheese and spinach inside pastry. Very good," he told us while smacking his fingertips against his lips to emphasize the taste.

The pastry was indeed delicious and had obviously been made in this village only hours before. It was still warm as if the arrival of the bus had been expected and these snacks had been specially baked for this occasion. We ordered another round of the strong and sweet Cypriot coffee while the driver was washing down his meal with a jug of village wine, and then a cigarette for dessert. This was going to take a while—slowly, slowly in fact. We paid a special low village price of £1.20 for our food and drinks, and before continuing our journey, we stretched our legs a little around the village before the driver polished off the liter-jug of wine.

There was no sign of young people our age. We did see infants, but the village was dominated by unperturbed elderly people who greeted us kindly as we peered at their houses, which were scrubbed spotless from the exterior. All parts of their gardens were filled with flowers, herbs, and vegetables. The larger gardens had goats, which shared their ground with the chickens. Stacks of firewood were everywhere. Some of the houses had sagging roofs and walls that have become crooked with age, but most were beautifully maintained and looked very cozy. It would be a fine place to live.

The driver was refueled with wine, and the bus picked up three more women passengers. The café also served as the village bus station, and for me, it was the most beautiful bus station in the world. After an hour, we drove directly towards the mountains where pine forests dominated the vegetation scene. Beautiful as it may be, this was not a good sign: coniferous was a synonym for cold. The tortured engine of the bus whined with strain and I was sure it would give out. We stopped at another village. This was Kato Platres, and the three ladies who came on board in the previous village got off here, but were replaced by half a dozen other people.

Still climbing, the bus deposited the rest of the passengers in the mountain village of Pano Platres; except us—we were continuing to Troodos. "We make break," the driver announced as he desperately sucked on his cigarette. Again, we stopped to drink coffee. As we stepped off the bus in our shorts and T-shirts, we were startled by the sudden drop in temperature, and my exposed skin took on an instant transformation—goosebumps on top of goosebumps. It was worse than stepping inside a dark monastery. We hurried back on board to pull out our sweatshirts, but our bare legs were still subjected to the sudden cold. This village looked even more primitive than the last one, and the streets were barely wide enough for two-way traffic. The café had the same dilapidated furniture, but there was no one sitting outside. They were indoors. We also stepped inside for a coffee, but were still full from the previous giant pastry. Instead of sweet mountain air, the village had to put up with swirling smoke, which puffed out of almost every chimney. It was bloody cold, and we were still driving to a higher elevation.

On the bus, nobody else joined us. Maybe they knew more than we did. Why wasn't anyone else going to Troodos? The grinding bus had to persevere with steep and narrow, windy roads, and the ever-protesting, churning engine threatened to blow up as it made a sound similar to a chain saw that was cutting down a stubborn oak. We felt the heat of the engine build up as our butts started to smolder. Feeling dangerously hot, we moved to a different seat. The bus climbed all the way until the road leveled out and it came to a stop. "Troodos!"

"Are you going back now?" I asked the driver.

"I'm going to sleep in the village. Go back tomorrow," and he was gone.

It was freezing outside. Spring hadn't yet arrived here. We were dropped off in a little square, which comprised of a hotel and a taxi office. Our guidebook mentioned no accommodation here for budget travelers. Now I understood why—there wasn't any. The only accommodation available was the fancy hotel that stood next to us. The price per night was the equivalent to what we had spent during our entire trip in Cyprus so far. "Let's walk down to the village and look for a room," Sally suggested.

But the village was dead. There was no sign of life; no children; no old people sitting around cafés; not even a café! Only smoke spiraled upwards out of chimneys where lucky people sat in their cozy warm homes. There *was* no other accommodation. We would have to sleep outdoors tonight. It had been our original plan to do so anyway, but we hadn't anticipated such cold—and it was still daytime. At night, the temperatures will plummet. There was no bus out of here until tomorrow, either. We were stranded.

"Let's go hiking," I suggested to Sally. The Troodos Mountains are rich in trails, and we walked back to the expensive hotel to pick up a trail guide. "We still have some food left and maybe we'll come across a cave where we can build a fire and stay warm." It was a good idea. There was still about three hours of daylight left, and hiking in the mountains would also help to keep warm.

"A cave would be nice, but *please,* no tombs!" Sally insisted.

The short hike in the mountains did warm us up, but changing into our jeans helped a lot, too. In the mountains, the air was crisp and pure, and the pine forests emitted the freshest air any lungs would die for. There were no caves anywhere, and the idea of a romantic night in the Stone Age soon evaporated. We were disappointed. "Let's go back to the hotel. They have a restaurant there. Maybe we can get some tea," Sally suggested. A hot tea was something I needed right now. Maybe a hot meal, too. We will freeze tonight.

Back at the square where the taxi office was located, a bus schedule was tacked onto the notice board. The bus driver was right: one bus a day. Without accommodation, it was impossible to stay in the mountains in this cold, and the hotel was ridiculously expensive. A young man was sitting at his desk inside the taxi office when he noticed our deliberating outside the window. "There are no more buses leaving today," he reminded us.

"We know. Just checking when the first bus leaves in the morning. It's too cold here."

"Where are you staying tonight?" He focused on the backpacks.

"Camping somewhere between the trees," Sally answered gloomily.

"You can't stay outside!" He looked shocked. "You'll freeze! The temperatures will be dropping well below zero this night. Why don't you stay in the hotel?" He pointed across the square.

"Too expensive," we answered in unison.

"Yes, I know. I couldn't stay there, either." He thought for a moment. "In that case, you should stay here in the office. I'm leaving shortly, but you are welcome to stay inside. He beckoned us into his tiny office, which consisted of nothing more than a desk, a phone, and one chair. There was also something that looked like an old-fashioned switchboard that was used for contacting taxi drivers. "If you have mats, and I see you have sleeping bags, you can sleep here on the floor, and you are welcome to put the

158

heater on. It's going to get really cold tonight," he reminded us once more. "If you like, you can stay more than one night, but I need the office back by 9:00 A.M. That's when I start work."

"This is just perfect," we told him. "You've saved our lives."

"It's no problem. I will leave the door unlocked for you in case you want to go out and eat in the hotel restaurant... it's expensive though. You can also leave your backpacks inside if you decide to go hiking tomorrow." He grabbed his bag and stuffed some papers inside. "Have a good night. I'll be here by nine." Then he got inside the car and drove off. Sally and I were speechless by such kindness we were confronting in this country. Complete strangers would go out of their way to help us.

"Let's get some tea now," I insisted. The hotel staff were also friendly and *of course* we could use the restaurant. We didn't want to waste the food we still had: salami, bread, haloumi cheese, mandarins, and leukomi for dessert. A tea was all I wanted, but we decided to come in for breakfast tomorrow. The hotel had very few guests who looked quite overdressed, or maybe it was us who were underdressed in such an elegant dining room where tables were covered in several layers of white cloth. It was a morose, superficial atmosphere, so unlike the cheerful *tavernas*. Laughter and loud voices would be out of place here. We left quickly, but not before taking advantage of the bathrooms.

It was already dark outside and the deep chill had set in for the night. Someone from above must have been watching over a couple of desperate backpackers, thus guiding us to the taxi office. We certainly would have frozen this night, had we slept outside. It was frosty in the office, too, but the small space heated up rapidly once the electric heater was switched on. Having failed to come across a real cave, we made this man-made one equally cozy by lighting a candle and huddling inside our sleeping bags, and only then we allowed ourselves to laugh about the day's events. It turned out to be a great night after all.

We had to switch the heater off middle of the night, or there was the danger of roasting to death. The early morning welcomed us with steamed up windows as a reminder how cold it was outside. It was almost 8:00 A.M. and time to make a move before the taxi person arrived. Another blow from the heater blasted the frosty air away before getting dressed, then we made our way to the hotel restaurant.

English breakfast was on the menu, but for a horrendous price. We ordered it anyway, and made sure to savor every last crumb. It was delicious. We were just enjoying our tea (the hotel had no Cypriot coffee) when an elegantly-dressed, white-haired woman leaned over from the adjacent table and introduced herself in Queen's English. "My name is Jane, and who may you be?" We introduced ourselves, but without the Queen's English. "Are you staying in the hotel? I don't remember seeing you before."

"No, we are sleeping on the floor of the taxi office across the square. We just came in here to eat," Sally told her.

"Oh, that is just marvelous," and she clapped her hands. "You two are real travelers."

"Yes, I think so. We are backpacking…, but on the cheap."

"That is the best way. I would also prefer to sleep on the floor of the taxi office." Then she lowered her voice and leaned forward. "People are so stuffy here, and all they talk about is the stock market, or how much they had paid for their jewelry," she whispered. "Now, tell me about your adventures," she demanded. "You look as if you've seen some wonderful places."

"We've seen a lot of Israel." We spoke about life on the kibbutz and moshav.

"Did you go into the Dead Sea? It is my dream to see it."

"We did," and we explained how difficult it was to swim inside.

"I'm backpacking, too," she suddenly announced, smiling. "Really! My rucksack is upstairs in my room. I have decided to travel around the world." She noticed our surprised looks and went on to explain. "My husband was a boring old sod who never wanted to travel anywhere."

"You left him?" Sally interrupted.

"Yes, you might say I did," she snorted. "He died. That was two years ago… and left a substantial amount of money behind. I had two choices: to grow old in England and end up in the old people's home with relatives checking in on me to see how soon they could cash in, or… I could use the money to enjoy the rest of my days. I decided to sell my house and all my possessions and see the world. I am 72 years old now, but I feel much younger than I ever did when I was married."

"Where are you going next?" Now *we* were fascinated by her story.

"I have it all planned. From Cyprus, I'm going to take the ferry to Lebanon, then travel overland to India. I might have to fly if politics don't allow it. I will then travel through Asia, fly to Australia, New Zealand, and I really want to visit those islands in the Pacific, then fly to South America, North America, and if I'm still alive... Africa."

"But that will take years," we gasped in disbelief.

"I have the rest of my life. The best thing that can happen to me is that I die while traveling, and *not* in a sterile institution in England." She was serious, and we both took a liking to this amazing lady, who spoke and dressed as if she had come from Buckingham Palace. She changed subjects. "By the way, are you still here tomorrow?" Sally and I looked at each other as we hadn't yet decided.

"Yes, we're going to stay one more night. We want to do some hiking today." I spoke for both of us.

"Splendid! In that case, do join me for breakfast tomorrow morning. It's very interesting talking to you. Shall we meet at the same time?" We nodded. "Good... and breakfast will be on me."

We went to check with taxi man if it was okay to stay another night in his office. "Of course. I wish I had something better to offer you. How was breakfast?"

"Expensive, but wonderful. We're going hiking for the rest of the day, and thanks again for the use of your office."

The air was starting to warm up again, and the amazing vistas from the ridge glistened in the morning dew. Without the burdening backpacks, the hiking was much more pleasant and we covered quite a distance, working ourselves into a sweat. The downside was that there was no possibility of a shower afterward, and we would have to wait for this luxury until tomorrow. The people who stayed in the hotel didn't do any hiking, but silently remained rooted in the restaurant, reading their newspapers. We saw them as we went in for some tea in the late afternoon; they were as rigid as statues, still frowning at the newspapers. "Boring old sods," I was thinking.

After another uncomfortable night on the stone floor, we walked across the square to meet Jane. She was already there, drinking tea and scanning through her guidebook on the Middle East. "Good morning, my dears. Ready for breakfast?"

"Absolutely. How was your day yesterday?" We asked.

"Positively marvelous. I walked down to the village and met some wonderful people there. They have so little, and yet, are so happy. It makes me feel so alive to be able to speak with *real* people." I knew what she was talking about and wondered if we also fit into her "real people" category. Her next statement reassured us. "I honestly commend what you young people are doing. Enjoy life while you can and see the world!" was her motto.

Jane embraced us as we left and we wished each other pleasant journeys, wherever we may end up. Taxi man was in his office, and we also shook hands and thanked him for his generosity. The bus to Limassol was waiting to take us back down to the warmer coastal regions.

From there we continued to Larnaca and immediately booked into a *pension,* where a nice warm shower was waiting. Larnaca was the hotter and drier part of Cyprus and had more of the Middle-Eastern flair, but I didn't find the city so interesting; rather decrepit and dusty. A nearby mosque (slightly obscured by haze) beside a salt lake marked the perfect setting for a picnic, but we were more captivated by the numerous pink flamingos that shimmered in the distance. The heat was back too, and so were our shorts and T-shirts.

Cyprus has the most impressive collection of churches, and one that is really worth seeing is the Church of St. Lazarus. The entire interior is covered in golden icons depicting saints, heaven, and hell. There was one icon in particular that stuck out and I was entranced by it. It showed a large table covered with mouth-watering food. Demons (complete with horns and spiky tails) sat around it with very large and extra long forks in their hands, but none of them were eating. They looked hungry; their eyes longing for the food. The Greek Orthodox priest noticed my gazing at this picture and came over to explain the meaning behind it.

"This is hell," he smiled. "The demons are permanently tortured by the lure of all this delicious food, but cannot eat."

"Why not?" We wondered aloud.

"Their forks are too long to bring the food to their mouths and they are not allowed to use their hands, and so, they starve for eternity. This represents selfishness. They are only thinking of themselves. The only way for them to eat would be to feed each other. That's why the forks are so long. Only by sharing and helping one another can they achieve happiness."

The icon made a powerful statement, and the artist couldn't have portrayed "selfishness" in a better way. The church had the scariest-looking pictures I have ever seen inside a holy place, and many of them depicted angels and demons, and all had a message to deliver.

The following day was our last one in this wonderful country. On the bus to Lefkara, we read about our next destination, which was famous for its lace. The village has remained as traditional as possible despite the influx of tourists, who were clicking away with their cameras, but it wasn't the lace that made it worth visiting: it was the people. In the village center, dozens of elderly women sat in front of their homes, sewing and embroidering. They all wore black, as all widows did amongst the Greek Cypriots. Were they in permanent mourning? They didn't look it as they happily stitched away while chatting amongst themselves, completely oblivious to the thousands of photographs that have been taken of them. At first, I thought that this was all staged for the tourists, but in fact, it was reality. This is what the village was famous for. As well as lace, there were eye-catching, hand-woven baskets for sale. I would've liked to spend the night in this gorgeous village, but our ferry to Rhodes was leaving in the morning and we had to make our way back to Limassol.

We stayed in the same *pension* as when we first arrived in Cyprus, and afterward, dived into the delicious kebabs that were still sizzling nearby. I wondered what happened to Thorsten. Sally suggested that he moved into a dairy that produced *halloumi* on a large scale.

The ferry to Greece came early the next morning, and we took up a corner on the deck once more. As it pulled away from the harbor, we had an opportunity to gaze at the endless coastline and all the stacks in the water that could have been representations of Aphrodite. Cyprus became history as it diminished into a speck, but the wonderful people I had met will continue to live on in my journal.

7
WHERE IS GREECE?

The crossing to the Greek island of Rhodes was much longer than to Cyprus from Israel. It also gave us an opportunity to experience the rich deep blue color of the Mediterranean, which resembled the sky. Flying fish sprang out of the water and attempted to race the ferry. I had never been on a cruise, but it felt very much like one as we passed the most beautiful islands; some of them too small to be inhabited. This is how Greek islands were supposed to look, and they certainly lived up to my expectations. On the ship was a bar serving *Amstel* beer and other beverages. I wasn't a beer lover, but needed a change from the regular water and sweet juice. The ice-cold beer tasted surprisingly good, and I made a mental note of the Dutch brand. The bar was open to whoever wanted to sit inside and admire the view from the windows. Filipino workers were either scrubbing the ship or painting it. Most of them worked in the engine room. This was the most perfect way to travel and I felt exhilarated to have had this opportunity. I thought of Jane, and her wise and beautiful words, which affirmed that there was nothing better in life than traveling. I hope she has a long life and gets to see the whole world.

The ship's vibrations ceased and sleep came naturally. The night was pleasantly warm, and we lay back and gazed at the clear stars above. We met a Swedish girl earlier that day: she had booked a cabin all the way to Athens. It was shared by three other people, but she decided to sleep outside on the deck instead. "It is terrible inside. I feel like a sardine. There is no air and it's so hot." Agatha slept with us this night, but unfortunately, we had to bid the blue-eyed blonde farewell as the ferry docked in Rhodes the next morning.

At the entrance to the harbor, once upon a time, one of the wonders of the world presided over ancient fleets—the Colossi of Rhodes. It is long gone now, toppled by an earthquake many centuries ago and reclaimed by the sea. However, the old harbor remained an enchanting way to arrive on the island. As we drew nearer, vast imposing walls, which looked very Roman, still spurred the mind's eye that this ingress had once been heavily-fortified. Any approaching enemy from the sea would have had to think twice before an onslaught of this city. The walls were very similar to the ones that had also protected Limassol.

Disembarkation was about to begin, but we waited until the cars drove off, then proceeded to immigration. Agatha was still madly waving goodbye to us from the deck as if we were parting company after many years of friendship. But it did feel like we had been friends forever. It felt strange and somewhat disheartening that we should abandon such a happy-go-lucky, brief friend who would have made a wonderful travel companion.

Greece had become a recent member of the EEC (European Economic Community), but despite that, immigration was still stamping all European passports. My pages were starting to look colorful. We were confronted with different currency again once we changed a couple of Traveler's Checks. The Greek drachmas would not last very long on this island.

There was no bus waiting this time, but that wasn't necessary: the Old City of Rhodes was walking distance, just behind the walls, where tourism in its most extreme form paralyzed every visitor. There was no sign of Greece anywhere. Stupefied (and horrified) by all the shops selling an overwhelming array of touristy junk, I couldn't understand why the British were lured to this island. In England, package tours to Corfu and Rhodes were always being advertised on TV and newspapers, but if people were expecting to experience Greece, they might be disappointed.

We found a pricey, but cozy *pension* in the Old City and decided to book it for two days. Accommodation was easy to find, but where was the food? We walked and walked, but could not find any food places or *tavernas*; not even a grocery store where one could buy bread. This was absurd. We were starving. Why couldn't we buy bread in this town? Where was the Greek food? *Where was the food?* Every single shop was filled with imitation Greek statues and vases, or T-shirts with stupid slogans, and postcards galore. There were shops selling leather wallets and there was…, "Oh, my God!" a pub—an English-style pub with red-faced Brits slurping huge glasses of beer. Other shops sold all possible souvenirs depicting Greek gods with giant erect penises in multiple sexual positions. Several T-shirts simply sported the word "Rhodos." Pricey boutiques sold brand name fashions, and the sport shops carried "Boss" gear. This was hell, and I had a flashback of St.Lazarus church in Cyprus, where such images were depicted in the icons.

Everything was expensive on this island, and we very quickly decided to cut our visit to the island short and look for a boat to Turkey as soon as possible. Staying here would make no sense. We wanted to get a taste of Greece, but it felt like a British seaside resort; only bingo was missing. But if this place resembled a British resort, surely there must be a fish and chips shop in vicinity? We checked out the harbor area. Nothing. No food. A little bit further, and… BINGO—the local chippie; complete with salt and vinegar on the counter like in Cyprus; like in England. It was good. Very good. Maybe a touch of Britishness in certain parts of the world may be forgiven at times.

But Rhodes was boring. We were bored. There was nothing to do except aimlessly wander from street to street; from shop to shop, and finally—restaurants. Sterile restaurants. Unwelcoming restaurants, where dozens of tables stood in perfect alignment and no chairs looked out of place. It looked as if someone had used a tape measure to make sure they were all equidistant. The tables were covered with snow-white tablecloths. Sparkling-clean glasses, shiny cutlery (arranged with white-gloved hands), was enough to scare-off anyone who was hungry. We already knew from experience that a cloth-covered table automatically multiplied prices threefold. This was worse: aloof, immaculately-dressed waiters with bow ties, shiny black hair and manicured fingernails stood by the roadside clenching a menu and tried to coax the tourists into their restaurants. This scene alone was enough to cause hyper-inflated prices to multiply even more. We glanced at the menu that was displayed inside a plastic case at the entrance, and our jaws dropped when we saw how much it cost to eat roast beef and Yorkshire pudding or Wiener schnitzel with two vegetables. There was no Greek food on the menus; neither were there any Greeks eating here. Where did *they* eat? I missed the casual Cypriot *tavernas* with Greek music, and battered, scratched tables with the scuffed chairs. I was in a superficial world, and I recalled Dorothy's words. Tomorrow, we shall look for a boat to Turkey.

Approaching the city from a different direction, we did come across a mini supermarket where they sold bread. It was sterile inside, like the restaurants, but the bread was not the freshest. There were some baked goods, but they were all packaged. We ended up buying some meats and packaged feta cheese imported from Denmark. It was a poor selection.

The Old City came to life as it got dark and English party music pounded out from the pub. We ignored the bunch of superficially-happy, fun-loving, "all-inclusive" tourists outside, who were doing strange things with their beer, and decided to check out some smaller alleyways that were more secluded. There, we found a small family-run eatery, *and* it was Greek —Greek music, Greek food, and a Greek menu. Oh! The Greek menu was in Greek. That was a good sign. There weren't any table cloths on the tables, either—a *very* good sign. We sat down and tried to make sense out of the menu. There were a couple of Greek families eating here, too, and the food looked mouth-watering. I spied upon a salad that tempted me. An elderly woman dressed in black came out to take our order. She didn't speak English, but understood the word salad. "Salada," she repeated.

"Yes, salada," I confirmed.

"And two coffees," Sally added, holding up two fingers.

The delicious Greek coffee came instantaneously, accompanied with water. The salad was brought out soon afterwards: two bowls of freshly-cut greens with chunks of tomatoes, cucumber, onions, feta cheese, and fat, shiny black olives, and all of this was swimming in olive oil. This was accompanied with freshly-baked bread, which, I saw from the neighboring table, was used for soaking up the olive oil. I attempted to try an olive (something I had always avoided in Israel); these looked so perfect. They were fantastic. I couldn't believe that I had eaten an olive and actually enjoyed it. "Mmm… these olives are amazing," I admitted to Sally while munching away at a leaf like a rabbit.

"Can't believe you're eating olives," she laughed. "You're right, they *are* the best ones I've ever tasted."

The woman came out to collect the dishes. "Olives good," I complimented her, pointing at the pile of olive stones on my plate.

"Olive Kalamata. Kalamata good," was her attempt to tell us that these were Kalamata olives and that they were special.

Back in our room, we made plans for our crossing to Turkey. People told us that the country is incredibly cheap and it's not necessary to be thrifty. "As long as you have Western currency, you can buy anything you want."

We made our own breakfast next morning with the not-too-fresh bread we had bought and then walked down to the harbor. There were no ferries going to Turkey because of the political friction between the two countries, but small private boats did business by taking adventurous travelers the short distance across the water. Within twenty minutes we had a ticket to Marmaris for tomorrow morning *and* I was very much looking forward to it.

With the ticket in hand, we had the day to relax and do some sightseeing, but that meant more Roman and Greek ruins; both of which were becoming repetitive. To kill the day (and the day was very long), we ended up trying to get lost in alleys that were not shown on the map, still hoping to discover the real Greece. I did find a small vendor selling olives and ended up buying a few hundred grams of the Kalamata variety.

Our short (but endless) stay on the island of Rhodes came to an end as we headed to the waiting boat. I was happy to leave, disappointed that Greece did not fulfill my expectations. There was another side to Greece, I had no doubt, but right now, we were adventurous free spirits and were more interested in the unknown and the mysterious. Turkey fell into that category as it had not yet been discovered by party-loving, beer-guzzling tourists.

I was shocked by the size of the boat—just a large speedboat with seats for about sixteen passengers. We were five, joined by a man in his fifties and another older couple whose language I did not recognize. The man was from England: neatly groomed, studious-looking, and was lugging a bulky suitcase. Striking up a conversation, he spoke about his travels through the Mediterranean countries.

The boat suddenly whirred into action and sped off as fast as I suspected it would, and that was the end of our chatter, as the coarse sound of the speedboat combined with the wind and made any further discussion incomprehensible. Rhodes vanished very quickly, becoming a distant outcrop on the horizon. Not everything was bad on the island. I will remember it as the place where I acquired a taste for olives. I love olives!

8
COTTON CASTLES AND CHAI

The full blast of sea air styled our hair in the most bizarre form as the boat skimmed over the waves with incredible speed. We all arrived in Turkey looking like victims of electrocution with hair all gone "frizzy." No brush in the world would help at this point. Well before arrival, we caught a whiff of pine in the air as the boat slowed down and approached the Bay of Marmaris. We found ourselves encircled by pine growth high up on escarpments and all the way down to the shore. The scent grew stronger and was a pleasant welcome compared to the acrid diesel fumes of Rhodes and Limassol.

Water arrivals should have gone through the same procedure as everywhere else—immigration, then change money. But we were met by the police as we jumped off the boat onto Turkish soil. They couldn't speak English, but indicated for us to proceed to immigration for checking passports. The immigration office was closed, and there was no place to change money, either. We went back to the three uniformed men. "Immigration is closed," we told them. One of them strode over to the office and banged on the door. Nothing. He came back towards us.

"Passport sleep." He made the international sleep gesture by putting the palm of his hands together and resting his cheek upon them. The English man burst out laughing.

"Immigration is sleeping?" He found that hilarious. The police officer spoke again, or rather, he tried. He put his fingers to his mouth then pointed to some shops across the road.

"You... food eat. You passport," then he pointed at his watch and put two fingers up and repeated, "You passport... no sleep," and he pointed at the immigration office. "OK?"

"Ummm... *okay.*" I responded a little cautiously to show my confusion. The Englishman came to the rescue.

"I think he wants us to come back in two hours to get the passports stamped once the immigration officer is awake again."

"Or maybe at two o'clock," Sally proposed.

"Hmmm...." Now the Englishman was puzzled.

"Is there a bank here?" I asked the police officer. He didn't understand. Mr. English came to the rescue again.

"Change money," and he rubbed his fingers together.

"Ah, change money." The officer pointed to the same area as where the shops were. "BANK!" he blurted out with a strong intonation on the "B." We thanked them and proceeded across the road to the bank. I changed twenty pounds, and to my utter delight, received thousands upon thousands of Turkish liras; money in all variations and sizes. I was rich. I was a millionaire. What a difference to the pitiful amount I got in Cyprus.

A few doors away the locals were eating. A huge piece of meat was rotating clockwise around a vertical grill and it smelled *so good.* It was not much different to the kebabs in Cyprus or falafel in Israel. The idea was the same, only the pita bread and the filling varied, but the taste buds remained satisfied.

I expected Turks to look somewhat different and to wear the funny hats with a dangling tassel, but that was a stereotypical image one perceives from watching *Murder on the Orient Express.* These people didn't look much different to Greeks, but what *was* noticeably different was the friendliness towards us, and I felt very much at ease, taking an immediate liking towards this country.

We paid several thousand Turkish liras (not even a dollar) for our kebabs. It cost less than a coffee in Rhodes. We were joined by Paul the Englishman, and after this delicious meal, we participated in the favorite Turkish pastime—drinking tea; known as *çay* (pronounced chai) in Turkey. It was served piping hot in small, slim, tulip-shaped glasses. It was drunk black (looked more red though) and cost a mere few cents. The Turkish men were playing backgammon on battered tables like in Jerusalem. I fell in love with this simplicity, and the funny part was that we were still here illegally. Officially, we had not yet entered the country.

Paul had visited numerous Greek islands and also the Dalmatian Coast in Yugoslavia. "If you have only seen Rhodes, then you have not seen Greece at all," he told us. "Each island is uniquely different, especially once you get away from the tourist mob. But you're right, Rhodes *is* awful."

I had no idea what happened to the other two passengers on the boat; they had simply vanished. Two hours and four glasses of tea later, we sauntered back to the immigration office. It was open, and inside sat a gruff, uniformed official who looked rather scary with his wide mustache. He had drooping eyes like a cocker spaniel, and greasy wild hair that also looked as if it had been styled on a speed boat. We handed him our passports for the required entry stamp. He leafed through the pages lackadaisically while clearing phlegm from his throat, sounding like a protesting camel. "Where you come from?" He mumbled.

"England," I answered, somewhat confused as it clearly stated on the passports.

"No, no, no," stammered the immigration official irritably, "where you come from?"

"Oh, I see. Rhodos. Boat from Rhodes," said Paul. "Office was closed."

"Yes, yes. I sleep," and to confirm his tiredness, he yawned again. While slouching, he turned to a blank page and pounded the entry stamp onto it as if he was flattening a steak with a meat tenderizer, and rudely tossed the passports back without a word.

"I don't think he likes his job," whispered Paul with a grin. "Seems to be annoyed that we disturbed him."

Now that we were legally in Turkey, we set off to look for accommodation. Paul already had his at one of the hotels he had somehow booked prior to arrival. We shook hands and watched him walk away. In the distance by the shore were a couple of high-rise buildings that looked like hotels, but so far we haven't seen any tourists. We didn't have a chance to look for a room because it came to us. A teenage boy came our way and asked, *"Sprechen Sie Deutsch?"*

"No, we are English."

"You want room to sleep?" Asked the boy.

"Yes."

"Come with me. My family has room in house," he beckoned. We looked at each other, shrugged our shoulders, and decided that he was genuine. His house was only two minutes away on foot; quite old and a little in disrepair. We entered a small courtyard, which reminded me a little bit of our excellent accommodation in Jerusalem, but this home was not as elegant. The boy called someone, and a woman appeared from the house. She was his mother. She didn't speak any English, but showed us a simple room behind a curtain that served as the door. There were four beds inside and a table with four chairs, and each bed had a bedside cabinet.

"We like it. How much?" He gave us the rate in liras, which was almost two dollars a night.

"Is good?" Asked the boy.

"Is good," we confirmed. But I needed the bathroom and asked for it. The lavatory consisted of a ceramic bowl set into the ground. The edge was ribbed; it was where the feet were placed while crouching. There was no toilet paper though, and I remembered people telling me to take some with me to Turkey. It wasn't used everywhere. Luckily, I had some tissues in my pocket. This was something I would never get used to. Why can't the world have standard toilets?

We took the room for a couple of nights to give us a chance to absorb this new culture, then went back out after dropping off the backpacks. There was a market near the harbor with a variety of colorful fruits for sale. Some of them I had never seen, and we pondered over them for a few minutes, wondering what they might be. They were the size of apples, slightly deformed, and very yellow with a thin layer of velvet-like skin on them that disintegrated when rubbed. The vendor said something in Turkish, grabbed one of the fruits and started cutting it up, giving both of us a thick chunk each. It was tough and tasted slightly of pineapple, but the more I chewed, the more pleasant the taste, and I felt compelled to buy a kilo. I found out later they were known as quince fruit.

Eating out was amazingly cheap and it was not necessary to buy supplies of food for preparing our own cold meals, but we ended up buying a lot of fruit which tasted as delicious as in Israel.

We took a walk by the harbor and watched fishermen tending their nets. People were friendly and greeted us on the streets; nobody bothered us. The sound of the muezzin suddenly erupted, which took me by surprise. I hadn't heard the call to prayer since Jerusalem, and this was a reminder that we were in an Islamic country. Walking eastwards, the road followed the shoreline towards the area where Paul had his hotel. This looked like the newer part of town, and quite a lot of construction was taking place near the shore: an indication that Marmaris was growing and will one day be attacked by mass tourism like in Greece. The beaches here were quite attractive, but today was not beach weather. It was totally cloudy and there seemed to be a threat of rain upon the horizon. Again, I caught that refreshing scent of pine, which the wind carried towards my nostrils. We walked down to the seashore despite the threatening weather and remained transfixed by the sublime beauty of this bay. The deserted beach continued to the rocks, where pines grew between the crevices. The cliffs stretched for miles, and where there was a break, sandy bays had developed. We deserted the beach, too, with the first spots of rain, and scrambled into the nearest café just as droplets came trickling down.

"Welcome, my friends, and you come from where?" Asked the waiter.

"England."

"Welcome, welcome. You like *çay*?"

"Yes, *çay*," we nodded, and the waiter went to a large samovar where the red tea was kept hot. Several backgammon sets were placed haphazardly on a shelf, and we helped ourselves to one, setting up a game while enjoying several glasses of *çay*. Meanwhile, other men escaping the rain, herded into the café and followed suit—*çay* and backgammon .The air inside was soon filled with cigarette smoke. We were the only ones who weren't smoking and were soon gasping for fresh air. The rain stopped and we shot out, stinking like an ashtray and walked back to our room. The air had turned cool.

Marmaris was very pretty, but not *too* exciting. We stayed in our room the rest of the evening while searching for an "exciting" destination in the guidebook. The nearby town of Fethiye was famous for its tombs that had been carved out of rock into a cliff and were worth visiting. It was easily accessible by bus from Marmaris. We shall go there in the morning.

At night, heavy rain pounded on the roof of the house and the muezzin decided to hold a call to prayer at the same time, adding to the din. Despite the noise, which I found hypnotic and mystifying, it did not disturb us, but had the opposite effect and caused us to drift off to sleep.

We were greeted in the morning with two glasses of çay carried in by the mother. I asked her if she could tell us about buses, but she merely shrugged her shoulders to indicate that our words were incomprehensible. She called her son. "No take bus to Fethiye," he warned us, "bus too slow. Take *dolmus*."

"Take what?" We looked at him with a sign of puzzlement.

"*Dolmus* small bus. Drive fast." We found out that these "*dolmuses*" were actually small vans, which pick up half a dozen passengers at a time and drive like crazy to reach a destination.

Large puddles had formed from last night's rain, but the air was clear and a brilliant blue sky transformed the Bay of Marmaris into a rich, blue paradise. We located the bus station easily, and there were indeed minibuses amongst them. The regular buses had the destination written on them, but the *dolmuses* were guesswork. The drivers stood by the side of their vehicles and shouted out destinations. I couldn't understand anything, so they approached us. "Where you go?"

"Fethiye."

"No Fethiye." The next one approached.

"Where you go?"

"Fethiye."

"I no Fethiye," then he hollered something to one of his colleagues in the distance. "You go... he Fethiye," and pointed at a bunch of other vans.

"Fethiye?" Asked the driver as we approached. We nodded and clambered into the white van where two remaining seats awaited us.

Immediately we were off, and the driver honked his way through the crowd and joined the oncoming traffic with hardly a glance. The other four passengers were a Turkish family with two small boys and neither spoke any English. They just smiled when we glanced at them. The driver rapidly veered out of town towards the mountains, and soon we were climbing and climbing, but the van sped along in low gear. I thought about the ascent to Troodos Mountains in Cyprus in a vintage bus with an engine that threatened to explode. I was astounded now to be sitting inside a very modern vehicle, which easily coped with the steep climb.

For some prejudiced reason, I had perceived Turkey to be a third world country and still living in the Stone Age. It was, in fact, more modern than Cyprus, and I wasn't sure whether I was disappointed or relieved by this revelation. Secretly, deep inside me, I had hoped for a lot more primitiveness, just for getting a kick out of traveling in such conditions, but that was my own selfish desire. Later, I found out that my original perception of Turkey did indeed exist, but towards the east, where the country bordered Syria, Iraq, and Iran, where the Kurdish tribes lived, and Western visitors were perceived as an exotic rarity. It was a region that was still shrouded in strict Islamic customs, and the guidebook warned of stoning incidents when indecent exposure of bare skin (legs and arms) had angered the locals. We had no intention of traveling to that part of Turkey. Maybe it was better to stay in the modern Western half of the country where the customs were not as extreme and women dressed in modern European clothing without covering up even though they were Muslims.

The mountain roads became narrow, but the driver expertly steered the vehicle with ease, as if he had made this trip hundreds of times. The road was not in the best condition, and at times, my heart jumped when I felt that he was driving too fast near a precipice, which dropped down to the unknown. The Turkish family didn't seem to care: they had faith in Allah. The man was twiddling with prayer beads while the woman had a bag of sunflower seeds on her lap and was cracking them open; picking out the seeds with her tongue like a parrot. Also in parrot style, she simply discarded the shells onto the floor. The boys were also eating what looked like a mixture of nuts and large green seeds.

The worst of the climb was over, but the roads continued to twist and turn like a writhing serpent, and then I decided to have faith in the driver who was not the least bit concerned. After almost three hours, the *dolmus* started making its descent towards Fethiye, but we had already spotted it from higher up, and it looked even more spectacular than Marmaris. The blue lagoon glimmered like a jewel and was set off by miles of sandy beaches and desolate islets.

The place was gorgeous, and I wished that we had taken all our belongings with us and stayed here instead of making a mere day trip. We still hadn't had any breakfast; therefore, filling up our stomachs was priority now. They were both rumbling with discontent as the *dolmus* terminated at the local market. Other buses and vans also parked to drop off and pick up passengers. This was perfect, and would be easy to find again on our return trip.

The market abound in food—cooked and uncooked. There were stands with all kinds of seeds, which Turks seemed to enjoy parroting on. Varieties of nuts and dried apricots were displayed in a heap. I also recognized *loukoumi*, but this was the real Turkish delight, and was sold in all shapes and colors. Small cafés, with locals sipping tea and playing backgammon, were scattered everywhere. It was a place which I found as attractive as the blue lagoon. We bought some meat and salad-filled pita bread and washed it down with pepsi. The meat was lamb, which was the most common meat in Turkey.

Our map directed us to the rock tombs we came specially to see. I don't know why we were so infatuated with tombs, but I found them more fascinating than the standard ruins of Greek and Roman temples, which the Mediterranean had an endless supply of; so did Fethiye. In town was a Roman theater and splendors of ancient Greek architecture, but we had seen an adequate amount of such ruins in Cyprus and Israel, and would give them a miss this time.

The rock tombs were visible from the road; carved into the face of a cliff high up. But how do we get there? We simply headed in that direction and ended up walking along steep and narrow roads that zigzagged all the way to the cliffs. The view of the bay area was stunning from this vantage point, but even more stunning were the dozens, or maybe hundreds of holes that had been carved into the rock. The holes led the way into the tombs, but the more astonishing entrances into the interior of the rock face were adorned with carved columns that looked as if they were supporting the entire cliff. These didn't look like tombs, but more like a temple hewn out of bare rock. We wanted to get up closer and venture inside those cavernous openings, but that was easier said than done. There was a trodden, but treacherous path, which led up from the road, and we were soon climbing upwards towards one of the several entrances. It reminded me of the tombs in the Kidron Valley in Jerusalem, but these were much more overpowering. It had never crossed our minds to bring a flashlight along, but that gave us a very good excuse not to enter inside. Most of the entrances were precipitously perched, and would have welcomed another couple of souls to permanently reside amongst the ancient ones. Nobody else was here. We were careful not to break our necks as we stealthily crawled around on all fours. The limestone outcrops provided an excellent grip, but the smaller crumbling stones created a hazard, especially on the slopes. We stayed here for two hours before making our way back down. The alluring beach was beckoning us.

So was the café, which we passed, tempting me with delicious-looking pastries, which promised total gastronomic satisfaction. After much physical exertion, I needed to sit down for a while and replenish the fluids… and the sugars I had just lost.

The beach was a dream and almost empty. It would have been nice to go swimming, but we hadn't brought anything with us. It was sufficient to stroll barefoot along the shoreline on the soft, light sand. Some sandbanks or mini islands could be reached easily, where the water remained very shallow, barely up to the knees. Looking back into town, a lot of construction was taking place by the roadside facing the bay and large buildings were taking shape. Like Marmaris, this place would also someday be ridden with tourists; at the moment, it was very much a place for backpackers, as these were the only other foreigners I met—Germans mostly.

Getting back to Marmaris seemed faster, but that was because I slept most of the way. The climbing in Fethiye had exhausted me, and we also happened to end up with a racing driver who caused my head to spin while taking sharp bends at suicidal speed. I was grateful to be overcome with fatigue, but even more grateful to arrive in Marmaris in one piece. It would have been so darn unlucky to career off the edge after admiring those tombs.

Evenings in this part of the world was an occasion for the local folk to come out and get together with families and friends, and restaurants and cafés soon filled up. Unlike England, where such places merely serve their purpose as "belly-fillers," here in the Middle East, people tend to stay a long time and *enjoy* the food—slowly. We were never strangers wherever we ate in Turkey, and people did try to communicate with us, but English was a language that was not really popular, and communication was therefore impossible. For some obscure reason, German was the language most people mastered.

A long bus ride was on the agenda. The posters I had once seen hanging in the moshav office in Tel Aviv were pictures of *Cotton Castles*, officially known as Pammukale. They were located far away inland near the city of Denizli. We boarded the bus one late evening and drove the entire night with several stops along the way. The bus was absolutely modern with upholstered seats and head rests protected by a white cover. As well as a neatly dressed driver, we had on-coach service, which catered for the comforts of passengers. The hostess hovered with moistened lemon-scented towels, which she handed to every individual with a pair of tongs—they were hot. I wasn't exactly sure what to do with it until I saw other passengers wiping their face, neck and hands. She then collected them again. I guess they wanted no smelly people on this immaculate coach. Drinks and snacks came afterward, and as it was to be a night journey, sleep was inevitable.

The bus pulled into the station in Denizli before dawn. It was chilly outside, and the dark city was still asleep when we stepped out. The large bus station was full of activity though, and as well as passengers, there was a large military presence, or they might have been police. There were dozens of them, dressed in white uniforms and white hats that looked more like helmets. They were congregated in a group, standing in line like soldiers are expected to, and did not look particularly friendly.

Denizli was at a much higher elevation than the coastal region, and the cold forced me to dig out my coat from the backpack. We didn't feel comfortable in this drab, dark and colorless city after spending so much time by the Mediterranean. The best thing to do was to get out—fast. We didn't see any buses to Pammukale, but maybe a *dolmus* was heading in that direction. "Let's check out those minibuses," I suggested.

"Excuse me, are you going to Pammukale?" An elderly man asked us in excellent English.

"Yes, how do you know?" We wondered.

"There is no other reason for tourists to come to Denizli unless they are going to Pammukale," he stated and shook our hands. "I'm going there, too. Let's look for a *dolmus*."

We followed him to the waiting *dolmuses*, and with his help, were soon sitting in the right vehicle. "Do you live there?" We asked him.

"No, I come from Ankara. I'm on holiday, too." He told us that he was a history teacher at a school in Ankara, but almost retired. He had never seen Pammukale, and this was as exciting for him as for us. "I am tired, very tired," he told us. "When I retire in two years, I will have more time to travel. Right now, I want to spend a few days in the hot springs. It's good for the mind and soul."

"There are hot springs there?" I was surprised. The book didn't mention that important fact.

"Oh, yes. Very old and full of ruins." The man was actually a professor and a real history buff. I loved history too, therefore, I didn't mind him giving us a lesson on the Romans throughout our journey.

Nobody else came onto the *dolmus*, so the driver set off with only the three of us inside. Dawn was breaking, revealing the ugly greyness of the city. I was glad to be out of here. Pammukale was about thirty minutes away, located at an even higher elevation. Snow appeared among the hills in the distance, but as we got closer, it turned out not to be snow at all, but the geological wonder we had come to see; perched like fairytale castles made out of cotton.

The *dolmus* dropped us off on top of the hill outside the entrance to the hot springs where steam rose upwards as it mixed with the cooler air. Below us were white terraced pools that looked like something out of fairyland. I expected to see winged fairies flapping around this magic kingdom. It was still extremely early and not a soul was in sight. The professor was excitedly telling us about the ancient city of Hieropolis, which was located on the top of these cotton castles, and whose ruins were widespread. It was all very interesting, but my head was already full of historical accounts ever since Israel, and I was more fascinated by these travertine terraces.

All three of us left our shoes and baggage on top while changing into shorts and steadily climbed down into the pools. The water was lukewarm and knee deep, but the crystal-clear water soon clouded over as we disturbed the cottony sediments, which felt as soft as feathers to the naked feet. We made our way down several levels until the formations jutted out directly above us. They were huge. These terraces gave the impression that they were attached to the sides of the cliff, like fungi to a tree, but each one held water in the form of a basin. We were looking from below at the underside that resembled boats. Constant trickles of mineral-rich underground water left behind deposits of calcium carbonate and produced natural artwork, making it look similar to stalagmite cave formations. With the softness under our feet and the sparkling whiteness that surrounded us, it did not take much imagination to picture oneself walking upon a cloud. Maybe a bottle of wine would have served well here.

We climbed back out of the pools and let our feet dry off. The professor was enjoying himself, too, happily wading through the pools like an excited child. "Let's go down to the village for breakfast," he suggested.

"Yes, let's do that," I agreed with this smart suggestion. We hadn't eaten since yesterday. The village was located at the foot of the hot springs, so we backtracked down the hill to a narrow street where chairs and tables were invitingly spread out outside like in Cyprus. Some early birds were already sitting and sipping çay.

"I think this is a good place to eat," the professor commented. People nodded and murmured a greeting as we sat down. The professor spoke to the waiter in his language. He nodded and left, but came back shortly with three glasses of coffee to our table; the rest would follow shortly. "I ordered breakfast for all of us," he smiled proudly.

While waiting, the professor told us a little about his passion for history, and we told him about historical sites in Israel. He had never been there, but was very knowledgeable about the region and vowed to make a long trip there after his retirement in two years. "There is *too* much history in Israel. I will need time to see it all. At the moment, my students don't give me any peace," he joked. "Aha, here comes our breakfast." He rubbed his hands gleefully.

Breakfast came: olives, cheese, sheets of flat bread, and small flaky pastries with an unknown filling. The waiter disappeared briefly and returned with çay. I had already gotten used to unusual foods during my travels and no longer turned my nose up at any unknown food item. I was prepared to eat anything that was placed in front of me as long as it had no eyes and didn't move. Eating was the other joy of traveling; discovering culture through food. The British food palate was pitiful in comparison to the rest of the world's, and now I understood why all the invading armies in the last millennia were unable to gain a stronghold in England. It must have been the repelling food that had forced them to retreat.

The professor insisted on paying for the breakfast, telling us that we were guests in his country. He exchanged some sentences with the waiter who was pointing at a building. "I asked him about rooms," he translated. "He suggested we try that building." He was also pointing.

The professor took a private room for himself, and so did we. The rate was unbelievably cheap, but the room was very basic with a thin mattress that must have been slept on a million times. We didn't mind as long as it was clean, as we always spent most of our time outdoors anyway. I could never understand why some people spent a fortune on accommodation in five-star hotels when two dollars a night was all that was necessary, and the fun part was that we never knew where we would end up from day to day, but that is how I enjoyed traveling.

After a wash, we met the professor outside and walked back up the hill to the hot springs, which were actually baths and have been used since Roman times when tired, ailing soldiers had congregated upon Heriopolis to submerge themselves in the water's therapeutic qualities. The professor was also here to recuperate like the Romans once did. We paid the small entry fee and went to the changing rooms. The entire compound was shrouded in steam, which had transformed itself into a cloud that stayed suspended above the pool area, looking like a hovering flying saucer. There was no wind whatsoever, and the vapor had nowhere to go. Mostly hairy, elderly men soaked themselves in the waters, no one taking any particular notice of the two Europeans who stood out like aliens. The Turks were too relaxed and their minds switched off as they lay there as if in a trance. The water was not as hot as the steam made it appear, but hot enough to form a smile, and cool enough not to be cooked like a lobster.

This was ecstasy. We let the water cover our shoulders and heard a sound of pleasure being emitted from the professor. "Aaaahhhh... I'm staying here forever," he murmured with a content smile. Then he switched off and joined the rest of the men on planet bliss.

This was no ordinary pool. Roman ruins were everywhere, even in the water. Tumbled columns and other pieces of ancient architecture were submerged in the springs, so it was even possible to sit down on some collapsed pillar in the middle of the pool. One had to be cautious though not to stub a toe, but this was not a place for wild water acrobatics; it was a place to relax, smile like a goofy village idiot, and ponder the simple pleasures of life. I envisioned Romans harnessing these pleasures of natural spring water; it was something they were experts at. Total tranquility surrounded us, steam rose, water trickled... we decided to travel to planet bliss. "Aaaahhh...."

After a couple of hours, we left the water before becoming calcified. I felt drained and somewhat dizzy as we made our way back to the changing rooms. The professor was, like he said, staying here forever, and had no intention of going anywhere. We would meet him later in the evening. For the rest of the day, Sally and I wanted to spend some time at the cotton castles, which were still fairly deserted. We met another backpacker there, from Australia. He was also traversing among the wonders of Turkey. He had just returned from another village he had been to, a short walk from here.

"Check it out tomorrow. The whole village is built around bubbling hot water... and it's *really* boiling, so don't fall inside." He was on his way east, having stopped in London for a long time to earn some money for his globetrotting. He admitted how easy it was to find work in England: a particular newspaper was specially circulated for Aussies and Kiwis. It was filled with travel tips and job offers for them.

"Do you have the same service in Australia for Brits?" I asked him. He shrugged his shoulders.

"Nah, don't think so. Nothing for Poms," he joked. The Aussie left and we continued to marvel at these natural wonders.

Back in the village, we ordered a mystery food from a menu that was entirely written in Turkish. Pointing at an interesting-looking word that looked tasty, I asked the waiter, "What's this?" He thought for a while, searching his mind for a translation.

"Soup," he proudly blurted out, happy that he knew the word. Soup was always good and we settled for it, but the waiter didn't have the vocabulary to explain what kind of soup. "*Sprechen Sie Deutsch?*" He hoped. We shook our heads.

The soup came. It was a thin soup with small, reddish-brown things floating around in clear liquid. "Some kind of meat," Sally commented suspiciously. I twirled the brown things with the spoon, flipping them over.

"Chicken stomachs," I said glumly. "Chicken stomach soup."

"Yuk!"

I tried it. "It's not so bad." It was tasteless. "Tastes a little rubbery, but not bad if you don't know what you're eating." I continued to eat the soup. Sally forced herself, but didn't finish the stomachs, swishing them around in the bowl with disgust.

We met the professor in the evening. He looked as pink as a shrimp and was very jolly. "I only came out to eat something. Have you eaten yet?" He asked. We told him about the chicken stomach soup. "Oh, how delicious! Where did you find it?" We also told him about the other village with the *very* hot springs.

"We will go there after breakfast tomorrow. Will you join us?" He shook his head.

"I came here to relax. I want to stay in the water all day."

Drowsiness took over and we were forced to have an early night on the most uncomfortable bed in Turkey. In the morning, we went back to the same café as yesterday and had the same breakfast and coffee. The professor was nowhere around. He was undoubtedly simmering in the Roman baths. We would join him later.

The village was a fair walk from here, along a deserted stretch of road with grass and sparse vegetation on both sides. It was cloudy this morning, and the atmosphere reminded me a little bit of the barren Yorkshire Moors. Our peaceful stroll was abruptly interrupted by a frenzied barking behind us. A large black dog was menacingly advancing in our direction, but without a wagging tail. This sinister canine meant business as it stopped a few meters from us and started growling, curling its lip to reveal very dangerous teeth. We stopped dead.

"Er... nice doggy... good doggy... go away now." I tried to shoo it away with my hand, but the demonic creature took that as a provocation. Everything happened high-speed. As fast as lightning, it sprang onto my thigh and tore through my jeans and flesh. Sally shrieked and grabbed a large something that was lying on the road and attempted to pound the dog's head with it. It yelped, so it must have been a hard something as it scampered away towards the hills. I stood there in shock, my jeans torn, and blood gushing out of my thigh. Sally was equally dumbfounded and had no idea what to do. She was still standing there with the rock in her hand she used for clobbering the dog with. I started to feel nauseous and felt like vomiting. For some strange reason, I was thinking of chicken stomachs.

"John, you look pale. Can you walk?" Sally worried.

"I was thinking of that awful soup we had yesterday." She looked at me as if I was mad.

"Can you continue to the village?" She repeated. "It's nearer than going back." We could see the first houses ahead. "Maybe there's a doctor there." This last statement she said with utmost doubt in her voice.

I used Sally for support as I hobbled along to the village, but every time I applied pressure onto my leg, blood oozed out. My whole right leg was now saturated in blood and I felt very much like throwing up. "Darned chicken stomachs," I muttered.

People in the village saw us approaching, and one guy who looked to be about our age, took one look at my leg, dropped his jaw, and took over the support from Sally. His English was enough for basic communication and understood the word dog. "You come my house," he ordered, taking me to one of the primitive-looking stone houses which looked as if they still belonged in the Byzantine era. The guy barked an order to a young girl who was gaping at my leg. She ran off, probably to prepare tools for my amputation at the local butcher shop.

We entered one of the homes where a woman was already preparing a bandage on the table. The girl who had run off was there helping her. "This, my little sister. This, my mother," he pointed at them individually. We were inside a room that was obviously the kitchen. The floor was stone, like the walls, and without color. The fact that there was no sign of electricity or gas didn't startle me. The channel of steaming hot water that was flowing through the room from one end of the wall to the other, *did* startle me. The mother sat me down on a rickety wooden chair, and with skilled hands, cut off more of my jeans to reveal my oozing thigh where the dog had deeply punctured my flesh. The skin had been peeled off, as if it was made of rubber. She spoke to her son. "You must take off jeans," he translated. It made sense, and I obliged. The woman got a clean pot and filled it up with the water that was flowing in the channel. She then got a cloth, dipped it in the water, and started cleaning my wound. I gritted my teeth in pain as she made contact with raw flesh, carefully dabbing and wringing out the cloth in the bucket, immediately transforming it to tomato soup. She said something to her son, and he took away the water and threw it outside. The process was repeated with another clean cloth, then came the painful part when she applied some gel from a tube, causing excruciating pain, which made me grind my teeth. The burning sensation continued for a short time, and after a while, started to cool. The mother put some material over the wound and wrapped up my thigh with a bandage. I felt immediately better, but the best medicine came from her son as he brought some glasses of tea, which settled my stomach and my nerves. I was grinning again, sheepishly, and so was everyone else. The mother put away her leg-repair-kit and spoke to her son again. "She say you rest leg... no walk now for one hour." He was right. Bleeding would start again if I attempted to put pressure on it so soon.

Mother came back carrying another metal pot, but this one had holes in it and looked more like a colander. Inside, were about a dozen eggs; some of them still with feathers attached. There must be chickens behind the house. She carefully placed the whole pot into the channel of water. Sally and I must have looked dumbfounded, but then the son started to explain. He told us that they used the spring water for cooking in. It is at a constant boiling point and is even used for heating all the homes in this village. This village relied entirely on thermal energy, and most important of all, it was free and in constant supply, like it has been for thousands of years. These channels were evidently ancient and looked as if they had been built by our Roman friends. But that was *my* uneducated guess, because these channels looked like the raised Roman aqueducts in Jericho, which surrounded the city. Here, they circled the village and were inside the houses. The houses must have come later though, much later. They were not *so* old.

The eggs were ready, and the mother also brought in some sheets of bread, olives, and an eggplant mixture. A feast was about to begin. It was then that I realized how bizarre this really was: sitting half-naked with my bandaged leg stretched out in a colorless stony room with *weird* thermal activity going on, holding a boiled egg in one hand and a glass of tea in the other. If it hadn't been for that dog, I would never have experienced this or met these nice people who did everything possible to make me comfortable. I was *very* relaxed until Sally whispered to remind me that I still wasn't wearing any trousers. I hurriedly pulled out my shorts, which I usually carried in my knapsack for changing into when it got too hot. I stuffed my ravaged, blood-stained jeans into the bag. I would throw them away later.

After I was allowed to get up again, the son showed me the rest of the house, which was also all stone, but there were nice rugs placed on the floors and soft sofas to sit on. I spotted a television, so they must have electricity after all. Pictures of family members decorated the walls. The water channels disappeared behind the walls and reappeared in the next rooms. I had never seen or will ever see anything like it again. Most bizarre.

It was time to move on, and I gratefully thanked the family for their generosity and for saving my leg, which felt amazingly better, and the bleeding had stopped. We firmly shook hands and continued to the waterfalls, which we were told about. They were just around the corner; not waterfalls as I had imagined, but a steamy, hydrothermal area, where boiling and blistering water bubbled up from somewhere underground and cascaded down a rock face that was covered in stripes of varying colors. I found out later that these stripes on the rock were produced by the various minerals which were found in the water, and it kept flowing century after century... never stopping. This was the same water that was running through these homes and whose energy was harnessed. It was probably the best cleansing fluid for wounds.

I was nervous walking back to Pammukale village, paranoid that the demon dog was waiting for me. We both grabbed a handful of rocks and kept a weary eye on both sides of the road. No dogs. We carried the rocks all the way back until that desolate road came to an end, and the conceivable safety of the Roman pool environs prompted us to discard our weapons. I was longing for the "pool of bliss," but that was not possible with my wound, and Sally didn't want to go in alone. Instead, we made plans for tomorrow when we would take the overnight bus to Cappadocia, over 500km from here.

Daylight diminished, triggering a signal that it was time to eat. Being cautious with our order this time and not wishing to play guessing games with the menu, we looked around at what the other people were eating. Focusing on someone else's eye-catching dish, I blurted out to the waiter, "We'll take that!" I pointed out the food and he said something incomprehensible; an attempt to teach us the name of the dish, but it was pointless. I was hopelessly inept when it came to the Turkish language: I couldn't grasp it. Arabic and Hebrew numbers, basic words, and names of foods, I had no problems with, but Turkish was a challenge. Our food came. What looked like a steak from afar was actually made out of minced-meat mixed with spices, and very mouth-watering. It was accompanied with a salad, the usual flat bread, and various small dishes containing different sauces and dips. It tasted fabulous. We stayed longer to drink tea and play backgammon. The professor appeared, looking very healthy and refreshed, as if years of strenuous teaching had dissolved and been washed away. The spring water did indeed contain magical qualities.

"You didn't come to the pool?" He asked. We explained the doggy incident and I showed him my bandaged thigh under the table. He looked concerned.

"Have you had a tetanus injection?" I told him I got vaccinated before leaving England. He was relieved, but still asked about the dog. "Was the dog foaming around the mouth? There is rabies here."

"No, he didn't look rabid… just a mean dog."

After frolicking in the rock pools the best part of the day, we made our way back to Denizli and took the night bus to Konya. The bus service was as impeccable as before and we made several (horrible) bathroom stops along the way. We tried to avoid these breaks (as long as nature permitted) if possible, as the toilets were usually foul and the stench was overpowering. Squatting in such conditions was a miserable affair in public places. Despite the vast distance, the bus made good time, arriving in Konya at daybreak. No lingering here, but an immediate transfer onto the next bus to Göreme, which is located in the region of Cappadocia. We slept all the way through, arriving in the afternoon.

The long bus ride was good for my leg, which needed much rest, but something was not right with my stomach. Usually after a long journey, I would start searching for a café or restaurant, but for some strange reason, I had neither appetite nor desire to see any food. "Shall we get some breakfast?" Was something I didn't want to hear from Sally.

"Er… sure… if you're hungry," I answered slowly. Food was the last thing on my mind. She looked at me quizzically. "Maybe we should find a room first and get rid of these backpacks."

Cappadocia was one of those places that appear in weird dreams after too much wine. It could also serve as a setting for a sci-fi movie, where the strangest rock formations protruded out of the ground like inverted cones and gave the impression that this was the surface of an alien planet. It was eerie, but astoundingly beautiful at the same time.

Backpackers have no great expectations with regard to accommodation, so when we found a *very* basic room in the village, we hardly battered an eyelid at the gloomy, dank room which was worth exactly the asking rate—less than two dollars. But we were not alone. Other hardy backpackers swarmed to this part of Turkey, driven by recommendations of fellow travelers on a shoestring, and guidebooks that focused on attractions off the beaten path. In such a way we were able to exchange tips and stories, and be informed about the latest changes—which hostels and restaurants to avoid, and which place had the best food (clean food); and so... we ended up in a typical locale that catered for the desires of such world wanderers. The travel guide also recommended *Lomotil* tablets in the event of a severe diarrhea—the one and only drug powerful enough to "put-a-cork-in-it." I made a mental note of this fact with an uncomfortable feeling that I may soon be needing it—very, very soon.

Sally dragged me to a restaurant for breakfast before we started exploring. I reluctantly sat down, but only ordered tea with a feeble excuse that I wasn't hungry. The sight of her eating made me nauseous, and my internal pipes and organs were noisily performing strange squirting sounds. "Are you okay? You're awfully quiet... and pale."

"Mmmm... my stomach isn't in the best condition. Maybe some more tea will settle it." I asked for more *çay*.

Nothing happened for the next few hours and I endured the discomfort while walking around the cones and other rock formations that resembled giant penises. The cones were not just rocks, but were hollowed out and transformed into living quarters. When the early Christians fled the persecuting Roman armies, they hid themselves by carving out homes and churches from these stone cones that had been formed by volcanic activity. From the distance it looked like a deserted landscape, but close-up, you could see that windows and entrances had been carved into them. Entire families had settled here and many of them are still inhabited today after 2,000 years. They would wave and greet with "Hello meester," and small ragged and curious children followed us around as we curiously meandered between cones and penises.

The pain in my stomach sharpened and I was forced to go back to our room. Just in time. I dived into the bathroom as I felt an enormous volcanic upheaval and an inevitable eruption. A simple hole in the floor was all I had; not even a ceramic toilet basin to squat on. This was not an ideal place to pick up diarrhea. There was no toilet paper, either. "Damn!" I cursed at the toilet. At the same time, the rest of my internal organs came out through my mouth as I vomited like never before, breaking out in sweat that was pouring off my face despite being cold. I continued like this until half of me disappeared into the hole and I trembled with pain, feeling suddenly weak. I had to strip and attempt to clean myself with my left hand, using ice-cold water from a short hose that was attached to a tap near the floor. There was nothing for drying oneself, either. I was a total mess and an embarrassment to the human race.

Moaning in pain, I went back to my room, collapsed on the bed, and decided to die. It was worse than the dog bite. Sally saw that all my color had drained from my face and she dashed out to buy the recommended Lomotil. "Get some toilet paper, too," I begged, "lots of it."

The pain, vomiting, diarrhea, and death continued the rest of the day and into the night until the tablets started to take effect. Next day I was still in pain, but didn't have to go to the toilet anymore. The bad news was that Sally started feeling sick, too, and before the morning was over, she also started to disintegrate and contributed a large part of herself to the hole in the ground. During these miserable days, our only friends were the tiny Lomotil tablets, which saved our lives, and as I attempted to go out and drink some tea in the evening, Sally remained in the room, moaning in pain. I felt better the next day; very weak and very drained. Sally was also starting to recover, but we both looked like characters from *Dawn of the Dead.*

Once we were reborn, we continued to explore the fascinating rock formations of Cappadocia, and after being outside for a few hours, felt some color coming back to our faces. We were healthy again.

The most fascinating part of Cappadocia lies below the surface. Numerous clandestine cities had been built underground; some of them several storys deep. They were also homes to the Byzantine Christians who hid from the Romans, but these underground structures dated to an earlier time. These were real homes with kitchens, grain and wine storage rooms, toilets, and public meeting rooms. There was even access to underground water, and for ventilation purposes, chimneys had been built. Entire communities could live here without venturing above ground. The former homes were linked and it was possible to walk from house to house through labyrinth tunnels. The underground city was vast and one could easily get lost if no notice was taken of the entrances. It would have been a great place to sleep, but accommodation was so cheap in Turkey that it was not necessary. One thing that has not changed in these 2,000 years I noticed, were the toilets. Maybe Turkey needed another 2,000 years for the bathrooms to evolve. I wondered what life must have been like then: to be forced to hide underground because of religious persecution, and how did they manage to build all this? This was just *one* underground city, and there could be over a hundred of these, still unexplored, still full of secrets.

Cappadocia was a mysterious place where people still lived in mysterious ways, and the alien-like landscape contributed to the eeriness that permeated the entire region. Remarkable as it is here, I felt a little quirky for some unexplained reason. It was even spookier in the dark when the conical rock formations transformed into deformed monsters, and the light that was emitted from the holes that served as windows, looked like eyes from a distance.

The last leg of our journey was to Istanbul. We didn't stop in Konya on the way, but maybe we should have done. It was the center of the sect known as the Whirling Dervishes: a small religious group that was famous for twirling themselves round and round into a trance. I had read about them, but still failed to understand their purpose.

The journey to Istanbul was endless, but in modern Turkish buses it was made bearable and we also had the advantage of night travel, which seemed to shorten the distance. The drivers, hostesses, and even passengers were always courteous and no voices were ever raised. It would be a perfect place for Israeli bus drivers to be sent to; in Turkey they would learn about courtesy towards passengers.

The arrival in Istanbul was timed perfectly; not too early; not too late. The city was humungous and most complex, but that was not surprising, history and age considered. With such a historical time span, decline and deterioration comes naturally, followed by dirt and extreme pollution. A sickly-looking gray haze enveloped the entire city, which was astonishingly busy this time of morning. It was barely nine o'clock. We left the enormous bus station and joined the crowds on the streets. It wasn't much different to an English city, actually. Also here, people from all walks of life were rushing to catch their morning commute, and the businessmen with briefcases wouldn't have looked out of place in London.

Despite clear explanatory directions in our guidebook on how to get to the Sultanahmet District, we soon realized what an impossible task it was. We had the local bus number, but that didn't help. We went back to ask at the bus station, but nobody understood any English and only replied with blank stares. *"Sprechen Sie Deutsch?"* They would ask. What is it with Turks and Germans? Asking pedestrians was pointless—they also couldn't understand us. Communicating with aliens might have been easier. We were well and truly lost even before we got lost, standing by the main road and looking as helpless as cow 166 amongst a herd of camels.

"Excuse me, do you speak English?" A voice from behind interrupted our thoughts—a clean-shaven man in an immaculate business suit. His English was impeccable. "Can I help you find something? You look very lost."

"Yes, we are looking for the bus to the Sultanahmet District."

"Oh, but it is not here," he informed us. "Istanbul is a maze. It is impossible to find anything unless you are born here. Come, follow me. I will take you there because you will never find it alone." He was right. It *was* a maze, and we ended up criss-crossing, zigzagging, and jaywalking through the most complicated streets that no cartorather in the world would have been able to plot. We plowed our way through crowds for about twenty minutes until we arrived at a small, local bus station. The kind businessman didn't simply leave us there, but even made sure that we boarded the right bus. He spoke to the driver. "I told him to let you out in Sultanahmet." I was about to pay the fare, but the man interjected. "Please, allow me. You are guests in my country." He paid and we shook hands, then he disappeared back into the crowd. We were both awed by such kindness, which seemed to be prevalent in this country.

The Sultanahmet District is the historic part of Istanbul and also a haven amongst backpackers who swooped upon this district with its cheap hostels. It was also near the Blue Mosque, which we planned to see later today. As instructed, the driver stopped and clearly hollered "Sultanahmet" towards us.

This was definitely the right place. A few other backpackers were making their way amongst the crowds. We simply strolled around in this fascinating part of Istanbul until we found accommodation at one of the numerous backpacker lodgings that abound in this area. Despite the long journey getting here, we were so excited to have made it to Istanbul that we simply dumped our backpacks in the room and dashed outside again without a wash or a change of clothing.

I was happy to pick up the *Herald Tribune* at breakfast to see what was going on in the world. Quite a lot apparently: while traveling in Turkey, America had bombed Libya as a response to a terrorist act, which had been linked to Colonel Gaddafi. But the front page was splattered with thick headlines—A nuclear accident had occurred in the Soviet Union at a place called Chernobyl. There were reports of a radioactive cloud heading towards Eastern Europe and Scandinavia. The news was shocking. How serious was it? Information was scant and there were no reports about any immediate danger.

Istanbul is not the imagined jewel of the Orient as perceived in old movies. The old trading routes to Constantinople, which were traversed by spice, silk, and incense-bearing camels have now been replaced by trucks delivering Japanese cars and electronic goods. It was, nevertheless, a "must see" city, and despite the dust, the noise, and traffic fumes, I found myself taking a liking to it. This was the location where Asia meets Europe and also an important hub for backpackers taking the bus to the Far East. We intended to take a bus to the Far West—London, but would look into that in a day or two. First, there was a lot to see and experience in this exciting city.

Carpet salesmen hovered on every street corner. They sat in open storefronts and pounced on anyone who happened to glance at their pile of rugs. It was like the Old City of Jerusalem and equally aggressive. We foolishly fell prey to one while pausing to dig our fingers into a silk rug, curious to know what it felt like. A bad move. "Ah, I see you know what a good carpet is. This is one of our best." He dragged the rug off the pile and rolled it out on the floor. "Come, feel how smooth this is. I make you a good price on this one." We were trapped like flies in a web.

"We don't want a carpet," Sally protested, but he had no ear for "don't wants," instead, he started digging through a pile for another silk rug while his assistants heaved it out.

"This one is very special. It comes from Persia." He placed it on the floor alongside the other one.

"We don't want a carpet," this time I repeated.

"You buy both I give you a special price." Then he said something to his assistant in Turkish who dashed out quickly. He started telling us about how many knots were used per square centimeter until his friend reappeared with a tray of the usual tulip-shaped glasses of tea. Now the spider was going for the kill. We were so trapped and couldn't even leave without drinking the tea. The carpet salesman decided to take a different approach, seeing that we were obviously not interested in his carpets. He started to make smalltalk. "You come from Germany?"

"No, England."

"Welcome. Now let me show you *these* carpets," and he started pulling others off the pile and explaining differences between the knots. Educational as it may have been, we were simply not interested and wanted to leave.

"We don't want a carpet! Even if we did, we can't get one through customs," I told him impatiently. I had read that when you import a carpet, the customs officials will count the number of knots per square centimeter, and this will tell them the quality of the item. They will then impose import tax based on their calculation multiplied by the size of the carpet, and this could even work out more expensive than the item itself. I told him this.

"Oh, that is not a problem. We can send the carpets directly to your home and you pay no taxes," he lied. "Now, which one would you like?" Just then, Allah saved us as the call to prayer emanated from the nearby minaret. The carpet people froze. Now was our chance.

"It's time to pray," I told them. "We will come back," and rapidly left the store and joined the crowd. The three carpet stooges stood speechless, but did not protest.

Attractive oriental items were for sale everywhere in the bazaars, but the pouncing sales people made sure that tourists didn't browse just for fun. The result was that nobody was buying, as scared off tourists rapidly made their way out of the area.

Since the sixty's, on-the-cheap hippies have been coming to Istanbul, as it was the first contact with the Orient. From this point, they continued their journeys to the mystical East. I was overjoyed that I had not entered Turkey this way. I might have developed a very negative image of this country, had I been exposed to such aggressive harassment from the outset. How happy I was that we had crossed into Turkey through the back door where tourists had not yet transformed the friendly laid-back towns into superficially happy all-night-party centers, but from the construction I had seen, it was bound to happen in the coming years.

Istanbul is a city of minarets, especially within the old district where the beautiful imposing Islamic architecture is something to marvel at. The Blue Mosque alone is adorned with six of them, and if this unusual feature is not enough, it is crowned with varying-sized domes as if the architect could not build enough of them. We visited the famous mosque after some brunch and were surprised that it isn't blue at all. Nevertheless, I was flabbergasted by the sheer size of this humongous monument, and the closer we approached, the more almighty it appeared.

There is a separate entrance into the mosque for non-Muslims, where a scatter of shoes reminded even the tourists that they had to be removed prior to entry, and as we wandered in, I was absorbed by the gorgeous intricate patterns of the tiles that dress the interior. I found the undersides of the domes to be the most striking feature, creating patterns, which are nothing less than a work of art. The *blue* part of the mosque can be found on top where thousands of blue tiles shimmer on the ceiling in natural light.

We picked up our shoes and walked over to the adjacent park, which was the site of the Hippodrome of Constantinople. During the Byzantine Empire, it was the center of political life. When the Romans built it, they competed in horse and chariot races. Now, it is a peaceful setting with park benches, obelisks, and afternoon strollers.

Because so many backpackers congregate in this area, many budget travel bureaus have sprung up. The Magic Bus which used to transport travelers on-the-cheap to exotic Asian cities, has now been replaced with equally inexpensive bus transportation. Whether heading east or west, the possibilities to purchase tickets to places such as Karachi, Damascus, and Delhi was, without any doubt, the utmost temptation for any seasoned traveler who was prepared to endure the long and uncomfortable drive, but at the same time be rewarded with a once-in-a-lifetime experience. I was captivated by such destinations and very tempted by the lure of the East.

We also bought a bus ticket, but to London. We would return to England to work for some months and continue traveling once the wallet was fattened up again. We paid a mere $100 for the bus ticket, but first had to obtain a transit visa for Bulgaria prior to the journey. That was a standard procedure and not a problem. We would be staying many more days in Istanbul, anyway.

After the visa requirements were taken care of, we visited the overwhelming Topkapi Palace where former Ottoman sultans had once upon a time resided and ruled their immense empire. It is now enclosed by high stone walls that lead to an impressive entrance, which wouldn't have looked out of place in the Old City of Jerusalem. From the courtyard are gates that connect to other courtyards and to various buildings that make up the palace. Over hundreds of years, each sultan added his own touch to this splendid example of Middle-Eastern architecture, and the result was dazzling. I had seen such places only on TV when tales of Sinbad and Ali Baba were made into a film, and ornate interiors of a palace with elaborately-dressed rulers, princes, guards, and eunuchs were always portrayed in the stories. Those might have been fairytale fantasies, but inside Topkapi Palace, those fantasies are reality. Such places *did* exist, and it wasn't difficult to imagine the power and wealth such rulers once had; masquerading as gods because they could utilize their power to take a man's life at the flick of a finger or permit him to live. Another courtyard led to the Harem, where the wives and concubines of the sultans used to reside, and where fantasies of 1001 Nights were fulfilled. Oh my! They did have a grand life.

Istanbul was a very fine place to end the journey in Turkey. We didn't visit any other sites in the next few days, but casually strolled through the markets, sat around in cafés to drink tea, and avoided the carpet salesmen like the plague. Our supply of *loukoumi* from Cyprus was long devoured, so we bought some Turkish Delights to take back to England with us. Somehow, the Turkish variety was not as fine and not as fresh as its Cypriot counterpart, but maybe it also depended where it was bought.

The bus to England left in the afternoon and would take three days to get to London. We had been spoilt by the luxurious Turkish buses that commuted long distances and my expectations were high. When we boarded a primitive, diesel-spewing, cramped vehicle, I couldn't imagine this "thing" traveling so far, neither could I picture myself stuck inside for three days. I had expected it to be full of international backpackers like the former Magic Bus, but only one other English couple were on board. The rest of the seats were taken by Turks; and not city people either, but bore a palpable resemblance to disheveled peasants. All the women wore a veil or a scarf that covered their heads. The unshaven men looked quite gruff in their tatty jackets and baggy trousers that had been worn out a decade ago. The amount of luggage these people lugged onto the bus was inconceivable; a large part of it consisting of food. The women carried bags of sunflower seeds and nuts and bottles of water. We also came prepared with our food bag, but didn't take the whole market with us like these people had done. Our food supply comprised of bread, cheese, dry sausages, and various fruits. I wasn't sure if it would last till England, but the bus would stop on the way... I hoped. It had to. There were no toilets on board. Two drivers commanded the bus, and neither of them spoke English, but German. They looked like the kind of people I wouldn't want to meet in the dark. I had a bad feeling about them and made a mental note not to leave any valuables on the bus when we made a toilet break.

The bus departed two hours late and the passengers had already started littering the floor with discarded sunflower seed hulls. I couldn't imagine what this bus would look like after a couple of days. It took another couple of hours just to get out of Istanbul, and once the congested city roads gave way to freer highway traffic, we were crossing the busy Bosporus—the bridge between Asia and Europe. Despite the misleading short stretch on the map, it wasn't until dark when we arrived on the Turkish/Bulgarian border. With the darkness came the cold, but not because of the decrease in temperature, rather from the cold atmosphere, which swallowed up any joy or happiness one may have possessed. We were approaching a communist country, and the Bulgarian border officials looked like trouble. With guns in their holsters and don't-mess-with-me uniforms, they approached the bus and indicated to the driver that he should park. "What's happening now?" I asked no one in particular. Nervousness took over and even the drivers looked ashen-faced.

9
THE RETURN

"Out!" commanded the border official. The Turks didn't understand this little word, but the get-off-the-bus gesture could not be misinterpreted; on the other hand, that was also the extent of the Bulgarians' entire English vocabulary.

We were herded like cattle towards a glass cubicle where another unsmiling official sat and scrutinized passports. While everyone formed a line, the discomforting presence of armed soldiers dissuaded any notion of "making a run for it," but that was highly unlikely: Besides delicious paprika salamis and the indoctrination of communism, I didn't think Bulgaria had much else to offer. My passport was treated with as much distaste as if it were a venomous snake, and the official leafed through the pages until he located the transit visa; there he went for the kill and pounded it to death with determination to emboss the Bulgarian entry stamp through the whole passport. Without any "please" or "thank you" we were allowed back on the bus, but could only stay inside until the last person returned, and then we were ordered to get off again.

"Out!" This time he pointed at the luggage, indicating that we take our bags out—everything! Again outside, we were lined up with our bags in front of us. Then the search began. Several uniformed men opened up everyone's bags and rummaged inside. That was not all, as a whole group of them, armed with flashlights, boarded the bus and started probing under the seats. They even looked underneath the bus. I was expecting to have a full-body search, but that didn't happen. After spending almost three hours at the border, we were allowed to take our bags onto the bus and return to our seats. Only then, did the barrier open up and allow us to proceed into Bulgaria.

Unfortunately, the drive through Bulgaria was in total darkness. There were no street lamps, and only the beam of headlights illuminated the way. After leaving the smooth Turkish roads, we now had to endure potholes throughout the length of this country. There would be no dozing tonight, as the bus juddered, shook, and slowly bounced its way towards Yugoslavia. The drivers changed at the border, and the new one cursed while fighting with the steering wheel and meandered between lanes. There was no danger of oncoming traffic… there simply wasn't any. It was as if the darkness had swallowed up the entire population.

Many hours passed as we slowly progressed to the Yugoslavian border. Amongst the lively chatter the incessant sounds of cracking sunflower seeds permeated the bus. Just about every passenger was noisily munching on something, and we also decided to dig into our food bag. There would be no stopping along the way in Bulgaria. Anyone who needed a toilet would have to tie-a-knot-in-it or plug-it-up until the next border crossing. Luckily, Bulgaria was quite small.

The rigid control of people in transit was ridiculous. Leaving Bulgaria was the same procedure as entering Bulgaria. Again, it was required to leave the bus, line up, have the passports pulverized with an extra forceful exit stamp, and to make more trouble, the luggage had to be lugged out and searched—again. This preposterous *modus operandi* caused fierce discontent, but we were powerless to complain or show any agitation. We were in the grasps of communist logic, and the border officials were making sure that everyone suffered as much as possible with the procedure. They wanted to show that all those fancy badges they wore gave them the right to exercise the full extent of their power.

Back on the bus and some meters further along was the checkpoint to Yugoslavia. Once more, it was the get-off-the-bus procedure and passport control, but luckily, it wasn't as rigid as its neighboring country. We didn't need a transit visa for Yugoslavia, and neither was the luggage checked. This crossing took less than an hour and included a Yugoslavian toilet break.

The roads improved a little and we were on our way through the most boring and monotonous landscape I have ever seen. It was daylight, and because of the excitement from the night before, the passengers nodded off to sleep. Sally and I did likewise as we drove past abandoned-looking farms that seemed to expand across the entire country. From the bus, Yugoslavia did not look attractive at all, especially as it was cloudy and caused the landscape to appear even bleaker.

The bus made another stop after some hours, and the Turks rushed out to empty themselves of parrot seeds. We went after the mad rush was over, delighted to be back in the land of *proper* toilets, even though they were not the cleanest. For some obscure reason I couldn't define at this point, the toilet seats were covered with shoe prints. Sally told me it was the same in the women's bathrooms. The worst part was that they weren't flushed after usage. I couldn't decipher why; the flush worked perfectly fine.

The roadside stop consisted of a cafeteria with hardly any food available... and no coffee, either. Frowning, heavyweight servers of unknown gender, wearing grease-stained aprons looked as unappetizing as the pitiful food they were offering. With their grubby, meaty hands, they picked up the food and slapped it onto chipped plates, which they rudely thrust towards the customers. We had no Yugoslavian currency, so we couldn't have bought anything anyway; neither did the Turks, but they did have German marks, which seemed to be an acceptable method of payment. I guess we could have used dollars, but decided not to ruin our stomachs here. It was still a long way to London.

The drivers changed once more and the bus continued towards Austria. Everybody was refreshed once again and I was starting to feel the pains of long-distance bus travel. The bus was also starting to stink, and the floor looked like the bottom of a parakeet's cage with seed hulls scattered everywhere. The terrain became hilly, and as we approached the Alps, snow-covered peaks captured the last fading light, and I was disappointed not to have seen them.

Leaving Yugoslavia was nothing more than an exit stamp. I was glad about the speedy process because the air outside became much cooler due to the higher elevation, and something I hadn't seen for a very long time appeared on my arms—goosebumps. Almost immediately, the Austrian border loomed up, and a barrier with *Zoll* written on it blocked further entry. I was back in my world—Western Europe. For us British, a simple flash of our passports was sufficient to get us through; for the Turks, it was hell. We four British citizens waited on the bus while the Turks were being interrogated. What was their purpose traveling here? Definitely not tourists. I'm sure they were not going to London to wonder at the Changing of the Guards, or to admire Big Ben. They didn't look like snow-loving people either, so they were not going skiing in the Alps. Migrant workers? Most probably. Now the Austrian customs officials were leafing through their passports and looking for a work visa. Or were they here to visit relatives? Not likely. This strange bunch of Turks were the most surly and most unfriendly I have ever met; neither of them made any attempt to talk to us (which was most unusual for Turks), and there was no offer of seeds to munch on.

The border took as long as the Bulgarian one, but after all the entry requirements were satisfied from the Turkish side, the bus parked in front of a restaurant building where they also had a bank for changing money. This was the most beautiful stopover point so far on this trip, and the restaurant offered an amazing array of mouth-watering goodies. The prices were in Austrian shillings, but we changed a small amount of money at the bank and splurged on some very fine food, which consisted of a schnitzel dinner and a coffee with a delicious pastry to follow.

Such a spotless place must surely have nice bathrooms. It did. Some of the Turkish passengers were still inside and they seemed to be marveling at the luxury. I opened the door to the toilet, which was slightly ajar and stopped dead in my tracks. There was a man inside, and he hadn't even bothered to lock the door. It was here that I solved the mystery of footprint-covered toilet seats: the man had climbed up onto the toilet, and with his feet on the seat, was crouching into it instead of sitting down. I couldn't believe my eyes as I rudely stood there gobsmacked, staring at this bizarre spectacle. The man thought that I was gawking at his enormous, serpentine-like penis, which was sticking out like the trunk of an elephant over the rim, then he freaked out and started yelling belligerently, but all I understood was, "Bulubulubulu." I scampered and went to the next toilet, which had already been used. The evidence was there—footprints on the seat and an unflushed load.

I came out to meet Sally. "I've solved the footprint mystery," I told her, relaying what had just happened.

"That explains it. It's the first time they've seen a Western toilet and have no idea how to use it," she guffawed, suppressing laughter.

The naked, crouching man stalked past and glared at me menacingly. "It was him," I nudged Sally.

Compared to Eastern Europe, Austria was a different world: brightly-illuminated highways that felt as if they had been covered with a carpet. Not a single crack or pothole hindered the bus. It was now the bus that infringed upon the perfection of this country where everything appeared untainted. Our bus was an abomination that shouldn't have been allowed to litter these beautiful roads... and why hadn't it broken down yet?

We were in the Alps; crossing the border to Germany. Again, the Turks were held up; this time by the Germans, who were trying to decide whether or not to let them in. Again, British passport holders were just waved away back onto the bus when they noticed our familiar black, hardback covers.

The bus miraculously made it to Germany, driving towards Munich on the famous German Autobahns where speeding was not an issue. The bus took advantage of the roads after the destructive potholes in Bulgaria, determined to show how much power it actually had. My body was in pain from the cramped sitting position and lack of sleep, and I vowed never to make such a bus journey again.

We stopped in Munich for a very long break where most of the passengers left, arriving at their destination with bulky over-stuffed canvas bags, some of which had come apart and were kept intact with string. Those who did not have enough canvas luggage also carried large, well-used plastic supermarket bags, which were about to burst. In their desperation to get off the bus, they squeezed through the aisle and shoved their bags in the remaining passengers' faces without so much as an apology. All the garbage they had was left on the floor and seats. I was disgusted by them, and still perplexed that they were allowed to enter this country. The group resembled a bunch of refugees and looked completely out of place in this elegant city, which glimmered in wealth, even in the dark.

The bus made several stops in Germany, each time letting out the Turkish passengers at some obscure location, away from any public bus stations, as if they were being smuggled into the country. By the time we arrived in The Netherlands the following night, there were just four of us left: us and the other English couple who looked as confused as we did. We were even more confused upon arrival at the ferry terminal in Hook of Holland where ferries were leaving for Harwich, England, and the driver told us to get off. "You change bus."

"What bus?" We demanded. "There is no other bus."

"You wait. Bus come," he lied.

"But we paid all the way to London... ON THIS BUS!" The other English guy raised his voice angrily.

"I no London. I go Istanbul. You go. Bus come." The two bus drivers looked menacing as they started yanking our luggage off the bus and tossing the backpacks outside. "You go," they spat.

We had no choice but to do as told. Without a moment's hesitation, the driver closed the door, reversed rapidly, and took off at top speed. We were left stranded outside the terminal building. I took down the bus's license plate and we all hurried into the building to look for the police. After asking at the ticket counter, a woman directed us to the police station, which was nothing more than a desk. We explained to the officer how we were deceived in Istanbul: having paid for the bus to London, but ended up getting kicked out here in The Netherlands. He commiserated with our story, but said there was nothing he could do because we had purchased the tickets in another country. We would have to pay again for the ferry crossing and the train to London.

The additional ticket to London was an expense I could have done without, but it was either that or staying in The Netherlands. There were still some hours to kill before the overnight ferry departed, and there was also good food available at the terminal. I still had some Dutch guilders left after changing money for buying a ticket, so I might as well get rid of them.

The ferry was a luxury I hadn't had for a while. Even though we only had seats, they felt wonderful after enduring discomforts on the Turkish bus. These seats were upholstered; they reclined, and at this moment felt as comfortable as a bed. This was an extra slow night crossing, which would time our arrival in London with the break of dawn.

The London-bound train was already waiting for the ferry passengers in Harwich. We were both quiet as we rolled towards the capital in darkness, both knowing that our journey was over. The train arrived in Victoria station at the crack of dawn. We sat on the bench for a while, observing the commuters who were hurrying to work. Had it all been a dream… this trip? We were back where we had started from—at Victoria station. It seemed like an eternity since we had come here for our mandatory meeting.

I picked up a newspaper at the kiosk. They all carried similar headlines —Chernobyl. Nobody seemed concerned about the nuclear accident; nobody was panicking; life seemed normal.

Sally came to Leeds with me after I had informed everyone of my arrival; meanwhile, she called her parents and told them that we shall both be there in a few days.

Leeds was as Leeds should be and always has been—gray. To make it perfect, it was raining. The people also looked miserable and gray, some of them enviously staring at our backpacks and deeply tanned hands and faces. I felt uncomfortable here, and instead of the feeling of coming home, I felt like a stranger. When I got together with my friends again, we had nothing much to say; like strangers meeting for the first time and making insignificant smalltalk. It was the same with my family, where TV game shows were more fascinating than my photographs and tales of the East.

My friend Billy was still the Billy I remembered and we both embraced, happy to see each other again. It was Billy who had given me the push to see the world, and this time it was *me* telling him about Israel instead of the other way round. "Is this your souvenir from Israel?" He laughed, hugging Sally. "What will you do now?" I told him about our plans to work and save up enough money for more traveling. "I'm glad to hear that. For a moment I thought you'd start settling down."

"Too early for that," I admitted. "You were right—the world is a fascinating place." It was the last time we would ever meet.

There was no other reason to linger in Leeds, so we both took the bus back to London and then to the south of the country—to Andover. Sally was not looking forward to going home, either. She did not get along with her family, and that had been the reason for her desire to stay away from England as long as possible. I was allowed to stay at her house until I found a job and a room to rent, which was almost instantaneous, but I took a dislike to her snobby parents immediately and pitied Sally who had to endure them. They were furious with her. She had spent too much time abroad and should have come back a year earlier. From that point, things went downhill between us. I did find a job and a room to rent, but Sally wasn't so lucky. We continued to meet, but our get-togethers became less frequent. She was not able to find work and her parents would not allow her to travel anymore. They also made a point that I was responsible for her long absence and tried to destroy our relationship. They succeeded. She became withdrawn and didn't smile anymore, turning into a stranger.

After half a year of working and saving, I was ready to leave the country again and return to Israel. Winter covered the landscape in frost, indicating that this was a good time to depart. I had contacted the kibbutz office once again and arranged to stay on another kibbutz. I didn't have to go through the same procedure as before, and my vaccinations were still current. I couldn't wait to get back to the Middle East, back to the caressing warmth of the winter's sun.

I tried hard to coax Sally to come with me, but she was afraid of her strict parents and the repercussions it may have. If she left, she would not be allowed back. We spent a gloomy Christmas together, and some days later, met for the last time. I felt depressed, having shared so many adventures with her, but she was not the same person anymore. We would never travel together again—that was blatantly obvious. I counted the days until my departure, never having felt so miserable. This was not the outcome we had planned. We should have been going to the airport together and flying to an exotic destination where further adventure awaited us, but I was alone. Very much alone.

10
BREAKFAST WITH CAMELS

The year closed with a recap of the worst nuclear accident in history. In the last nine months, the media had been pumping out stories on the most affected areas that had played host to the radioactive cloud. There was still not much information about the Chernobyl disaster from the Soviet side, and the extent of the leakage continued to be hushed up by them. Maybe all of Europe was going to be radioactive now, so I considered myself lucky to be going back to Israel, which was well out of range.

I was on my way to Gatwick Airport on this bitter cold and gray winter's day; the kind of drab, depressing gray which manifests itself only in England and festers for an eternity. It was already dark (actually, I don't recall it ever being light today), and I was just in time to check in and undergo a thorough baggage and body search for the upcoming night flight. As usual, this unpleasant but necessary task was performed by Israeli security, specially trained to seek out potential threats to their country, and they didn't trust anyone else doing such a thorough job. That was fine with me, as I also felt much safer boarding a flight to Israel these days when it was not unusual to hear about a hijacking.

The focus was still on Libya, which had been bombed eight months previously by Americans, thus destroying Gadhafi's headquarters, but at the same time making the Libyans quite angry and increasing the risks of terrorism. Maggie Thatcher, of course, allowed Ronald Reagan to stage the attack from British bases, so now, we didn't have any diplomatic ties with Libya either, and that meant no more of those delicious Libyan dates.

I tried not to think about what had transpired these last few months in

England. I felt awkward traveling alone this time and already was missing Sally terribly. I couldn't bear the thought that we were to become "letter friends" only. The air hostess was distributing the *Herald Tribune*. Not surprisingly, Chernobyl was still making the headlines.

The flight left at 9:30 P.M. and arrived at Ben Gurion airport at 3:50 A.M. local time. Unfortunately, there were no New Year celebrations in the air as first expected. It was not the end of the Jewish year, so this occasion was unimportant and irrelevant.

The instant climatic change brought on a smile; more likely a smirk, when I thought of all those poor souls freezing in England; waiting for spring, which never comes; and the summer, which is more like a cheerless spring. I was back in paradise and felt immediately energized.

"Happy New Year," some of us exchanged wishes with one another.

"Yes," I was thinking, "*will* it be a happy one?"

"Happy New Year," came an Israeli-accented greeting as we were met by a very friendly kibbutz representative and whisked away to Kibbutz Nir Itzhaq near the Gaza Strip. So far, a very friendly welcome to Israel. New years day *was* observed on the kibbutz for the volunteers today, therefore, no work for them. I noticed some were still recovering from the night before. There were a couple of sun-worshiping Danish girls, who were busy tanning their bare breasts so early in the morning as I walked by to my new accommodation. They raised their hands in a "hi" gesture and continued toasting. I also spent the morning enjoying the sun and blue sky and getting to know the other volunteers whose length of elapsed time spent on the kibbutz could be counted by the shade of their tan. The topless Danes looked about six weeks in service, a happy Swedish couple looked more like three months, and there was also an anorexic French girl (also topless, but titless), who was still on the lighter side, and couldn't have been more than ten days. There was a bunch of New Zealanders, a couple of South Africans, and a very drunk Irishman, who all had reached their tanning limits, thus having the status of long-term volunteers. The several British volunteers were easy to spot as they always competed with freshly-cooked lobsters, and *their* length of stay could be measured by the amount of skin loss. I was to share my room with a Brazilian, who had also arrived recently, and we became the best of friends in the days to come. In fact, all the volunteers here were easy to get along with and I felt my spirits uplifted after those calamitous months in England.

The Irishman came from Cork, and so did his dialect, which was impossible to understand while he was sober. When he was plastered with alcohol, his jaw became heavy and his speech slowed to a more comprehensible level; only then, it was surprisingly feasible to have a conversation with him.

6:00 A.M. was the typical start to the day, and for my first day at work, I was put into the orchards to pick avocados. In England, I had only known the standard green, avocado-shaped avocados, but here they came in various sizes and shades: there were bulbous, glossy-green ones, which were more rounded and without that skinny tail; there were long ones, which looked like only the tail; another variety were small, dark purple, and with a dimply skin. I tried them all and decided that the round, glossy green ones were my favorites due to the mild taste. We also worked in the gardens—pruning juniper trees and then potting the young shoots after dipping them in some rooting powder.

On my first day off on *Shabbat*, I went off to explore my new surroundings of this kibbutz. Recreation facilities were in abundance: with swimming pool, volleyball and tennis courts, as well as basketball. This was more of a holiday resort. A bunch of us played volleyball and spent the rest of the afternoon enjoying the warm winter sun. Friday's "special" dinner (like on the previous kibbutzim) welcomed the Sabbath with the now familiar chicken or turkey in various forms. Saturday's lunch was equally delicious and there were also tasty desserts to choose from. Overall, the food on this kibbutz was excellent and even surpassed any other kibbutz food I had eaten in the past. The usual fruit-filled crates outside the dining room were also available, and one crate even contained avocados. I usually took several oranges back with me for squeezing. By our rooms we had a small kitchenette with basic utensils, glasses, and a citrus squeezer for our freshly-pressed orange or grapefruit juice. This was healthy living and I was ravishing it.

Sabbath was over and we were back at work clipping avocados off the trees. The branches were laden with fruit, so heavy that they trailed on the ground. We only picked the firm ones, gently placing then into baskets. These were for export for the European market. The soft ones and the not-so-pretty ones were separated and placed in a different container for the kibbutz consumption.

Afternoons were filled with free time, and for the first outing, I, together with two other volunteers, borrowed bicycles from the kibbutz and cycled the short distance to the Gaza Strip checkpoint. Here, vehicles to and from "The Strip" are stopped and the car occupants' ID's are checked, but only the vehicles with the white license plates, which belonged to the Arab residents. The cars with the yellow license plates were allowed to proceed—these belonged to the Israelis, who had the freedom of movement. Cycling seems to be unknown in this country we noticed: Gaza Arabs jeered and waved as they slowed down in their jam-packed vehicles while tooting their horns, but the gestures appeared to be more friendly than hostile, confirmed by the amazed looks on their faces. The guards at the checkpoint also proved to be friendly, except one surly soldier who was combating his boredom by loading and unloading his machine gun. If his intention was to make us nervous, he succeeded, and I got the impression that he couldn't wait to use it.

Things had changed in Israel while I was in England: new money had been introduced; they knocked off three zeros from the larger denominations and made shopping less scary; inflation had also been brought under control, and prices were no longer doubling before my eyes. That was the good part. The bad part was that violence in the Gaza Strip and the West Bank had erupted, and the *Jerusalem Post* was reporting more bombing incidents. But Israel felt as safe as usual, and I remained undeterred despite these new developments.

Next day, the lemon picking started. I never realized that lemons grew on thorny trees, and after the first hour, my whole arm was covered with deep scratches and blood. "Ouch!"

"Ow," came another sound.

"DAMN," from someone else.

"Zis is merde," came a French accent.

"I'm bleeding," whined the Danish girl.

The Irish guy said something incomprehensible, but it was an obvious statement of displeasure.

"Beautiful lemons!" was the comment from the Israeli side. For some strange reason, the Israelis' arms looked normal, without a single scratch. They dived into the trees for getting every last lemon, no matter how many thorns guarded it. Were these people actually human? Why didn't they feel the pain? Did they coat their arms in some newly-invented, anti-scratch lotion?

Our work hours were from 6:00 A.M. to 2:00 P.M., but the actual physical work was only about six hours, as we never worked more than ninety minutes without a coffee break. Twice, during this time, we drove over to the dining room: first for breakfast at 9:00 A.M., and lunch at noon. Everything was so easy going, the kibbutzniks were very friendly, and the food was absolutely excellent. Most of the days the sky was clear and it was warm. The orchard trees were rich in ripening fruit, giving the impression that this was the Garden of Eden. The only disadvantage of working outside were the cold mornings; made even more uncomfortable by the dew-sodden fruit trees, which saturated our clothes, and the high grass took care of permeating the canvas boots. After breakfast, we peeled off our coats as the sun rapidly heated up the orchards and dried out the moisture. Once lunch was over, it was warm enough to wear shorts and go topless (for the guys at least).

After the scratchy lemon trees had turned my arms into something that resembled a city road map, we switched over to grapefruit picking a few days later, where I discovered how a grapefruit is supposed to taste— very sweet and very juicy. I had only known the extremely sour ones in England, where they are eaten with a generous sprinkling of sugar. Fruit picking continued for the next three weeks. We picked various species of avocado, oranges, lemons, grapefruits, and pruned trees in between. One of the "in between" days was spent cleaning empty chicken food bowls and preparing the chicken houses for the next batch, which was due in a couple of weeks. The kibbutz had two chicken houses, and chicken farming was also one of their endeavors. Now, they were both empty, all the former occupants having got eaten.

One month after arriving on the kibbutz, it was time to do some traveling again. Together with Carlos—the Brazilian I had recently befriended, we took the afternoon bus to Be'er Sheva and immediately transferred to the Eilat bus, which runs every hour. It was already evening by the time we arrived in this expensive Red Sea resort, and too late to cross the border into the Sinai. Cheap accommodation was non-existent in this plastic tourist trap that catered mainly for the Israeli population, so after grabbing a delicious falafel in the center, we walked to Taba and spread out our sleeping bags on the beach. It was January, the night was cold and windy, and the surf was rough. Even the wolves weren't serenading as they had done during my last visit here with Sally over a year ago when the nights were sweltering. The memory brought a lump to my throat.

Very early in the morning, we walked over to the Israeli border, paid our departure tax, and boarded a white minibus, which drove us less than a hundred meters to the Egyptian side. Between these two borders is no-mans land, and walking across is strictly forbidden—border bus transportation only! It was only a 15-second bus trip to the Egyptian passport control, but it was an instant time warp into the past; from the bright and modern concrete air-conditioned Israeli immigration building, to the ramshackle structure with "natural" air-conditioning on the Egyptian side. Gone were the flowers and trees and irrigation; gone was the potable tap water; and gone (very sadly) were the Western toilets: it was all squatting for the next few days.

An austere portrait of President Mubarak hung on the wall of the office, where the greasy, unshaven customs official with scuffed, worn out shoes was stamping the passports. Looking important and adorned with dozens of badges on his ill-fitting military uniform, he gave the impression that *he* was the president. Right next to the office was another small ramshackle building serving breakfast; what kind? I didn't know, but after the customary entry stamp, we headed inside and ordered whatever was being served for less than a dollar: it was a plate with pita bread, goat's cheese, olives, hummus, and a glass of Turkish coffee. It really was delicious and my hunger was satisfied. The official who stamped our passports also came in to lounge and sip coffee.

The rickety bus (without windows) to St. Catherine's village arrived shortly after our scrumptious feast, and that was exactly where we were heading. We traveled through totally barren, stony desert landscape, where occasional black Bedouin tents were the only sign of possible life, but most of them looked abandoned. The Red Sea shoreline was also void of any habitation, with miles and miles of alluring deserted beaches. We passed several former Israeli settlements; now completely forsaken and looking like ghost towns. After the Sinai was given back to Egypt, these settlements were either blown up or converted to police and military outposts. Some had goats living inside, and for some reason all buildings were windowless. Where crops had once thrived, there was now dust, goat shit, and camel shit. There was no more irrigation anywhere. One may think it's a shame that the Egyptians had completely destroyed Israeli modernization and reclamation of the desert, but I would hate to see this coastline turn into another Eilat. I loved it the way it was—this primitiveness, and how it's been for thousands of years.

Upon arrival in St. Catherine's (Santa Katerina), curiosity got the better of me as I walked around stupefied by the crudeness of this village. The only inhabitants here were extremely friendly Bedouins, constantly uttering, "welcome" as we mingled amongst them. My nose caught the scent of something baking, so I followed the pointy thing and it led me to (of course) a pita bread bakery. There was even a sign written in English (kind of English) with an arrow pointing to "The Bokery." Here, I was to taste the most delicious pita bread imaginable. I bought five rounds of freshly-baked, spongy bread with plenty of roughage (sand) inside for just a few cents. It was tasty enough to eat without anything on it. I also couldn't get enough of the Bedouin-style coffee, which contained a high concentration of cardamom and possibly other spices I couldn't identify. There was a small store in the village selling almost nothing, but I did buy some goat's cheese, dried figs, dates, and cartons of thick, pulpy mango juice. Bedouin children with weather-beaten faces and matted hair harmlessly followed us around. I had never seen children with such huge feet, and their hands looked as if they belonged to old men who had physically labored their entire lives. I managed to get some good pictures of them after handing over some *baksheesh*. The Bedouins loved to chat, especially over several glasses of coffee while they pressed questions. "Where you from? Where your wife? Why you no marry?" We said goodbye to the friendly locals and walked the two kilometers to the monastery where we hoped to get a room for the night.

It is believed that St. Catherine's Monastery is the oldest un-restored example of Byzantine architecture in the world. Built in the fourth century and rebuilt in 527 AD, nothing has changed. There were no crumbling walls or ruins, remarkably preserved in this very dry, arid terrain. Here lies the tomb of St. Catherine—a martyr who lived in Alexandria and was persecuted for her belief in Christianity. Greek Orthodox monks momentarily occupied this holy place.

The monks of the monastery ran a very basic hostel within the compounds, segregated of course (as we were on holy ground and any night-time passion was a big no-no). Our payment of five Egyptian pounds also gave us the full use of the kitchen: useful for making hot drinks. Shortly after unrolling the sleeping bags, one of the monks came in with sweet mint tea and a bowl full of macaroni with pieces of goat's cheese. He told us that they usually cooked too much food for themselves, so they had plenty left over for anyone staying in the hostel. Nevertheless, this was such a kind gesture. There were only a few thrill seekers here today, but when masses of Greek pilgrims come, the dormitory fills up rapidly, and I couldn't imagine monks bringing food for everyone then.

The only reason to come here (if not on a pilgrimage) is to climb to the top of Mt. Sinai to witness one of the most spectacular sunrises in the world. That is why I was here, forcing myself to get up at 3:00 A.M. at the highest altitude in the Sinai in the middle of winter. Inflicting torture upon myself, I had decided to climb this mountain in complete darkness and bone-chilling cold. There was no heat in the hostel, and getting out of bed itself was already an agonizing act. I was secretly praying the monks would have bacon and eggs with fresh coffee ready, but even here, where the commandments were handed down to Moses, my prayers were not answered.

Equipped with a flashlight and the glow of the moon, we searched for the Camel Path, which (we were told) was just behind the monastery. I forgot to ask where the front was, as any part of this monstrous, fortified edifice could have been the back, especially in the darkness, but I was guessing it would make sense having the path on the mountain side. Our small group searched with flashlights, and before long, we happened upon the well-trodden trail. The way was fairly easy at the outset, but soon there was a noticeable variation in the ascent about an hour into the hike when the icy cold wind lashed our faces with brutal force. The higher we climbed, the steeper it became, and the pace slowed as faint patches of ice and snow confirmed the fact that this was a mountain, and not to be disillusioned by the desert. Gradually it became foggy, but then we noticed it wasn't fog at all, but clouds, which were lingering around the valley sides, as if protecting the snow from the inevitable sun. Our small group eventually overtook these clouds and it became brighter suddenly, but not from daybreak—it was still a couple of hours away, but by the moonlight, which illuminated the rest of the path in silvery light.

A foul smell made me pause; a rancid, decaying stench that did not belong here, where only the purest air is breathed. Camels! Of course… usually smelt before seen, but these were the stinkiest camels I have ever whiffed, maybe because of the sharp contrast at this elevation between fresh and foul. The beasts of burden did look rotten and well used—their patchy tufts of matted fur looking as if they had been haphazardly glued on to prevent further fur loss. Their skeletal, misshapen bodies stood rigid against the forceful winds; not the friendliest looking creatures either: they really looked mean, groggy and miserable—just like me at three o'clock in the morning. The Bedouins accompanying them were selling camel rides up the mountain.

"Meester want gamel?" Asked one of the Bedouins as we approached.

"Maybe so," I was thinking, but Mr. Camel certainly didn't look as if he wanted us. What if one of those things decided to bite my leg with those carious, yellow teeth?

The last part of the climb required the most effort, stooping and using both hands to grasp the jutting rocks for holding on to. A handrail had been installed to heave oneself the last few meters. The mountain did not want us here, as the wind blew with such force to cause total numbness of my face. Imagine going up here on a camel with its spindly legs; surely they would snap.

The summit of 2285m was finally reached, and the ferocious wind was now howling. I was also howling as my ears and nose were about to break off. My eyes and lips were sore, and I attempted to wrap myself up in the blanket I had borrowed from the hostel, especially to cover the ice block that used to be my head. We were too fast getting here and it was still dark for another hour until the slightest hint of the sun's rays would appear on the horizon. Standing on top of the mountain and waiting to freeze to death was not a brave act I attempted to endure. The relentless trembling wouldn't stop, even with layers of wrapped blanket around me. Fortunately, there was a large cave underneath the small chapel built on the summit. It is here where Moses is said to have hidden himself when he first came face-to-face with God. It is also the place where we all clambered in to shelter from the biting cold, only to stumble across a group of Egyptians who had spent the night in this cave. We disturbed the wrapped-up, slumbering mummies with our flashlights. "Welcome, welcome," some of them murmured, and room was immediately made for us as they shoved along.

The sunrise was certainly worth waiting for; not just *a sunrise*, but a most spectacular act of nature that provoked "ooohs" and "ahhhs" amongst us, awestruck spectators. Look above, and the sky was clear; look below, the clouds were swirling in and out of gorges and valley sides, tinged slightly pink like cotton candy from the first rays of the rising sun. The cold did not diminish, but I had forgotten about the numbness, too transfixed by this stunningly majestic view. The air was crystal-clear and free of pollutants—you could see for endless miles. "On a *very* clear day it is possible to see Saudi Arabia and the Gulf of Aqaba," one of the Egyptians proudly told me. I could not imagine anything clearer than this, but I guess he meant when there were no clouds swirling around and the wind was not blowing so harshly and picking up the dust in the valleys. I felt like I was standing on top of the world; especially with the clouds below instead of above, and the rapidly rising sun now fully illuminating and revealing the endless barren desert terrain that was made up solely of jagged rocks and boulders.

I lost my nose and ears again from the sheer cold, forcing me to climb back down. Such suffering I had to put up with, and I wasn't even able to take any pictures to show for it as the low temperature had killed my battery in the camera. We took a different route down this time, trudging down 3,750 eroded steps, which had been carved out by a single monk in order to fulfill his pledge of penitence many centuries ago. He must have been *very* naughty. We came across a 500-year old cypress tree at Elijah's Hollow, where the prophet Elijah is said to have heard the voice of God. It seems that every place where the voice of God had been heard, a chapel was erected, and there were several of them here on the mountain. Here, we met Ahmed, an Egyptian tourist who accompanied us for the rest of the time while in the Sinai. He gave us some berries to eat, which grew on the nearby so-called "demon tree."

"It cannot be grown from seed or reared as a plant," explained

Ahmed. "It just springs up naturally from the ground," he added. The tree did look somewhat demonic; the most gruesome-looking tree I have ever seen, and I was glad I didn't come across it in the dark. It was gnarled, tightly twisted like a cloth being wrung, and every square centimeter of it was covered with extremely long thorns. I never did find out the proper name of this tree. Demon tree could just have been a word-for-word Arabic translation, but very appropriate. Only the horns were missing.

Back at the monastery, we returned the borrowed blankets which had saved our lives. There was no wind anymore and it was good to feel the warmth of the sun again. We were shown around the grounds of the monastery and the Burning Bush, which was the only one of its kind in the Sinai. Mysteriously, this tree also cannot be multiplied—its offsprings would not grow anywhere else. I would have loved to see inside the monastery, but visitors are not allowed inside except by special permission for important people. I was not VIP. St. Catherine's monastery has a library, which contains ancient books and manuscripts dating back to the biblical period; written in Aramaic, ancient Greek, and Hebrew, as well as other ancient languages. I wondered how many secrets are hidden amongst all those ancient texts. On the monastery grounds is a chapel; it is used as an ossuary, containing the skulls of monks who had died here since the sixth century. In this rocky terrain, there is hardly any soil for covering up the dead. After being buried in the cemetery, the bodies are then exhumed when they become nice and bony and added to the collection. As well as monks, hundreds of ghosts must be living here, in secret passageways leading to secret rooms that probably haven't been opened for hundreds of years, and kept in eternal darkness while spiders had woven cobweb designs for over a thousand years. I shuddered at the thought.

Time was running and it was time to leave St. Catherine's; not a problem—we would just look for a taxi. Like everything else in Egypt, it was necessary to haggle over the price. Whatever the price, it was still dirt-cheap. The taxi fare came to twenty-four Egyptian pounds divided between the three of us. Ahmed joined us to our destination—Sharm-El-Sheikh—a four-hour descent through the mountainous terrain down to the Red Sea coast. The taxi made a stopover for breakfast in Dahab—a traditional Bedouin village with swaying palm trees and the usual scabby camels shading themselves by the concrete lean-to structures that managed to provide sufficient protection for them. We were back on the coast, and it was shorts and T-shirt weather again.

We arrived at a Bedouin-style restaurant; more of a temporary home-made shelter, where food was prepared and eaten under a black canopy that protected against the sun, but was open from all sides to allow the sea-breeze through.

The taxi driver was having breakfast with the other Bedouins, who simply squatted on cushions on the ground in their customary circular form. Inside the circle was a straw mat with a bowl of evil-looking gruel that was passed from person to person. Other larger bowls, containing unfamiliar dishes, were placed in the middle, where hands went in simultaneously, but only the right hand, as the left one was used (with the help of water) for... er... "after toilet functions." If the right hand was missing due to some misfortune, the poor soul would be shunned away—to eat alone. Pita bread was also used for scooping up the food with, and whatever liquid dripped onto the fingers, was licked and sucked clean, and then the hand went back into the common bowl, which was already mixed with other people's lick. Flies that were sunbathing on the nearby camel dung decided to join in the feast, too. There was no concern over hygiene. Carlos and I, as well as Ahmed, had our dinner (Western style) at a table next to the Bedouins, where we did not share our food. The Bedouins did share their delicious coffee with us, which suited me fine. I'm quite sure their food was very tasty, but admittedly, I could not join in their food orgy. I was still too fresh from the West and was not yet ready for such culinary practices.

We were closely observed by about half a dozen camels; all chewing something, and all twitching from the bothersome flies that found some bare skin on their bodies and moisture around their eyes. The Bedouins were well protected with their head scarves and full body garments. Only their huge, callous feet were subjected to flies, but their skin was so thick, it didn't bother them. The flies bothered us though. They were desperate for any moisture, and when I tried to eat, they would attempt to go inside my mouth as a bonus side dish. It was a constant battle: with the right hand, put the food into the mouth, and with the left hand, swat them away. They would land on the fingers, feet, and legs... and bite. The Bedouin were oblivious to this.

Now came the part I always dreaded in Egypt—when nature was calling. You never knew what was going to be behind that closed door, and sometimes the door was only a curtain. I would rather have gone out into the desert to do my business there. The worst part was the stench and the flies (the same ones that shared the food). Actually, I'm wrong. I *knew* what was behind the door, but how well was that hole targeted was the real question. Despite squatting above the hole, people still tended to miss. Hesitatingly, I opened that door and... my biggest toilet nightmare! The dirt floor was covered in piles of shit—in every corner! There was a jug of water for cleaning yourself, but even *that* had some brown stuff on it. I gagged and went back out immediately and went to ask for another toilet, but they just looked at me as if I was really stupid.

"That *is* the toilet," the restaurant owner told me, somewhat puzzled. He didn't seem to understand what my problem was. Carlos went pale when I told him—he also needed to go. No way! I was going to hold it till I burst. I didn't burst for a while, and willed myself to hold on until we got to Sharm-El-Sheikh, which was still a couple of hours away.

Never made it! On a nice stretch of this rocky terrain, panicking, I screamed at the driver to stop. He did—immediately, almost causing me to fly out of the windscreen. I dived behind a rock. Absolute bliss—fresh air, very clean... perfect!

We continued to our destination with our Egyptian friend, traveling through the most rugged, spectacular scenery I had seen yet—the same terrain that Moses and his tribe passed through after their Exodus from Egypt. Nothing has changed in those thousands of years. The coastal area was just flat, sandy desert, but the rest of the Sinai interior boasted mountains of unprecedented beauty. In Sharm-El-Sheikh, we said goodbye to our most courteous Bedouin taxi driver and he went in search for passengers for his return trip to St. Catherine's. They never go back with an empty vehicle.

We rented a tent on the beach for a little more than a dollar per person per night. Surprisingly, the tents contained very comfortable camp beds with the open end facing the Red Sea, and revealing palm trees that swayed in the light breeze. Oooh... this was such paradise. I immediately went into the sea to dip my feet.

"Hmmm, not too cold," I said. "Let's do some snorkeling tomorrow."

That was our plan, but for tonight we were in for a treat. The evening was spent sipping coffee around a campfire, which had rugs and large, firm cushions placed around it. This was so much more pleasant and cozier than sitting on coarse, bare sand; even better was the fact that we were the only two non-Egyptians amongst the group of six Bedouins, and of course, Ahmed from Cairo. This was one of the moments where the image will forever be embedded in my head: sitting on the mats around the fire, listening to the gentle waves, and observing the now silhouetted swaying palm trees with tethered camels against the moonlight. The drums came out, and the catchy pounding filled the night with mystery and invoked a feeling of being very, very far from the world I was used to. The pounding of the drums added a special mood to this seventh heaven at the southern tip of the Sinai Desert. Arabic music was put on (very loud), blaring out of the ghetto blaster. It was a lively rhythm with a lot of drumming and the haunting sound of string instruments. It was the first time that I truly appreciated Arabic music. Anything else would have been out of place. It was well past midnight when the fire burnt itself out and everyone started to disperse. A few of the Bedouins were already dozing on the mats by the fire where they stayed all night. We retired to our tents, left the flap open, and went to sleep with content.

It was time to change money and to replenish our dwindling food supply; so right after getting up, we hitched a ride to the nearby village. By Western standards, everything was amazingly cheap—almost free. Our staple diet consisted of pita bread, dried figs, dates, goat's cheese, olives, and thick, pulpy mango juice. Other times, we ate at local eateries (cannot use the word restaurants as that would be too far-fetched). A dollar a day was sufficient to survive here if one wanted to solely live on local food and not pay for accommodation, but doss on the beach. Hippies abound in the Sinai, and they did look as if they survived on *less* than a dollar, preferring to spend their money on hashish instead. In Israel, you could barely buy an ice cream for that amount.

The village consisted of the usual ragged children running and yelling, "Hallo meester," and covered up women doing chores, and lazy men sitting around under the shade of trees doing nothing, but staring into the desert together with their camels. There were some other backpackers and hippies around, but no real tourists. They would come some years later, and in droves, and this would no longer be a small cozy village, but a major tourist destination with tour buses running to all parts of the Sinai. There were already signs of construction taking place everywhere, and some beautiful hotels did exist, but they catered mainly for the Cairo residents. There was a proper bank for changing money and some eating places serving Western-style food. We skipped the modern, plastic-looking Westernized restaurants and went instead to a local run-down establishment that was serving pita bread, falafel, hummus, salad, and two rounds of sweet mint tea. The whole filling breakfast came to $1.50 between the three of us, *and* we had the pleasant company of camels who were munching on their breakfast beside us.

We found the bakery and bought fifteen rounds of bread for about thirty cents. The procedure for buying pita bread was like this: form an orderly line at the windowless window, have the right change ready, then simply give it to the grubby-handed pita man standing inside the window. In return, piping-hot bread was collected very rapidly from the moving conveyer belt, stacked up according to how much money was given to him, and the whole stack was simply handed over straight into my hands. Bags or wrapping did not exist; the result was a loud yelp, a few jumps in the air, and singed fingers, then I passed the stack to my friend who did the same while I was trying to blow my fingers cool; at the same time, the bemused locals regarded us as if we were completely crazy. They must have skin made out of leather. Even the camels glowed over us pitifully.

There was a shack renting out snorkels, masks, fins, and scuba diving equipment. We took the masks and snorkels and spent the day in the Red Sea amongst some of the most spectacular coral reefs in the world. The numerous fish were of every color that could possibly exist. The smaller variety swam in schools and seemed to be in a hurry, and the extremely large innocent-looking ones tended to be loners and more placid. I found out later they were parrot fish. There were also vibrant yellow dumb-looking fish that could have been swimming lemons. Some had thin, pointed snouts and looked as if they were wearing lipstick. I tried to imagine what each variety resembled, but then decided just to enjoy this amazing fish show. It was even better than in Eilat.

This was our last evening in the Sinai, and we spent it the same way as yesterday—with Bedouins, camels, fire, coffee, and drums. This night was absolutely still and there was just a gentle sound of waves lapping upon the shore. Tomorrow we have to return to Israel, as we only had a seven-day permit to stay here. Anything more would require a visa.

We said goodbye to Ahmed who was returning to Cairo. He embraced us and urged that we visit him in the city when we come to Egypt again. We left Sharm-El-Shekh early in the morning by vintage bus to Taba—a 3-hour journey for a mere two dollars. The bus stopped at an oasis nearby Nuweiba for the usual coffee and lunch and the twitching camels. I loved the lifestyle here—slow and easy going, and I really enjoyed these bus breaks whenever the driver felt like having one, which seemed like every hour. It reminded me of Cyprus. A regular bus timetable was something non-existent. There was also no feeling for time, as we soon found out. The supposedly 20-minute break was much shorter than expected. After a visit to the local shop to buy snacks and mango juice, we came out to gape in disbelief with our mouths open—the bus was gone! Vanished! Disappeared... with all our belongings on board! *But we still had three more minutes left!!!* So... here we were, stranded at an oasis in the middle of nowhere, surrounded by desert, Bedouins, camels, and Toyota pick-ups. Luckily, one of the Bedouins, who was still lunching, quickly assessed the situation and offered to drive us to Taba or to catch up with the bus; whichever came first, but of course, he wanted money for it... and quite a substantial amount. We fell into an argument over the price, and meanwhile, the bus was getting further and further away towards Israel.

After finally agreeing on the price (still a rip-off), we rapidly sped away at 140kph. This was to be my fastest, craziest car journey ever (getting our money's worth). The driver totally ignored all the traffic signs indicating "dangerous curves" and speed limits; he even sped straight through an army checkpoint, leaving a trail of dust lingering behind. We could see the contorted, raging faces of the Egyptian soldiers waving their guns in the air. I was surprised they didn't come after us. After a suicidal chase over about ten kilometers, we noticed hovering dust on the horizon, and a few minutes later, our runaway bus in the distance. Our driver did not slow down, but instead, accelerated even more and started to honk his horn and flash his lights. The bus driver didn't seem to notice. We caught up, and now, both vehicles were speeding along side by side with only a few centimeters between them. Our driver was still blaring his horn, and I was waving frantically at the astonished passengers, trying to indicate to them to stop the bus. The bus driver, finally realizing that we were not maniacs trying to outrace him, pulled over and stopped. This was quite an entertainment for the passengers. After getting back on board, the driver just smiled slyly and said, "I knew you would find a way to catch up." Our belongings were where we had left them and the seat was vacant.

We were back in Israel after the usual border formalities, but not before undergoing a brief interrogation on the paranoid Israeli side, having to answer all the where, why, who, what, and when questions. It didn't take long; we didn't look like terrorists, so they let us through. We immediately went to the bus station and boarded the next bus heading north. It was evening by the time we arrived back on the kibbutz, but supper was still on, and the dining room was where we headed.

After the Sinai trip, it was back to work in the orchards. The mornings were still quite chilly, and a warm coat was a must until the sun gained some power later in the day. I would have preferred to sleep in today, but instead, found myself in the orchard picking lemons at 6:00 A.M.—not exactly fun in the cool morning dew. I felt better after breakfast, after some rounds of strong coffee. The work went on for most of the month, alternating between citrus and avocados. I befriended the two Israelis who were in charge of the work in the orchards—Yosi and Ariel, who I sometimes visited in the evenings. The work here was most enjoyable, extremely slow and relaxing, and it had the feeling of a holiday camp. A wonderful bunch of people—a mixture of Israelis and international volunteers worked here in the orchards, which was a place for fun and laughter. There was no stress, no hurry, and no yelling—just good-humored bantering and constant snacks.

On the way to the dining room one day, Yosi was driving the tractor while we all sat at the back on the trailer as usual, only to hear him shriek something in Hebrew and make an abrupt stop, causing us all to almost fly out. He then sprang off the tractor and started running off into the desert, yelling something unintelligible. We started after him, thinking some desert insect had probably bitten him and now he was delirious. Then we saw it. He was running after a huge lizard, trying to catch it. The poor lizard realized this crazy Israeli was gaining on him and started to rapidly burrow a hole in the ground, frantically throwing sand behind him in the last desperate measure to save itself inside a hole. Not fast enough! Yosi caught up to him, and by the time we arrived on the scene, he was pulling the lizard's tail with full force, and then managed to extract the mini dinosaur completely out of its hole. It was huge: about seventy centimeters long, hissing, and very angry—its sharp, clawed toes trying to take a slash at its captor. "This, in Hebrew, we call *ko-ach*," he told us gleefully.

"It means power," added Ariel, whose English was much better. An appropriate name for this lizard I thought, as it really was very strong. Yosi was wearing thick leather gloves for holding him with, otherwise his flesh would have been ripped to shreds. Having won the strength contest with the lizard, he gently released it again. The lizard hesitated for a moment to give Yosi a nasty reptilian look, then attempted to burrow itself again. Other times, the crazy Israeli would be catching snakes and releasing them. He knew his desert fauna and flora and was always eager to teach us about the animals here, showing us the differences between poisonous snakes and the harmless variety.

The harmless variety broke into my kitchen cupboard that night, thrashing wildly once I switched the light on and opened the cupboard door. I was happy to discover it was a coin snake, so I caught it like I was shown and let it wind itself around my arm for fun before releasing it into the bush. All kinds of reptiles and insects inhabited this area, and I was told always to check shoes before putting them on in the morning, as scorpions liked to rent them for the night.

Some nights later, I was woken up by a screaming Carlos, who suddenly leaped out of bed and hit the light switch. His face was covered in blood and he was frantically trying to blow his nose. Something came out of his nostril then—a huge cockroach, and it was still alive as it fell onto the floor and tried to scarper. Carlos whacked it several times with a shoe until it was well and truly splattered, creating a big mess on the floor. His eyes were still wide with shock and horror once he realized what had been inside his nostril. He jumped into the shower while I scanned the room for other creepy crawlies.

In the coming weeks, I also had an incident—not with a cockroach, but a yellow scorpion. I had already gotten used to the procedure of pulling back the bedding to check the bed before climbing in, in case any insect had the idea of spending the night with me. As soon as I pulled back the blanket, a yellow scorpion, woken up from its slumber, rapidly darted around for cover, but as it fell onto the floor, I gave it the "shoe-job," and once again, we had to deal with a gooey mess.

I told Yosi and Ariel about the scorpion the next morning, but there was no sympathy from that side. They found the incident hilarious.

Together with another friend, I hitched a lift to the Gaza Strip checkpoint located only twelve kilometers from the kibbutz. We were heading to Rafiah, which is situated south of the Gaza Strip on the border to Egypt. The area has suffered total unrest and violence for many years now, and has the highest number of people per square kilometer, making it one of the most densely populated areas in the world. It was also an area I was very curious to see. The first lift from the kibbutz took us directly to the checkpoint, where we had to stop first and inquire about the safety, but also to let them know where we were going—two crazy tourists venturing to a no-go region.

"Is it safe to go to Rafiah?" I asked.

"As safe as can be," was the strange answer. I guess if it had been dangerous, they wouldn't have let us in. We hitchhiked from the border while watching the Arab vehicles being stopped and checked by the Israeli soldiers. The second lift was in a van, driven by an elderly Arab (I think one of the soldiers asked him if he could stop for us), and the kind driver dropped us off at the Rafiah intersection. The third lift came almost immediately, bringing us to the center of town. This last lift demanded money for the ride, so we gave him a shekel, which sufficed. Getting here was fast.

It was the most startling sight in Rafiah—surrounded by poverty, disease, and ramshackle, derelict buildings. There was dirt everywhere, as well as an intense stench of urine in the air (would be worse in summer). We strolled through the Bedouin market, being the place I really wanted to see for its originality, looking the same as it would have done many centuries ago. Unlike the famous Bedouin market in Be'er Sheva, which is quite touristy and "safe," this one had retained the traditional flair one only finds in places unknown to tourists. We were the only outsiders here and felt the hundreds of eyes boring holes into our backs. All kinds of rags were for sale, but very few decent items of clothing. Pitiful-looking fruits and vegetables were displayed in a haphazard way on broken sheets of cardboard. Assorted spices, different kinds of sweet, honey-dripping Arab cakes and other snacks I could not identify were for sale together with the flies that came for free. The animal section of the market consisted of sheep, goats, and donkeys. The purchaser simply paid for the beast and took it away on a leash. There were no camels!

Not surprisingly, a number of beggars eyed us suspiciously and followed us around, but to my disgust and astonishment, there were also lepers on the streets. I had never seen one, except in historical films. Several people with deformed limbs, twisted and gnarled feet, shuffled along the dirt-ridden ground, some with mouths wide open as if in pain, revealing rotten teeth. Everybody we saw had the same rotten brown/black teeth, half of which had long dropped out. Amongst the crowd were a few blind people, and some with milky, clouded over eyes showing evidence of eye disease. It was a scene out of poverty-stricken Medieval England, where a village idiot always appeared and where the homeless made lean-to structures, which they shared with goats. Here, this was reality, and it could have been any century in the distant past, but not the twentieth. I had only traveled about an hour to get here, at the same time I went back several hundred, or a couple of thousand years in time.

Indeed, we stood out like sore thumbs, attracting more attention than the Israeli army. *We* were the village idiots here—an entertainment for the locals. People started whispering to each other and speaking in hushed tones. That was unnecessary, as we didn't understand a word of Arabic. The creeping feeling of unease became omnipresent as the locals descended from all directions and decided to tag along—us, being the center of attraction (or distraction).

Rusty bicycles, donkey-pulled carts, half-starved and bony horses, made up the bulk of the traffic on the roads, as well as sidewalks. We decided to go into a café and muse over the world in front of our eyes. It was not a pretty sight. Some of the few cars which did exist, meandered in between the crowds, the donkeys, the carts, and running children. There were no traffic rules. Vehicles simply went where there was space; even on sidewalks, which were no more than an extension of the dirt road. An occasional jeep would drive by, filled with soldiers in riot gear and equipped with loaded machine guns. An extra large automatic weapon always commanded the rear of the vehicle. The general atmosphere was very tense in Rafiah; the area being prone to rioting and stone-throwing incidents, especially in the last three weeks, as a protest against the Israeli occupation.

After a few hours in this town, it was time to leave. My curiosity about the town had been satisfied and there was no reason to stay any longer, unless I wanted to experience a riot, which I didn't. Prolonged lingering would have been much too dangerous. The tense atmosphere could be cut with a knife... and it felt like the calm before the storm. An Israeli military jeep pulled up. "Why are you here? Where are you from?" They demanded. They found it totally inconceivable to actually see any tourists in this town; must have been the first time for them. "Meshugah," (crazy) I heard them murmur amongst themselves and shake their heads in disbelief. They ordered us to leave town immediately before we got stoned (physically), and there were plenty of good-sized chunks of rock lying around everywhere. I most certainly didn't need any persuasion to make an exit and happily took their advice; actually, it was an order!

By this time, we were being shadowed by about thirty people: a couple of them crippled, and a young man with twisted feet that shuffled along with the crowd. I felt like I was in one of those zombie films, where the corpses come back to life and start following you around in droves. Some of them came right up to my face to stare into my eyes—real spooky. The leper I had noticed before was amongst them and I was afraid he would get too near me. A bus sent from heaven was coming our way, which we gratefully hailed down, delighted to leave this chaotic place. Unfortunately, this bus drove off in the opposite direction to where we wanted to go, and we ended up at the Rafiah/ Egyptian border crossing. A taxi finally took us to our destination—the Israeli checkpoint. The driver dropped us off a couple of kilometers before the border, forcing us to walk the rest of the way. I think he tried to avoid being anywhere near Israelis, as they might have contemplated searching him.

A long, straight road extended ahead, and rich, fertile fields with crops on both sides of the road were being harvested. Donkeys helped the farmers with this arduous labor, overloaded with field crops. While walking towards the checkpoint, we were picked up by two Bedouin girls on their donkey and cart, so we enjoyed the rest of the trip in true Bedouin style amongst girlie giggles. Trying to chat with them in English brought on more giggles as they also made an attempt to make themselves understood in Arabic. A second donkey and cart caught up from behind, and as we were dangling our legs, sitting at the back of the first cart, it was difficult to avoid being nibbled by the oncoming donkey that was also steered by two giggly girls. They purposely came as close as possible. We hopped off at the turn-off, thanked the girls, and continued the last few minutes on foot. More giggles. I think that had really made their day. After a brief questioning session, the soldiers were happy to have a chat with someone "different" and invited us to eat some oranges with them. Two full crates were stacked inside the cabin. They also made us coffee on their camping stove and explained how boring it was for them to be here day after day and checking vehicles. The sun was almost gone as we made our way back to the kibbutz. This time we didn't get a lift, and after walking the twelve kilometers on the lonely desert road, it was very dark by the time we arrived.

There was a temporary work pause in the orchards, and most of the volunteers had to help out in the chicken house instead. A small truck arrived with 29,000 baby chicks. These tiny, yellow, chirping fluff-balls had to be unloaded and put into the chicken house, which had already been prepared for them, complete with heat lamps and small cordoned-off areas that kept them in groups. There were two such chicken houses side by side. The chicks were released into their compounds and huddled together under the heat lamps. These buildings were huge—you could play football inside. Here, they would grow into roasting chickens. The following days we were on "chicken patrol," making sure that none of the yellow fluff-balls fell into their water and drowned. A lot of them did, so our duty for the day was to collect the corpses in buckets.

After being in Israel for so long, I decided that I wanted to study Hebrew. The office that organizes all that is two hours away in Tel Aviv. I went there together with my Brazilian friend Carlos who also wanted to study. Such Hebrew study courses are known as *ulpan*. They take place on a kibbutz, where 50% of the time (four hours daily) is class study; the other four hours would be voluntary work for a period of five months. A great deal, and it costs nothing—food and accommodation included. Well, *nothing* if one is Jewish!

"Impossible!" Growled the woman from the Jewish agency. "This program is only available to Jews. Non-Jews can participate, too, but you have to pay for the course." After getting to know Israelis, I have realized that "impossible" doesn't have the same connotation as in English. My friend Carlos was quite proficient in Hebrew after having spent much more time in Israel than I. He continued talking to her in Hebrew and tried to convince her that we were for real and had a genuine desire to learn about Judaism and to study the language. She eyed us like a toad trying to decide what to do with two bothersome insects, and I caught a slight tensing of her lips. "You come back one week from now to this office for an interview; the decision is not entirely mine," she admitted; whereas, we had to bring with us references from our previous stays on a kibbutz. With the present one also helping us to get onto the language course, it may not have been so impossible after all. We left the office happy, knowing that we would be accepted. It was just a matter of discussions and interviews the following week, and doing some paperwork of-course. Anything that starts with "impossible" or "definitely not" is always a good sign in Israel.

One week later we were back in that office handing over references, which were scrutinized by the deep-voiced toad. This was not the end of it; she sent us to another office in Tel Aviv, where the interviews took place and we had to answer questions like: Why do you want to study here?" And, "Why do you find Judaism so fascinating?"

In one of the offices, two women questioned us about our affection for Israel. I was honest with my answers, telling them I loved the language and wished to learn it. I also admitted that I felt very much at home in Israel, more so than in England. This was also true: Israel had a strange, invisible pull on me, and I felt exuberantly happy here. Despite the many rude people, the constant military conflicts, occasional bombs, I really loved this place. The woman studied me, then said, "I think you have Jewish blood in you somewhere down the line and you may not know it." The other woman continued asking questions about my family.

"There was a Rabbi with the same surname as you," she suddenly blurted out.

"Oh!"

The other office had application forms for the *ulpan* course, which we filled out together with our passport information. That was it then. They would inform us by mail whether the selection was a success. They probably discussed my possible Jewish past, and that would be a very good reason to let me attend the course. Carlos had made a good impression on them, too, with his first-rate knowledge of the language. They were deeply impressed that a non-Jew could speak so well. We did want to go to the same place, but it was obvious he would be several levels higher than I; whereas, I would be starting with A,B,C, or in this case: Aleph, Beit, Gimmel….

At every possible opportunity I always tried to go on a trip somewhere —usually dangerous. The so-called "dangerous" places always turned out to be the most intriguing ones in the end and not as life threatening as people made out. The rule was to use common sense and listen to your gut feeling. This time we borrowed bicycles from the kibbutz and cycled over to the beach in the Gaza Strip. The Israeli soldiers at the checkpoint maintained their friendly approach, offering us refreshments and their endless supply of oranges. After cycling only a couple of kilometers, it was once again a time warp several centuries into the past, passing through the rich, modern, and high-tech farms of Israel, where the latest *John Deere* tractors were harvesting carrots and potatoes, and where computers automatically measured and distributed every drop of water onto the crops. Immediately on the Gaza side, it was the usual overworked donkey with baskets on its side that plodded through the fields, but was more environmentally friendly and always deposited free manure along the way. The Arabs still harvested everything by hand and plowed their fields manually by donkey. The Bedouin women and children would wave to us and shout greetings as we whizzed by on our bicycles. They were harvesting peas nearby rows of almond trees. We passed many such folk along the way where the women were doing all the work. Some smiley-faced young girls helped with the herding of goats. There were no men in the fields. It seemed that the entire male population just sat around cafés; sipping coffee and smoking. They leered as we pedaled passed them. Occasionally, they would make a strange, guttural sound and shout something. Never could figure out what it was that they hollered, but probably something obscene as it set the others off.

The desert landscape acquired its romantic beauty as we neared the beach, with its perfect sand dunes shaped artistically by the wind. It was a shame to see all this spoiled by the many-scattered, poverty-stricken refugee camps made up of rags, sticks, sheets of rusting, corrugated metal; in fact, anything that held the other piece together. The children ran about in their dirty, ragged clothing, some of them playing in the sand dunes, where they climbed to the highest one and slid down to the bottom. That looked like fun. They soon spotted us. "Hallo meester... where you from? Give me *baksheesh*."

"Where's the beach?" We asked.

"Give me *baksheesh*," was the reply.

We stopped a passing army vehicle to ask for directions to the beach. It was equipped with the usual automatic weapons. One of the soldiers recognized me from my previous trip into the Gaza Strip. "Hey, *Shalom*," giving me a firm whack on the back. The beach was finally reached after cycling through "dangerous" territory for thirty-one kilometers and arriving in Qatif. We were the only people there. Unfortunately, the upper part of the beach was a favorite drop-off spot for local garbage—rusting cans, plastic containers, car parts, and even a car battery, but where the sea lapped the shoreline, miles of fine, litter-free sand stretched all the way to Egypt, and there wasn't a soul in sight. An abandoned military command post with a badly-weathered sign, written in Arabic and English, warned people not to trespass on the beach. It might have belonged to the British during the occupation prior to 1948, as today that sign wouldn't have made sense... or would it? Why wasn't anyone here? Take away all this garbage, build some cabins, and the result would be a magical transformation. The beaches here were totally untouched (except where they got bombed), and much more attractive than the Israeli ones, where hotels and food places dominated the coastline. Obviously, the locals didn't share my thoughts as nobody would dream of enjoying the beach, and if they did, they would be fully clothed like in Egypt... like in Victorian England.

The return trip back to the kibbutz was just as pleasant, without any bad encounters or threats whatsoever: no stone-throwing; no shooting; no stabbings; no bombs. The most life-threatening moment would have been on the beach—stubbing one's toe against a sharp, rusty can. *Dangerous!!!*

11
THE CURSED JOURNEY

Back on the kibbutz I was happily re-allocated to work in the orchards. Acting as an undertaker for chickens was not my cup of tea. Usually, the volunteers were rotated to work in different areas, including the kitchen, dining room, or the dishes. Yosi had me permanently assigned to the orchards, as he also preferred not having to show the ropes to newcomers every couple of weeks. Dirk, a recent arrival from Germany, was my new good-humored friend working together with me in the orchards. He had a deep fascination in Israeli farming methods, having grown up on a farm in Bavaria. Like me, he continued to marvel at the geography of this country and wanted to experience it first-hand by renting a car for two weeks, with which he would try to visit as many corners of Israel as possible. Not wanting to travel alone, he invited me to join him, which I gladly accepted. We would be roughing it: sleeping in the car sometimes, and not being able to wash either, but that sounded perfect....

The first day started... no... actually, the first kilometer started as a probable jinx or a curse, which I hoped would not haunt us on the entire trip. Was it a prelude of things to come? The rented Fiat Uno blew two tires after only one kilometer from the kibbutz—a double puncture. What a blow! This couldn't be true. We were not left stranded, but cheered up a little when many of the passing vehicles stopped and offered us assistance. The car had one spare tire, and the other flat was repaired by a passing

Israeli who merely shrugged his shoulders after a "thank you," and insisted it was nothing.

On the road again, we continued towards Jerusalem and spent our first night in the Old City. Being most familiar with the city's layout, I guided Dirk to the same private hostel where I had first stayed two years previously with my girlfriend. Nothing had changed since; the rooms looked the same, and it was as lifeless as before, but I loved the ambiance and the location of the place. A Christian Arab family lived here—three generations under one roof, but still had enough space to transform two extra rooms into a hostel with about six beds in each, for which they charged a very fair rate. Nothing had changed one bit. The very ancient grandmother still continued to offer sweet Arabic tea as a welcoming gesture.

We found *our* spot for the night, but the car was a slight problem. It was not safe to leave it just anywhere, as Jerusalem had recently become famous for its tire-slashing incidents. Our tires had already suffered enough, so the best we could do was to find it a safe parking place, and the safest ones were in front of the very big and famous hotel chains in the modern part of Jerusalem and far away from the Old City where we were staying. The walk back was endless, but getting into a car which was still in one piece the next day would actually save us time.

It was already well into the night, so a walk around the Old City was out of the question, as one never knew what was lurking in those shadows in those ancient, spooky alleys. The muezzin's call to prayer sounded especially eerie and raised the hair on my arms. Had I been a dog, all my fur would have been standing up. We avoided the Christian and Muslim Quarters, and instead, decided to hunt down some food in the Armenian section of the Old City. Food aroma wafted into my nostrils before long, then we discovered an Armenian eatery where they were baking interesting pizzas; not the regular kind one is familiar with—these were very flat with slightly spiced ground meat on top and sprinkled with sesame seeds and a green herb that tasted of coriander and thyme. These flat things were shoved into a stone oven and baked over a fire. The taste was out of this world; very simple, but very tasty. We washed it down with a glass of tea.

It was still pretty cold in Jerusalem at night in March, and the warmth of the flaming stone oven was a welcome relief. The Armenians sitting inside were most surprised to see a couple of foreigners wander in, especially at this time of night, enjoying their traditional foods instead of heading to the usual tourist eating establishments where the food tasted like the surroundings—plastic. While chatting to the woman who made the pizzas and also ran the restaurant, we learned about the Armenian people and their religious beliefs. Her English was rather good. "We originate from an area between Turkey and the Soviet Union by Mount Ararat, which is very sacred to Armenians," she told us, "and we have our own language, too," she added. We found our first encounter with the Armenians very friendly, and to prove how friendly they were, several people insisted shaking our hands as we left.

On the way to the Wailing Wall we took the long way round in order to avoid those dark, scary alleys in the Arab Quarter. Luckily, we arrived in good time as an army swearing-in ceremony was taking place. The security at the Western Wall was quite dramatic; not surprising, as the previous ceremony that had taken place here came under attack of petrol bombs.

We continued our journey the next day along the West Bank, but not before a visit to the Arab Quarter to indulge ourselves in some of the scrumptious cheese and apricot cake saturated in honey. This is an Arab specialty and a very fine breakfast with a couple of glasses of strong Turkish coffee. Oh... I could eat this forever. It had been a long time since I ate here—with Sally... and I started to miss her again.

Our trip took us through Ramallah—an Arab town in the West Bank, which boasted a higher standard of living compared to other towns in the area. Nablus (or *Schem* in Hebrew, pronounced like sch-chem *and* with some phlegm on the "ch"), on the other hand, was a complete contrast—it was the next town we drove through. Nablus is famous for its riots and stone-throwing incidents, which occurred quite frequently when it was time to release a little of the tension in the West Bank. This was the town which was most featured around the world when they reported "trouble" in Israel. Israeli soldiers patrolled up and down the main streets, armed with their favorite weapons and ready to use them at the slightest hint of disturbance. We soon stuck out in town as our car was the only one with yellow Israeli license plates. All the other cars carried the usual blue Jordanian ones. Some scuffles broke out within the crowd involving Palestinians and the army as we drove along the main road, which took us directly through the center. We didn't wait to investigate what the commotion was about, but quickly sped out of this trouble spot and made a rapid departure out of Nablus.

The West Bank (also known as Judea, Samaria and Palestine) contains the most awesome, breathtaking scenery; although very barren in parts, the terraced landscape supports many species of wild, indigenous plants and orchids not found anywhere else. Olive terraces cover large areas of the West Bank—some of those gnarled and twisted trees looking extremely ancient. This biblical landscape with its own rugged beauty could only be in Israel. All those Bible stories had taken place here, and surveying the surroundings, it wasn't hard to imagine the Crusaders, the Canaanites, the Romans, and the ancient Israelites all having passed through these hills, and it would have looked the same then as it does today. Distracted by the scenery and its invocations it had upon us, we took a wrong turning and ended up in another Arab town—Tulkarm. This place really looked as if all hell had broken loose. It was worse than Nablus. Whatever happened to that serene environment that had been just around the corner? Driving through the West Bank is never boring, with its ever-changing scenery around every bend of the road. Much of the land was being farmed by the Palestinians using the usual manual method—donkey pulling the plow along. Also here, like in the Gaza Strip, there was no sign of any modern farm machinery. It was hard to imagine that people in the West Bank had a higher standard of living than their counterparts on the other side of the River Jordan, we were told by a Palestinian.

North-bound now, we continued driving along the scenic routes, passing through gorgeous olive groves and small Arab villages, which had more atmosphere than the larger towns. It felt safer and friendlier, too, and there was no sign of any Israeli military presence. Our route along the Jezreel Valley took us through Druze villages Isfiya and Daliyat Al Karmel, which we found very disappointing due to their lack of anything attractive or interesting. There was not even a decent place to eat here, as food should also be enjoyed together with the surroundings, and *these* surroundings were nothing to boast about. Modernization and industrialization of these villages had relieved them of any character they may have once possessed. The Druze people were out-and-about, recognizable by the men's thick mustaches and flowing white head-dresses, whereas the women wore black robes with white shawls.

Driving up to Mount Carmel now, the scenery changed dramatically to pine-forested slopes, revealing its white limestone and black dolomite, which the mountain is made up of. This was too glorious to simply pass by ignorantly, so we stopped the car and honored the mountain by hiking amongst this beautiful countryside where the air was filled with the aroma of pine. But nature didn't really want our presence here, sending in black clouds and forcibly cutting the hike short. Those looming dark clouds suddenly discharged their voltage above our heads, together with a torrential downpour that soaked us instantaneously.

We arrived in beautiful Haifa at last, where Dirk had a contact address of a German woman who would put us up for the night. Haifa was surprisingly humid after the dry deserts I had become accustomed to, and I was still soaked from the rain. Although it was night, the city was full of activity and in full swing. The city is built on three levels—downtown, middletown and the upper terraces of Mt. Carmel. Middletown is where all the action takes place and where all the restaurants can be found. Haifa Port was a colorful sight with all the illuminations flickering in the warm night sea breeze. It felt good to be here, and the arrival in the dark made it even more enchanting.

First stop the next day (south of Haifa) was Beit Shearim. This was the gathering place of the Sanhedrin who used to be the highest authority of all world Jewry. It had also been recognized by the Roman Empire in the second century CE. About twenty caves have been discovered on this site, but the amazing fact is that they form an underground network. It gets even more astonishing: its walls are lined with dozens of intricately-adorned sarcophagi. It reminded me of the catacombs in Pathos, Cyprus. As well as the catacombs, archaeologists have also discovered an ancient synagogue, and there may be other surprises still awaiting discovery.

Mount Meron was our next destination in Upper Galilee. Despite the bad weather, which was determined to disrupt our trip, the drive through the forests and valleys was out of this world, made more dramatic by distorted sunlight that was in confrontation with determined, ominous clouds. We were being followed by the blackest cloud I have ever seen, at the same time the surrounding countryside was lit up in blazing sunlight. To our left were the rising hills of Galilee; to our right was the completely flat landscape of Emeq Hula. The contrast in the land was breathtaking.

After parking the car alongside the IDF (Israeli Defense Forces) radar installation based on the summit of Mt. Meron, we were given suggested walking routes to take by one of the friendly guardsmen. Mt. Meron is the highest mountain in the Galilee at 1208m; for that reason, it became rather cold as we hiked along the trail up to the summit. The cloud that had been following decided to burst and bombard us with hail, thus drenching our clothes… again. It was bitter cold, wet, and windy so high up, and I had to force myself to take out my camera with my frozen hands and take a picture of the marvelous, panoramic view of Lebanon, which revealed itself in full sunlit glory. Cold, wet and miserable, we hobbled back to the car, put the heater on full blast, and drove off towards a nearby Druze village to buy groceries.

The village of Hurfeish was more like the Druze village I had imagined. Here, it was completely void of tourists. The very handsome people gracefully strolled along in their traditional costumes, barely battering an eyelid at our presence. At the grocery store we were offered my favorite coffee with cardamom and had some very tasty Druze snacks. We were given *lebanha*, which is made of large sheets of paper-thin bread filled with pickled goat's cheese and folded up umpteen times—not my favorite snack, but interesting nevertheless. Maybe the taste would grow on me later. The people were extremely chatty and friendly, wanting to know the usual things…, "Where are you from? What is your name? Where are you going?" But it was genuine interest and not the usual aggressive demands one is confronted with in the Arab *souk*.

We drove on to Qiryat Shemona—the forbidden town; so-called by us as the entire town is decorated with "do not enter," "private," and "forbidden" signs. This town still retained the scars of constant PLO attacks from Lebanon: Some buildings still had large chunks missing from them. Bullet holes splattered most of the buildings, as well as bus shelters and roads, which had played host to katyusha rockets. It was hard to believe that anything could happen in this sleepy, dormant town. It was forbidden to have tea at a restaurant for some reason, so we ended up having cocoa at a bar, which was not forbidden after parking just outside on a forbidden spot. Inside, it was dead and totally void of people. Only the sound of *Fred Astaire* type of music haunted the empty space—obviously a place lost in its past. The barman/waiter looked as if he had woken up after fifty years of sleep and had forgotten to change the record. Nevertheless, we spent the evening in this weird place and desperately took advantage of the warmth inside. This was a good time and place to make travel plans for the days ahead.

We skirted the whole town along forbidden routes looking for a place to spend an evening, but found no accommodation. Even if there had been, we decided against spending the night here anyway. We looked for a place to sleep outside town, as sleeping was probably forbidden here, too. The entrance to Horshat Tel Nature Preserve was an ideal place to crash out, where oak trees, some two thousand years old still survive. It was planned that we wake up in time for the opening in the morning. This was our first night in the car. Outside, the temperatures plummeted and the windscreen was soon fogged over.

Morning 6:00 A.M. The weather was beautiful; the sun was shining and the sky was blue, but this image was deceptive—it was freezing. Snow-covered peaks on the surrounding hills were a stunning contrast against the greens and the blues. Waking up to the sound of gushing water and the aromatic scent of pine forests was most invigorating and put me in a good mood after yesterday's morose influence of Qiryat Shemona.

The nature reserve did not open. It was closed for the winter: a disappointment, but feeling nonchalant nonetheless, we did the next best thing—a scenic drive around the Golan Heights. Although I had been here times before, I was still awed by the hypnotizing beauty of this craggy landscape. This time of the year it was even more beautiful than in the dry summer months. Spring flowers were blossoming, and on the higher altitudes, snow gleamed against the blue sky. Pink and white blossoms from the apple and pear trees bordered the roads. The Druze village of Majdal Sharms looked most striking against this background, like a village out of a fairytale. Majdal Sharms means "the Tower of the Rising Sun"—a most appropriate name.

Our plan was to drive around the perimeter of Mt. Hermon—the highest mountain in Israel located on the Syrian border, but this was not possible. An endless line of traffic heading up to the mountain was at a standstill, and we hadn't moved for an hour. This mountain is a popular ski resort for Israelis, and it looked as if the skiers would have a long wait before reaching the slopes. Congestion was not the issue here: the roads were blocked by snow, and we were waiting for the snowploughs to come through and clear the way. Unfortunately, they only managed to clear the first ten kilometers; the rest of the way being impassable, as drifts caused by a (mountain) snowstorm the night before blocked even the snowploughs. We drove back via the Druze village of Mas'ada, situated at the base of Mt. Hermon.

The Druze in the Golan Heights are unlike those at Mt. Carmel. Here, they continue to support Israel's enemy—Syria, and refuse to become citizens in their new country. They were in a tricky spot: no longer part of Syria, but neither belonging to Israel. They have been separated from their families and brethren on the other side of the mountain since the Six-Day War, and still continue to raise Syrian flags on public buildings. Very few tourists ever venture this far, and this lack of intrusion sets the town aside to retain its traditional ways, and thus allow the Druze to continue the practice of their secret rituals.

Out in the distance on a hill stands Nimrod's Castle, and we took advantage of the opportunity to visit this huge fortress, which is said to have been built by the first mighty man on earth.

We trekked along a footpath from this point across rough terrain covered with basalt and limestone, which had been eroded to fantastic shapes. Two hours later, we arrived in Banyas—the site of an ancient Greek sanctuary dedicated to Pan, the god of nature and shepherds. This is also the spot where Jesus had chosen his first disciple. Mesmerized by history and nature, we didn't realize the number of miles hiked, and walking back to the car would have taken too long. At that moment, as if sent by God, a vehicle on this desolate road was passing our way. The driver was one of the local Druze residents, and he was more than happy to offer a lift back when asked. I had the impression that he even felt honored.

Another disappointment that day while traveling to see Tel Dan and the fauna and flora museum—it was (of course) closed. Winter season! That evening, we decided to leave the north as it was far too cold and continue our way south via Emeq Hula. History tells us that 20,000 years ago, flowing lava from the Golan region stopped the Jordan River in the south of the Hula valley, thus forming a big lake. Later on, Egyptian farmers made their way north to cultivate papyrus and breed water buffalo. The lake had become a swamp when the first Jewish settlers arrived at the end of the nineteenth century and founded the first settlement of Yesod Ha

Ma'ala. Life was an adversity then as the settlers desperately fought against harsh conditions—swamps and malaria, but to no avail. About thirty years later, the Jewish National Fund organized the draining of the mosquito-larvae-infested swamp, but it wasn't until the late 1950's that this accomplishment came to prevail. The region around this settlement has been preserved in its original state and declared a nature reserve. Among the still-existing papyrus growth are living beavers, wild cats, wild boar, and herds of water buffalo. It continues being induced by the cold water from the Jordan and warm spring waters nearby. Although the driving was hazardous along the full 15-kilometer stretch of the pothole-ridden road, the swampland scenery made up for it.

Once again, we spent the night in the car, but in Tiberius, by the shores of the Sea of Galilee where it was considerably milder.

Milder it was, but the weather turned foul the next morning, enticing us to sleep in a bit. First on the agenda was a drive around the Golan Heights and a visit to Gamla. A similar tragedy occurred here as in Masada when the nasty Romans laid siege upon this religious city. It was packed with 9,000 Jews at that time—enough fighting power to massacre the stunned Romans as they finally pierced the walls of the city. When the news traveled back to headquarters, they were furious about the outcome, and a second, harsher attack followed some weeks later. It was too much to withstand the legions this time; therefore, the Jews hurled themselves over the ridge rather than be captured and turned to slaves, or even herded to Rome to play in the lion arena.

The ruins resemble the hump of a camel (from which it bears its name) whose hip form steep slopes descending into ravines of two tributaries en route to the Sea of Galilee. The only access to the steep walls is along the narrow strip of land, known as the Camel's Tail. Above us, vultures soared high up in the air as if waiting for another mass massacre. Could these be the descendants of the vultures that witnessed death on a large scale some 2,000 years ago? We arduously endured the heavy rain and ice-cold winds, observing these birds as they circled above; not a very encouraging sign, as there was an endless drop into the valley at the side of our footpath. They were probably hoping we would lose a foothold and smash ourselves on the rocks below, thus providing a scrumptious feast for the above hopefuls. We had to disappoint them evidently. Their nests were perched high up on the precipice—a beautiful sight against the background of a waterfall plunging fifty meters down.

A visit to the archaeology museum was a must, so we drove (very wet) a few kilometers to the (not so interesting) town of Katrina, where we also had to replenish our low food supply. The rest of the evening we spent touring the scenic routes along the barren eastern side of the Sea of Galilee.

Tzafat was our stopover for the night—a picturesque artists' center set on Mt. Canaan. Nothing much to do here except eat and walk around the attractive artists' quarter of the town, where beautiful local paintings were exhibited inside expensive galleries. A penetrating ice-cold wind was blowing with a promise of snow on the way. It was time to make our way back into the warmer regions. We slept in the car outside Kibbutz Degania, which was the first kibbutz to be set up in Israel, and very impressive with its beautiful landscaping and architecture.

Next day's highlight was Hammat Gader on the Jordanian border. The site comprises of spectacular Roman ruins, complete with baths where hot spring water was still gushing in *and* it was open to the public 2,000 years later. This was a prize the Israelis had taken from Jordan in the Six-Day War back in 1967. Bubbling-hot sulphur pools were letting off steam nearby, filling the air with the odor of rotten eggs. An alligator farm had been added as an attraction, and I wasn't sure whether they were there to gawk at or converted to handbags after their reptilian exhibit. These content-looking alligators had been imported from Florida, USA, and to see them, a suspended bridge goes over the swamp where one can get an excellent view of these animals in their natural habitat.

After freezing ourselves these last few days in the north, it was absolute bliss to submerge ourselves in the hot sulphur pools, getting a massage at the same time from the eternal gushing water that had been channeled off by the Romans and was still pouring into the pool at several locations. The idea was to let it cascade onto your back and shoulders—it felt *so good*. Many Israelis, Arabs and Druze also come down from afar to enjoy the soothing powers of these waters. The only thing which was missing was ice cream. There were no other foreign tourists to be found here, and the only reason why we ended up cooking ourselves in these pools was because a kibbutznik mentioned it as one of the places we should stop at. He was right.

Back in the car again and heading south, Jericho was our next destination. The drive along the Jordanian border enabled us to view the rich variety of agriculture, which thrived in these rich, fertile soils and making use of the entire valley on both sides of the River Jordan, which defined the border from the north to the south. In the Palestinian areas, the fruits and vegetables would be harvested by women folk and sold at the roadside by men and children to the oncoming traffic. But that was in the coming months; for now, families were still planting with enthusiasm—transforming the Jordan Valley into an endless green strip.

Jericho identifies itself to be the oldest and lowest city on earth. We didn't dispute that claim as we drove into the old city where extensive archaic ruins symbolized its ancient history. A short drive eastwards brought us to Allenby Bridge (King Hussein Bridge, as it is known on the Jordanian side), the border crossing to Jordan, which was closed until politics between the two countries improved. On the way there, we were surrounded by the endless sight of refugee camps and hordes of children roaming around in ragged clothing. These were the displaced Palestinians.

Inside Jericho there is a Greek monastery built on the Mount of Temptation: the site where Jesus was tempted by the devil, and where he fasted for forty days and forty nights after his baptism in the Jordan River. The monastery is perched high up on the edge of the cliff, and the arduous climb to reach it was well worth the effort for the splendid view we were rewarded with—the entire city of Jericho, and beyond... the desert wilderness and the northern shore of the Dead Sea, where a slither of turquoise looked like an accidental brush stroke on a painter's canvas.

Jericho beckoned that we stay. We did... and spent the evening strolling around the city, but actually, it was more like an oversized village. The friendly local Arabs were a pleasant contrast to the harassing mob one finds in the Old City of Jerusalem and the Gaza Strip. Beautiful and sweet-smelling flowering bushes permeated the air, and the streets were crammed with traders selling the most awesome varieties of oranges and grapefruits available on the planet. It was difficult to pass by without splurging out on the most delicious oranges I have ever tasted—even better than from the kibbutz. We bought a whole box. Jericho, I was told, is supposed to have the sweetest apricots on the planet, but this was not the season to test that theory.

Spring is the best time to come to Jericho; this time of year is much more pleasant and bearable compared to the first time I came here with Sally in the summer months. Then, we could hardly breathe or move in the scorching, merciless heat, and couldn't wait to get back on the air-conditioned bus.

In the late evening we dared to visit the local hangout where the male Arab population spends its leisure time playing *sheshbesh* (backgammon), drinking tea, and smoking whatever they smoke from the water pipes. The locals were so bemused to see two foreigners venturing into such a place, that for a moment, everybody looked around, but very quickly a table was cleared for us and the usual "welcome" muttered. The only thing to do was to order *sheshbesh* and coffee—that seemed to prove the point that we weren't just a couple of dumb tourists, but knew what to expect and how to behave.

The hospitality of the Middle East, as described by travelers of days long gone by, is an unforgettable experience. The company of these friendly Jericho residents proved the point that modern times have not changed this concept, as we were treated with extreme courtesy and respect. We did likewise, and stayed there until well into the late evening hours and then moved on to have a feast of oranges, falafel, and olives. It was time for our sleep-in-the-car routine—this time on a banana plantation on the outskirts of town.

Still in Jericho, a trek along Wadi Qelt was on our agenda the next morning. The wadi (dry river valley) descends 395 meters below sea level, revealing an oasis that is rich in gleaming springs, various plants, and many species of wildlife. The valley threads twenty-eight kilometers between limestone cliffs, providing a desert lover with the most captivating rugged backdrop, and offering the adventurous hiker a most challenging, but rewarding trek inside a bone-dry canyon that lies below sea level.

The outset of the hike is from St. George's monastery—another Greek monastery built precariously into a cliff. I could never understand why the Greeks always chose the most inaccessible sites for erecting a monastery. What puzzled me most was how they managed to transport all that building material up to the top? This structure dates back to the fifth century; built on the spot where it is said that the prophet Elijah was fed by ravens on his way the the Sinai. He was escaping the wrath of Jezebel, the

Queen of Samaria. I wasn't sure what he had done to upset her so much.

Near the monastery are the Elijah springs, but first, I wanted to see the monastery itself. We knocked on the door, hoping to be allowed entry. The heavy, antiquated door was opened by an amicable, smiling monk and he beckoned us to come inside. "Please... come in." The young, studious monk was overjoyed to have visitors. Being very chatty, he told us stories of monk life and explained how some of the more devout ones became hermits, spending the rest of their lives residing inside one of the many surrounding caves that dotted the cliffs, which were even higher than the monastery. The only way up was by rope and pulley system, and that is also the way that food was sent up to them. They shut themselves off completely from the outside world in order to be in total isolation. As a result, a lot of monks take up wood carving as a way of deviating from the eternal boredom. We were shown several impressive carvings that had been produced, and as he offered us tea, he continued to explain how monks are sent to serve in monasteries all around the world. He took pleasure in enlightening us with this information and told us we were welcome to stop by for a tea and a chat anytime we were in the area. In the following years, I would return several times.

The trek along Wadi Qelt took up most of the day. We were surprised to see so many others taking the same route, thinking that we'd be the only insane people attempting this hike. This seemed to be the favorite torture point for exercising new army recruits, who were being forced to trek the entire twenty-eight kilometers in their full combat gear, which included lugging heavy arms. Wearing just a pair of shorts was strenuous enough: the steep wadi sides prevented any inflowing breeze, and the result was an oven effect. When the noisy soldiers finally passed, what remained was just an echo of the trailing voices and the desert dust that had been kicked up. Even the slightest movement of the smallest stones being dislodged from the sides and trickling downwards caused a resonance. We were covered head to toe in dust and sweat, and I had no idea where and when the next shower would be. Sitting down on the boulders and devouring some of our oranges, I thought about the past few days when we froze our bones in the snow and icy winds... and now we were practically naked.

There was still time to see Herodium near Bethlehem—the hideout of King Herod, the crackpot king, who was eternally haunted by the fear of assassination. As with all other ruins in Israel, Herodium was magnificent. We left the car at the bottom and climbed up an endless hill that resembled a volcano; in such a way, we felt the immensity of this ancient, colossal project; so vast, it was inconceivable how it was constructed. The view from the top was to die for, especially towards the east, where the harsh and unforgiving Judean Desert stretched as far as the eye could see. One could imagine King Herod atop his fortress-palace commanding the Judean hills and nervously seeking out any signs of potential enemies advancing from valleys afar. It was worth coming up here just for the view and a fine place for a picnic.

As Bethlehem was nearby, it seemed like a good idea to visit the town and see the famous Church of Nativity—the site where Joseph and Mary arrived and passed the night in a manger. Inside the church are various levels: one descends into dimly lit passages and stone stairways, which have been worn out by pilgrims throughout the ages, and in the last decades, by tourists coming to see this sacred place. The ancient construction with its musty air caused a claustrophobic feeling within, and I couldn't wait to get out into more open spaces.

Bethlehem, as a whole, is a far from attractive town; it's even less attractive when one is constantly pestered by the Arabs to come in and buy something from their tourist junk collection. Not wanting to spend an evening in this place, we traveled onto Jerusalem, where we found a lovely bar and were seduced by cleanliness and comfortable chairs. It was good to see civilization and people again and to regain some of the vigor we had lost over the last few days: from the cold and cramped car seats. Having already seen most of this area, we drove on to our next destination—the Dead Sea, with a night stop at Qumran, where the famous Dead Sea Scrolls were discovered, and now can be seen in the Shrine of the Book—a museum in Jerusalem. We were finally back in the true desert, which I preferred this time of the year (March).

We woke up the next morning to a lazy day ahead and traveled to the southern part of the Dead Sea—to Ein Boqeq. The water was inviting and luring us to come in and wash off that grime and dust that had accumulated in the wadi. Swimming wasn't possible in the Dead Sea, so we just floated and then dried off in the sun. Our former sand-covered bodies were now replaced with a thin layer of salt, but at least I felt cleaner. I wanted to see

Newe Zohar—the site of the famous and much photographed Dead Sea salt crystals projecting out of the water, or so they *were* the last time I had come here two years before. We made several excursions up and down the coast looking for these awesome wonders, all the way to Sodom, but none could be seen. All that was visible in the water were huge mechanical, clawed monsters removing the mineral deposits from the Dead Sea, at the same time destroying what was left of these salt crystals. I was shocked that this was actually permitted, and even more shocked that this area was not protected or dedicated as a National Park.

Disappointed, we drove to Sodom to look for the famous pillar of salt known as Lot's Wife. Lot's wife was turned into a pillar of salt by God for breaking her promise not to look back upon the wicked cities of Sodom and Gomorrah, which God rained fire and brimstone upon in an attempt to obliterate these sinful places from the face of the earth. There is nothing left of Sodom today except the Dead Sea Works, which Dirk wanted to visit (for some obscure reason), but visitors were not permitted. The entire jagged terrain here is made up mostly of salt. The water and dissolving salts had created caves in this area on and around Mt. Sodom—one of the best examples being Arubotaim Cave, locally known as The Chimney, because of its enormous conical-like chimney opening. Looking back towards the Dead Sea (like Mrs. Lot once did), an endless expanse of the most beautiful desert imaginable stretched before my eyes, painted mostly in white, light gray, and tan, colored by the salt crystals, chunks of which could be broken off and placed on the kitchen table ready for use—so pure it was.

Countless undiscovered caves still abound in the region, waiting for the next archaeologist to stumble onto some biblical treasure or ancient hidden secrets. There were even ruins of a fortress built atop a salt hill, and then the question—who was this built for? A fortress in this location with such a strategic view could only be used in defense. From whom? The desert has seen too many ruins and invading tribes and ancient armies dating back thousands of years. Today, the armies are still present, fighting with Palestinians and nothing has really changed, and definitely not the landscape. Being in Israel was like being inside a history book.

We found Lot's wife—the pillar of salt, and I ran my hand over the brittle thing, whereas a large chunk broke off. "Oops"—hope it wasn't her nose! There was a cave nearby that looked rather inviting and had a decent-sized opening, so we sauntered in, a little hesitant at first, and then found ourselves ankle-deep in bat excretions. The stench was overpowering, but curiosity made us continue cautiously along the passage, which didn't seem to have an end to it. Distracted by "clicking" sounds, we shone the beam of the flashlight upwards and exposed a vast number of bats hanging upside down—they seemed to be having a conference; disturbed by the light, they flapped around us in protest and retreated to the darker interiors of the cave. We left the bats in peace, a little disappointed not having found anything valuable except a good source for garden fertilizer.

Once again, our grocery supply was starting to look rather dismal—we had only three oranges left. Arad came up on the map as the next town, and the one we drove to for replenishing our supplies. A well-stocked supermarket was located in the center with an assortment of good food, which we bought plenty of, as the next couple of days would be spent in the heart of the desert. While in town, it was hard to resist a delicious falafel, pastry and coffee. I felt human again and very happy. The only attraction in Arad is the pollen-free air because of its location in the Judean Desert. People with pollen allergies tend to move here, but nevertheless, Arad is a very beautiful contemporary town, boasting uniquely-designed, futuristic-looking architecture. It looked as if the whole town was run on solar energy; sun being something there was not a shortage of. It is also the cleanest town I have ever seen without a scrap of garbage anywhere.

Next day was desert day; ascending from Arad into the heart of the Negev Desert, where we traveled through the most treacherous terrain imaginable in our tinny and fragile Fiat Uno. The bottom of the car would annoyingly scrape the boulders and other protrusions, which were trying their best to rip a hole underneath. The going was almost snail-pace due to the constant breaking in order to avoid the potholes. The passing four-wheel-drive vehicles, looking as if they belonged in this rough terrain, would stop and wish us good luck, and we *did* need it. We conquered the infamous and treacherous route known in Hebrew as *Ma'ale Akrabim*, roughly translated as Scorpion's Descent. Other people called it the Serpentine Descent, appropriately named as the track coiled like a serpentine for several kilometers, and it felt as if we were descending sideways. Our poor little car was being jolted with utmost cruelty, but it kept moving. There was no road at all: just gravel, stones, potholes, and rocks that had come hurtling downwards from above—probably dislodged by other vehicles that had driven too near the edge. This was not a simple drive down a steep hill, but an actual winding descent down a sheer and dangerous precipice. Dirk, who was driving, had such a firm grip on the steering that his knuckles turned white; in fact, we both turned white. Coming the other direction was an ascending jeep with Israelis inside staring in disbelief at our ridiculous car. They whooped and cheered us along; I don't know if in mockery at our stupidity or applause at our bravery.

We continued torturing the car towards Har Tzor—famous for its unusual rock formations caused by wind erosion. Unfortunately, we failed to find it and almost ended up getting completely lost in the desert. Yet again, the desert had changed. In the previous deserts, there were always some indications of past civilizations, but *this* desert was pure virgin. If virgin forests could exist, why not virgin deserts? As far as one can see in all directions, there is just unforgiving, rugged, harsh terrain with thorny bushes, and we started seeing the low and wide acacia trees more frequently. But lifeless it was not; there were usually some small lizards scurrying around, and I'm sure there were plenty of snakes hiding under those boulders.

Small herds of wild camels placidly roamed around in peace and solitude, and occasionally would block our way; whereas, we had to "shoo" the creatures away. They took no notice of us, but looked down their noses at these two pathetic human beings with their laughable car, which could probably fit under a camel; and *this* vehicle was meant to shoo them away? They didn't budge... but turned their not-so-pretty-side in our direction and decided to meditate. That was it! This meant war! Reaching the end of our tether, we both shot out of the car like a bullet and ran towards the dromedary creations. With flailing arms and screaming like lunatics and making (worse-than-camel) noises, we launched a verbal attack. It worked, and we proved the fact that size was no factor. We saw only one other person—a lone Bedouin, but, like the camels, he also took no notice of us as if we were invisible. He seemed to be in a world of his own. His face was so charred and weathered, it reminded me of a pickled walnut I had once seen.

It was impossible to continue along this horrendous track... and the car was suffering. The wheels were getting stuck in the sand more frequently now, churning it up without being able to grip anything. We had to abandon this insanity and turn back, having taken six hours to travel a mere twenty-five kilometers.

Consulting the map, we were able to get onto a better road (without camels) and eventually an asphalted one again. Now we were heading south again to King Solomon's Mines in Timna Valley, an area that has been mined for copper for several thousand years. It was a quick tour as we were trying to beat the encroaching darkness. More elements were against us—a sandstorm started to blow, painfully blasting our exposed flesh, but it was worth the endurance as we gasped at the most fascinating works of natural erosion by wind and sand upon red sandstone and granite. With the sinking sun, the last pink rays made these natural wonders dazzle.

We came to a stop after another 30-minute drive, having traveled from the most northern point to the southern tip of Israel. In Eilat, we became part of the tourist mob for a few evening hours, enjoying our last evening. I was not sorry to end the trip, as sleeping in the car had become quite intolerable for the body. Tonight we left the vehicle and crashed out on Taba beach among the usual howls of wild dogs or wolves or whatever howled out there. The wind was fairly strong and the sand was drifting, but at least it was dry and warm, and that was the important thing.

Huddled in our sleeping bags didn't help. The blowing sand found its way inside. My nostrils and ears were full of it, as well as my scalp… and my hair was so matted, the brush wouldn't go through it. Being in this embarrassing state the next morning, we didn't venture into town for breakfast, but made do with the food we had and ate on the beach. Eilat is full of clean, shaven, and neatly-groomed tourists staying in nice expensive hotels, and we didn't want to scare anybody, looking as if we had just entered the Promised Land after forty years of wandering. It was much too windy to go for a swim and the Red Sea was wild, so we just had to make do with our sandy bodies and wait until we got back to the kibbutz tonight. Oh, I was so much looking forward to that shower!

Being the last day, we saved the best till last; something we had been looking forward to—the Hai Bar Biblical Nature Reserve: a wildlife sanctuary constructed to repatriate animals native to the region in biblical times. The park warden pointed out areas on the map for the best animal sightings. We soon noticed we were practically alone in this reserve, as we slowly drove between small herds of ibex, gazelles, wild donkeys, addax, oryx, and ostriches. The majority of these animals had been imported from the East African continent and have adapted to this region due to similarities in vegetation and climate. The landscape is made up of sand, dry brush and low acacia trees—a typical savanna which is found in large regions of East Africa. A sandstorm was still blowing, and quite surprisingly, rain started falling, too, but this didn't last long.

While making a brief stop to have lunch in the car, a sharp, loud tap on the window alerted our attention. Nearly choking on food with fright, I found myself face to face with the ugliest ever, freaky-looking ostrich. It seemed to have appeared out of nowhere, but maybe it had been hidden amongst the bushes nearby, taking us by surprise. It was *very* interested in our food and I was grateful we were not eating outside, having at least the window between us and that monstrous bird. The tapping on the window became more rapid and the ostrich became more frenzied while approaching the car from all angles and doing its best to get inside. The best thing to do was to start up the engine and drive away… but it was no use. The monstrous bird started giving chase, attacking the car from behind. We were getting very nervous as this nasty animal with its wide open beak, and with a crazed, primordial look in its eyes, started kicking the car with its powerful hoofs (or whatever ostriches called their feet) and possibly causing serious damage to it. How would we explain this to Budget Car Rental Agency? I didn't think there was anything in the insurance coverage clause referring to ostrich assault. Still being chased and attacked, we approached an area where the addax roamed, and these wonderful animals chased off the unsuccessful over-sized bird, and we were left in peace with rapid, beating hearts. "Hooray" to the addax. "Down" with ostriches!

On our return journey back home now, we drove through a region that picture postcards are made of—Red Canyon Gorge and Moon Valley. In addition to being an area of geological wonder, it is also a hiking dreamland. The only word we could muster to describe the scenery was… "wow." We desperately wanted to get out of the car and do some serious hiking in this area, but the fierce wind and incessant lashing sand made it impossible to even open the door. It was also unusually cold for this region, which is usually one of the hottest areas in Israel. The drive towards

Makhtesh Ramon (a giant meteorite crater), which we also wanted to see, was not easy as the storm picked up in intensity. The further north we drove, the stronger the wind became, making it most difficult to keep the vehicle centered when the road started to move, or appeared to, when the sand drifted across. Occasionally, our view would be totally obscured by a sudden spurt of sand in front of the car, and we had to stop. We reached the town of Mitzpe Ramon just as it turned dark and a torrential downpour was upon us.

The Negev town of Mitzpe Ramon was much worse than we had imagined. It made sleepy Qiryat Shemona (up in the north) look like a cheery party town in comparison. Because of the almost nil employment, most of the residents here had long since moved out, leaving over 400 apartments empty. This really was a good example of a modern-day ghost town. The anticipation of finding at least a café to have a hot drink and some food, rapidly diminished to desperation, if not urgency. This town was dead! Deader than the Tombs of the Kings in Cyprus. We were dead, too: totally bushed and famished, and there really was nothing here. Nothing—a mere ghost town in the desert... or maybe all the residents were hiding from the storm.

Not wanting to spend another night in the car in this horrendous place (and hungry, too), we decided to continue home and brave the now atrocious weather conditions. The rain had let up for a while to let the sandstorm have another lash, then to our utter amazement, it started to snow! *Here* in the heart of the desert—*insane.* At once, we were forced to make an abrupt stop as the blizzard conditions completely obscured our view. All elements of nature were upon us, trying their best to get us stranded; only fire and brimstone were missing. What had we done to deserve this? Did we invoke some curse or bad luck from some ancient spirits we had accidentally offended during our journey? Even the animals had attempted to disrupt this journey. But we battled on—through the snow—rain—wind—sandstorm— and came out victorious.

Our list of "must see" places was not completely checked off—thanks to the freaky weather. Proceeding any further would have been futile. These sandstorms tend to last for days. Our arrival back on the kibbutz coincided with *Purim*, and everyone had gone mad that evening—dressed up in bizarre costumes. It was carnival time, and the kibbutz was as wild as the weather. Loud South American music was blaring out of giant speakers, and there was (wild) dancing, with drinks and food galore. It felt so good to be back for a well-deserved sleep *and* to have some good food down our system. I was simply too exhausted to participate in anything and just yearned for a real bed after the shower, which soon filled up with sand from my body. An African bushman in a grass skirt and scary face markings whacked me on the back when he saw me, then threatened me with a spear. It was Carlos dressed up. "We got into the *ulpan*," he told me with excitement.

"When did the letter come?" I asked fuzzily.

"Last week. The language course begins in May. It's on kibbutz Ein Shemer, near Hadera... and... you look *terrible*... you don't even *need* a costume."

"Thanks. Where's Hadera?" I wanted to know.

"North."

Oh, well. I would check the map tomorrow to see where it was located. Right now, I just wanted to sleep, but Carlos the bushman kept talking. I was even too tired to share the excitement. The wind outside was still blowing and rain was falling on the parched desert landscape. This was good: in a couple of weeks the desert will bloom in spectacular colors.

While we were gone, a Jewish group of lively South Americans had arrived to spend six months in the Promised Land. Portuguese and Spanish now dominated our group: they came from Brazil, Uruguay, Argentina, and a couple from Peru. The Peruvians were strange and kept mostly to themselves. The Brazilians came (with high expectations) mostly from Rio's affluent Copacabana region, *and* were complaining about their simple accommodation. The Argentinians reminded us English that The Falklands belonged to them, and considered themselves the more superior of the South Americans. I liked the Uruguayans the most, who were very content with everything here without a peep of complaint. Overall, it was a very interesting group of about fifteen.

We still had the the car for a couple more days, and to take advantage of this, made short trips to the nearby towns of Ashkelon, Ashdod, and further north to Jaffa, then the car deserved a thorough wash before returning it to the car rental agency in Tel Aviv. The Fiat Uno had endured as much abuse as an all-terrain vehicle: persevering through snow-covered roads in the northern mountain regions; being pelted by sandstorms; leered at by the Israelis in their fancy desert-terrain vehicle; snubbed by wild camels, who pointed their rears in mockery, and the demented ostrich who thought that anything smaller than "it" was worth bullying. The bumper had some noticeable dents in it, but nothing *too* bad.

The very friendly woman at Budget greeted us. "Can I help you?"

"We're returning the car." She sent someone along to pick it up. He had a pad in his hand, probably for listing all the damages. The man just checked it over inside and walked briskly around it, hesitating at the rear while feeling the dents with his fingers and scribbling on his pad. "From an ostrich," we told him.

"What?" He didn't seem to hear while still taking notes.

"An ostrich attacked the car." Only after saying this, we realized how bizarre this excuse actually sounded. Car rental man just looked at us, shrugged his shoulders, and that was it. I didn't think he really cared; after all, any damages were covered by insurance—ostrich or whatever!

"Thank you, come again," was all he said. We were gone in a flash.

12
HEBREW IN A PUFF OF SMOKE

I left Kibbutz Nir Itzhak together with my friend Carlos to go and study Hebrew on yet another kibbutz—Ein Shemer. Such Hebrew study courses are known as *Ulpan* and are designed for new Jewish immigrants who seek a total immersion course with the intention of settling in Israel. The Hebrew word for this procedure is *aliyah*, which means "to go up." This is how Jewish immigration to Israel is perceived. As well as studying, there will also be some organized educational trips. I couldn't believe how I ended up being so lucky to get onto one free of charge, and I was really grateful for it. The duration of the course was eighteen weeks—until the end of September, and they reminded me of the absolute intensity of this course. The studies take place four hours each day, six days a week, and we also had to contribute four hours of work a day *and* find some time to study, too. It was going to be tough.

As soon as we arrived, we were shown to the students' housing and led to our basic rooms, which had four beds, a couple of tables, and several chairs. It was sufficient, and typical for student accommodation. I was to share the room with Carlos and two American guys—one from a small town in Virginia, the other one from Detroit. They were the perfect roommates, and we soon made friends. The remainder of the students, numbering about thirty, were all from various Central and South American countries, and Spanish was the dominant language.

The course started the next day and we were divided into two groups: those who already knew some Hebrew (like Carlos), and those who knew nothing (like me). Our teacher's name was Astrid, but we ended up calling her *Ashtray*, as she was a chain-smoker with a permanent overflowing ashtray on the table. She even smoked in class and was constantly coughing while teaching. When her coughing spasms took the lesson over, she lit up another cigarette, and this miraculously subdued her cough. There was incessant chatter in Spanish throughout the lessons, making concentration very difficult. Ashtray taught in Hebrew and English in her rough, smoky voice, and it didn't take me long to realize that she was not a good teacher; not even being capable of controlling the Spanish chaos in the classroom. The result was that I had no idea what was going on or what we were supposed to be learning. Some of the students didn't speak a word of English *or* Hebrew, so they *really* look confused. My Virginian room mate was in my group, too, and was also having a hard time trying to comprehend what the hell was going on. We received tons of homework every day and lots of vocabulary to learn. Four hours of work went on top of that, so there wasn't really much time for lounging around. I was assigned to the kitchen—quite easy work, taking dishes off the conveyor as they came around. I was quite adept at this after my first experience on Kibbutz Ha'ogen with unloading hot dishes.

The kibbutzniks here were quite aloof; in fact, it was the most unreceptive kibbutz I have been on so far. Mostly elderly people lived here, and they didn't seem to like the intrusion of the temporary visitors. Without the young *ulpan* students, Kibbutz Ein Shemer would have acquired the gloomy atmosphere of Qiryat Shemona. We certainly didn't feel welcome at this place, and I couldn't understand why the kibbutz offered this language course here if they didn't wish to be bothered? None of them made an attempt to engage us in any conversation, so the result was, I continued speaking English and the South Americans carried on with their Spanish.

The food replicated the ambiance of the kibbutz: rather bland and repetitive, as every day was the same unappetizing breakfast. They hadn't discovered spices or salt at this place yet; maybe the ancient Spice Route never made it here. All the vegetables were overcooked, and even the chicken was tasteless. There were no nice desserts or halva to go with my coffee. I was going to starve to death here, I knew it. The South Americans played around with their food, too, and made contorted faces.

The following week, Carlos and I returned to Kibbutz Nir Itzhaq: our friends were getting married and we were invited to the wedding. The celebration provided an opportunity to fatten up before the onslaught of Hebrew studies.

After yet another week of study, I took a few days off to spend my birthday in Jerusalem. Not wanting to travel alone, I asked my American roommates to join me—my umpteenth visit to the Old City. I simply enjoyed being here surrounded by ancient monuments and strolling through the aromatic Arab *souks*. This is one place one can never tire of, and there was always something new to discover; not surprising, as there are thousands of years of history in this city, mostly underground though.

A visit to Jerusalem is incomplete without a stopover by the Wailing Wall, and to round off this pleasant evening, a feast of roast chicken and watermelon. I couldn't imagine at the time a finer way to spend a birthday. This day was also the height of Ramadan—the Muslim time of fasting, with a record number of Arabs arriving to pray in the Al'Aqsa Mosque. Jerusalem is the third most holy place to Muslims after Mecca and Medina, and they all wanted to be here today. All the roads were congested due to this mass of people; so much in fact, that some of the drivers had lost patience waiting for the traffic to start moving, that they resorted to driving on the sidewalks. Chaos and madness had set in Jerusalem, and I considered myself lucky having found accommodation so easily, but that was only because I had now become very familiar with most of the alleys, twists and turns, and steps leading into dark, spooky, uninviting places, where undiscovered antique shops, cheap and basic hostels, and amazing places to eat offered the adventurer the true spirit of Jerusalem. Regular tour groups would shudder at the thought of entering such areas. It was in such an area in the Arab Quarter where we stayed and the full flavor of the city manifested itself upon us; its eerie vibes sending a chill down my spine —a thrill that I relished.

That night, there was a PLO demonstration and a riot among Palestinian youths outside Damascus Gate. A petrol bomb was thrown at a passing Israeli bus, but nobody was hurt. The Israeli army came in to disperse the crowds.

I spent the Sabbath in the Old City—touring the whole perimeter on top of the city wall known as Rampart's Walk. This wall is like a miniature version of the Great Wall of China, and it is possible to view the city from a different perspective. This was my first attempt at this fascinating walk to see the different contrasts in standards of living; from the ancient living quarters of East Jerusalem, to the more modern high-standard artist centers in the Jewish Quarter. The walk upon the wall also took us through the Armenian Quarters and the many churches that abound in the Old City. The riots which had taken place at Damascus Gate the previous night were over, and life there continued as it had done for many centuries. It was a good spot to rest and pick up a delicious ring of sesame-coated bread. I bought more of those rings and other Arabic goodies to take back to the kibbutz to help me through the hunger pangs.

A month of Hebrew studies was over—my head was full and so were my lungs with Ashtray's smoking. Learning Hebrew on this course was much more complicated and difficult than I first anticipated. The lessons were terrible—unplanned and without any structure, disrupted by the disturbing, incessant chatter during class. I was now convinced that Ashtray was not a real teacher. I did get something out of the course though—a hot-blooded Israeli girlfriend (Tamar), who I finally met in the dining room one day after eyeing each other up the last couple of weeks. We got together in her room in the evenings, but she wasn't much help in practicing Hebrew as her English was perfect, so we ended up speaking English all the time. Her parents had immigrated to Israel from Iraq, but she was born in this country, which makes her a *Sabra* (A Jew who was born in Israel). In the next months, I diverted my attention to "other" Israeli studies... and lagged behind with my homework.

All the *ulpan* students ate in the usual communal dining room together with the kibbutzniks. We were there three times a day—for breakfast, lunch and dinner. We didn't really mingle with the kibbutzniks, neither did they make any attempt to befriend us. One evening while sitting together with all the other students, Carlos asked me to go and ask for some more chocolate spread from the kitchen, as I had already finished eating. "Sure, no problem. What's chocolate spread in Hebrew?" I asked him. He gave me the word and I went off to the kitchen to ask for "shit spread," and from the bewildered look I detected from the kitchen woman, it suddenly dawned on me that Carlos had purposely given me the wrong translation. "What on earth did I say?" I wondered. Back at the table, everyone was in stitches and Carlos was killing himself with laughter. "What did I say?" I demanded.

"There's… no more… shit spread… here… " He tried to squeeze the words out, still guffawing and half choking with tears streaming down his cheeks.

"OH, MY GOD! I SAID… THAT?" I mentioned the disbelieving reaction from the kitchen woman, and that brought on more fits of laughter, and I laughed with them this time. In a dull kibbutz such as this, it was essential to have fun.

I still hadn't seen Nazareth, and the following Sabbath morning provided that opportunity as I regrouped with my friends and attempted to hitchhike all the way. Instantaneously a car stopped, which took us a part of the way, then another friendly, chatty driver brought us to the center of the city and briefly educated us on the history of Nazareth.

Despite its exotic past, Nazareth today is a modern Christian Arab city full of churches, which were built to commemorate Christ's childhood. The overall city is not so interesting unless one is a church freak. A stroll among the Arab market was another disappointment—it was crammed with touristy bits and pieces and innumerable Holy Family memorabilia. An attractive church courtyard captured our attention as we wondered in to look around. It was probably lunch time, as the door we came through was slammed shut behind us suddenly… and locked. We were stuck inside… and the high stone walls surrounding the gardens prevented any means of escape. This was most amusing, and we had no idea when the gate would be opened again. Not wanting to find out, we had to look for an alternative exit. The only way out was to climb up one of the lower walls and trespass across someone's garden.

We also visited the beautiful Basilica of Annunciation: a modern, but impressive piece of architecture built on the site of Mary's house, where Gabriel the angel announced to the world at large that the Virgin Mary had conceived. Despite the pleasant churches, the atmosphere was marred by the number of mass-produced artifacts of Mary and Joseph belligerently thrust into people's faces. Ensnared tourists searched for an escape passage inside this trap while hounded by Mary and Joseph. The demise of Nazareth was rampant, and if I were to list the top five most boring places to visit in Israel, Nazareth would be there. After a feast of falafel and some coffee, we effortlessly hitchhiked back to the kibbutz.

The trips continued: this time an organized one by the kibbutz. We traveled to a holocaust museum and Rosh Hanikra. The holocaust museum was based on a kibbutz near Haifa. There, we were shown a film about the holocaust and many disturbing original scenes that had taken place under the Nazis. A survivor from Auschwitz hosted the program and gave a real life description of her sufferings in the concentration camp. She was still disturbed to this day and still could not have any contact with a German. There is even a sign at the entrance to the holocaust museum forbidding entry to Germans. An interesting discussion was held afterward, which could have continued forever, but we were running out of time to our main destination.

Rosh Hanikrah is a coastal resort situated on the Lebanese border. What attracts all the tourists here are the beautiful chalk-white cliffs and grottos, sculptured by the ever-pounding waves. A cable car is used to descend to the grottos where it is possible to wander around the caves and rock pools filled with clear blue seawater. This is a beautiful part of the Mediterranean, and I'm sure the coastline becomes even more striking inside Lebanon. The breathtaking panoramic view of these two countries can be witnessed from the perfectly perched café high up on the hill. Next to the cafeteria is the border station where Israeli troops cross over on their way to and from Lebanon every time they decide to make group excursions inside the country. This café is also the Israeli army hangout because of its location. They can cozily sit here and drink coffee while keeping eyes open on any new cross-border developments.

Meanwhile, here we were, lounging in the café and enjoying the view, being totally oblivious to the fact that we were sitting in one of the most dangerous places to be in the world—a place where a katyusha rocket can be launched at any time from Lebanon, and land directly in the café. But everything seemed so peaceful around us, and any potential threat (if there was any) was well disguised. Israeli holiday makers still came to this border beach resort, but this demonstration of "everything-is-okay" was just an illusion. The lingering reminder of the danger was the constant presence of armed soldiers. This is typical of Israelis: to build a resort directly on the border to an enemy country, to make a point that they are not going to cower.

After a couple more weeks of studying, I took off once again with a bunch of friends to Ein Gedi—the Dead Sea resort. It was becoming increasingly challenging trying to get some time off from studying to make some trips… and the teacher was *not* too happy about it, especially as I was *not* the best student. I was either going off somewhere or spending my time with Tamar. There were four of us—myself, the two American guys, and an American girl, who was also studying Hebrew. We took three days off, and once again attempted to hitchhike to our destination. We split up into two pairs, but I was not so lucky with my partner, being unusually unsuccessful this time. We ended up having to use the public transport all the way. As we had split into two groups, we met on Ein Gedi beach in the late afternoon. The other two had better luck with hitchhiking. A German girl and a Canadian guy we bumped into later that day joined our jolly group and accompanied us for the rest of the trip.

It had taken most of the day to get here, and it was too late to do anything physically exhausting, as we were worn out ourselves. The fierce July heat was at its peak and there was no escaping these baking temperatures. A pleasant float in the Dead Sea was an attempt to cool off, but even *that* had little effect, especially as it was well over 40°Celsius outside.

Locating a perfect spot on the rocky beach was not a simple matter. A palm tree provided partial shade from the fierce sun's rays and seemed the likely spot to roll out our sleeping bags. In the evening, we hunted around the beach for firewood and charcoal that was always left behind by previous visitors. Turkish coffee was soon cooking over the open fire… and served together with sandwiches and sweet goodies from the kibbutz that we had managed to scrounge for our trip. Somehow, coffee and food seem to taste better when eaten during camping trips around a fire. We discussed our Hebrew course and the disruptive classes, then the conversation was steered to plans for the next day.

Sleeping turned out to be a challenge due to the endless pounding of *darbuka* drums and oriental music being blasted out most of the night.

Today being Friday—the Muslim holy day, some of the Arab population of Jerusalem was spending their day off camping with their families. Constant arguments would break out between them throughout the night, some of them sounding quite violent. These people never seem to have a quiet discussion; it's always loud arguments, or maybe it's their way of having a polite conversation. Israelis were the same, and often waived their arms around while shouting. We were the only bunch of foreigners sleeping on the beach, surrounded by mostly Arab families, and what looked like Orthodox Jews, recognizable by their black *kippahs*. Some women, dressed in oriental garb, cackled in an unrecognizable language, but they must have been local—maybe Armenians from Jerusalem? Overall, it was very mixed, and I couldn't comprehend what all the fighting was about in Israel when everybody here seemed to have one thing in common—peace.

Oppressive heat made sleeping difficult. We were sprawled over our sleeping bags, stripped down to shorts and lying under the stars, waiting and hoping for the slightest breeze. Sweat was pouring off me so much that I couldn't stand it any longer... and went back into the Dead Sea, which was warm anyway. The water looked as black as oil in the darkness and was absolutely still, like a mirror. Not a ripple disturbed this perfectly still lake. I did. I was soon joined by my roommate who was also melting. Being in the Dead Sea in the middle of a beautiful summer night evoked a feeling of magic. On both sides of this rift valley are the silhouetted mountains of Jordan and Israel, which were responsible for the lack of air movement. There was no moon out this night, but the light given off by the trillions of dazzling stars was enough to see the shapes of ghostly rock formations. The drum pounding and yelling had stopped a while ago, and the only sound was the faint trickle of water caused by us—the insomniacs, getting back out of the Dead Sea. I showered off the salt under the nice cool showers that aligned the shore and went back to lie down on my towel without drying off, trying to make myself comfortable with a smooth rock as a pillow under my folded T-shirt. I finally drifted off to sleep.

Our group started off on an extra long hike the next morning through the Ein Gedi oasis. At the outset of our hike among low acacias, we came across frolicking hyraxes and herds of ibex. The hyraxes were too busy chasing each other among the bushes to notice us; neither did the ibex pay any attention as they carried on eating anything green they could find.

The first part of the trek took us to a waterfall, where we did the most logical thing in this heat—to strip off and have a cold shower underneath the falls. The German girl stripped quite a lot off, but I assumed she was *really* hot. We continued to climb steep crags—difficult in the heat, which made me feel nauseous. It was still early morning, but the sun was already merciless, scorching every living thing in the desert. From one of the peaks, the vast expanse of the Dead Sea was barely discernible as the heat haze obscured most of the view, making it appear like a shimmering mirage. The landscape looked equally unforgiving with its maze of twisted canyons, eroded by sudden flash floods, which occurred during freak storms. It was a lunar type of landscape: very bleak and colorless in parts, with intricately-shaped rock formations caused by wind erosion. Beautiful as it was, it was deadly to get lost in this area. At this point, after two hours, one of the participants in our group (my Virginian roommate) dropped out due to the intolerable heat, and returned to camp.

The next resting place was the cool shelter of Dodin's Cave, where cold water trickled through each crack. All the water in this area is potable as it comes from underground springs—quite delicious and cold. Taking advantage of natures refrigerated offering, we filled up our almost empty containers, but even with full ones, it was still not enough. It was being drunk at an alarming rate, thanks to the salty air which added to the permanent thirst. Without the natural spring water, it wouldn't have been possible to attempt this hike in summer. We would've had to carry several more containers, but didn't have enough hands.

Continuing the trek, we passed ruins of a Chalcolithic temple that has been dated to around 3500 BCE. The Chalcolithic Period even predates the Bronze Age. Although intriguing to archaeologists, who are able to decipher the historical significance of this site, to the naked eye, it is just a jumble of rocks. After five hours, we reached the Ein Ghedi spring. Here, another participant dropped out (the other American) and returned to camp because of the unendurable heat and arduous trek. It was only another hour's walk to the largest waterfall in the area at Nahal Arugot. The four of us pressed on, determined to reach it. As long as I had a supply of water, it was possible to go on. Surprisingly, the hiking and dodging of loose rocks was becoming easier. After just over six hours, the thunderous sounds of the waterfall could be heard in the distance. We made it. Arriving there, we found the place swarming with people—mostly soldiers having the same idea of cooling off as we did. Most people (the soldiers too) kept their clothes on inside the rock pool—a good idea as this would help them to stay cool in this heat. I hated wet clothes clinging to my body, no matter how hot outside, but I had no other clothes on except my shorts, which I took off to keep dry as I entered the pool and waterfall. The water was freezing—a stark contrast to the surroundings, but the stimulating powers of this instant cooling would invigorate the return trip.

Feeling fully charged after that refreshing dip, we decided to make the return journey along the main road, as nobody could face retracing the same route back. It would have taken another six hours, and we would soon have run out of drive. By using the road, it was only about a third of the distance. True, it was not as picturesque, but our concern was to return to camp before dark. We only stopped once: this was to let a large herd of ibex cross the road in peace. After two more hours, we finally reached our spot on the beach, only to find the other two members of our group enjoying ice cream and cold drinks and having a conversation with some soldiers. I did the same: bought an ice cream and a can of my favorite mango juice straight out of the fridge. The nearby hotel also had a small refreshments store for desperate Dead Sea survivors who were dying to get their tongue on anything cold.

Most of the campers from the previous night had already left, so the beach appeared almost desolate. Our backpacks and sleeping bags were where we had left them. There was still one large group of Arabs staying here—they were drumming into the night around the fire. I was glad they were here; it was a reminder that we were in the Middle East, and without them it would have been *too* quiet. They beckoned us to join them. "Where you from?"

"Different countries," we explained.

"Welcome," and they offered us some delicious freshly-brewed coffee.

We collected leftover wood for our fire, also dry ibex dung, which are amazing fire starters (we were informed by the Arabs), and after cooking our dinner on open flames that evening, the lot of us took to the Dead Sea again and formed a human chain while performing water aerobics. We ignored the "max-stay-20-minutes" sign, as the high concentration of salt is supposed to do nasty things to the body if the soak in the water is exceeded. We stayed for about two hours. All the cuts and scratches inflicted by the day's hike came into fierce life in the water while the salt ate and tortured them. It was painfully agonizing, but the minerals would give the wounds a good cleansing, and after a while I didn't feel the pain anymore.

It was very dark and the current was surprisingly strong this night, and without realizing it, we had drifted right out to sea (lake) towards Jordan. The lights along the shore were only a dim flicker now, but on the Jordanian side, they had grown bigger. This was very frightening: either we would drown or get shot by the army for illegally trying to cross into a country that Israel had no diplomatic relations with. The borderline was in the middle of the Dead Sea, but the middle was still (luckily) far away. Panic stricken, the six of us started to swim back against the current, a difficult task due to the density of the water, and it required a lot of energy. It was necessary to avoid splashing, as any drop getting into the eye can cause the most excruciating pain, causing one to panic and splash even more. That is how a lot of people drown in the Dead Sea, even in the shallow ends. The shore lights grew bigger, and eventually we all arrived safely after nearly half an hour of hard swimming in very dense, oil-like water.

Fresh-brewed coffee and food soon made everyone get over the recent fright, and we were soon laughing at the incident. Afterward, myself and one of my friends returned to the sea with tubs of ice cream (from the hotel shop that never seemed to close), eating them afloat and making sure we stayed near the shore. We spent the night under the stars once again, and also fought with the rocks to try and get comfortable. I was trying to figure out the position I had slept in last night, but the rocks seem to have moved. This night, I had sharp protrusions under my sleeping bag, which I could have sworn were not there the previous night. Even my rock pillow didn't feel as smooth. Strange! The drums died out, so did the fire, and only the occasional, final crackle of the dying embers was the only sound that broke the perpetual silence in this vast, desolate, and barren rift valley. And I tried to imagine how it would have looked when nomadic tribes wondered through during the Chalcolithic Period, then the early Israelites, and the battle-ready Romans on their way to Masada. All must have gathered in Ein Ghedi at some time to quench their thirst in this oasis where natural spring water has been flowing for thousands of years.

We split up into groups again and hitched rides to Jerusalem the next morning, and then caught a late afternoon train back to Hadera. This was my first and last train trip in Israel. In such a modern country, the railway network is surprisingly primitive, for the simple reason that trains are very rarely used, even though they are a cheaper alternative to bus travel. The journey to Hadera took over three hours compared to just two on the bus. Nevertheless, the pleasant train ride wound through a different part of the country, where steep, craggy hills dramatically boasted the most beautiful countryside, intermittent with lush, green vegetation; already a different planet compared to where we had just come from. The train chugged along very slowly... so slowly in fact, that it would have made any Cypriot happy.

Our arrival on the kibbutz coincided with the late evening dinner, and next day it was back to Hebrew studies. I seeked out Tamar in the dining room and filled her in on our Dead Sea adventure. We spent the rest of the evening together, and the following day I was dead in class with my mouth in a permanent yawning position, but Astrid didn't seem to notice... or she didn't care. Tamar was usually free in the late afternoon, and we often took advantage of those few hours and hitchhiked to the nearby town of Afula, where we usually ended up in the ice-cream shop.

My friend Carlos decided to leave the course and the kibbutz, as none of the lessons were advanced enough for him. He was wasting his time here, not learning anything. His only conversations were in English, Spanish, and Portuguese, but not Hebrew. He left, disappointed and disillusioned. I never saw him again after that.

Couple of weeks later, we had another organized excursion: this time to Nablus where we attended a seminar on Jewish values. This was for three days and it was in English. Once again—no Hebrew practice. I felt somewhat out of place here as I wasn't Jewish and I wasn't sure about my values, either. I became a listener rather than the participant. We met other *ulpan* students from other kibbutzim, which was the part I enjoyed the most. There were people from every corner of the globe, and a lot of potential immigrants amongst them who would add to the small population of Israel. I envied them for being Jewish and being able to settle in Israel at any time, but that would mean going to the army, too. The seminars taught us about the different wars Israel had had with its neighbors, how they started, and how Israel gained land because of them. We were now in the

West Bank, the part that used to belong to Jordan before Israel took it in the Six-Day War. These seminars were performed outdoors, while we sat on the grass in a shaded area, listening to stories about Israel. It was partly biblical, too, reminding everyone how Jews escaped from the Pharaoh in Egypt and made their way across the Sinai to the Promised Land. I enjoyed these seminars, finding them fascinating and most importantly, we were fed excellent food and desserts throughout the day. We learned how settlers came to this wilderness and tamed the land by planting imported trees from Australia that absorbed the swamps... and the introduction of irrigation in the deserts, where they became green. Everything to do with Israel was covered in this seminar, and I was sorry when it was over. Had I been a Jew, I would have been a very proud one after those three days.

My other roommate from Detroit decided to leave the course also. It was not serious enough for him. He would go to a *Yeshiva* in Jerusalem: an institution where the Jewish holy books are studied—the Torah and the Talmud. There, he would continue studying Hebrew. Being Jewish himself, he decided to take the orthodox path.

I was showing what I was learning to Tamar one evening and she cracked up laughing. "You can't say that in Hebrew," she argued.

"Why not? It's what we're learning; it's in the book," I countered.

"Because nobody speaks like that!" she assured me. "This is too formal and old-fashioned." She continued giggling at the phrases I was supposed to learn, but gave me different versions to what was in the books, assuring me that this was the colloquial form. True enough, after thinking about it, all our lessons *were* from books and no role-plays ever took place. We had to memorize phrases and words and that was all there was to it.

I stuck it out with the *ulpan* a while longer, then also decided to leave the kibbutz and the Hebrew studies, as I felt that we were not participating in the most important thing in my opinion—conversation practice. The lessons consisted of doing exercises from the same text book; also, the lessons were now performed solely in English instead of sticking to Hebrew. This also slowed down the learning process. I felt I had enough material to study on my own accord now; most important of all, I needed to be engaged in Hebrew conversation—something that never occurred in Ein Shemer as all the people I had met so far showed no desire to talk to any outsiders.

I did however, make some good friends with some of the young (but very few) Israelis during my stay, but they had to leave to go to the army. Sadly, that included Tamar, who was leaving at the end of the week—her military service would last almost two years. Without Tamar, prolonging my stay was meaningless. Carlos was gone... and so was my Detroit friend, who had decided to become religious and become a West Bank settler in the future. It was time to make a move again.

After a visit to the moshav recruiting office in Tel Aviv, I managed to procure a place on Moshav Ein Habsor, only 10km from the old Kibbutz Nir Itzhak, so naturally, I took the first bus to the kibbutz to see all my friends again. As the moshav was so near, it was very easy to hitchhike over to the kibbutz each week, especially for the tasty Sabbath dinners. The South Americans were still there, and the gorgeous, dark-haired, dark-eyed, dark-skinned Uruguayan girl (Rachel) I had been lusting after ever since the group arrived, had miraculously become available, so I took advantage of that situation. Now I had another good reason to visit the kibbutz.

The arrival on Moshav Ein Habsor was again a new chapter for me. Nicknamed "Dallas" by the locals, it is the richest moshav in the country. This moshav was founded by people who previously attempted to settle the Sinai by establishing a settlement there, but had to give it up once Israel gave the peninsula back to Egypt. The government then gave the misplaced tribe (once again escaping Egypt) sufficient funds to relocate and start a moshav here next to the Gaza Strip. I think *more* than sufficient funds were splurged out when I saw the affluence portrayed in the fancy architecture—certainly not what one would expect from pioneers. The living conditions for the volunteers were pretty good, too: with a great kitchen, toilet, shower, a separate dining room, TV, and a large sofa. Not bad at all. I hoped the people were friendly here.

They weren't. From my first impression, they seemed rather gruff with a chip on their shoulders. Maybe they were still irate about being uprooted out of the Sinai Desert. My boss was a questionable character; I wasn't sure what to make of him. He seemed friendly, but there was something about him that put me on guard. My gut feeling told me likewise—not to trust this character. The only good thing was that his English was much worse than my Hebrew; therefore, I had an opportunity to converse in his language.

This moshav also kept ostriches as I found out one evening while sitting outside and pouring the desert out of my boots. A boy was taking an ostrich for a walk... on a leash, as casually as if it had been a dog. After a physically exhausting day, I thought that I might be seeing things, but this was real.

Some of the farmers specialized in ostrich meat, which was exported to South Africa. There was also a separate building where ostrich eggs were incubated as they lay under heat lamps, waiting to be hatched. I momentarily felt sorry for these huge birds... being eaten, but quickly changed my mind again as I realized that they were actually monsters, as I recalled how my rental car was attacked by the same bird variety... "EAT 'EM ALL!"

At 7:00 A.M. the next morning, I put in a couple of hours of work, stretching enormous plastic sheets over the earth. Several rows had already been done. The idea was to suffocate the weeds. After sealing off any remaining air gaps, gas was pumped in to kill off any alien bodies. Wow! This was so unnatural. I asked the farmer what kind of gas he was using, but he wouldn't tell me. Was it even legal?

I went back to the kibbutz to spend the rest of the day with Rachel. My Israeli friends had also prepared a lot of nice food for me to take back to the moshav. This was most generous of them, as food is very expensive to buy here. I was also given a good supply of various fruits.

I was now back at work: weeding and trimming bushes. This was to take up about a week. The afternoon shift was spent planting flowers and chives. These would be ready for picking in winter—packed and shipped to Europe. The moshav occupies a vast area; bigger than any other farming communities I had seen in Israel. This used to be just another piece of desert wasteland, but irrigation changed that to rich farmland. The areas that were not being irrigated remained as parched as the wilderness described in the Bible.

I was invited to a party on Nir Itzhaq. My friend Yosi arranged a car to come over and pick me up. I think everybody on the kibbutz went crazy that evening. It was more extreme than Purim earlier in the year. There were people dressed up as clowns, and the club was turned into a posh cocktail bar while sex movies were being shown in the bomb shelter. Ice cream, cakes and drinks were in rich supply. There was no shortage of anything. It was a great evening, and I had to laugh when I thought back to Kibbutz Ein Shemer, trying to imagine something like this taking place there. It would cause a revolution. I stayed the night on the kibbutz, and as tomorrow was the Sabbath and my day off, Rachel and I tagged along to the beach near Rafiah with a group of Israelis who borrowed a minibus... well, the minibus was not actually borrowed, as everything on a kibbutz belongs to everybody, and all they needed to do was to sign up for it.

This is the perfect life here. After a week of arduous work in temperatures soaring to 44°Celsius, I really felt that I deserved this treat, and it felt like paradise just to swim and relax and do nothing. The kibbutzniks brought tons of food with them—enough for the whole kibbutz, and an endless supply of sugary, sweet watermelons. As with all excursions, the Israelis are never without their machine guns, especially in the disputed Gaza Strip, and two of them carried them around constantly, keeping a weary eye on the surroundings, but everything was perfectly peaceful. My blissful thoughts were discomforted by the inevitable return to work on the moshav tomorrow.

I was given an extra job of teaching English to the farmer's son for one hour each evening. A good move for me, as I also picked up more Hebrew this way, and it gave me good practice for teaching English in the future. (I was planning to make South America my destination, and once I finally get there, teaching English would be my key to earning money). The downside was, that the son was a bit on the thick side and did not really want to learn English, neither was he capable. He preferred to speak in Hebrew, which was okay with me, but I persevered, viewing this as a challenge.

The next couple of weeks were spent doing quite horrible work, which was to dip about 1,500 sticks in tar and then to place them at equal distances on the ground. These would be used for trailing tomatoes. I expected to hammer the sticks into the ground, but there was a more ingenious way of doing this. The holes were made by forcing water (from a metal nozzle, which was connected to a hose) into the rock-hard, sun-baked ground. When switched on, the force of the water shooting out of the nozzle breaks down and washes away the soil, leaving a neat hole for inserting the sticks into. This may seem like a waste of water, but the ground *is* rock hard here, and not even a sledge hammer would be able to penetrate a metal spike into it, so it makes sense to make holes by using this method—nothing can stop the sheer force of water. The pressure of the water came out in such force, it could easily tear off flesh from the bone.

I worked on this together with Abdul—a Palestinian from Rafiah who also worked for the farmer. Abdul was an older man who didn't speak a word of English, and his Hebrew wasn't much better either, so we didn't communicate much. Despite that, it didn't discourage his sharing his food with me, which I gladly accepted: it was always delicious, and to refuse would probably be taken as an insult. His pita bread was quite unique. He explained, in a mixture of Arabic and Hebrew, that one of his wives (he had three) bakes it at 4:00 A.M. every morning on a hot stone coated in olive oil. It was the olive oil that gave it this distinctive taste. He also made known, in a hushed tone and darting eyes, how terribly wicked the farmer was… and that I should be wary of him. Shmulik (the farmer) really was disliked. Many times I witnessed him treating Abdul like a slave—shouting obscenities at him in Arabic (which I understood). Poor Abdul just cowered. He needed this job for supporting his large family, and to answer back would have gotten him fired—he did not deserve such treatment, and I really despised Shmulik for this. His son was treated the same way, and I could see that he didn't think too highly of his father, either. In a nutshell, Shmulik was a bastard!

It was time to make plans for Europe. Both Rachel and I intended to travel together, and we both wanted to make Spain our destination, but it was difficult to decide how to achieve this. Whether to fly direct (too boring), or take a ferry to Greece and/or hitchhike from Athens to Seville (sounded more fun). The situation was not fantastic here on the moshav. The farmer was becoming too demanding, wanting more work out of me, and also starting to treat me like a slave. I even had to share the house now with three scowling English people who never seemed to shower and sat around in their work clothes all day long. Out came the booze, the loud music, and the usual innuendo of sobersided remarks. I looked forward to the weekends when I could go to the kibbutz for a couple of days and to be with my friends. Rachel came back with me one day and I noticed the English guy's eyes pop out. "Lucky bastard!" I heard him mutter.

Rachel decided to join me for the remainder of the time on the moshav, but this arrangement only lasted a day as the boss fired us both. His reason was that we spent too much time snogging instead of working. That was ridiculous; we did no such thing during our work... well, maybe a peck here and there. The farmer had a severe psychological problem, but I was thankful for this anyway—I absolutely hated this place. We both went back to the kibbutz, hoping to stay there as volunteers until we left for Greece in a couple of weeks.

There was more bad news the next day: We were informed we could not stay on the kibbutz as volunteers even though I was asked by Yosi and Ariel—to come and help pick mangoes before leaving Israel, but as the new volunteers' leader resented us both, his word was final. (Before I had left kibbutz Nir Itzhaq, a nice lady used to be the volunteers' leader. While I was away, she had been replaced by a *chach-chach (chach-chach = Israeli men of Eastern origin who display their hairy chests to the world at large, and everything they possess is transformed into gold and hung around their necks. They also listen to oriental music and consider themselves cool)*. The new "cool" *chach-chach* made a point that we could not stay as volunteers; instead, we ended up staying as guests of Yosi and Ariel. There was nothing the leader could do about this, no matter *how much* gold was wrapped around his neck—he was not able to deny anyone a guest. That made him furious and he completely ignored us after that. Next time we bumped into him, his shirt was buttoned up. Maybe he had ripped out his chest hair in fury.

The following day we went to Tel Aviv to buy our ferry tickets, some basic camping equipment, and to make travel inquiries. Our boat for Crete was two weeks later. We still had plenty of time to enjoy the city and stroll around some shops and cafés. I was ecstatic with the actuality of traveling with Rachel and couldn't wait to hit the road with her.

Mango picking had officially started. Finally, a dream came true—to pick and eat mangoes straight off the trees. This was the first time for me and I enjoyed every minute of the work. In the first hour, I did nothing but eat mangoes. There was mango juice all over my face and clothes, and the flies were also loving it. I was not the only pig—my friends were ferociously devouring with equal intensity. It felt good to be working together with them again, like back in winter in the citrus groves and avocado plantations. This time, they were speaking Hebrew with me and not English. I was amazed how much I had learned this year, and chatting in the orchards with them was more educational than during the Hebrew classes.

Everything has an opposite. The past few days had put me in a state of euphoria—today, I was devastated. Rachel had a phone call from Uruguay to return to her country immediately—her mother was very sick and in hospital. Suddenly, all our plans we had made were over—dashed—destroyed. So... what to do now? It was the second girlfriend I managed to lose in a couple of months. The Israeli girl left for the army, and now Rachel was being recalled back home. I was not having luck with girls. I went back to Tel Aviv to change the ferry ticket and bring the departure date forward by a week. Three other South American friends from the kibbutz wanted to join me on this trip. That was okay with me, I didn't feel like going alone.

Rachel was suddenly gone—on the plane back to Uruguay, but I had no time to be miserable about it... later though; right now, mangoes had to be picked. I spent the next few delicious days in the orchard again, picking and devouring, and almost bathing in mango juice. I was in an eating frenzy, like a werewolf tearing up flesh, but for me it was the mango flesh. Anyone who hasn't tried freshly-picked mangoes ripened on a tree has not attained the ultimate bliss on planet earth.

I finally left Kibbutz Nir Itzak for good and went to spend *Shabbat* with my Detroit friend in Jerusalem. He was doing his religious studies at the *Yeshiva*. He did ask me to come and visit him when opportunity arose. The students there (mostly Americans) were most welcoming, and I was invited to stay there even though my friend was away at the time. The Sabbath began with prayers in the evening; an alien performance I witnessed for the first time: confusing and very difficult to follow. Prayers were also chanted throughout the entire course of the meal. Sometimes it wasn't easy to know what one is supposed to do during the feast, as it was constantly interrupted by singing, praying, or having to get up to wash ones hands, then chanting a prayer once again before the hands were dried. I was told that the reason for this was to distract oneself from the food and concentrate solely on God.

During the Sabbath at the *Yeshiva*, one is not allowed to drive, to operate any kind of machinery, to switch on a light, flush a toilet, or even tear off a piece of toilet paper from the roll. Instead, ready-torn sheets of toilet paper are prepared before the commencement of the Sabbath, and all lights are left on. It would be a great sin to flick a switch. It is forbidden to listen to music or watch television, or even walk great distances or do exercises of any kind. For these people, *Shabbat* is to spend time in prayer and to be with ones families and friends.

I felt strange being here amongst all this. I felt it to be very lonely and cut off from the real Israel I knew. I was glad that the orthodox were a minority in this country—I couldn't bear to imagine how they would rule with religious fundamentalists in power. How could my friend have chosen such a life?

I went to the Old City after a tasty lunch at the Yeshiva, breaking one of their rules and thinking about the delicious food. A sin. Walking a great distance was another rule broken, therefore exerting a lot of energy, hence rule break number two. Another sin. Exerting energy meant a lot of exercise. Oh, dear—three broken rules! I was such a sinner! REPENT! I continued to sin and managed to change all the shekels I had into dollars, at the exchange rate of 1.70 shekels to the dollar on the black market. There was no legal way to change shekels into other foreign currencies

The last day in Israel! It was a good way to end it with a visit to Mea Shearim, the ultra-orthodox community in Jerusalem. The neighborhood has not changed for over a hundred years. Known as *Haredim*, they dress in the traditional way as they had done back in Eastern Europe two centuries ago. They are devoted to studying and living by the Torah—their holy book. Most of them live in crowded conditions, as most are poor. These people oppose the State of Israel, believing that only the coming of the Messiah can proclaim Israel into existence, otherwise Israel cannot exist. Neither do they serve in the army, but do enjoy a generous financial support from the religious political parties.

Signs around the neighborhood state that visitors must dress modestly and not to enter bare-headed. There was a pile of brown paper *kippahs* at the entrance to the neighborhood, which I donned on my head. I felt very much an intruder amongst these outlandish people. It was impossible to take any photographs—the rude people would yell at me (in American-accented English) to put away the camera... or they would cover up their faces when they saw the evil "picture-taking-thing." I had to be careful here. These folk wouldn't hesitate to take the camera and smash it, or even smash *me.* They are well known for their violence with the police and the public. Recently, they caused riots as a protest for showing movies during the Sabbath. The religious law forbids this. I wondered where they find this law in their ancient holy books where modern entertainment rules are spelled out. These ultra-orthodox fanatics had even burnt down bus shelters that had posters advertising bikinis on them. It is not unusual to read in the newspaper about gangs of ultra-orthodox men throwing rocks at passing vehicles who dare to drive on the Sabbath. Mea Shearim failed to inspire me with goodness and spiritual purity. It was a neighborhood inspiring hatred and zero tolerance towards anyone who was not one of them. Not my idea of religion—this was mere fanaticism from the Middle Ages. It was time to leave.

Saying goodbye to Jerusalem, I took the bus to the port of Haifa in the afternoon and walked the short distance to the ferry terminal. The Ba'hai Temple commanded the hill overlooking the city, and the golden dome glistened in sunlight. That was always the first thing I saw when I entered Haifa, but also the last, upon departure on the ferry. After finding my South American friends, we were split up at passport control where the Israelis interviewed us individually with the usual security questions. I already knew them by heart and was prepared with my answers.

At 7:00 P.M. it was goodbye to Israel. A very sad goodbye it was as the ferry made its way from Haifa port. I couldn't believe I was leaving Israel; all that had happened to me here, the experiences I had had, the places I had seen, but most of all—the close friendship I had forged in this fascinating land. I became very close to many people I had met, and now, as Israel was shrinking on the horizon, everything seemed like a dream. In a short time, everything would be history, and only my travel notes would remain as an emotional reminder of this wonderful life I was experiencing. The notes would help me remember, but friends' names would get mixed up, and faces would become a blur. It wasn't the end, I knew, but just the beginning of the next chapter and what lay ahead. I had to go on now and try to realize my plans to work in Europe and be in South America as soon as time permitted. I didn't know when I would return to Israel, as I had given up making plans. Now I took things as they came.

The crossing was good and so was the weather. There wasn't much to do on board except eat and play dominoes with an Israeli I met. His

English was atrocious, which was good for me—we spoke Hebrew all the time. I was feeling gloomy though, because my plans with Rachel didn't work out. It would've been so much fun to travel through Europe with her. Her English was quite disastrous, too, but she spoke Hebrew, and that was the language we had communicated in. Too bad she had to fly back home. She left me her address in Montevideo, Uruguay, so that I could stay at her house when I finally reached South America. Somehow, I knew I would never see her again—just a gut feeling. I couldn't explain it; maybe it was my karma, and this was the path my life was supposed to take.

As darkness descended, we all went to the first class lounge, which was out of bounds for deck passengers like us, but after a change of clothing we looked no different to those who paid through their noses to stay in private cabins, and our class was never questioned. We spent most of the night there listening to a live band performing very lively Greek music played on the mandolin, and as the night progressed, the music got louder and faster, and our jugs of wine became emptier and emptier.

Our first stop was Limassol in Cyprus. It was possible to disembark and visit the island for two and a half hours—sufficient time for me as I didn't need more than that. Together with my friends, I took the waiting bus to the city to seek out the tastiest kebabs in the world. It was just like I remembered it two years previously. I also took advantage of buying the popular and tasty Cypriot bread that is coated with sesame seeds and tiny flecks of liquorice. Fresh, it's delicious to eat by itself. At 12.30 we were back on board and continuing the journey to Crete, which was another twenty-seven hours away. More Greek bouzouki music and wine in the late evening proved a fine introduction to the arrival in Greece.

13
THE SEARCH FOR OLIVES

Crete is the largest of the Greek islands: unique with its mountainous landscape and miles of beautiful sandy beaches, some of them pristine and untouched by mass tourism. The northern part of the island is as touristy as Rhodes, while the south remains unspoiled and is a more attractive destination for the independent travelers or adventure seekers. Heraklion, the capital of the island, is the point of entry. This is where we disembarked in the second part of the afternoon, not knowing what to expect in the coming days and weeks.

Entering the country was very simple—there were no questions asked, no baggage looked into, and no passport control. We simply strolled off the ferry into the port and away into the city. The lack of security is always shocking after being used to the Israeli immigration. Heraklion is definitely no romantic Greek city or a nature lover's paradise. It is a typical dirty, noisy, polluted conurbation, and it could have been anywhere in Europe. It was as Greek as Liverpool and as charming as Manchester. Not wishing to hang around in this expensive city, we took a bus to Nikalaos, just to escape. The 90-minute bus ride brought us to the touristy eastern side of the island; not exactly what I was looking for, but considerably better and cleaner than Heraklion. The town resembled an English seaside resort, full of lobster-colored English sun worshipers and thrill seekers. Despite that, we did find some nice accommodation with a kitchenette and bathroom for 400 drachmas per night. At the current exchange rate of 130 drachmas to the dollar, it was quite a bargain—and sparkling clean. Having fun is what the people were doing here, and having fun we did likewise.

I went around the town on a motorcycle with the Israeli I met on the ferry, getting to see what there was in vicinity—not much! Mostly restaurants. Compared to Israel, meat is very cheap and delicious in Greece, so I quickly reverted back into a carnivore after a couple of hungry visits to various restaurants. There really wasn't anything to do here except eat and stay on the beach, then eat again. I couldn't understand why people chose to make such holidays and to travel so far if this is all they demand. Fun as it may be here, after the second day it becomes monotonous, and then it is time to leave. I was the lucky one—I could do that. The holiday makers were doomed for two or three weeks in their package deal (rather ordeal).

The English drink like fish and become louder as the moon rises, turning into monsters and behaving in a way that would not be tolerated in Great Britain. Such behavior was ubiquitous in all resorts where the British were bunched together. The sad part was—British passport holders were automatically tagged as violent drunks and hooligans—and not civilized tea drinkers who sat down for their afternoon rituals. Was drunkenness a way to relieve their boredom? Nobody would admit it—they will fly back home, burnt to a crisp, show stupid pictures of themselves in a bar while intoxicated, and tell everyone, "It was the greatest time ever!"

We intended to check out the work situation in this British town, where the language barrier would not be an issue, but our hopes were dashed: being September, it was practically the end of the tourist season and nobody was hiring in resorts this time of year. On our rented motorbikes, we drove the fifteen kilometers to Neapolis, a small town that has managed to retain its Greek atmosphere (and good coffee), despite the nearby Anglo-Saxon invasion. This place was ready to close down for the season and the whole town appeared deserted. The cafés and restaurants were open, but were void of customers. We were the only tourists enjoying the coffee and serenity of Neapolis, but the peacefulness was soon disrupted by our noisy motorcycles—the noise of the engines even more amplified in the narrow streets. The locals stopped to give us disapproving looks, as if to say, "Just go home now and leave us in peace." We did zip around a little longer though, to see as much of this pleasant town as possible. In the evening we let out some energy at the local disco in Nikalaos.

Enough! I can't stand tourist resorts for more than a day: that's why we hopped onto the first bus in the morning and ended up spending the entire day following the coastline to the western part of the island. The 300km sluggish and mind-numbing ride brought us to Chania, where the prospect of finding work was multiplied by the sheer array of activity in this town. We checked into the youth hostel for a very reasonable 350 drachmas per night—a squalid place with cold showers and nowhere to make food or coffee. The proprietor was grotesquely overweight, greasy-skinned, sweaty and dirty. He reminded me of *Bluto*, the cartoon character in *Popeye*. He was stuffed with food *and* money: his huge, round stomach overpowering the rest of his body, and a small, stubby head wobbled as he spoke. Despite his disheveled appearance, he did have work for us when asked, but only in construction. We could start tomorrow at 7:00 A.M. Well, might as well have a go at it, nothing to lose.

First day at work... and the last! My Israeli friend and I ended up doing all the heavy, difficult laboring while the regular Greek workers preferred to stand around and relieve their duties upon two foreigners. As we toiled, they sniggered with perverted pleasure while an innuendo of obscenities was passed around amongst the Greeks—directed at us, of course. We were digging out the earth in order to make a foundation for a building—one of many that were being erected. The seven hours of hard labor came with a good breakfast and put 2,000 drachmas into my pocket—not much, but at least it was a start. The boss however, turned out to be good-natured, unlike his primordial team, but I didn't think I could do this kind of work—it really was not for me.

Back at the youth hostel, we just collapsed onto the bunks and died for the rest of the day. Bluto was already sprawled out on his throne with an empty plate next to him. He was snoring with his mouth open, and I was so tempted to put a cockroach down it—I'm sure he would have enjoyed a little extra snack.

I didn't want to stay in this awful place, so we rented a small apartment next to the attractive Venetian harbor for 2,000 drachmas, divided between the five of us. This beautiful and modern accommodation had a nice clean bathroom, a kitchenette, and hot showers—quite a luxury for us. The little extra for this comfort was well worth it, and the location couldn't have been more perfect—directly in the center. Town centers would normally put me off, but in this beautifully picturesque harbor town it was *the* place to be. The nights here are particularly lively with blaring Greek *Bouzouki* music; shops and restaurants are open and everybody is happy. The most beautiful setting are the rows of tavernas and cafés lining the Venetian harbor, providing an uninterrupted view of the lighthouse. I loved this place even though it was filled with tourists: mostly Germans, British, Dutch and Danish, as well as Greeks from the mainland. Somehow, this town has managed to retain its Greek heritage without resorting to mass tourism like on the eastern side of the island.

We bid farewell to the two Brazilian girls. The stress and the feeling of insecurity was too much for them. They were hoping to pick up casual work in a café or restaurant, but as before, nobody was hiring this late in the year. The girls never had to work before for a living, so it finally dawned on them that they may need money to survive. To their amazement, dollars did not simply fall from the sky. They went back to Israel where they could be looked after.

There were now three of us left—Avner the Israeli, Edmundo the Brazilian, and myself. We did try out work in construction again; this time with a different boss who was paying 3,000 drachmas for a day's work, including food. We didn't do any digging this time, but the work was equally strenuous, having to lug bags of concrete from the trailer and to pour out the contents onto a surface that had already been cleared for forming a foundation. This was weird. The concrete powder was not mixed with water as it should have been, and then the liquid poured into a mold. No, after all the powder was scattered around, the boss picked up a hose and sprinkled water over the powder. Nothing was mixed or formed. I hoped the ancient Greek architects were watching from above; they would have turned in their graves. We did this for a couple of days, but I absolutely detested this kind of work and decided to quit.

Platanias is another small town located twelve kilometers east of Chania, which we checked out for possible work. Nothing. We walked there and back, mainly for the fun of it. The scenery here is really gorgeous, and going on foot was the only way to absorb it. Our Brazilian friend was not so impressed with the hike, brooding most of the time, but for me, I found the countryside fascinating, and I loved walking.

The central part of the island is made up of steep mountain ranges, with desolate, scattered villages completely hidden from the more touristy areas. It is how everyone imagines Greek life to be, and this can be found in the mountains of Crete. This is where we ventured, taking the local bus south this time—fifteen kilometers to the village of Skines. From there, we walked the two kilometers to an even smaller village—Fournes, set amidst beautiful hills and surrounded by an abundance of orange and olive plantations. In the distance, loomed the 1820m peak of Mount Lefka Ori. Nobody spoke English so far inland, but they did manage to comprehend that we were looking for work in the orchards, but it was too early in the season for olives or oranges. Despite the disappointment, we still enjoyed the fresh, fragrant mountain air and a stroll around the villages.

The last remaining Brazilian (Edmundo) said goodbye and returned to the comforts of Israel. His was a very short adventure, and he was definitely not made for traveling. The three Brazilians I originally came with all came from wealthy families and had different perspectives with regard to adventure—more suited for all-inclusive package tours and pampering. They whined incessantly when things didn't work out and always gave up easily. I was now left with my only friend—Avner the Israeli. We would persevere with attempts to find some kind of employment, even in construction until the olive season began. I needed the money, as it was costing over ten dollars a day to live here, and the funds were quickly diminishing. Nevertheless, we were having a fine time in Chania—sightseeing, playing backgammon, and drinking Greek coffee during the day, and in the evenings we ate out at our favorite Greek hangout, which catered mainly for the locals, thus providing delicious traditional cuisine. I especially enjoyed the fresh calamari (baby squid), deep-fried and served with the freshest salad imaginable. This was always washed down with jugs of *retsina*—the very potent resin wine. A jug of wine on the table for families (kids drink it too) is as standard as water.

The September heat departed together with the Brazilians, and the beginning of October was indicated by a sudden drop in temperatures—from their usual 30's to only 20°Celsius. The wind picked up, making this a very stormy day with rough seas. The tethered boats in the harbor bobbed and swayed with the waves, which came crashing down against the ancient sea walls and over the pier. Chairs and tables had been gathered and people sat indoors. I was taking a stroll along the pier then, together with another Brazilian I had met earlier in the hostel. He was also looking for work. He was traveling alone and had entertaining tales about China he had recently visited. He had taken the Trans-Siberian Express from Beijing all the way to Moscow, and then continued to Berlin.

After a walk around the lighthouse *and* on top of the sea wall, we returned to the hostel to get changed. It was difficult to avoid being sprayed, as the pounding waves came cascading over the top. We spent the evening at the local disco looking for girls, but the place was overrun by stocky, hairy-chested Greeks who resembled the Israeli *chach-chachs,* with golden chains around their necks, open silk shirts and rolled-up sleeves that revealed gorilla-like arms. They hovered around the blondes like hungry vultures waiting to tear up the flesh. Girls were outnumbered by about 20:1... so we left.

As the days went by, the temperatures continued to plummet, hitting the fifteen mark. It was time to put on jeans and a coat. The sea was still rough, and there was not much to do except laze around. Chania started to empty itself of tourists, too, and especially in this weather the town had lost its liveliness; even the lighthouse adopted the loneliness and looked vulnerable as it throbbed from the continuous battering waves upon its walls. Nobody walked the usual crowded pier, which used to be lined with pistachio nut vendors.

Costas is a café near the port where all job seekers gather from 7:00 A.M. until someone approaches asking: "Are you looking for work?" It is the place where I found myself one morning doing the same thing as the others. Avner and I were offered work for two weeks—putting tiles down on the floor, even though we had never done anything like it. The pay was 2,000 drachmas a day and included a meal. After the first day, I realized it would be another week until we actually started putting tiles down. What our boss didn't tell us was that the floors had to be prepared first, and sand and cement to be carried in. This was very unpleasant work, but I would stick with it until finding something better in the next two weeks (easier said than done). The place of work was in Kournas, located 45km east of Chania. We were picked up at the café every morning and dropped off at the end of the day. The delicious meals were provided fresh on the building site by the boss's wife: wine, sausages, salad, sesame bread, olives, feta cheese, baklava, and coffee. When it came to feeding, the Greeks were extremely generous and made sure we were well and truly stuffed.

What I had noticed about Greek villages is that there is a large concentration of very old people—mostly men. Young people are not seen. I think they leave the lonely life here and move to the cities. The old men are usually found sitting together outside a café, supping the local wine and smoking heavily. They all look in pretty bad shape as if they've had a very hard life, but it could also be the constant consumption of alcohol and cigarettes, making people appear even older than they really are. Maybe it is also the diet, as Greek food is very meaty and fatty. I wasn't sure about the salads either, as they swam in olive oil. True, olive oil is extremely healthy, but when the equivalent of a glassful is poured into the salad and sponged out with white bread, leaving a clean bowl behind, it cannot be good for you. There is no such thing as a light meal, so a strong Greek coffee is one way to relax the bloated stomach. The elderly women look tough and are solidly built; the men are more slight, all unshaven, with wiry bristles that looked sharp enough to scour a burnt saucepan. Their greasy-looking skin could have been olive oil seeping out of the pores.

One day there was nothing going on, so I just spent the day eating and playing backgammon. While working, I managed to spend less money as I didn't have to buy any meals. I had developed an addiction to souvlaki though, and I was grateful that they only cost 100 drachmas—less than a dollar. I went through three of them a day. We had become regular visitors at our local restaurant, too, which was located across the road from our room; so regular in fact, that the owner didn't charge us for wine anymore —it was always on the house. Most of the time after 10:00 P.M. he was drunk anyway, and, not being able to carry the plates to the tables, he sent one of his waiters out with the food. I also noticed that our portions had gotten bigger. Avner's English was terrible, so we spoke Hebrew all the time. A Danish girl sitting at a table next to us was staring while we were talking, then she came over to ask, "What language are you speaking?"

The restaurant owner's name was Jorgo (Yorgo). I had the impression that 49% of Greek men are called Jorgo and the other 49% are Costas. I didn't hear any other name, but there must be that missing 2% somewhere. Jorgo invited us to go to some kind of night club with him, to listen to some Greek music. It was already after 1:00 A.M. and I was really worn out; also, there was something about the guy I didn't like—another one of my gut feelings. Avner, however, did go... and I didn't see him again until daylight. He came back excited. "John, you should have come... you should see his house... he is sooo rich." He continued telling me that Jorgo took him to his house afterward, and it was expensively furnished with high quality oriental rugs in every room. "He hates Jews though," he went on.

"What do you mean he hates Jews? He invited you, didn't he?"

"He said I killed Jesus," he lamented.

"He was drunk, as usual," I assured him.

Avner was dead for the rest of the day, having ruined his biological clock, but I was fit and awake and getting tired of Chania. I was writing down notes at Costas Café when Avner appeared in the late afternoon. He looked bad... probably just got up. "Coffee?" I offered.

"John, I need a girl!" He sounded desperate. I looked around.

"You've missed the tourist season... they're all gone, and I don't think a Greek girl will be so easy to catch." I was joking around, but he was serious.

"Come, I want to show you something." He pulled me up, dragging me along. I followed him for ten minutes to an unknown side street where I noticed red lamps hanging on the buildings. Whore houses!

"No way!" I was speechless.

"Okay, but come inside with me," he begged.

"What for? I'm not going in." I was wondering how he knew about this place, anyway: Jorgo must have told him. I knew there was something weird about that guy, but I went in out of curiosity. Pictures of available girls were hung on the wall; all you had to do was point at the one you fancied and she would be summoned. An elderly smiling woman came towards us. I felt most uncomfortable. "Avner, I'll see you later. Have fun," I told him and dashed out very quickly back to the café.

Last day in Chania—tomorrow I will travel to the southern part of the island for a change of scenery, and hopefully, work. The employment situation in Chania was dismal, as all available jobs were only in construction, which I disliked. All around this area, new buildings were springing up, getting ready for the future mass-tourism assault. I was informed that there was better work available in Paleohora and they paid more, too. I was also getting sick of the Israeli guy. He had almost squandered all his money on many pieces of *Boss* clothing—new sport shoes, and a trek-suit. I didn't know how much the prostitutes were costing him, but I didn't think he could survive much longer on his splurging. He was planning to travel the world, but that would never happen.

The bus journey from Chania to Paleohora was certainly not boring, as the speed-happy, chain-smoking driver swerved around the sharp mountain bends trying his best to tip the bus over. One of the bends was so sharp, and he was going much too fast, that the doors swung open and our luggage shot out onto the road. The two round barrels of olive oil and feta cheeses weren't as lucky, as they went tumbling down the mountainside. The passengers went rabid, screaming at the driver to stop to pick up the luggage. That was not a problem, but the olive oil barrels had to be retrieved further down the mountainside as the bus descended. We found them still in one piece, but dented by a tree that stopped them from rolling down further. The feta cheeses ran out of momentum half way down, as they were in square metal containers and didn't roll down as much. We all helped to retrieve the runaway food, except the driver who had caused this in the first place. He was now silent and brooding, knowing that he would not break the speed record to Paleohora, and was now driving normally, but sweating profusely after having absorbed verbal attacks in all languages. The olive oil and cheese owner was still seething, muttering Greek curses and boring holes into the driver with his livid eyes. *"Ma-la-ka"* I heard him repeat venomously several times.

The 77km trip to Paleohora took several hours, despite the prior speeding. Some areas were so steep, the bus had no choice but to crawl. This gave me a chance to enjoy the amazing views from the center of the island—acres and acres of olive trees with tiny desolate villages scattered amongst them. The air was the freshest I had breathed since Mt. Sinai, but already a lot cooler at this altitude compared to sea level. Winters must be severe up here: it was already so cold in the middle of October. We descended down into flatter land on the southern side of the island, and here was Paleohora.

This town is much smaller than Chania, less touristy, and overall a lot more pleasant. It had a long, sandy beach with just a handful of people. It was also warmer here than on the northern side. Yes, I really liked this place, and the positive ambiance put me in an optimistic mood. I immediately set about finding accommodation, which shouldn't have been a problem, as even here, most visitors had already left. It *was* a problem... I went to one *pension*. "Do you have a room?" I asked the woman. She shook her head. "Oh!" I was surprised, as it *did* look empty. Never mind... I would try the next place. "Do you have a room?" Again, the next one shook her head, too. "That's strange," I said to myself. There was nobody here. I walked off and noticed the perplexed expression on the woman's face. I was also baffled. The third place I found, after searching around, looked so deserted it must have had a room. There was no doubt. "Do you have a room?" I was becoming a repetitive parrot.

"Yes," she said with a shake of her head. Now I was *really* bamboozled. Why was she shaking her head? I repeated the question.

"Do you have a room? I NEED A ROOM... TO SLEEP!" I repeated a little forcibly this time. Again, she shook her head. "BUT YOU JUST SAID YES!" Was this a joke?

"Yes, come inside," she also repeated with an equally puzzled expression, not comprehending why I was being so rude. She had *lots* of accommodation, and I picked out a nice room for 600 drachmas.

I was still somewhat agitated by the strange responses I had gotten. Later in the evening, I mentioned this to some people I met in the restaurant. They killed themselves laughing. "Here, when people shake their heads, they mean *yes*, and a nod indicates a *no*." I burst out laughing, too, suddenly realizing that British gestures may have different meanings in other countries. No wonder the other women were confused after my walking away when they *did* have accommodation. At the same time, I tried to find out how to find work in these parts.

The same work-searching technique was used here as in the other town—sitting outside a particular café (Costas of course) early in the morning and waiting to be picked up. There was not so much competition here either, and people kept telling me that there were a lot of jobs available, but I had no luck today. I ended up walking around this small and attractive town, and to the beautiful beach where I happily spent most of the day. It really was an ideal place to stay, and it didn't have the large influx of tourists. All the travelers I saw were individuals who had made it here on their own accord: Some were on their way to hike the famous Samaria Gorge; others wanted to see isolated monasteries built into the cliffs; some were looking for casual work for financing their next move on the travel board (like I), and some were pot-smoking hippies who had no plans *or* desires to go anywhere. There was a total absence of holiday thrill seekers, and all this made Paleohora appealing and unique. I fell in love with this place.

Next day, I hiked over to an out-of-the-way village together with a French guy I had met at *Costas'*. We shared similar goals—both attempting to finance our travels. The village of Azogires is located eight kilometers up in the mountains, which meant a steep climb up a narrow dirt road snaking its way up the mountainside. It was so narrow that two cars would not be able to pass, and on one side was a sheer drop down to the gully, but no cars came from either direction—a clear indication how deserted this place really is. The heat was back, too, and so was the sweat, but the view from here was well worth the ordeal, and everywhere were gnarled olive trees laden with fruit. The village looked as if time had abandoned it a very long time ago, and I was wondering if they even had electricity and plumbing. I doubted it. Azogires had more than enough olive trees, but it had no work for the simple reason that the fruit was not ready for picking. People in this village were overwhelmingly friendly and said they would ask around for possible employment for us. We were to return in the evening. To kill time, we walked another five kilometers to the next prehistoric village—the name I could not make out, neither the Cyrillic script.

The pleasant walk turned unpleasant—not from the heat, but because of thousands of flies that surrounded me—they were all over my body. With every step I tried to kill a few, but more would come. What attracted them? I was taking two showers a day, so I couldn't have stunk! Even in the deserts of Israel and Egypt, I had never experienced such swarms. The incessant buzzing and biting (yes, these flies were vicious) gave no respite as we made our way to this dormant village which consisted of only a few buildings. There was no sign of life here whatsoever. It was as if the inhabitants had been abducted by aliens, and the stone dwellings left for nature to take over. There was no reason to stay here, so we walked back to Azogires. This was a wonderful day for the flies: they had been enjoying us for eighteen kilometers, and I couldn't wait to get back down the mountain and submerge myself in the soothing waters of the Mediterranean.

We came across a smiley hippie German couple who were also looking for work. These jolly, friendly people shared the information that they knew of a farmer who owns 5,000 olive trees. "His name is Jorgo (another one) and he is bald-headed with a mustache." And so, the four of us went to search for him. We entered an area which looked as if it had thousands of trees and were suddenly greeted by an elderly couple who were beckoning that we come into their garden. They didn't speak a word of English and we didn't understand any Greek, but they continued talking and smiling all the same, gesturing that we should sit down at their table, which was placed amongst flowering shrubs. We did, and were given food (fried fish) and a glass of village brew known as *krassi*, but it could also have been rocket fuel... so strong it was. They had a distillery set up in their garden, which they proudly showed off to us; pure lethal alcohol came out in droplets and into a large glass jar. We stood and gawked in amazement.

We walked back to the café and waited until dark. The mustached olive tree owner did not come. We were told to come back on Sunday; maybe he would be here then—maybe! This café is the best place I have eaten Greek food at so far; the entire kitchen being run by an old lady who didn't speak a word of English. She was famous for her omelets, I was told, and this is what I ate. The café was very simple inside: nothing more than aged furniture and without any decor. It merely served its purpose. The chairs and tables looked as if they had been used for at least half a century, and the elderly locals were the only clientele who occupied this place off the beaten path and spent their days there. It was also spotlessly clean, and I now realized after being in Greece so long that such simple, basic-looking places always served the best-tasting food, using traditional recipes. They always seemed to be run by an old woman who didn't speak a word of English.

The walk down the mountain road was not safe in the dark, and without even the moon illuminating the way, it was impossible to see. One foot wrong, and down you go. We returned to the café for some light—so dark it was. The kind owner/cook/waitress gave us some candles and matches, and in such a way, we made our way down the mountain with hot wax dripping down and singing our fingers. Once the sun disappeared, the temperatures plummeted and the pesky flies were gone, but the night was now filled with the shrill sounds of crickets, some going immediately silent as the candlelight disturbed their night calls. There were no other sounds— no cars, no voices, no wind. The way back in the dark seemed much longer than on the way up, even though it was all downhill, but we *were* dawdling and having fun.

I took to the German hippies—they were a very likeable and positive couple, thoroughly enjoying themselves, laughing a lot with not a care or worry in the world. Their sole existence was here and now, the future being irrelevant. They were a complete contrast to the Brazilians I had originally come with. We arrived some hours later back in Paleohora, hungry and cold.

It was Sunday and I set off once again to Azogires together with the German hippies to see if we could meet Jorgo. This was another two-hour hike in the mid-October heat, but we knew that there was wonderful food to be found in Sophie's Café. I didn't have an omelet this time, but wanted to order something different from the menu. The menu was in Greek, so that didn't help with the choice. Sophie beckoned us to follow her into the kitchen, where she showed us the available, prepared dishes by opening large pots. I sniffed one of them, satisfied with the aroma, and chose it. "This one," I said.

"*Mikro.*" She gave me the name for remembering in the future.

"*Mikro* is good," I acknowledged. It was the word for pork.

Greek salad automatically accompanied all meals, drowned as usual in olive oil. Torn chunks of sesame-seed-coated bread came with it, too—it was used for absorbing the oil. Fries, known as *patates*, were also included with most dishes, baked in olive oil and lemon juice.

It was well worth coming here just for the food, and Sophie made sure we had a good portion. Again, it was a wasted effort as Jorgo never showed up. When asking about him, people would respond with, "Which Jorgo?"

"The one with the 5,000 olive trees." They would shrug their shoulders in response. We also asked some men in the café. "Where is Jorgo?"

"Come back Tuesday, maybe he will be here then." They communicated in Greek and with gestures. The German hippies had spent a long time in Greece and knew some basic vocabulary. We searched the village for the mysterious bald-headed man, but there was no sign of him. Everybody knew him though, telling us that he was very rich with thousands of olive trees, but I could see from the trees that the fruit was nowhere near ripe enough for picking yet, so what were we doing here wasting our time? We returned to town.

Next day, Avner and I were offered work with tomatoes while waiting in the café, but this was only for four hours. We accepted it anyway, being the only offer we had. The following day we had better luck—a job for several days in the olive plantations—not picking, but the grass and thorny growth around the trees had to be cleared before the nets could be rolled out. Any sharp protrusions would tear the netting when they are collected again. This was very enjoyable work and the boss was quite laid-back, unlike some other slave drivers I had worked for on the island. The seven-hour day was paying 3,000 drachmas, including a very excellent filling meal. He did not work over the weekend, but I managed to find a similar kind of job with another friendly farmer meanwhile, and he was paying 500 drachmas per hour. On Monday, I resumed work with the first farmer. We finished clearing around the olive trees, and now the nets were put down around them. They were evenly spread out, covering the entire ground of the olive terraces. When the olive season starts, there are some varieties that are shaken off the trees; others fall down naturally into the nets as they ripen. They are then gathered together with the olives and immediately replaced with a fresh net. Once this starts, there should be plenty of work available, which is what we were all waiting for. Everybody was also waiting for the rains to start, as the weather had been too warm and dry, and the crops were thirsty. I thoroughly enjoyed working amongst the olive plantations, especially when the boss was the friendly and respectful type. Most farmers here spoke enough English for giving instructions and making small bits of conversation, having had many years of practice with foreign workers.

We didn't have to wait too long for the rains, as some days later, the storms lashed out in full fury, thus ending the dry spell and sending the temperatures plunging once more to a cool 13°Celsius, the coldest I had felt in about eight months. Also, my work with the olives was over, so it was back to unemployment once again and sitting around the café in the early hours of the morning. During that time, I rented an elegant two-bedroom luxury apartment together with a Syrian I had befriended. The monthly off-season charge was 20,000 drachmas, which was less than three dollars a day per person—a real bargain. It came equipped with bathroom, kitchen, refrigerator, table, and sofas. It looked more like a luxurious business suite and had all modern appliances. I could certainly spend a long time here this way, if only I could get permanent work.

I said goodbye to Avner. The Israeli had spent all his money and was returning back to Israel—broke. All the people I had originally come with were now all gone, but I made some good friends in Paleohora and wanted to stay longer and experience more of the Greek culture, which I was enjoying.

It was November, and I once again found myself working in the olive plantations, doing a similar kind of job as before—clearing ground around the olive trees. Transportation wasn't so good, having no choice but to sit at the back of a pick-up truck together with my Syrian friend (Mario), and traveling twenty-five kilometers to a village where the olive trees were located. Now I knew how cattle must feel after being transported on bumpy roads, exposed to all weather conditions. The work was enjoyable, though, and once again, the boss was fairly friendly. There was however, a crazy, cackling old hag constantly arguing with herself. She was the boss's mother, and unfortunately, was working with us. The shriveled up human looked about a hundred years old and was keeping a weary eye on our work, not letting us stop for one moment to chat or wipe sweat off our foreheads. As soon as we hesitated, she would scream "DULYA! DULYA! APOCHI! APOCHI!" (work, work, here, here) pointing at the enormous weeds as if we were blind.

"Oh, get lost you old witch," I mumbled, tempted to put her out of her misery. The Syrian was grinning maliciously, fantasizing her torture and cursing in Arabic while giving her the evil eye. Our boss was working equally hard, sniggering at the scene and shaking his head with amusement; poor guy: he had to put up with his senile mother all hours of the day. When she wasn't screaming at us, she was talking to herself.

Talking to oneself seems to be common practice here in Greece, especially in the villages. I used to think it was only the old people going

289

senile in their age, especially the very old women, who tended to shriek in high-pitched voices. Old men usually just mumbled to themselves and stared into nothingness or reminisced on a distant memory they tried to visualize. I also noticed this behavior among the younger generation... not only the old.

Feeling hungry one evening, I wondered into a small, local restaurant that was empty; well, almost empty except for a ravishing girl who was sitting alone at a table waiting for her order. Our eyes locked for a moment, and her sweet smile prompted my instantaneous assessment of the situation —and to keep her company. The blonde angel was a godsend, and as we had (very quickly) taken to each other while polishing off a plate of squid, conversation came naturally, and after the second jug of wine, it felt as if we had known each other forever. Katrina was a *real* tourist from Berlin, and had a month's vacation for backpacking around Crete. She had also fallen in love with Paleohora, where she was renting an apartment in town. There were some places nearby she still wanted to visit, so we made plans to go together, as we were getting on *extremely* well.

A week later, all the backpackers/workers/travelers had a special treat. A festival was taking place in one of the mountain villages, eight kilometers from Paleohora. A whole group of us walked up to the village in the dark, full of eager curiosity and glad to experience something different instead of olive trees. The sound of musicians playing traditional Greek music on a mandolin infused the festival with positive spirit. The *other* spirit came out of a distillery that was set up—producing the famous local *raki*, where people could go up and help themselves to as much as they wanted, filling up their glasses at the dripping tube. Everything was free, including endless gallons of village-brewed wine standing in casks, and mountains of roasting chestnuts, emitting a wonderful aroma. They must have been harvested from the village trees. We were all having a fantastic time and everyone was well and truly drunk, especially the locals. They were preoccupied with firing guns into the air. (In Crete, carrying a gun around is a sign of being a man, so much that the entire male population wants to prove their manliness, and the result is, everybody carries guns around with them. I have heard stories of Cretans falling into an argument and shooting each other. I was hoping this wouldn't happen here as alcohol and fire power don't mix well together.) The police from Paleohora were there, too (drunk), and I also spotted the police officer who was always bothering the campers on the beach. He was shooting off a few rounds into the air, hardly being able to balance, so intoxicated he was. He did recognize us though, waved, and hollered, "HALLO ENGLISH!" To him, all foreigners were English, and then continued shooting into the air while holding a glass of alcohol in his left hand.

All foods and beverages that were available had been produced locally, and there was nothing that came from a packet or bottle. It was village life in its purest form, as it always has been for hundreds of years, and there was no sign of any influx from the outside world. We, the guests, were extremely lucky to experience this Greek version of the "Wild West" last frontier life, and I was grateful that we were given the opportunity to participate. My olive boss was also here (without his mad mum), and raised his glass in a greeting gesture.

As the night progressed, the fiddle and mandolin players put themselves into high gear and played so fast that I expected smoke to materialize from their instruments as the crescendo was also notched up a few decibels, and the men became drunker and wilder, dancing to the music by the enormous bonfire in a wild, primeval style. By now, there must have been more than a dozen guns being discharged sporadically, adding to the din. My head was spinning from the noise and the wine, which was the most delicious wine I have ever drunk. Such a wine could never be bought in a store, and it had the distinct taste of pure, natural ingredients and ancient recipes handed down from generation to generation.

On the way back to Paleohora we were all singing and dancing on the main road, having been transformed into Greeks. There was Mario the Syrian, two French girls, A French guy, the German hippie couple, the German girl Katrina, and two Canadians I had met earlier—one Franco, one Anglo. After a couple of kilometers, the ten of us got picked up by a large minibus, which we piled into, and were driven to town. Midnight—still early, so we spent a few hours at the local disco, which was a small and pleasant set-up with a good mixture of Greeks and foreigners.

Samaria Gorge is a National Park located not far away from here, but getting there was quite tricky: It meant going back to Chania to take a bus from there to the outset of the gorge, or one could take a boat from

Paleohora going to the other side of the gorge and attempt the hike in the opposite direction. Katrina and I took the boat with a couple of other tourists. The boat made some stops at other seaside villages, and then arrived about an hour later at Agia Roumeli, which was actually the back end of the gorge, where it ended at the Libyan Sea. The tiny village of Agia Roumeli was only a place for stopping to take a rest, with the usual small café for refreshments. We didn't need a rest as we had just arrived, but a nice Greek coffee I could never pass by. It was not on our agenda to do the entire hike along the gorge, as it can take up to six hours, but simply to traverse this famous place of natural beauty for a short time, then turn back to catch the six o'clock boat back to Paleohora. This small village is surrounded by beautiful bushes and oleanders, as huge as in Galilee in Israel. In fact, it looked very much like the Galilee area with its natural pools of water and similar plants.

The path, we were told, was easy to spot... and it was, so we followed it immediately after downing our coffee, making the most of our time. The park was officially closed, as this was the end of the tourist season: we weren't really supposed to be here—but who cares? Katrina didn't, and neither did I. We just wanted to hike mid-way at least. We started out the easy way—the place where the gorge flattens out. Coming from the north, this would have been a great way to end the hike, but as we were heading the opposite direction, for us, it meant the elevation getting steeper. We walked and walked and saw no other hikers. It was November, and the last autumn heat was trapped in the gorge. The German hippies had come here in the middle of summer when the temperatures soared well above 40°Celsius—they must have fried. I'm glad it wasn't *so* hot—this was perfect temperature. The route was quite easy as it followed a creek, and we noticed after about an hour, the gorge sides were becoming steeper and the path was narrowing; the oleander and bushes disappeared behind us now. We stopped for a break—water and sesame bread with feta cheese. The easy, almost flat path became rocky and huge boulders started appearing, starting to look more and more like the wadis in Israel I had hiked previously. In Israel, at least it is permissible to sleep in one and make a fire, too, but here, it was forbidden for some obscure reason. It's not even permitted to sleep on a beach in Greece, but a lot of backpackers ignored this rule anyway, and I'm sure a number of hikers had slept in the gorge despite it being prohibited. Had I known it would be this wonderful, I would have planned it better so that we could have spent a night here, but that would have meant taking more equipment, as well as a sleeping bag. After seeing what was ahead of us, it was good this way, with a minimum load.

We hiked, clambered, and dripped with sweat for the next hour. The landscape was breathtaking… well… actually, there was no more landscape. We reached a very narrow point where it was possible to almost touch both walls with outstretched arms, and the canyon walls were so steep we had to look straight up to confirm that it was still daylight. Our path was disrupted by enormous boulders that lay on the ground—huge rocks that had come tumbling down from above, and it was hard to tell when the last one had fallen. It could have been this morning or ten years ago; there was no way of telling, and all those loose boulders above would one day come hurtling down and flatten a hiker. The path became even steeper and more perilous as our hike slowed down tremendously while clambering over more boulders; meanwhile, daylight had become mostly obscured in this part of the gorge. This was about the half-way point, where we rested again, and then decided to turn back down to the village. Attempting the hike from this end is really not a good idea; it is much more difficult because of the steep gradient, but I was satisfied with what I had seen. Going back down was much easier—following the creek again. We saw the oleanders in the distance and knew that the village was nearby.

The only café in the village was also serving food, so we ordered a fine stewed pork dish and ate hungrily. This was a fantastic day with Katrina, both of us being well and truly exhausted. We left on the six-o'clock boat back to Paleohora and were there an hour later.

The pleasant work in the olives was regrettably over, and now there was only arduous "tomato" work available. Horrible work made horrible bosses, and that was exactly what I experienced the next day, spending ten hours without a break planting tomatoes—row after endless goddamned row. This strenuous, back-braking work only paid 2500 drachmas (without food), and we were treated like vermin. It didn't help demanding more money from these arrogant people—they would not pay more. I was livid and vowed not to work anymore for such farmers. It was a bad day, but a good meal and an evening at the disco with Katrina perked me up. They were playing the same *Madonna* songs and repetitions of *Moonlight Shadow*.

Next day after a late breakfast, Katrina and I walked over to the beach and joined our friends who were camping amidst such paradise. A new hippie appeared on the scene—an American from Los Angeles, who was patching up holes in his well worn-out jeans. The others were discussing their travel plans—where to go next after Greece. Another Israeli I had met earlier was flying to South America; the French guy wanted to go to Pakistan, but was running short on cash; one of the Canadians was planning to go to Egypt; the other to Israel, which he had not seen yet; the American, like the German hippies, had no plans. JP the French guy was telling us about his earlier trips to Pakistan.

He told us that he smuggled rubies out of Afghanistan and Pakistan, then sold them for a considerable amount of money in France—this is how he financed his trips. He went on to tell us about his adventures in the Himalayas and the people he had met: "In Pakistan, every woman is covered head to toe, and even her eyes are blacked out with netting." He now informed us about his ruby-smuggling scheme: There is a place called Chitral Valley in the Hindu Kush mountains, which borders Afghanistan. Most of the people who live there are light-skinned, have blue eyes, and brown or reddish hair: known as Kalash People, they are said to be descendants of Alexander the Great's soldiers, who decided to settle down and make their home on that spot, inter-marrying with the locals, hence causing any future offspring to have lighter, Caucasian features. He explained that he crossed into Afghanistan illegally with the local villagers and made his way to a border town, where every imaginable illegal item could be found: every kind of weapon, grenades, kalashnikovs, and precious stones. He bought the stones there and smuggled them back to Pakistan, and then immediately flew directly to Paris, fearful each time. Once discovered, it would mean a spell in a Pakistani jail.

David, the Israeli, was telling us about Israeli backpackers in South America—how they usually follow the same route as all other Israeli travelers, and how they leave messages for each other at certain locations. "There is a book we buy in Israel, in Hebrew though, and there are addresses inside which tell us where we can stay for free with Jewish families. The book gives information on where to locate Jewish communities and contact information of rabbis, and where to find kosher food." He went on to inform us that Argentina and Brazil had the most addresses.

The German hippies had been living on the beach all summer (they looked it, too), and were attempting to make Goa, India, their ultimate destination. It was the center of the hippie world. They told us some things about the area around Paleohora; that there are scores of caves nearby, some of them occupied by hermits. "There are also monasteries built into cliffs where monks stay in complete solitude," they mentioned.

"Oh, just like St. George's monastery in Jericho, in Israel." I described to them the monastery and what the monk had told me, and I went on to talk about St. Catherine's in the Sinai.

"*We* lived in a cave when we came here in spring, as it rained a lot then," they surprised us with this revelation. Yes, they were *real* cave people —wild.

Katrina told us how awful it was in Germany: how she hated it there, and how unfriendly the people were, but she had to go back soon, to her job in the office. She fit in perfectly into our group, and I could tell that she longed for the same adventures we had experienced.

"That's why we are never going back," the German hippies chimed in unison. "We are going to India!"

The American hippie was now "hippie weaving" —fastening the threads to his jeans with a safety pin and making bracelets. The German hippie couple had a guitar they played quite well, and the setting by the sea was ideal for this. I was, meanwhile, telling my listeners about weird places in Turkey I had seen last year, and about places to visit in Israel. There was also a very tall Dutch guy in our group. He took over the guitar for a while, and the German hippies were now sprawled out on the blanket, stroking each other like chimpanzees. For a moment I thought they might start picking out fleas from each other's matted hair and eat them. Mario and David seemed to be getting along very well, despite the two countries being in a state of war. They spoke about the Yom Kippur War, about losses from both sides of their families during the conflict, and they both wished there was peace between their countries. There was absolutely no animosity between them.

This was how we spent our November days—listening to fascinating travel stories, to the sounds of the waves and the crackling fire, with sleeping bags and mats sprawled out on the sand. The rest of the beach was deserted, void of tourists who had long gone home. We were a strange mixture, but also the most wonderful bunch of people I have ever met. I would never again get to meet such amazing people. We were all from different backgrounds, but felt a kinship amongst ourselves: karma had brought us together. Ignoring our watches, we always went by the sun—the sunset indicated that it was time for dinner, as we walked over to our usual restaurant for some delicious fried squid, salad, and the usual jugs of wine. We returned to the beach afterward and re-lit the fire, and talked until people started to drift off. Most stayed on the beach; some had rooms. I went back to town with Katrina, where I was staying in her apartment for the past few days. She was a "special" friend.

I managed to get another day's work with tomatoes again, but with a different and equally unpleasant boss who paid 3,000 drachmas for seven-hours work, but again without any break or food. These tomato farmers were a different breed of people compared to the placid olive growers. It was not worth the unpleasantness or the money, especially as no food was provided. I was still working with Mario, and even he was not content. The other workers were surly, uneducated Greek rednecks that created a very unpleasant atmosphere where nobody talked. I was overjoyed when the seven hours ended and I could go back to town (home).

Two weeks passed. We had another great evening at our favorite restaurant, where all the beach people hung out to eat, drink, and play backgammon. After a good meal and several jugs of the lethal *retsina* wine, there was so much noise, we were almost thrown out. It would have been bad for the restaurant's business though, as everyone in the restaurant knew each other… so… more wine… and… more noise! The cheerless owner/cook/waiter was frowning heavily with disapproval at this rowdy bunch, but he knew his livelihood depended on keeping us happy. Word among backpackers soon spreads like wildfire, of places to avoid or to recommend. We stayed there well into the night and many of us ordered more food, snacks, and coffee with baklava… and more wine towards the end.

After so many eventful evenings, I needed some peace, and the most peaceful place I knew was the mountain village of Azogires, which I wanted to introduce to Katrina. We both needed to clear our heads and infuse ourselves with fresh mountain air. The famous Cave of the Forefathers, recommended by our beach friends, was another 40-minute walk up the mountain from the village. At this altitude, the temperatures dropped rapidly with the increasing wind; black rain clouds were gathering nearby. We found the cave on the mountaintop, marked by a large cross as described to us. The cave itself was huge, and inside were a number of tunnels leading in different directions. Impressive as it might have been, our flashlight was quite dim, and the light it emitted was not enough to penetrate the consuming darkness. Disappointingly, we left the cave, not wanting to venture into the deep, endless black hole. This was not the only cave in the area; there were others that had been converted into churches.

The hiking however, was fantastic, where we spent the day clambering over rocks and enjoyed breathtaking views of the coastline in the distance. It looked as if it was being bombarded by torrential rain. Also near the village there are deep rock pools with mini waterfalls, making it an ideal spot for swimming, but not at this time of year. It would have been ecstasy in summer. Crickets were still singing; not with such intensity as before, but with barely audible, desperate dying sounds, indicating that winter was just around the corner. I took Katrina to Sophie's restaurant, urging her to try one of her famous omelets. This restaurant was so small; it only had four tables set up. Usually, there were always some locals around, but this time we were alone. Katrina fell in love with this place *and* the omelet. As usual, I ended walking back down the mountain in the dark, and now rain was falling here, too, bringing down the temperatures even more. We huddled together to keep warm. Our dim flashlight gave out the last micro voltage, and then died. But nothing mattered as we made our slow (very wet) way back to Paleohora—the day was wonderful.

After getting changed into some dry clothing, we made our way to the rowdy restaurant. The usual noisy crowd was already there, and so was the busy, frowning owner running around with plates of food and jugs of wine. We talked about our future travel destinations and our experiences with the Greeks—good *and* bad. This evening was special for us all, as it was the last evening we would be together. Most people were leaving tomorrow… and sadly, Katrina, too—she was flying back to Germany. We were especially silly this night, making the owner crazy, but also it was a way of showing the trust and deep friendship that had developed between us all and bonded us together. It was an evening I will never forget, and one that will never be repeated. We all exchanged addresses, and there were some watery eyes and affectionate embraces; even the restaurant owner seemed to ease off with his frowning and sensed that things were changing, and tomorrow his restaurant would be quite empty. Soon, he could close down for the season.

The next morning arrived, and a very sad day it was as I watched most of the people boarding the bus to Chania… and so was Katrina. She did suggest my coming to Germany with her, but by not being selfish, she didn't try to persuade me to do so, convinced that I would die there in misery, not being able to adapt to the environment, and she was happy to remember me as I was. Coming from the northern part of England, I knew what she meant. We clung onto each other tightly, treasuring those last moments, and that was it. Gone! I felt abandoned and very much alone as I watched the bus pulling away with a watery-eyed Katrina. I hobbled over to the beach (also wet-eyed) with the few remaining friends that were left here. I also spent my last night in the apartment I had shared with the Syrian, as our lease was coming to an end tomorrow. I hadn't slept there for over two weeks anyway, so it didn't matter. Everything was coming to an end, and I felt miserable.

We vacated the apartment the next day, and Mario also left Paleohora —another friend gone. I had to reconsider what I wanted to do now, and I suddenly had the feeling that it was time to move on—not really wanting to stay in Paleohora anymore. There wasn't any point leasing another room, as I wasn't sure what to do next. This had been the greatest place on earth for me for a time, but now the atmosphere was changing; almost all backpackers had left, and the Arab workers were moving in, getting ready for the olive-picking season. This was catastrophic for the working tourists, who had been desperately waiting for this seasonal work in order to earn some good money, and then be on the move again. The Arabs would do the same job for half the pay, so naturally, they were chosen for the picking. Later, Polish workers would come and undercut the Arabs, so the idea of actually earning a decent amount was diminishing.

Maybe a couple of days on the beach would clear my head a little and bring in some fresh ideas; therefore, I decided to camp there with the remaining group. I had a bad cold (from the wet walk in Azogires) and a splitting headache, neither of which cheered me up. The few remaining beach settlers made the usual night fire. There wasn't much conversation between anyone sitting around the glowing embers this time: we were all preoccupied with our own thoughts. There wasn't even the usual guitar playing which took place each night. Strangely enough, the drunken local police didn't show up as they had done on numerous occasions to harass the campers/backpackers by checking the passports and putting out the fire. They seemed to enjoy making problems for us; clearly making a point that they did not like on-the-cheap travelers doing things for free.

All I had was a sleeping bag, a mat, a gas cooker, and a couple of pans. Some of the others were better equipped—with a tent and better camping gear. It was sufficient though, and I soon turned a small area of the beach into my living quarters next to the other "illegal" campers. Tomorrow, I would be back in the café looking for work.

There was none. It was my last day in this town. Being unable to find a job was the last straw, not that I really cared, as I really did want to move on now. A small group of us decided to walk up to the mountain villages and see about employment possibilities in the approaching olive-picking season. There were five of us—the two Canadians, the Dutchman, JP the French smuggler, and of course, myself. I cheered up a little (not much) as it got warmer again and the 18-kilometer hike cleared my head. Sleeping on the beach helped to eliminate my cold and headache; also being in the company of these cheerful guys perked me up somewhat. Along the way, we picked and ate ripening mandarins and leftover, overripe figs. Almonds had fallen to the ground—these we smashed open with a rock to get into the nuts. By walking along this particular route, it was not possible to starve. We rested on some rocks by a stone house: the setting was in a village, which was adorned with colorful bushes, pomegranate hedges, and potted flowers, still blossoming in the last days of November. After some minutes, an old woman came out; speaking Greek, she carried a bowl of small, fried fish, which she placed in front of us, gesturing that we eat. (Fish again! Greeks must have a secret supply stashed away for tourists.) I couldn't believe the generosity I had experienced here in these desolate villages. The kindness of these people made up for the arrogance and selfishness I have had to put up with in Greek tourist towns and the various bosses I have had to work for, but when I think about it, it was actually just a few joy killers. We exchanged a few words in Greek with the woman and thanked her sincerely, then made our way back to town. There was an empty, rickety bus coming our way, and it stopped. "Paleohora?" Asked the driver.

"Yes, Paleohora," we acknowledged by shaking our heads, and hopped on, grateful for not having to walk back the eighteen kilometers. A couple of other passengers came on the bus along the way—the usual old people, struggling with the familiar containers of olive oil and feta cheese. Like in Cyprus, we slowly chugged through other out-of-the-way villages, dropped the olive and cheese passengers off, then continued to town—only eighteen kilometers away, but ninety minutes to get there.

I had my last good meal in Paleohora and then went to sleep on the beach. Looking around this place, it was easy to fall into the trap as some of the travelers had done—to be stuck here for a great length of time. Paleohora had a strange, seductive pull and would not let anyone go easily. Quite a few of the people I met sleeping on the beach had been around for six to eight months, having run out of money and not able to find regular work. I was gradually sinking into the same pit, having just under $200 left. I had to get out of here whilst I still had the chance *and* money.

The first bus out of Paleohora, and I was on it next morning. I was supposed to go together with the French ruby smuggler, but he was taking the next bus. Police raided the beach again last night, while I was in the restaurant, and took his passport, which he had to pick up from the police station with the promise that he would leave town immediately. Passport checks on tourists had become a regular occurrence. I guess they were trying to scare off the few remnants of straggling backpackers left over from summer, as they wanted to finally clear the beach settlement. The corrupt police always stank of alcohol, but it was better when they were drunk—they didn't bother us then. JP and I were supposed to meet in a mountain village called Valukalies, which is the centre of olive oil production. There, I had an address where I could get work and a place to stay for the winter. Well, it was my last chance—I had nothing to lose.

The village people gave me odd, but unpleasant looks when I got off the bus in Valukalies. They were probably thinking: "What the hell is a tourist doing here at this time of year?" I showed the address I had on the slip of paper to some mean-looking men, and the suspicious folk pointed the way, hesitating at first. I was on my way, once more hiking up a mountain into the most isolated village I have seen yet. Nikaleos was the olive man I was looking for. Everybody knew where he lived, but what incredible bad luck—nobody home. The locals were very mistrustful and most unfriendly here, glaring at me as if I was some kind of criminal.

"What you want?" Was one question thrown at me.

"*Dulya*," (work) I replied.

"Here no *dulya*," he hissed. "Nikaleos have no *dulya*. You go." The nasty, bristled old man eyed me threateningly.

"You rude bastard," I was thinking, not believing him at all. Nevertheless, I wasted no time getting out of this unwelcoming village and its hostile inhabitants, who obviously wanted no outsiders intruding in their clandestine community. I also did not want to be the focus of attention, so I hastily retraced my steps back down to the equally unreceptive Valukalies. I was in time to meet JP on the second bus as it was just pulling in. "Don't get off here," I warned him, and pushed him back onto the bus, "we're going on to Chania."

"Chania? Oh, no!" he protested, not liking the idea, but I told him what had just happened in the village and he surrendered.

Things were getting from bad to worse. I also found out in Chania that it was even more difficult to find work there, due to the many hopeful workers who had descended upon this town, compared to a couple of months ago—most of them from Arab countries. Tomorrow, if the weather is good, we will visit the surrounding villages to see if the orange-picking season has begun yet.

The weather *wasn't* good the next day—rain and cold. That morning, we met our American hippie friend from Paleohora, known as LA. He told us about our friends on the beach—the police returned, rounded up everybody, and demanded their passports. Few of the people were found without work visas and were now being deported. How lucky I was to have left yesterday. I didn't need a visa, but I couldn't bear the harassment from those crooked police. They couldn't be trusted. It wouldn't surprise me if they had even planted some drugs on the tourists as an excuse to have them arrested and deported. I was hoping my Canadian and German friends were okay.

Sitting in Costas café the next morning, watching the rain fall and drinking coffee with my friends, I came to a conclusion—I give up! The weather turned miserably cold and it kept raining more often now. "I'm going back to Israel," I suddenly blurted out.

"If you go to Israel, I come with you," said JP, amazed at my decision. He had never been to Israel and wanted to see it.

"Me, too!" LA joined the club.

Because of that darned rain on that particular morning, we were on the ferry to Piraeus, where we would take the one and only weekly ferry to Israel. In the winter season, there are no direct links from Crete to Haifa, as there are no tourists coming here this time of year, so all Israel-bound travelers have to go all the way back to mainland Greece. Today was Wednesday, and ferries to Israel leave once a week—every Thursday. It's a 12-hour night crossing to Piraeus, so we should easily make it.

I was on the move again, and what a great feeling it was to be leaving. Pleasure overwhelmed me with the realization that I would never be stuck here, and I was my cheerful self once again. But what a fantastic time I had on Crete, also strange moments with seedy people. Many of the Greeks I met were uneducated, arrogant, and most insulting. The police were a farce —drunk and corrupt. Many villagers looked upon foreigners with suspicion and did not accept outsiders, but restaurant owners gladly took their money. I found it difficult to imagine that Greece is a part of Europe, and now a member of the EEC. The island of Crete was far away from that reality, and I felt the folk would make sure to keep it that way—as it always has been.

On the other hand, I can honestly say that Greeks are also the most generous and kindest people I have met. Their food and wine is out of this world, and I love their music and village culture. They should not be absorbed into the rest of Europe, as this would destroy their individualism and the traditions they still behold. The people are unique (if not always pleasant), but that is Greece, and I would hate to see it any other way. My thoughts are contradicting, but so is this country. I hate it and I love it. Crete is weird.

We arrived in the grubby port of Piraeus at 6:00 A.M. with ten hours to kill before the crossing to Israel. The famous Acropolis I wanted to see was not so far away, but nobody had the energy to make the effort of going there. We had breakfast together, and then bought our ferry tickets, which cost a mere $70. It was cheap, but nevertheless, it left me with only $60 now. We spent the day shopping for food we would need for the three days on the sea, and at 2:00 P.M. sharp, it was time to check in.

We said goodbye to Greece, and without any regrets, left this strange country where police take the law into their own hands. However, I felt a bit of a failure by not fulfilling my original plan of working through Europe, but I did start the wrong time of year, and it was much too cold now. The rest of Europe was now freezing; certainly not something I wanted to go through. I wondered how Katrina was coping with the cold and with all the things she didn't like in Germany. It felt great to be returning to nice, sunny and warm Israel once again. It is where I felt at home, and I wished that Katrina was coming with me.

As Israel loomed up in the distance, I felt somewhat anxious, hoping they wouldn't want to see how much money I had on me for support, otherwise I would be in dire straits: $400 was the minimum entry requirement.

There were five of us together now: myself, JP, a Canadian we met on the boat, and LA was here, too—still patching up his jeans, and we were also recently joined by a German called Wolf, but we called him Germany. Germany was well into his mid-fifties, divorced, with little money, but dressed like a millionaire and brandishing two bulky suitcases, as well as an extra piece of hand luggage containing alcohol and endless packs of cigarettes. He was stocky—built like a tree trunk; tall, with bulging eyes, and a stomach that proclaimed that he enjoyed his food; his eyes were on the verge of popping out of their sockets, forced by the pressure in his body—and his English was bad, bad, bad.

I always made sure to look presentable—shaved, hair washed, and wearing a fresh T-shirt when going through customs. I never encountered problems then.

"Oh, you are back in Israel," commented the customs official as she leafed through my passport.

"Yes, I really love it here… there is so much to see… still," I told her truthfully.

"Are you going to stay on a kibbutz again?" She asked.

"No, I'm going to a moshav." I switched to Hebrew.

"Ah, you speak Hebrew. Are you Jewish?" She also changed over to Hebrew now. I was subconsciously praying she wouldn't ask about my funds, trying to steer the conversation far away from that subject. I didn't answer her directly with regard to my Jewishness.

"I attended the *ulpan* before for several months," I continued telling her. She smiled and wished me fun in Israel, handing me back the passport.

Everybody got through okay except LA. I had a feeling he would run into trouble at customs. He looked like the perfect victim. We waited outside for him for two hours, then he plodded out, ashen-faced and looking more disheveled than ever.

"What happened to *you*?" We demanded. He looked embarrassed.

"They... strip-searched me. They took everything apart—all my belongings." He looked distressed, but we all burst out laughing. They even took the metal seams off his mini chessboard, looking inside for drugs. Unable to find anything suspicious, they then x-rayed the chess pieces to make sure nothing was hidden inside.

I took everybody to Acco, the ancient Crusader city nearby Haifa, where we all sat to sip coffee in one of the gazillion Arab cafés that lined the ancient port. Afterward, we took the bus to Tel Aviv to look for a place to stay for the night. The recommended hostel turned out to be a squalor and had long since gone to the dogs. It attracted strange, shifty people you wouldn't wish to meet in the dark. We immediately abandoned the idea of staying there and went to look for a better place.

That night, we all hit Tel Aviv, whooping it up and splurging out on restaurants, cakes and ice cream. I didn't really care about overspending, even though I had about $30 left; we were all having a great time. Germany had a remarkable humor, and we found him quite amazing in his ways, constantly muttering, "*Ja, ja*, is good... cigarette?" He was forever passing out cigarettes to everyone. Although our age difference was over thirty years, he was really young at heart and in the same boat as the rest of our group—with little money and hunting for work. With his infectious good mood, the difference in age was barely noticeable. For some intrinsic reason he hated Germany (the country) and the German people, whereby, he had decided to sell everything and set out to travel, never to return. Looking at his outfit, baggage, and behavior, it was obviously his first time out of Germany.

Laundry was the first important chore to take care of the following morning. The five of us strode off to the nearest laundromat, lugging huge bundles of grotesquely dirty clothing, looking as if they had never seen water. That taken care of, it was the moshav office next... and yes, they did have immediate vacancies for work. After paying for the insurance, I was now minus $50, which would be deducted from my first pay. I felt pretty destitute.

This was the last time we would be together, so it meant an extra good time in Tel Aviv. Germany had a perpetual habit of buying German newspapers (about 3 daily) and telling us what the temperature was in Frankfurt. He also had an incessant craving for meat. *"Ja, ja...* I want meat... cigarette?" At this rate he would go broke in no time, as meat in Israel cost a king's ransom.

We said goodbye to LA who went to try out a kibbutz. It was a great idea, as on the kibbutz he would have all the time in the world for patching up his jeans and making bracelets. Germany stayed put at the very decent Momo's Hostel in Tel Aviv, hoping to find work there. Three of us remained, and we made our way to Moshav Sde Abraham, which was situated to my horror—right next to my old Kibbutz Nir Itzhak.

14
FLOWER POWER IN ISRAEL

Moshav Sde Avraham was made up of Argentinean immigrants, which was good for me, as I wanted to add on to the Spanish vocabulary I had picked up during the Hebrew study course—thanks to the constant Spanish chatter in class. The family I was to work for was young and amazingly friendly and spoke excellent English, so it was an instant goodbye to my Spanish *and* Hebrew practice. They made a good impression on me from the start, and I took a liking to them immediately, but I wasn't at all too enthusiastic about the work, knowing it would be tedious and boring. My accommodation was pretty good, though—a three-bedroom bungalow with kitchen and living room, complete with TV and a couple of worn-out sofas. The bedrooms would soon fill up with other people very shortly, but right now, I was to share the house with the Canadian I met on the ferry—known as Dave. JP ended up in a different house because his farmer owned a different property.

Just as I had imagined the work to be, that's how it was—tedious and boring. I started at 6.30 A.M., twining tomato plants around strings that came trailing down from above. The plants would be trained to climb upwards. We were in a huge greenhouse, where only tomato plants were grown; these, I was told, were "special" tomatoes destined for export to Europe. They would grow into perfectly-shaped, blemish-free fruits without any taste. There were endless rows of them.

In the afternoon, we started preparing a piece of desert for irrigation. An area had to be cleared free of weeds, and then irrigation pipes were laid out in rows, then connected to the main irrigation system. After the water was turned on, it dripped out very slowly at even spots. In the desert, every drop of water is precious and has to be used sparingly.

Next day, the cabbage planting started. We planted thousands of them, together with Bedouin workers from the Gaza Strip. When they found out that I spoke some Hebrew, I was bombarded with dozens of questions: "What's your name? You married? Where you from? Are there many Arabs in your country? Are there many Jews in your country?" It was always the same annoying questions. There were also the constant invitations to visit their homes and to spend a night there—in Rafiah. I declined the invitations as I had no inclination at that moment to go into the Gaza Strip, and especially as I didn't know these people. I had just met them and needed time to size them up first before being too friendly with them. It was too early to tell whether I could trust these workers... and *how* can they invite me to their homes after having just met me? This didn't make sense, and I never did go to visit them, mainly because I had no desire to answer the same questions over and over again, probably to the entire family, which presumably numbered a couple of hundred. If they were disappointed, it didn't show, but I remained friendly and respectful towards them. The Bedouins soon accepted me into their circle, and I always ate together with them during our breaks.

It is certainly understandable that electronics and machines have replaced the work of people, but I would never have imagined it possible to replace the work of bees. This was exactly what I did the next day—I became a bee! As we didn't have any of these insects around here, I did the job of one by pollinating the tomato flowers using a battery-operated vibrator. I went from flower to flower with a buzzing vibrator in my hand and feeling very silly indeed. All that was missing was a black-and-yellow-striped uniform and a pair of wings. Where do I make the honey?

Very few volunteers were working here; one of them (Sasha) came from the Soviet Union, and he had been on the moshav for an eternity. For anyone who has never met a real Russian, and the stereotypical image one conceives is that of a vodka-guzzling lout, this is 100% correct. I met him in the shop one day while buying groceries. He was buying vodka and arak.

Alcoholic fumes were already emitting from his body, and I was sure that he would burst into flames while smoking and tottering with his bottles. His poor English was mixed with Russian, and he was grinning incessantly as he attempted to invite me over to his place. I went over in the evening with Dave. His home was astoundingly spotless, and the stone floors glistened, unlike our dump with dirty floors. He was still drunk, but managed to cook a delicious *borscht* (beetroot soup), which he offered us. Out came the vodka, too. How did he manage to keep this place in such tip-top shape in his condition?

On our first day off, and a very warm one it was too, we walked over to a monument a few kilometers down the road. Built in the desert, this circular monstrosity contains dozens of enormous columns with car engines, wheels, farm machinery parts, weapons, all cemented onto each one. Each column had a strange object atop of it. In the center was a staircase where one could climb to the top and be rewarded with a fantastic panoramic view of the landscape—the Sinai Desert, the Mediterranean, the Gaza Strip, and the numerous moshavim and kibbutzim that had transformed the dry desert lands into rich green farmland. At any rate, this monument remained a mystery to me. There was no placard or even a hint of what it is supposed to represent—it was quite hideous, actually. I could imagine historians several thousand years from now scratching their heads at this spectacle.

We discovered a mango plantation on the moshav in the evening, and of course, the few surviving ones at the end of their season soon found themselves in the kitchen. Also in the kitchen (already cooking) was our new house member—Hassam from Egypt. He introduced himself in a very English accent, having been educated in Britain. Now there were three of us in the house. In the weeks to come, we became good friends and conversed into the night and covered every subject under the sun. Meanwhile, my friend JP from Crete decided to leave, as he didn't like the farmer he was working for and had no fun in his work. It was the last time I saw him, and I wonder if he ever went back to Pakistan for more rubies.

Flower work was slowly starting—carnations. This was to be my work until I left the moshav. The Arabs picked the flowers while I stayed in the packing house, selecting and packaging the carnations. Today was the beginning, and only a few hundred were picked, but in mid-season, thousands would be carried in as they opened up quickly.

It was mid-December and a few days before Christmas when the start of the Palestinian uprising, known as the *intifada,* began. The aftermath of this violence cast a very dark shadow on Israel, and from that day on, it would never be the same again. Times were changing in this country, but for the worse.

The flowers were now coming in larger quantities, but these carnations hardly seemed natural. From the first stage while they are growing, they are constantly fed and sprayed with chemicals. After they are cut, cleaned, and packaged, two kinds of chemicals are added to their water: one to open up the flower earlier, and one to keep the stem rigid (the farmer called it LSD). This resulted in a very beautiful flower with no scent whatsoever. They might as well have been plastic carnations.

Sandstorms started with the intifada, and the Negev Desert was on the move. The wind was howling and the sand was lashing out everywhere and leaving ripples on the ground, making it look like a beach at low tide. Winter had arrived.

Christmas was upon us, and what better way to spend it than in the ancient city of Bethlehem, where the Christmas story had taken place? Well, by the time the day was over, I could have listed a dozen places where I would rather have spent this day. Had I known that the whole world was on its way to Bethlehem, too, I certainly wouldn't have attempted this trip at all. The buses to Bethlehem were packed to bursting point, and there was almost no standing room. Never mind, it was only a short trip.

The day was freezing cold. We left the warmth of the desert and arrived to only a few degrees above zero. To top it off, it was pouring with rain. It was a difference of almost 20°Celcius—I should have brought warmer clothing.

The security in Bethlehem was very tight due to the uprising which had errupted lately in the occupied territories, and Bethlehem did not escape the sting. Even though it is a predominantly Christian city, the army was not taking any chances at all. They had to protect pilgrims and tourists who had traveled from various countries just to be here on this special day. The soldiers were swarming everywhere. While walking up to Manger Square, soldiers on both sides of the street welcomed each visitor with a suspicious glare, remaining spaced out equidistant from each other; they were even standing on roofs of houses; all looking tense, but also alert and ready with their automatic weapons. It was one of those scenes normally shown on the ten o'clock news back in England. I could just imagine the headlines: *Israeli Army Dampens Christmas Celebrations*. Well, I couldn't deny that. It certainly did *not* feel like Christmas here, and the military presence was not exacly jolly.

Entering Manger Square required a full body search: to walk through a metal detector, and then I had to do a strange thing—to take a photograph. They wanted to hear the "click" of my camera to make sure that it really was a camera. Pity—they didn't let me take a picture of them, but to point the camera to the ground. Well, if it made the soldiers happy, I let them hear the "click" of the shutter (and what a waste of frame). A few minutes later, I had to go through the whole procedure again while trying to get into the Church of Nativity, supposedly the place where Jesus was born, and this church commemorated the spot.

You have never seen a packed church until you have been to this one here on this day: It was jam-packed with people from all corners of the world. Pilgrims and tourists had traveled far to be here tonight—to pray and sing carols. Inside the church, built upon this very holy site, I was shocked to see a plastic doll in the badly reproduced manger, where believers would go up to it, kiss it, and weep over it. I was mesmerized by this scene and actually disgusted when I noticed a label sticking out of the doll's rear end, which looked like a "Made in China" tag.

There certainly was no Christmas spirit around here. The people (including ourselves) were miserable due to the persistent rain and having to stand several hours to go through endless security checks. There was also a lack of decorations, which should have been suspended on all buidings and trees. The only colourful objects were the umbrellas preventing the people from drowning. A lone, unhappy-looking Christmas tree stood in the square, also with pitiful decorations. Most of the shops were closed and boarded up: I didn't know if by choice or by order. It just didn't seem logical that they would not remain open when the city was swarming with tourists looking to buy a holy souvenir or a can of holy air. Reporters and film crew swooped around the whole place. I hoped they had to click their cameras, too.

After our Christmas dinner of barbecued chicken, we went to see the carol singers in Manger Square. School children and choir groups from many parts of the globe were performing here. This was to continue for the next four hours until the start of the procession at midnight. I certainly had no desire to stay around waiting for this event in atrocious weather conditions and freezing to death. It was imperative that we find some sort of accommodation—any, just to to have a warm bed to crawl into. If we had, maybe I could have endured this penetrating cold for a couple more hours. There were no vacancies to be found anywhere in the city; even the most basic, dirtiest, cheapest forms of accommodation were all taken. The only possible solution was to get back to Jerusalem and find a place to sleep there.

A couple of hours later, we found ourselves back in the Old City of Jerusalem, still looking for a room. It was absoloutely deserted; a complete contrast to Bethlehem, but at least there were no soldiers standing on roofs. We did, however, surprise an army patrol scouting the alleys as we suddenly bumped into them on the corner. After realizing that we were not terrorists, even they went out of their way to try and find a room for us, but no luck. All beds (and floors) within 50km radius of Bethlehem had been taken. Definitely no sleep for us tonight. We had to do something, but what? Now I knew how the Three Wise Men must have felt. There were no more buses back to the moshav at this time; not even any shops that were open where we could have gone in to kill time... and I couldn't stop shivering.

Christmas day: it is well past midnight now. We were still wandering around the dark, deserted ancient alleys in this eerie biblical city and constantly bumping into the same army patrol. We did discover an all-night Arab café—a real sleazy joint, but at least it had a gas stove for keeping warm. Warmth is what we needed now, and I didn't care what kind of place this was as long as I was able to thaw out. I was soon downing my second glass of hot chocolate—it felt so good, and I felt my body being revitalized. The army patrol came in shortly after, gave us a nod, and also bought themselves a drink. The mood amongst the Arabs was suddenly very subdued. Israelis were not welcome in this part of the city, *especially* the Israeli army. I was not sure whether *we* were welcome even. The soldiers, despite being fully-clad in army gear, did not escape the freezing temperatures as they stood by the stove, toasting their hands. I was hoping they would stay for a while as this was not the safest place to be in. What was this place? It seemed a regular hang-out for bad guys and malevolent characters. They didn't stay. After polishing off their drinks, they left abruptly.

I spontaneously decided to do some pre-dawn sightseeing—*anything* to get out of this seedy place. I had never seen the Wailing Wall so late into the night—now was the opportunity. During the day it is always packed with tourists and religious folk. Luckily, I knew my way around the city and it wasn't long until the Wailing Wall compound came into view. It was floodlit in the darkness, which made it even more captivating; more so than during the day when there are too many distractions and you cannot absorb the magic of this place. At night, all is peaceful... and the only sound is the call of the muezzin emanating from the numerous minarets. Especially in the dark, the call to prayer would send a chill through the body, but it belonged here, all these different religious groups sharing this ancient part of the city. That is what makes this place so enchanting. I stood there for a while, absorbing this image, gazing at the Temple Mount with its beautiful Dome Of The Rock jutting out behind the wall. I was surprised to see some ultra-orthodox people praying at the Wall at this time of night. Nothing stops fanatics.

Well, that was almost two hours I managed to kill. What to do now? It was another three hours until dawn. The rain was still falling in bucketfuls, and the temperature dropped even more. Maybe it felt colder because of sleep deprivation. There was only one place to go—back to that awful café and wait. At 6:00 A.M. we would catch the first bus out of Jerusalem.

More sleepless and bedless tourists found themselves at the café. They also had no luck finding accommodation. It was amusing to see other stranded wanderers ending up inside the only place in the Old City that was open. The extra company brought with them a feeling of relief, as this helped to loosen up the strange atmosphere here. Rock music was now blaring out of the stereo, and the owner was as drunk as a lord. Was he trying to create a more inviting atmosphere for us? A strange way of doing it: He was mixing tea with coffee, beer with milk, spilling drinks all over the tables, and smashing glasses. All this time he was laughing deliriously, nor was he able to keep balance. He managed to stagger outside and throw up, and then staggered back inside, collapsed on a bench, and started snoring. What happened next was really amazing: With the owner completely knocked out, the café became self-service. People were making their own drinks behind the bar, while the owner was in a different world. Around 5:00 A.M. the owner's friend came in, summed up what was going on, and charged everybody for what they owed, then kicked everyone out and locked up. Obviously, he would pocket the money and tell the owner (once he's back on planet earth) that all the customers had left without paying.

It was only an hour before the first bus left, so we pulled over a taxi bound for the bus station and froze there until 6:00 A.M. What a strange Christmas it turned out to be; definitely an unforgettable one. It was still raining, but also the day was breaking, and in a few hours I would be back in the desert warmth.

Today was Friday, that meant no more buses from Be'er Sheva back to the moshav until Sunday. Sabbath wasn't supposed to start till sunset, so why were there no more buses so early? It wasn't even noon yet. The only way to get back was by hitchhiking. This was usually not an issue, but on Fridays one always had to compete with the soldiers who were returning home to spend the Sabbath meal with their families, and they were always given priority with lifts. The advantage was they never had to wait more than a few minutes, and quickly made space available. At least it wasn't raining here: the sky was blue, and it was warmer—much, much warmer. I love the desert!

Traffic was sparse on this lonely desert road, but very soon, a farmer from a nearby settlement, noticing that we were most probably volunteers, stopped and took us all the way. Upon arrival, it was the obvious—shower and bed; lovely, lovely bed.

The year was at an end, and the New Year's party was taking place at our house to the sounds of *Heart, Bryan Adams,* and *Bananarama*. All the volunteers were here—a mixture of nationalities, all chatting in different languages. It was goodbye to this year, and a very eventful one it has been for me, but I felt the coming year would bring many more unexpected surprises. New world developments were also occuring, and the Soviet

Union was keeping the media excited; not the Chernobyl disaster (that was old story), but TV cameras were pointing at Mikhail Gorbachov—he had captured the attention of the world with his reforms known as *Perestroika*, bringing political and economical reforms to his country, thus a more relaxed style of politics and pro-Western tendancies. Such a poignant move was turning him into a celebrity and the world was paying close attention. There were also rumours of an end to the Cold War. I was following this political development very closely, as I was yearning to visit Poland, and if there was any relaxation of the Soviet politics, it would make travel to and within that country much easier, without having to worry about secret police and the fear of being watched all the time. The border crossing from Turkey to Bulgaria had put me off the Eastern Bloc.

The world population reached the five billion mark, and continued to grow at a rapid pace, especially in India and China. Margaret Thatcher (the Iron Lady), had been elected as the Prime Minister of the United Kingdom for the third time and was still gathering momentum, plowing forward with her hard-line politics, determined to becoming a British empress. This was also the year when the work on the Channel Tunnel had begun, joining the European continent with the UK for the first time since the last Ice Age. The French started drilling from their side, and the British from theirs, and somewhere along the line under the Channel, they would meet in the middle and shake hands: Quite an amazing engineering project.

This had been, politically, a bad year for France, who decided to blow up and sink the Greenpeace ship *Rainbow Warrior* for protesting against nuclear testing on the Pacific islands. They now had to deal with world condemnation and political fallout with New Zealand. It was not good to be from France and be traveling around the Pacific at this time: there were a lot of angry folk out there whose paradise islands were being nuked by the French. Maybe JP should return to Pakistan's Chitral Valley and stay low for a while.

I was looking into the future though, and mentally making my plans: to be in Egypt by end of May, hitchhike through Europe, and visit Poland in June. In July, I intended to find work in Canada, then hitchhike through America and be in Mexico for the end of the year. If all this had worked out, it would have been a miracle, as I always ended up adrift with other plans due to meeting new people, new relationships, and the work and money situation played a factor, too.

New Year's Day, but no day off for me. The flowers didn't remain closed on this occassion. What a way to start the new year! I was five hours late for work with a hangover. Mountains of carnations greeted me on this day, begging to be cleaned, selected, and packaged for the start of 1988. I worked late into the night, lacking sleep and dying to go to bed, but the flowers had to be put to bed first. My boss and his wife worked equally hard and *did* keep me alive by feeding me throughout the day, and made sure I had enough caffeine for my hangover. They were good people and respected our need to celebrate the new year. There was nothing said about my lateness, but they continued grinning at my hangover.

A letter from Germany was waiting for me—from Katrina. I had written to her that I was back in Israel. She wrote back on a beautiful Christmas card, complaining about the cold in Berlin, and how miserable all the people were. She missed our time in Crete, and wished that she had continued traveling with me. I wished it, too... and wrote back telling her so. It wasn't too late.

Two Palestinian men worked with the flowers on a regular basis, returning each season. The farmer drove over to the Gaza border crossing every morning to pick them up, and then took them back when the work was done. One of them was an older man, wearing the traditional Bedouin garb with a red and white *kefiyeh* he always wore on his head. His body odour was intense, reeking so much that it was torture standing next to him for any length of time. The other man was much younger—dressed in jeans and T-shirt, but without the odour. He also had the *kefiyeh*, but wore it around his neck. They brought their food every day and always invited me to sit and share their meals with them, which I gladly did. Their wives baked pita bread on hot stones over a fire each morning. It was always fresh, and they used it for picking up the food with. Canned tuna appeared on a daily basis, and the homemade goat's cheese and egg plant dishes were also popular and delicious. I always looked forward to these breaks.

There was also a Bedouin girl who worked together with me in the sorting house while the two men only picked the flowers and carried them in for us to cut to size, sort, clean, and pack. She was wrapped up top to bottom in a *chador*, with only her eyes visible. At first, I was a little disappointed, having to work with a non-speaking black ghost whose eyes always followed me around, but after some days she started to open up... and so did her clothes, realizing that she didn't have to behave around me. She took off her *chador* one day, and underneath sported a tight pair of jeans and a bright pink T-shirt. Wow! There was actually a human being underneath all that, *and* a very pretty one, too. Fatma was her name, but she couldn't speak a word of English, and her Hebrew was very poor, but it was enough to chat and giggle all day long. Her coal-black eyes were always on me whenever I glanced at her, tempting me with her provocative smile. I was dying to snog her, but I couldn't bare to imagine what would happen to the girl—probably would have her throat slit by her brother or cousin if such a scandalous thing should occur. This is how it was day after day, making tedious work fun, and I ended up enjoying working with Fatma... very tempted each time. When she heard voices outside, indicating that the men were coming in with bundles of flowers, she hurriedly put her *chador* on again and retreated to the far side of the packing house, doing other chores in silence with her back turned. She was always ignored by the men; in fact, she was totally invisible, and there was never a hint from them that she actually existed. When the men were present, she also pretended that *I* didn't exist, thus giving everyone the impression never having cast a single eye on me. At meal times, Fatma always sat alone in the corner; not speaking, while the men sat at the the other end with their backs to her. This was the same procedure every day, and when they went back to their picking, off came her covers, and there was the human being once more. I will never understand this strange mentality amongst these people; their code of conduct so bizarre to Westerners.

The constant fight with the radio in the packing house was relentless: my boss loved listening to sport commentary, whereas his wife would switch it over to (easy listening) Hebrew songs as soon as he stepped out. When I was working alone with Fatma, we had it tuned to Radio Amman, broadcast from Jordan, where they always played English pop music—mostly *The Bangles* and *Cyndi Lauper*. At lunch time when the Arab men came, they took over control and put on their awful, howling Arabic music, which to me, always sounded the same. With two against one, I had no say... and neither did Fatma, as she didn't exist. It was automatically changed upon their departure. The worst was the soccer commentary, which always sounds the same no matter what language it is in, and for that reason, it was always a sigh of relief from everyone (the wife too) when the boss left. Even Arabic music was better than *that*.

The flower power continued for another couple of weeks before I had a chance for a day off. It was the Sabbath, but there was nothing much to do with it as the weather was in a rage and another sandstorm mixed with rain was upon us. It was very cold, and the only thing to do was to sleep and make smalltalk. Two girls had since joined us in our house: Anke from The Netherlands, and Mirjam from Surinam. They were traveling together and making money along the way. This made our home somewhat livelier with the five of us, and very soon, word spread that there were two female newcomers in our house and everybody wanted to visit.

My house had become the major gathering point now, and it was sometimes difficult to get rid of the people when I wanted to sleep. There was the daily guitar playing around the electric fire instead of the real outdoor kind, but still cozy. Sasha the Russian, was permanently drunk, spending his entire earnings on arak, the lethal spirit tasting of aniseed. I never saw him sober or was able to have a proper conversation with him, puzzled at the fact that he still seemed to be able to perform his work and always got up on time. There was nobody else from Britain here; most foreigners being from South America—a jolly lot, with the exceptian of a Peruvian, who was more somber and concentrated on smoking his hashish all the time. As usual, I steered away from both—the alcohol and smoking —neither would give me any pleasure—wine was an exception.

This month had seen endless violence in the occupied territories of Israel, especially near my moshav alongside the Gaza Strip. Around the towns of Rafiah and Khan Yunis and various refugee camps, curfews had been imposed. Gangs of Palestinian youths were hurling stones at the soldiers. The result so far—over forty Palestinians have been shot dead by the army. This led to worldwide condemnation of Israel, including its closest ally—USA. Before, the Palestinians used to shun away from the soldiers, now they were starting to fight back. In the Gaza Strip, the people were turning more to their religion—Islam. The outcome of this was more and more fanatic Muslim fundamentalists were being recruited to die as martyrs while in confrontation with the Israeli army—stones against automatic weapons.

On the moshav at night, the entrance was guarded by an armed soldier, and now it was forbidden to venture outside the perimeter of this settlement after sundown. I started to feel like a prisoner here. We stayed indoors anyway, as bitter cold had now descended and the electric heater was on full. The five of us played card games, chess or backgammon, and spent the evenings talking endlessly. The girl from Surinam always wanted one of us to give her a massage, and even took her T-shirt off for it. This was our daily winter routine. Every Friday, my host family brought over a batch of freshly-made hummus and a cake, which I shared with everyone, as the others didn't seem to have such a generous family to work for as I did.

Nevertheless, this had been a wonderful month, as far as my savings went: with only one day off this month, and working the rest of the thirty at an average of twelve hours a day, I managed to save over $500. If the family hadn't been so nice, and the work had been horrible, I wouldn't have done this. I was being treated like a family member, and jolly Mrs. Boss was making sure I didn't go hungry or thirsty. The Gaza Bedouins I worked with were also very friendly and had an equally good rapport with the boss—they were also treated with respect. The atmosphere couldn't have been better... and I still fantasized about kissing Fatma... and other things....

During the night the alarm went off. This signifies that we are under attack, but I didn't really have any reaction; I just wanted to know what was happening as all the men of the household rushed inside, grabbed their M16's and sped off to the center in their cars. The women stayed at home with the children. It was exactly what I expected—only a drill. They just wanted to know how long it would take for everybody to prepare during a real attack. The time taken was two minutes and fifty seconds.

My three-month visa was already coming to an end: it was imperrative that I travel to Be'er Sheva to renew it. I couldn't believe how quickly the time had gone by: it felt as if I had just recently arrived from Crete. It turned out to be a wasted day, as I never did get an extension on my visa— the official form from the moshav office was missing. I had to return to the Moshav for the sacred document that would grant me another three months. It would have to wait another day.

The immigration office was as big a mess as I remembered it almost three years ago: None of the officials spoke English, and there were scores of Arabic-speaking people sitting around in the waiting rooms, on the stairs, and even outside. Everything was dirty and nothing was organized amidst the mass confusion, and nobody had the faintest clue which department they should be in, or the correct forms to fill out. The place looked like a house full of refugees. There were several African people wearing *kippas*, also waiting for visas. These must be the ones I had read about in the *Jerusalem Post*—the recently-discovered Ethiopian Jews who claimed to belong to one of the lost tribes, and were now trying to prove their Jewishness.

The next two Saturdays I managed to get a day off. It was time to contemplate my next move. Three months on this place was more than enough. Now I wanted to get away from this growing boredom—from these damn flowers. Living and working in the city was a tempting thought. I most certainly didn't want to transfer to yet another moshav, but that may be the only way of obtaining permits to stay in Israel for any length of time. This place suited my requirements for a while, as I really needed a temporary home where I could rest, do some Hebrew studying, and make plans. Greece had tired me out—physically and mentally, especially while moving around from place to place. It felt good to settle down again for a some time, but my feet were starting to itch.

I took a chance to walk over to Gaza together with Dave and the girls . The violence was still continuing in the occupied territories, so I was most surprised when the soldiers at the border let us through into the Gaza Strip, especially when numerous world government officials and reporters were being denied entry to this area. Twenty minutes inside, walking towards Khan Yunis (I really wanted to see with my own eyes what was happening) we were picked up by a jeep full of soldiers who whisked us away and drove us back to the border. The driver apologized, saying that he was ordered to bring us back across. High ranking officials inside the Strip radioed the patrol that it was much too dangerous for us to proceed at this time. They had been alerted by the soldiers manning the checkpoint. "There is a mini war going on there," he informed us. True enough, on the horizon over the cities of Rafiah and Khan Yunis, we could see smoke rising; probably from petrol bombs, burning tyres, and burning vehicles.

We stayed with the soldiers at the border while they prepared some coffee, still apologizing for not permitting us to walk to Khan Yunis, but they couldn't afford the risk. They appeased our disappointment with oranges. We ended walking back to the moshav after stopping off shortly to see a war monument by Kibbutz Sufa.

Things were deteriorating: terrorists gunned down a bus in Be'er Sheva, killing six people and injuring many others; the bus was carrying workers to Dimona. All buses were now being searched around this area. On top of that, violence continued in the Gaza Strip, with two more people shot, numbering well over sixty now. The uprising didn't seem to be abating, instead, it was becoming more extreme. I didn't it realize it at that time, but there would be no more visits to the Gaza Strip—it was to become one of the most dangerous places in the world.

At night, helicopters circulated this area, heading to nearby Rafiah and Khan Yunis—the main trouble hotspots. They were doing overhead surveilance, preparing for more violence. During the day, fighter jets worked on their maneouvers, flying low and breaking the sound barrier each time. The explosion of air would vibrate the ground and buildings. Israel was showing the rioters how much power they were up against.

The last day of work on Moshav Sde Avraham had finally arrived—with relief. I thought the day would never come. I was supposed to stay here only two months, but ended up staying almost four, not because this was a very exciting place—far from it, but I managed to save $1200 during my stay, which was a great achievement. It was a good place to save money, and my host family were the best people I ever worked for. That day, they presented me with a large, gooey, delicious "good luck" cake, and I received all my money with an open invitation to return the following season for more flowers—No bloody way!

Now the flower picking season was over and the labour force had been cut down, with almost all volunteers leaving this month. There was only a maximum of about fifteen volunteers on this moshav, and luckily, each one of us got on with everybody. The two girls were also leaving, as well as Dave and Hassan. We had spent the winter together in that small house and had grown fond of each other. Our parties, silliness, and laughter, broke up the monotonous flower-sorting, but we all had different plans and destinations: more friends, more goodbyes, and more sadness. It was the moment I always dreaded and the saddest part of travel—to get close to people—and then, the painful goodbyes... and it didn't get any easier as every additional "goodbye" was like another wound, which would fester and consume the soul.

The next day I had all my laundry done, packed, sent off letters, and now ready to leave (with no regrets). My boss had found work for me at a steak restaurant in Tel Aviv: one of his friends was the owner. He recommended that I try it out, and that is where I was heading in a few days, once I managed to convert the shekels into dollars. Living and working in the city will be so much more different (more expensive, too) to the isolated life I had gotten used to in a desert farming community.

No more flowers... HOORAY! I couldn't see anymore flowers now... FREEDOM!

I left the moshav for good today and traveled to Jerusalem to see my Detroit friend at the Yeshiva study centre. It was only a brief meeting with him as everybody from the center was heading to Tel Aviv to demonstrate against returning the occupied territories back to the Palestinians. There was nobody left here and no reason to linger, so I also went to Tel Aviv and checked in at Momo's hostel.

Amazingly, Germany (the German man I came to Israel with back in November), was still there where we had left him—at the hostel, but not the same person I had gotten to know. We were overjoyed to see each other again, but I sensed a little sadness in him as well as boredom. He had lost a lot of weight and some of his sense of humour. Working and living in this city had certainly changed him, but *not* his English. He didn't even tell me about the temperatures in Frankfurt, nor did he offer me a cigarette.

15
ANGUISH IN PARADISE

Car fumes hit me full force in the noisy city as I walked along the palm-lined Ben Yehuda Street. The owner of the Argentinean steakhouse was expecting me. Business-like, he was: friendly enough, but somewhat reserved at the same time. He didn't have any full-time work for another two weeks, but suggested that I put in a day tomorrow. I think he wanted to try out his prospective employee beforehand. I was offered 500 shekels a month, including accommodation and free restaurant food (steaks every day). For that, I was to work eight hours a day, and my tasks would be mainly kitchen and cleaning duties. The word "exploitation" sprang to my mind. WHAT??? 500 SHEKELS!!! Nowhere near as much money as I had expected. I earned more on the moshav…, but maybe I would give it a go anyway just for the experience. In addition, I could move into my room immediately instead of paying for the hostel each day.

I wasn't told about the living conditions, and was not prepared for what I saw—three rooms, no kitchen, and five Arabs living there already. The place was putrid, dirty, and stank of filth. There was no furniture in the apartment, neither any beds. They sat and slept on cheap, flattened mattresses on the floor—on no account would I live here. There were no introductions, and the unfriendly occupants stared at me suspiciously while Arabic music was wailing out of the radio. I left as quickly as possible; told

Mr. Argentina Steak that I'd move in tomorrow after work, but I had no intention of doing either. What on earth was he thinking? That I had just come off the street somewhere? Actually, the streets were cleaner than his so-called accommodation that was more suitable for cockroaches. I went back to Momo's hostel, still in shock.

A lively evening at the White House Bar was a good way to blow off steam together with Germany and some people I met at the hostel. I fell into a hostile argument (my first in Hebrew) with an Israeli over an insignificant thing such as, "*I was sitting here first at the table.*" It amazed me that an adult was seriously arguing over a childish issue as this *and* he wasn't willing to share the table, either—there was plenty of room. Such aggression is typical in Israel, but primarily in large cities, where life is fast-paced and "me-first" cohorts are rampant.

Staying in the city was even more expensive than I had anticipated. I had no inclination to waste my hard-earned cash here, where there were many possibilities to having a good time, and *good time*s had a price in Israeli cities. It was not like Crete, where one could live very cheaply. The unfriendly city people made me think twice about staying here and looking for work. For anyone who arrives in Israel for the first time and spends time in Tel Aviv, they would get a very negative impression of Israel. Only by leaving the city to seriously travel around the entire country for a prolonged time, this view would change.

Observably, I knew that I could most definitely find work here and earn more money than on a moshav, but it would mean having to live in a youth hostel. This was something I was also not prepared to do. I appreciate and enjoy youth hostels while traveling from place to place, but I certainly cannot make one my home for a few months: to be with strangers, and having to worry if my luggage was safe every time I was out. In addition, spending much more money here was inevitable. Not having facilities to cook and being forced to buy ready-made food was also an added expense. I could have put myself on a permanent falafel diet, I suppose, but there was a limit how many of them one could consume. Maybe the city was not such a good idea after all.

What were my options? I visited the moshav office, only to find it empty. The moshavim were crying out for volunteers, as there was a shortage of labor due to the unrest that was scaring people away. Once again, Israel was in the media spotlight, letting the world know how dangerous and risky it is to travel to the Middle East. Such nonsense I could not abide because every country in the world has its risks, and the media should instead focus on the more positive aspects of a country instead of stone-throwers in Israel.

Entering the office, I was greeted with enthusiasm. "Well, HELLO! It is good to see somebody today." Yehudit was the only person in the office, and it was her job to place volunteers on a moshav. She recognized me from before. "How did you like your moshav?"

"The people I worked for were very nice," I told her truthfully.

"That's always good to hear. Hope I can find you another nice family to work for." I was presented with several destinations, but I wanted to be on a moshav where paid overtime was available. Tonight, I would make up my mind where to go and return to the office tomorrow.

I decided on Moshav Neot at Sodom, near the Dead Sea, as I liked the location. "Good luck!" she wished me… and back to the desert. According to the map, the moshav was located in the boons of a forgotten land. The time-consuming journey would take up most of the day: buses were infrequent, but I loved driving this route, and to admire the sudden approach of the desert after the lush green vegetation on the Mediterranean side.

What a beautifully weird place this was. The bus was traveling through a desert where scorpions and reptiles thrived, and the next moment we were inside an oasis. The moshav was encircled by eerie emptiness; not the usual dull yellow color, but mostly white, being the salt formations caused by the Dead Sea that used to be much higher hundreds of thousands of years ago than its present level today. On one side were these serrated, soaring, salt-rock cliffs, looking brittle against the azure sky. A vast expanse of flat desert brush dominated the adjacent side and persisted all the way south along this Great African-Syrian Rift Valley, which continues beneath the Red Sea and emerges once more in East Africa. The stumpy, broad acacia trees with their thorns supplemented the region with natural beauty. The air was motionless and oppressive, with only the clamor of the chattering birds that were grateful for this haven. There was that strange feeling in my ears again, just like the first time when I came to the Dead Sea by bus. Those cliffs looked invitingly tempting, and I was already planning future hikes up there; even If I did get to the top, I would still be below sea level. I was thinking it was going to be great working here.

I couldn't have been more wrong. After seeking out the moshav leader, things got off to a bad start when his vibes clearly indicated "Mr. Nasty Man," and I took immediate dislike to him…, which I also made obvious. He allocated me the farmer I was supposed to work for and left briskly without another word. "Mr Evil Man" was my farmer. He marched me to my living quarters—very simple room, small, with two beds and a cupboard, a nice kitchen and dining area combined. It was sufficient. My boss didn't say much, not even so much as a smile or an acknowledgment of gratitude that I was here to help with his farming. His presence made me feel very uncomfortable. He was an Orthodox Jew, wearing his black *kippah* at all times, and there was also something uncanny about him I couldn't quite grasp. Pure evil he was for sure, but the question was, how evil? He didn't offer me anything to drink or eat, and I had to ask twice to have some bedding. As for the shop, it was up to me to find it and get myself some groceries. I felt as unwelcome as an intruding scorpion and would probably be treated as such.

In most parts of the world, when entering a grocery store, it is deemed normal to grab a shopping cart and fill it up *while* shopping. Not here though, where one was used for different purposes. Once you enter a supermarket or grocery store, you grab the vehicle, run as quickly as possible, and stake your place in line with it. If anyone gets in your way—run them over! At the cash register, you will see a line of empty carts waiting for their owners while they shop frantically, returning every few minutes, hands full with groceries which they toss inside, nudge them down a bit more towards the cash register, and run around doing the rest of their shopping while always keeping a beady eye on the line, lest any impudent intruder should sneak ahead. Nobody shops with their carts as I did that day, and when I was ready to pay, there were about eight unsupervised carts in front of me. Naturally, I went to the front (as nobody else was there) and then all hell broke loose. From the aisles, raised voices chastised me and demanded that I get to the back of the line. The enraged shoppers appeared with their wicked eyes upon me, daring me to proceed. I did, ignoring their pathetic behavior. The cashier just sniggered to himself, paying no heed to the commotion and not wanting to get involved. Quite miraculously, the angry mob behind me had suddenly finished their shopping simultaneously and were gnashing their teeth and mumbling amongst themselves about this impertinent, bad-mannered foreigner who didn't know how to queue. I was to witness this procedure in many shops throughout Israel, and after some time, ended up staking my place with an empty cart in line, too, and feeling very foolish and selfish about it.

My Egyptian friend, who had shared the house with me at Sde Abraham, was here, too, I was told by Yehudit from the moshav office, so I went to seek him out. Hasan was astonished and delighted with my sudden appearance and gave me a big hug. "How is this place?" I asked him.

"People are so weird here," he confirmed my assumptions. "Not only the farmers, but also the volunteers." Afterward, we went to the volunteers' bar to see what sort of crowd congregated here. Well, it was a long time since I had seen such weirdos. Nearly all the volunteers were English and Irish, drinking heavily, and looked as if they had spent the entire day rolling around in the desert. Unshaven and sordid they were; their clothes in tatters... and not the most friendly-looking bunch, either. Several of them were stoned and oblivious to anything. The strong stench of hashish and stale beer pervaded the interior. I thought this was a refugee gathering. "See what I mean?" Hassan eyed me.

"What *is* this place?" I asked, but more to myself. It was clear to me that I did not belong here. The more I saw of this moshav, the more anomalous it felt. Maybe it was just a bad day and things would be better tomorrow at work.

There was no work the next day. I started off with a free day. Everybody worked Saturdays here, so a Thursday was taken as the official day off. I took advantage of this extra time and went off to do some hiking out of the moshav towards the beautiful desert landscape; first walking through vigorous-growing date palms and then the spiky scrub. It was March, and already pretty hot, and I was forced to wear shorts, which enabled the thorny bushes to tear at my legs. Within an hour, I was covered in scratches. Small lizards scurried about everywhere, sometimes scampering over my feet. In the sand there were familiar hoof prints of ibex —the desert goats, and several other animals I couldn't identify. Afterward, I walked over to the jagged white cliffs to the top of the canyon with its winding wadi below, and from above, was the captivating picture-postcard view of the Dead Sea in the remote distance—very blue, sparkling like a sapphire at the foot of the tinted pink mountains of Jordan, illuminated by the sinking sun. I stayed atop for a while and watched the sun set in the west. The green fields of the moshav were a startling contrast against the harsh desert mountains. Irrigation had certainly brought this place to life. I felt revived again, and yesterday's bad start now seemed irrelevant.

In the evening, my boss came over and laid down the rules and regulations. Cold-blooded and stern, he talked down to me as if I was some uneducated fool; neither did he pay for overtime: here, you were given time off instead. One thing was clear—I was to work for an asshole *and* a psycho. I needed to take a walk in the night to decide whether I should stay here; not for the work, but to explore this astonishingly striking landscape with its endless hiking possibilities. Walking outside the moshav at night wasn't very safe, I had been told, as wild pigs tend to roam. They are extremely aggressive, come charging out of nowhere, and can easily kill a human being. That was okay; I really did want to see one, and I was convinced that they couldn't be worse than the people on this moshav.

Today was my first and last day of work. It was to be one of those bizarre events: after only working four hours in weeding, my wacky boss suddenly materialized, escorted me to the house, and ordered me to pack all my belongings and *get-the-hell* out of this moshav and never to return—I was speechless—it was all very sudden—I had done nothing wrong. I knew my work had been good enough, even in those few hours, so what was the problem? He would not offer any explanation and rebuffed my questions. My feelings were confirmed, he *was* mentally disturbed—a psycho. I wasn't even allowed to take a shower or make a phone call to the moshav office or see the volunteers' leader; being told that he didn't want to see me, but wanted me out of here as soon as possible—again making the point—"Never to return!" The farmer took me out of the moshav by car, with the intention of leaving me out on the lonely desert road by a bus stop where I could take the next bus to Jerusalem (this bus came twice a day), but his cowering wife, who was terrified of him, pleaded with her husband to drive me into the city, as they were heading that way anyway. He relented somewhat, and a very long, silent journey followed until we reached the suburbs. His wife also offered no explanation why I was suddenly whisked away out of the moshav without being able to speak to anyone. She just shrugged her shoulders, avoiding conversation and afraid to speak. I couldn't even say goodbye to my friend Hassan.

"Out!" He simply ordered when we arrived in the city. I needed no urging and gave him the finger once I had my things.

In Jerusalem I felt a little out of place: wearing shorts and a T-shirt. People were looking me as if I was mad; it was so cold here. Everybody was dressed appropriately—trousers and coats. I wish I could have explained that I was not a summer idiot, but had just been whisked away from the desert by a very demented, orthodox moshav-madman. Feeling conspicuous, I wasted no time, but took a room at the Jaffa Gate Youth Hostel in the Old City for a couple of nights, put on some warmer clothing, and went out to exchange some money on the black market. What a day! Like a bolt from the blue, wandering within the narrow alleys, was a face I recognized—Pascal—my French Canadian friend from Paleohora, Crete. I recalled once more the memorable times we had spent together in Greece, together with the other beach people: Katrina, my friends, and the beach scene sprang to mind and brought a lump to my throat.

I adopted the role of a tour guide and took Pascal round to see some of the famous sights in Jerusalem, as he seemed quite lost. He had been in Egypt, and was now looking for work in Israel. Pascal brought me up to date on the events in Paleohora, Crete: After my departure, the following day, the police raided the beach and arrested everyone; they were all thrown into jail for the night, even the European passport holders. In the morning, the troupe was escorted onto the first bus out of town.

For several months now, the Old City of Jerusalem has been a ghost town: the Arab shop owners were on strike as a protest against the Israeli occupation of the territories. This time of year, the Old City should have been thriving and swarming with tourists, but the narrow alleys were deserted, and for the first time ever, I was able to walk normally here instead of edging myself sideways through the crowds. Some shop owners only opened for two hours a day, just for the hope of a little business for getting by... but there were no buyers. All the tourists had been scared off because of the unrest. The uprising had a negative effect on the Palestinian population—they were only hurting themselves with it. Only armed soldiers were discernible in some parts, awaiting further trouble. I couldn't believe how much it had changed already, and there was now an uncanny feeling of tension in the air—something I had never felt before.

I took Pascal to see the ultra-orthodox section of Mea Shearim the next day; my second visit here, and something every visitor to Jerusalem should witness. What strange people they are! There were many of them lurking around this time, but nobody seemed to be having a conversation or joking around; nobody was smiling, and even the children looked solemn and bloodless from their sickly, pale white skin color that hardly sees daylight. It was the skin tone of a person who spends his/her entire life indoors. The young boys were also dressed in black ultra-orthodox garb— with a wide brimmed hat and looking very pious with their side locks. We were totally ignored; invisible, unhallowed beings who had no place on this earth. I was happy to finish the tour guiding and to get away from these eerie zombies.

There was not much to do in the evening. The Old City shops were boarded up, and outside, the weather was cold, wet, and miserable. Feeling a little despondent myself, I braved the downpour and went off to the modern part of Jerusalem outside the Old City walls, as everything would be open there and coming back to life, now that *Shabbat* was officially over. Surprise again. I bumped into my other friend—the Detroit guy from the *Yeshiva* and his group of orthodox buddies. We embraced, overjoyed to see each other again. He asked me to join him at the cheesecake restaurant with his fellow students, which I gladly obliged. I told him about my adventures since our last get together, while he filled me in on his religious study sessions. I noticed he was growing side locks, but did not comment on the evident transformation that was taking place, and instead, I wondered how much longer he would be allowed to associate with heretics.

Yehudit, the woman at the moshav office in Tel Aviv, was surprised to see me back so soon. She was quite upset when I told her what had transpired, that she immediately called the volunteers' leader to demand an explanation. We were both surprised to learn that he had absolutely no idea what had taken place and was very angry with the farmer for having acted in such an unorthodox manner. He asked me to come back, saying that he would pay for the transportation, but I refused, as I didn't like that strange atmosphere on the moshav anyway, and with all those horrendously drunk and stoned volunteers there, I really had no desire to return. A pity, as the location was a place that dreams are made of. Yehudit, meanwhile, made a point to the leader that the farmer is not to get another volunteer, otherwise she would suspend the service to the moshav. She was very apologetic about the whole episode, also admitting that there were some nutcases out there, some of which were not allowed to have any volunteers. Now she had another name to add to her blacklist. Yehudit had another arrangement for me; not a moshav, but to work for a private farmer. He was to meet me at the bus station in Hadera.

Two hours later, he was shaking my hand at the bus station, and after brief introductions, I took a liking to this good-natured, but quiet man. He spoke only Hebrew, and explained that this was the first time he had taken on a volunteer, and I was to tell him what things I would need and to explain to *him* the rules. This really amused me, as it was supposed to be him telling *me* the rules and regulations. I am convinced that we would have gotten along very well, but there was just one dilemma—the accommodation. It was in extremely poor condition. He was going to convert his office into a bedroom, but there wasn't even a shower in the building—just a sink. "Er, where do I shower?" I inquired, somewhat bemused.

"Shower? Oh, I'm going to get a shower put in."

"No thanks, it's no place for me," I told him, and requested that he drive me back to the bus station, which he obligingly did. There was absolutely no way that I was going to stay in this cold, lonely, desolate, rural place, with or without a shower—to alienate myself from humanity? One week here would have driven me crazy. He was very understanding and still remained friendly, apologizing that the accommodation was not suitable.

I don't understand the Israelis: they are extremely clean people who live in very comfortable and cozy homes, but they expect foreigners to live in dirt and squalor. It would never cross their minds to make a place habitable for any workers, neither are they able to comprehend that some of these foreign workers actually lead a higher standard of living back in their countries compared to them, and are only here for pleasure and experience. Not having a shower was the last straw. We shook hands and I wished him good luck and left. It was pouring with rain outside, and I was cold and miserable *and* in a bad mood. The bus to Tel Aviv had just left, and I didn't feel like waiting an hour for the next one, so I resorted to hitchhiking.

The lift took me into Netanya, but I decided to stay a while and grab some food. I was starving, still feeling dejected and pissed off—nothing seemed to be working out. I stayed in the café for a long time, also missing the second bus while brooding and watching the rain, which persisted throughout the day. I thought of all my friends I had to say goodbye to in the last three years, convinced that they were all having a nice time somewhere, but that made me even more miserable. In my present state, only negative thoughts entered my head, accentuating the fact that I was once again—alone. Before getting depressed even more, I took the next bus to Tel Aviv and went back to Momo's hostel for the night. I was overjoyed to see "Germany"... so much in fact, that I hugged him. We went out together after his shift was over and I was grateful for his good-natured company, which perked me up somewhat.

Yehudit couldn't believe I was back yet again. "What? He doesn't have a shower?" She yelped, finding that too incredible. "He's *not* getting anymore volunteers. A shower is one of the requirements." She said that harshly, then took out her book and also blacklisted him. "I have just had a request from a very nice farmer on Moshav Fatza'el, by Jericho. You will like him," she declared with a confident smile, suddenly transforming into a sweet angel.

"Do you promise?"

"I promise," she assured me.

16
INVASION OF THE GRAPES

I was on my way to the Jordan Valley where the moshav was located
—twenty minutes north of Jericho and directly on the Jordanian border.
"Oh, my," I mumbled to myself, it's so beautiful here... and these hills....
However, my present mood wasn't so positive. In fact, the way I was
feeling right now—unmotivated and apathetic, still simmering from the
"desert eviction," I was charged with negative electrodes, which overrode
any positive feelings.

I checked out the accommodation... hmmm, not bad (even though I
had to transform it from a coalmine into something livable); what a hassle!
Well, it *was* a real house at least; hmmm... pretty good, actually. I met my
boss—Shimon, who seemed genuinely friendly (but so do lions before they
catch their prey). I didn't trust him... too friendly in fact. At that moment I
didn't trust anyone after my recent experiences. Work starts tomorrow—
brushing grapes. Brushing grapes???

Yes, I had heard correctly. Brushing grapes it was, on an early, cold
morning. Each bunch of grapes has to be thinned out when they are still in
seed form; this has to be done before they flower. What a strange job, but
quite pleasant and easy. A small brush is used (a kind that is used on
poodles) to carefully brush off about 50% of the baby grapes, being careful
not to harm the remaining ones on the cluster, or do it too hard, in which
case the whole bunch would snap off. There were thousands of them, and

332

endless rows of vines. I worked with two other English volunteers, who were not particularly friendly, but come to think of it, neither was I. Our boss worked with us, making polite conversation while playing soft Israeli music on the radio. The atmosphere was actually pleasant, and I started to relax. We took a couple of breaks for freshly-brewed coffee, and then it was time for lunch. We were driven back and forth on the back of the tractor, accompanied by the farmer's dog who sat by the gear stick. This was a floppy-eared, docile gray thing who answered to the name of "Max." Actually, he didn't answer at all. He was as dumb as an ostrich: he didn't even *know* his own name. I liked him nevertheless and we became good friends.

This moshav also had a bar. It was open on Tuesdays and Thursdays in the evening. I didn't even bother to investigate it, knowing exactly what to expect, but I did happen to walk past it one evening, and the sounds of *The Doors* infiltrated the entrance, but also the whiff of hashish.

A few days later, we had a change of work—picking artichokes. One walks up and down between the rows and clips off an artichoke that is protruding. They are tossed into an open pack, which we carried on a frame on our backs. This work was also pleasant and easygoing. I grabbed a couple for dinner.

It is end of April—Land Day. There were more demonstrations in the territories. A three-day curfew was imposed in the West Bank and the Gaza Strip. Nobody was permitted to enter or leave those areas. During that time, violent demonstrations were expected as a protest against the overtaking of Arab lands. I suppose this meant more bloodshed and more tear gas.

The highest point in this area is Mt. Sartaba. It is where I found myself at 4:30 A.M. before it got too hot. I was attempting this hike together with an Israeli guy (Zev) and his Italian girlfriend (with a strange name) who were also working on the moshav. These recent arrivals were my neighbors; never went to the bar, and kept to themselves mostly. The Israeli was a fitness fanatic and I often saw him stretching outside before the birds woke up. Macho man was leading the way—a strenuous walk over the hills. But this was just what I needed, and trying to keep pace with the tall, long-legged Israeli was no fun at all, as he tried to show how fit he was, forcing me to almost trot to keep up with him. His girlfriend was not amused, either. "What's the hurry?" I yelled.

"We have to get to the top before the sun comes up," was his lame reply.

"Take it easy, it's not Mt. Sinai."

The first pink rays of sun appeared over the horizon at 5:30 A.M. and it was a moment I always cherished—when everything comes alive again. This area was teeming with wildlife, and to prove itself, we invaded the privacy of several snakes that were enjoying this moment, too—the first warmth of the day. They angrily slithered away into the grass.

The coarse, desert grass is razor-sharp in these hills, as my ankles soon found out when the barbed spikes hooked into my flesh, making it bleed. The spikes succeeded penetrating my canvas work boots, through socks, and into my feet. Several times we were forced to stop and de-spike ourselves. We had a marvelous idea of wrapping up our feet, first in toilet paper, then the socks on top. It helped a little. Toilet paper is always good to have for all kinds of emergencies.

We passed caves that were used as dwellings by the Bedouins who lived here, and whose lives usually evolved around sheep, shepherding them from pasture to pasture. It was a scene straight out of the biblical era— same place; same lifestyle; different times.

After three hours of good hiking, we were standing on the summit, grateful for the wind that materialized from nowhere and dried off the dripping sweat... and what a breathtaking view it was from here, even though daybreak had taken place over an hour ago. The other side of the valley was Jordan, and the border was noticeably visible next to the fields where we worked. Jordan Valley was sprawled out in the distance from the north to the south, rich in farmland, and the green hills, which would soon be parched by the strengthening sun, trapped the valley on both sides and caused an oven effect. These valleys would soon dry out, shriveling vegetation as the desert heat takes over in the long summer months ahead.

Atop of Mt. Sartaba are the ruins of a fortress built by King Herod for one of his many wives—a place where she was confined. As the Romans passed through, they destroyed the structure, and the scattered ruins can still be seen today. History continues—this mountain was also used as a beacon by Jews in ancient times when fires were lit to announce religious holidays and the beginning of the month. Camels used to traverse this parched land as part of an ancient trading route, bringing in goods from further east to the ancient ports on the Mediterranean. It is not unusual to still find Roman coins along this earliest road, I was told. Today, all is silent, and the only sound was that of a distant tractor on the way to the field.

Back at home I dived into the shower and discovered what had been causing me discomfort between my legs throughout most of the hike—some of the barbed grass had pierced through into my balls and was embedded there. It was excruciatingly painful when I pulled it out, then blood started oozing out. Oh, no, what should I do? Go to see the doctor? No way! That was too embarrassing. I would leave it, and hopefully it would heal, but maybe I should put on some antiseptic. I borrowed some from my boss, telling him it was for my cuts, but didn't tell him which cut. I ended up putting a plaster on, but it pained and worried me for some days. My balls healed again. Damn the grass!

Taking advantage of my second day off, I decided to follow one of the nearby wadis to see how far I could get. Wild crab apples were growing everywhere—delicious when dried out naturally by the sun. The three of us (same group as before) visited one of the many-found caves in this limestone country, only to find the ground covered with empty bullet cartridges and bomb shrapnel. Apparently, this place had been well used by the Israeli army; not surprising, from this commanding position, it's a very good vantage point to the wadis lower down, which the enemy had no choice but to traverse and expose themselves.

Enough cave exploration: we continued our hike along the wadi until the way became narrower, and the sides were no longer gentle banks, but smooth, sheer rock faces caused by sudden winter flash floods. We were forced to turn back due to the growing presence of scary-looking bees—bright red in color with yellow stripes, four times the size of the humble bumblebee and a sting like an erupting volcano. Hovering overhead, they sounded like miniature helicopters. Taking a detour on the way back, we visited one of the many strange monuments found all over Israel. They all look beautiful, but pay tribute to war and death. No monument ever seems to commemorate a happy moment in history.

I was starting to enjoy myself here; living in such a stunning location, and the work was fun, too—much more fun than those endless flowers.

Local side trips was something I always looked forward to. Zev's brother stopped by to visit him one day. He was also keen to tour some local hard-to-get-to places, and so, I tagged along with them as they had a car. First, we went to see a Greek monastery (Mar Saba); this one is situated smack in the middle of nowhere between Jericho and the Dead Sea. Hardly any tourists ever came here. It is so remote that not many people are actually aware of its existence. In order to reach the monastery, "leg power" was put into action, as we traversed the short distance from the road and climbed, what seemed like, hundreds of steps to reach the outer walls of this extraordinary structure. However, it was a wasted journey: wearing only shorts, we weren't allowed inside. What else could we wear in this heat? But the exterior was magnificent nevertheless, and the panoramic vista of total barren desolation and solitude was an experience that made up for the denial of entry. If aliens were to land on this spot, they would be convinced that there was no life on planet Earth. We ambled amongst the grounds of the monastery until a busload of Greek pilgrims pulled up alongside. Amazing! I thought this place was supposed to be cut off. The Greek chatter made me think of Crete.

Back on the road, and we stopped briefly at the nearby Nebi Musa mosque, also located in the middle of nowhere. It is said that this mosque contains the tomb of Moses. The compound was protected by a high, rectangular wall that we skirted briefly. Next to the mosque are ancient tombstones, some of them so old, the Arabic script had disappeared from erosion. The Israelis didn't attempt to enter this holy Muslim site, and I wouldn't have been allowed in anyway, with my shorts on. There was not a soul visible and no sound whatsoever. We continued.

Our next stop was Qumran, where the famous Dead Sea Scrolls were found and are now exhibited in the Shrine of the Book in Jerusalem. There was an entry fee to see the caves, but none of us wanted to pay the ridiculously inflated amount, so we didn't proceed. I have seen enough caves, and there was nothing inside them now, so why pay to see an empty one?

Coming back through Jericho, I noticed what a ghost town it had become. All the stores and restaurants were boarded up and shut down. Jericho, at this time of year should have been bustling with happy tourists, polished-up camels, and eager locals. There were no tourists to be seen, and the camels were stripped of their regalia and were now standing in the unemployment line. The few locals looked melancholic—aimlessly shuffling around with hands in pockets and kicking at the dirt. The place where I had once sat to drink coffee and play backgammon was also boarded up, and the rich fruit markets now stood abandoned. The atmosphere inside Jericho was extremely tense. Evidence of recent rock-throwing incidents was on the roads, probably from the night before. Huge rocks now obstructed large parts of the main road, forcing vehicles to drive around and dodge them. The Israeli army was out in full force in their riot trucks, equipped with tear gas and a large machine gun fixed onto the rear of the jeeps. Each vehicle contained several soldiers dressed in extreme riot gear with helmets and loaded weapons, looking like ferocious combatants out of *Star Wars*.

What happened to the Jericho I had grown to love last year during my trip here with Dirk? Then, it was full of gaiety, and I remembered all those packed restaurants and the friendly fruit vendors selling crates of oranges. All that was over now. It was a different time then, when Israelis and tourists mingled with the Palestinians. What went wrong so suddenly? I felt saddened by this. When I had first realized that Fatza'el would be so near Jericho, I was excited, but now I felt sickened. Even the ever-flowering bushes and fruit-laden papaya trees failed to convince that this situation was temporary.

We accidentally saw what no tourist should have witnessed at one of the refugee camps. An army truck had stopped; the machine gun on the back was trained at a Palestinian who was being forced by some soldiers to wipe off what seemed to be pro PLO slogans off the wall. What I assumed to be his family, were gathered outside, petrified by the military incursion. The children were crying and clinging onto the skirts of their mother. Would the husband be arrested now? Would their metal, ramshackle shelter be bulldozed? I had no idea what happened to them—we did not hang around to find out.

I was glad to be back on the moshav, disturbed by what I had witnessed in Jericho; a town that is usually trouble free and made foreign visitors feel welcome. Things had indeed changed so much since the uprising, and there was no sign of it abating. I cheered up a little with a wonderful barbecue in the evening under a heavenly night sky, listening to the haunting music of *Tracey Chapman*. It was perfect for such a night.

May 1st, is Labor Day in Israel, like in most parts of the world. Despite that, we were working. It had been quite a good month after all, and I was happy to have met some nice people after my mistrustful and pessimistic stance in the beginning. Many of those brooding beer guzzlers I had seen when I first came here were gone, and newer, more interesting backpackers were swiftly appearing—from different parts of the world—from Australia, New Zealand, The Netherlands, Denmark, Columbia, and also a new breed from Britain. The new Brits were so unlike their predecessors—these were alive—and jolly, and I made good friends with some of them. The two English I had worked with were also history, and an English girl and a new Israeli guy were now working with me. I had also been given the use of the tractor, and Max the dog now sat next to me on the way to the vineyards. Our boss didn't come with us anymore, but dropped by later in the mornings to join us for coffee. I had the impression that he enjoyed that moment—to sit inside the vineyards together with his workers and make smalltalk. The three of us got on like wildfire, and the work didn't seem like work at all. Despite fooling around a lot in the vineyards, we made good progress, and our amicable boss left everything to us while he visited his other fields to check on the irrigation.

Handling thousands of grapes can become monotonous at times, but there was a weekly opportunity to make occasional short trips; even to Jerusalem (it was less than an hour away), which I tried to visit at least twice a month and to buy two loaves of the most delicious *challah* in Israel. It was sold at the bakery on Jaffa Road every Friday. The Old City became my regular haunt and where I did most of the shopping for replenishing my food supply. I got to know the Arab shops where they sold the best apricot jam, olives, goat's cheese, freshly-roasted and ground coffee, and of course, most importantly—I couldn't leave without a decent stash of Arab cakes. Returning to the moshav was like going back home. When there was a longer break in work, the short distance to the Dead Sea was my favorite destination—where I always slept outside under starry heavens. Life was so good and I felt ecstatic. I was living in paradise.

The work with the artichokes had finished; no despair: corn and onions were now ready for harvesting. That still left the watermelons, but they needed a few more weeks for ripening. The vineyards still took up most of the time: training the branches into upright positions and still thinning out grape bunches, this time with pointed clippers. This work was going to continue until the start of the picking in two weeks.

During that time, Israel invaded Lebanon. Reports indicated that 2,000 soldiers had entered Lebanon and 1,000 bombs had been dropped overnight. This was due to the persistent terrorist infiltrations in the Galilee area, threatening the security of settlements close to the border. Here in the valley, life continued as if nothing had happened. After two more days, the operation was reported a success, and Israel withdrew back out of Lebanon with a number of arrests as souvenirs.

Hot desert winds that come in from the Eastern deserts are known as the *sharav*. Arabs call it the *chamsin*, meaning "five," as these winds usually last for five days. This *sharav* attacked Israel, bringing in fiery-hot winds and forest fires. Temperatures spiraled to 45°Celsius in the shade, and the night tortured us with a sickly thirty-five. I had not felt winds like this before. It was like standing next to a fire, while the wind blew flames around the body. While returning from the fields at dusk, it was necessary to drive the tractor at snail-pace to avoid the full force of the wind, which stung the eyes. The wind from hell picked up the dust and sand and obscured most of the view, and the track I usually drove on, appeared to be moving. My face was wrapped up with my T-shirt, but I still needed my eyes. Now I understood why Arabs always have their *kefiyeh* on hand—very smart. At night, everybody was down at the swimming pool, still sweating in the water. This wind didn't blow for five days, but three; nevertheless, that was enough to cause a lot of damage to the crops around the country. There were raging fires everywhere, especially in the Jerusalem forests. Here on the moshav, many of the farmers had their grape crop ruined as the fiery winds shriveled up the unripe fruits into instant green raisins, thus roasting them in mid-air. The irrigation wasn't able to keep up with the sudden demand for water.

During that time I was doing the worst work possible—picking watermelons. They had suddenly ripened prematurely and had to be picked fast before they split. This was heavy, exhausting work, which became sluggish as it measured down to a slow-motion point. Our boss was also suffering, with an equally agonized look on his face. He made us drink huge quantities of water every five minutes, warning us that this heat was especially dangerous; we may not feel thirsty, but were losing water at a very fast pace.

At the bottom of the field was the barbed wire fence designating the Jordanian border. A wide stretch of sand runs by the side. This is patrolled by the Israeli army many times a day, in search of any disturbance in the sand, which would indicate border infiltration—terrorists. As the army jeep patrolled this stretch of sand, it smoothed it out again by dragging chains that were attached to the back of the jeep. This brought on a cloud of choking dust upon us.

Here in the sun, the temperatures soared to above 50°Celsius, and the wind was equally hot. Despite being inside an oven, I was not sweating at all. Any moisture would instantly evaporate, but my throat felt parched. Constant drinking couldn't keep up with the rapid loss of body fluids. I was afraid I would also turn into a raisin. This was unreal. It was only May! Maybe I had died and was really being tortured in hell. I couldn't even enjoy a cool watermelon—they were baking hot inside. I accidentally stepped on one and started to totter, losing balance, and then I stepped on another one which, to my luck, was already rotten, and my foot squelched inside the hot, putrid, slimy, oozing liquid that produced a stench like a rotten carcass, and my canvas boot was covered in it.

"John, don't step on the watermelons," my boss hollered through the blowing wind.

"It's a new game," I retorted sarcastically and raised my foot to show him my shoe.

"Eugh!" He looked aghast. The watermelons were picked and placed on the ground in rows, scattered amongst the field. These heavy buggers are much bigger than the versions one is used to from a local supermarket in England, and these monsters now had to be put onto the trailer. By forming a line, the four of us threw the bombs to the next person in the row, who caught them (hopefully) and passed them on. Sometimes, one of these bombs would miss, then explode on the ground, splattering and sending red watermelon shrapnel in all directions. My boss was by the tractor, did the last catch, and placed the precious fruits onto the trailer. We cleared the field in such a way and were done by evening. It was a great accomplishment, and our boss showed us his gratitude by inviting us all to dinner at his house.

At last, the grape picking started, also prematurely (thanks to the *sharav*), but the work was disappointing. It was boring, finicky, and very tedious. The grapes were brought in from the fields, which we picked in the mornings before the cruel heat, and then we spent the rest of the day in the sorting house selecting them. Rotten ones were picked out, small ones were cut out, and each cluster was loosened, thus bringing them up to export quality. They were then put into refrigeration, packed, weighed, labeled, and taken to the main packing house and awaited to be picked up for European export. I preferred the work before, when our boss wasn't working with us, so we took our time with everything and messed around a lot. The English girl had left as her time was over, and she still wanted to travel around Israel before returning to England. She was replaced with an Israeli girl (Mili), who had recently finished her two-year stint in the army, and the Israeli guy was still here, too. Mili was fun to work with and told me about her plans to earn some money then travel around the world. It was what a lot of Israelis did after their service. We became very close as we spent more time together.

Weeks went by and there was no end in sight. Because of the amount of work, my boss had employed two local Arabs who ended up doing all the picking now. We three stayed inside and did the sorting. The doors remained shut to keep the heat out, and the air-conditioning unit was on full with fans operating at maximum speed. It was over 40°Celsius every day now, and I often felt nauseous from the heat, which was affecting me. I was snappy and had reached the end of my tether… feeling really pissed off with this place now. There was no more time off for traveling since the grape invasion; nothing to do anymore, just grapes, grapes, and more goddamned grapes—I didn't even eat them anymore—I couldn't see them anymore! —grapes became the enemy—the terrorists—the most despised.

The grape invasion was in full force, and each day had become one and the same, causing many volunteers to pack up their bags and seek out cooler pastures, or they continued with their travels. A feeling of despondency descended upon the moshav, as people remained indoors hugging the air-conditioners and sticking their heads into the ice-making compartment of the fridge. It was even too hot for the swimming pool, which had also lost its allure. The days of fascinating conversations were over: the people I had befriended earlier had long since departed, and only hardy ones remained. But I had enough! I just wanted to leave now. Everyday I was melting and feeling nauseous. My appetite was gone and I lost several kilos. The heat was too extreme, and the fun was over—truly over. Tomorrow, I was going to tell my boss that I was abandoning ship. I was furious with him for firing Mili yesterday. She had only been with us for a month, and we had grown very fond of each other, but his argument was that she was too slow. She had been the only sane person left around here, someone whom I was still able to have fun and a friendly banter with.

My other Israeli friend turned out to be bipolar: he didn't talk anymore and had constant bad mood attacks. (Maybe it was the grapes.) He harnessed a deep loathing towards Israel, Israelis, and being here, and he couldn't wait to leave for Australia, never to return. The hatred stems from the day he had refused to serve in the army, whereas a spell in jail made him think twice. When released, the army was waiting for him, anyway (and you can't escape military service if you're an Israeli). Only pessimistic remarks came out of his mouth. He became intolerable as the arguments became futile: The historical significance of Israel, the deserts with their lost civilizations, the one of its kind—the Dead Sea, the hypnotizing Old City of Jerusalem, magnificent temples—these were all boring places for him. Everything was better in Australia, and that is where he was heading… or said he was. It crossed my mind to go to another moshav with Mili, but Egypt was calling me at the same time. I had enough money to travel now.

Next day arrived, and I felt less snappy as the temperatures dropped below 40°Celsius. I changed my mind about leaving after being informed that the season was ending at the end of the month. I was offered a bonus of 500 shekels upon completion of the grape harvest. It would be worthwhile to stick around for another three weeks, and foolish to lose this bonus, which would boost my finances. Those 500 shekels would buy an airline ticket.

Two weeks left, and I managed to wangle a couple of days off to spend some time with Mili, who lived in Jerusalem. It was a lazy day— getting up late and setting off late. At least I managed to cash my previous check, but failed to buy dollars on the black market due to the imposed restricted opening hours in the Arab areas. I spent the night at Mili's house in the suburbs of Jerusalem—a beautiful setting overlooking vast expanses of forest.

Decision time: Where should we go? Ein Ghedi at the Dead Sea was a likely spot. We both loved the place, and it had already been a year since my last visit to this oasis, when I swam in the sea with my friends from the *ulpan*. We attempted the prominent route along Nahal Arugot, walking through the encircled, lush palm tree entrance at Kibbutz Ein Ghedi, where the prized quality, extra plump dates were grown. The main entrance to the National Park demanded a fee that I refused to pay, as I believed no fee should be imposed on nature. It should be free of charge for everyone to enjoy and not to profit from. The other reason was that I tried to avoid *any* fees if possible (traveling on-the-cheap invokes "stinginess" that is necessary if one is to survive on the road long-term). It was the same place I went to before, with its natural springs and waterfalls. How I loved it here, but our enjoyment was soon spoilt, as we became targets for Arab schoolchildren throwing stones at us from the top of the wadi. We could hear them yelling in Arabic. One hit me on the shoulder, but caused no injury. We reported the incident to the guard at the entrance, but as expected, he didn't want to get involved. "I'm not the boss around here, I can't do anything," he waved his arms impatiently. He told us to talk to the guy in charge at the next reserve. Typical Israeli procedure: nobody wants to get mixed up in something that doesn't concern them; nobody cares; everybody complains, and the end result is that nothing gets done… on the other hand, maybe the incident was a retribution for getting in for free.

The excruciating heat turned each footstep into an agonizing gasp under the tormenting blowtorch from above; alas, we shouldn't have continued the walk as frazzled Mili developed signs of sunstroke and became very sick from dehydration, despite guzzling large amounts of water. Staying in the shade, provided by the scarce foliage in the oasis, and soaking in the cool springs, brought a little relief. Last time I had come here a year ago, it was full of people. Now, we were alone and enjoyed every minute of it.

We caught the bus back to Jerusalem, but I had to jump off at the junction just outside Jericho, whereas Mili continued home to the city. I started to hitchhike towards the moshav—not the best idea in the conflict-prone West Bank, but it was the fastest way back. The whole area was teeming with soldiers, which made me feel very safe. After a surprisingly long wait of almost thirty minutes, I did get a lift in an army jeep filled with the usual soldiers in riot gear and machine guns. I have long realized that no matter how much trouble there is in this country, the soldiers always respect and remain courteous towards foreigners. Others may have different opinions, but that was my personal experience.

Back to the grapes and only nineteen rows left to pick—about a week's work... I think. I longed for the end, and many times I simply felt like walking off. I had nobody left to talk to; even at work, everybody was solemn, moody, and totally uncooperative. The morose Israeli didn't speak anymore, but frowned at the grapes with hatred; my boss and his wife hummed to the awful "soft" Israeli music on the radio; the sullen Arab workers didn't say a word, either. There were four of them now. Maybe the tense atmosphere was because of the Arab/Israeli conflicts that were taking place outside. Here, they couldn't kill each other. The Israelis needed the Palestinians for labor, and the Palestinians needed the Israelis for work. Neither could survive without the other. My visa expired today, but I couldn't renew it as all the government workers were on strike, together with the hospital workers, etc, etc, etc... I read in the newspaper that the Arabs were burning down Israeli forests; meanwhile, the soldiers were demolishing the Arabs' houses. What an insane country this was turning out to be.

Just a few days left now, and I was all alone. There was nobody working with me except the gruff, unfriendly Arabs—so different to the ones I worked with on the previous moshav. I was now living alone, too; the messed up, bipolar Israeli who had been working with us cracked up yesterday and flew the coop, just days before the work ended. What a fool to have lost his bonus. It would have contributed greatly towards his ticket. The sickening heat, the Arab/Israeli conflict, the horrid grapes, all added up to the tense, eerie silence. If I had endured this deadly silence much longer, maybe I would have been able to qualify as a Trappist monk and settle in one of the monasteries in the hills of Jericho. At least Max came to visit me every night. I would miss him after I left. If only I could survive these next few days, the torture and grape nightmares would come to an end.

They did. The day I had been waiting for was finally here. It was 1:00 A.M. and I couldn't sleep. It was too hot despite the air-conditioning; also, there were too many things on my mind preventing me from sleeping: past events, and the beginning of the next adventure. I got out of bed, made myself some coffee, and sat outside on the doorstep. Piercing sounds of insects kept the night alive, assuring me that I was not alone; a huge camel spider clicked its way along the concrete footpath looking for a midnight snack. These ugly insects, although deadly looking, are actually harmless to human beings—they prefer to feast on scorpions. Black lizards clung on to the warm concrete buildings, positioned to capture the first rays of the sun a few hours from now. It was 3:00 A.M. —my last day here—another coffee—4:00 A.M. —too excited to feel tired—another coffee. A distant wail from an Arab village summoned people to prayer, leaving me in a bit of a daze. The night was beautiful.

Today we picked the last of the grapes, finishing before noon.

The end!

I left Fatza'el immediately after receiving my paycheck with the promised added bonus and headed straight to Jerusalem to stay with Mili for the weekend. We spent the day relaxing, eating ice cream, and took a nice walk around the Jerusalem forest—beautiful with its aromatic pine trees. Next morning, Mili went on ahead to her new moshav where she had already started a while ago—I would follow later after converting my earnings into dollars. The money-changing situation had not improved, and I was still having problems changing my shekels due to the closure of money changers in Jerusalem Old City. Stuck with shekels, I traveled down to Moshav Kadesh Barnea in the Negev desert, where Mili was working. I would stay here for a couple of weeks until I was ready to go to Egypt. Kadesk Barnea is the place where the Israelites, after having wandered in the Sinai Desert for forty years, crossed over to the Promised Land.

I wish they had chosen a better place to cross. What a horrible location! Truly—in the middle of nowhere—situated directly on the Egyptian border. Sinai Desert was just behind the house. It was surrounded by—NOTHING! On one side was an ugly, barren, flat desert landscape, and on the other side were sand dunes. The moshav itself is built on top of a sand dune, and not exactly a welcoming place, either. There was not even a store here, the nearest being ten kilometers away. I looked around; there were no trees here. Really! No tree at all—only sand dunes! —HELP!!! I didn't think I could stand this place. It was too much madness, this existence here. —WHY? Why do people want to live in such a place and put themselves into self-exile?

I spent the next day practically in bed; nothing to do as Mili was working somewhere by the sand dunes. I didn't really want to work here, it was too depressing, and I had more than enough money now. We went for a walk in the night to see only armed soldiers about. It was not possible to venture outside the moshav compound for security reasons; even inside, armed soldiers patrolled the grounds. The barbed wire fence just outside was the border, and the security was tight due to the infiltration of terrorists nearby, which had gunned down a bus in Be'er Sheva a few months previously.

I tried the work the next day, the one and only time. This work was so horrifying, and there wasn't even a possibility to make it fun like with the watermelons. We had to pull up plastic sheets and dead tomato plants in temperatures that well exceeded 44°Celsius—in the shade. To do two lines, it took six hours. There were forty lines left to do. I was horror-struck. This location was so desolate that an eerie silence persisted all around. It was not a comforting peace, as the night was void of all animal sounds that usually brought the desert to life. It was also the silence that anticipates the worse. I didn't bother returning to work in the afternoon, but slept instead. I was dead—from the heat, and the bed was full of sand, and I couldn't stop sweating... and the biting flies... mosquitoes... HELL! How on earth did Mili end up here? This must be the worst, woebegone place in Israel... and I was hungry. Anyway, it was too hot to eat. The cold showers weren't cold enough. I was taking six a day, desperate to have some contact with something cold. As soon as I stepped out of the shower, I felt even hotter than before. Despite being acclimatized to desert conditions, my body simply refused to function under these conditions, and I felt myself becoming delirious—I was tempted to climb up to the sand dune and scream, but that required energy, something I didn't have. I had never, ever suffered from heat such as *this*, and couldn't bear it any longer. Because of the situation here, things didn't work out between Mili and I, and so, we decided to part company. I really had to get out of this place—fast.

Strangely, my only thoughts were to get onto that nice air-conditioned bus.

The next morning, I took the first bus out and traveled back to Jerusalem to try, once again, to buy some dollars. Again no luck. The past ten days, the dollar had been steadily climbing, making it more expensive. I booked in for the night at my usual Jaffa Gate hostel, but ended up going to Tel Aviv instead, as I suddenly realized that I had to get to the Egyptian embassy to apply for a visa by tomorrow. The embassy is closed from Friday to Sunday. Today was Wednesday, and it was crucial that I arrive in Tel Aviv tonight. I wanted to get out of Israel quickly because once leaving the financial safety nets of a kibbutz or moshav, life is extremely expensive, and my hard-earned cash would just be wasted otherwise. I went to Momo's, where I bumped into a friend of mine from Brazil. We worked together once on Moshav Sde Avraham… and, of course, Germany, who now resembled a melting candle in the very humid city. We all went out for a drink together in the evening when the temperatures abated. While in Tel Aviv, I miraculously managed to convert all my shekels into dollars, *and* I was in a fantastic mood—loaded with money and on the road again.

17
PHARAONIC DREAMS AND
EGYPTIAN NIGHTMARES

I was in a very modern, purring, air-conditioned bus on the way to Rafiah—the Israeli/Egyptian border crossing in the Gaza Strip. Just by chance, Hassan happened to be on the bus, too. He was going back to Cairo with his Israeli girlfriend. Such a small world—I seemed to be meeting old friends everywhere. Crossing the border was a little irksome, as the several foreign passengers beset the Egyptian officials with the challenging task of identifying all those colorful passports and looking for the required visas. In a quagmire of utter confusion, they yielded to the simplest analysis of the situation and decided to "stamp away" and let everyone pass through... still, with a baffled expression on their faces. With all the bothersome buggers out of the way, they could carry on with their dozing.

Finally, we were in Egypt, in the northern part of the Sinai—an area I hadn't been to yet. Impressive high dunes bore a banal resemblance to a desert one perceives from tales of faraway places in the mysterious East. Those dunes, I knew, extended all the way to Kibbutz Kadesh Barnea, where Mili was still being tortured in the tomato fields. The beautiful scenery of the desert and beaches was marred by half-built concrete places of abode that jutted out of the hinterland. On the northern side is the very alluring Mediterranean Sea that looked even more dazzling between a plethora of palm trees that thrived in this scorched and waterless region, where ordinary human beings would wither away. However, ordinary human beings did not inhabit the Sinai, but the people of the desert, who have remained here for thousands of years—the Bedouin. Unfortunately, the Bedouin had absolutely no eye for floral splendor or natural beauty; garbage was scattered everywhere—the roads, the beaches, and rusting cans and plastic containers piled up at the bottom of sand dunes. This could have been utmost paradise... what a shame... and a waste of natural beauty.

Now we were traveling on an Egyptian bus after switching at the border. No longer was it a luxury coach, but a rickety-rackety thing on wheels without suspension and broken air-conditioning. This was only the beginning of a long and uncomfortably hot journey. Despite the dirty windows, I could make out people everywhere: they were on bicycles; on donkeys with carts; on donkeys without carts, and on foot. An absence of motor vehicles made it look even more primitive. Scruffy, dirty children were all over the place, some running after the slow-moving bus, which seemed to be the highlight of the day. Despite the suffocating heat, groups of fully-clad men lounged around in the shade provided by the few palm trees while smoking, staring, and completely insensible to their surroundings: there was not much else to do. Women would be doing likewise (not smoking though), but sitting in their own separate groups, wrapped up head to foot in their black cloaks, hence they should encounter any seductive gazes form the men and be drawn into close, physical contact. This, for a woman, could mean grave punishment: men are never guilty of such transgressions—it is the women who cast a spell upon the males, causing them to succumb to lust. Such stories, I had heard time and time again, and I recalled my time working with Fatma, and her stance amongst the male workers.

By late afternoon, the bus made a stopover in a small village for refreshments. An amazing sight caught my eye: we were surrounded by total desolation... and a ship was sailing past just in front of me—out of the blue. It took me a moment to realize this was not a mirage, but the Suez Canal, and the only place in the world where one could sail through the desert. Here was also the ferry crossing, which linked Asia to the African continent. I was now geographically in Africa, back on the bus, and proceeding into the heart of Cairo. Sand dunes gave way to lowland regions, where farms thrived on the rich silt deposits of the Nile delta. Mango trees and bountiful cornfields provided a stunning backdrop amongst rich, healthy-looking, luscious vegetation that enveloped the main road on both sides... and so did the garbage, unfortunately.

It was a late evening arrival, after being shaken and jostled around for over twelve hours into the heart of Cairo. Madness! Noisy and chaotic; cars playing dodgems; blaring horns, and hordes of people everywhere, and... of course—the ever-present garbage. Acrid fumes soon found their way into my nostrils and lungs. A permanent stench of rotting waste hung suspended in the air. In parts, along the River Nile, where high-class hotels were situated, it was most attractive and I was impressed at times, but most of Cairo was, in a nutshell—ugly. As far as I could see, the city consisted mainly of apartment blocks—tall, gray, decrepit-looking structures with windows that have never seen water.

Somehow, I ended up with three Australian fruit cakes I had met on the bus, and we all had to find a hotel for the night. It was very late... and I was spent. Hassan and his girlfriend had already gotten a taxi to his parents' house, but we would meet tomorrow. I don't know how I ended up with the Australian girls, but I found their abrasive accents irritating, especially as they were very shrill, and one of them sounded like a constipated goat when she laughed. Nevertheless, we latched on to share a taxi together and to haggle for a good rate at a hotel. As there were four of us, it would be easier to bargain. In Egypt, bargaining is an obligation... even for water.

A taxi came our way (one of many) and slowed down. "Taxi? Taxi? Need a hotel?" The driver slowed down to ask, hopeful for some late night business. We gave in and drove around to look for a hotel. We tried several, but all were fully booked. Even the helpful taxi driver went round asking about vacancies, but even he had no luck. I was becoming exhausted looking for a place to sleep and would have taken anything right now, being so tired and sweating like a pig... yearning for a shower, and contributing immensely to the Cairo air. It was difficult to comprehend the logic, but all the hotels were located on the top floors of apartment buildings—usually the ninth or tenth. This meant climbing all the way up to find out there were no vacancies, and then back down again with heavy backpacks. My heart was pounding wildly. I desperately needed to sleep, reaching that couldn't-care-less-anymore point, and ready to plop down anywhere in the corridor. There were lifts of course, but we did not trust these rickety, shaky boxes after having experienced one, thinking the chains would brake with so much creaking and trembling.

It was almost midnight when we finally found rooms in Horus Hotel, at a rate of seventeen Egyptian pounds, which was about seven dollars. It was not so cheap, but now, anything would have been suitable, and I didn't care how much it cost. I didn't like this place: it was very upper class, and only well-dressed, dull businessmen stayed here. We looked out of place in our shorts and backpacks. Older, scowling businessmen from other Arabian states lounged around in the posh lobby in their very white *thobes* and equally white *kefiyeh*, but their grimy, callous bare feet, impertinently resting on the ornate adjacent chairs, shattered their stately image. Their eyes drilled into the Australian girls while one character was making strange camel noises, trying to bring up some stubborn phlegm.

Once total exhaustion takes over the body, a bed is the best thing in the world, and I don't remember ever having enjoyed a bed as much as last night. I woke up hungry and in a good mood, ready for Egypt. The first thing to do was to find a cheaper hotel, but that proved as difficult as last night. All cheaper places turned out to be full, but by noon, we came across Amin Hotel in an area known as Tala'at Arb, for seven and a half Egyptian pounds a night, which was more like the price I wanted to pay. It was even better than the previous more expensive place, so we all booked for the next few nights. We met a local resident inside (not by chance I'm sure), who informed us he could organize a taxi for a "cheab brice" for the day, as his friend was the owner of one. He would take us to the pyramids and other places of interest. We were to meet him in the evening and discuss the price. Well, that suited me perfectly; meanwhile, I phoned my friend Hassan to arrange a meeting place—at Wimpy's (Wimby's in Arabic) in the evening.

The rest of the afternoon I spent walking around Cairo, forcing my psyche to adjust to the total pandemonium. Grey was the dominant color— even the few palm trees that attempted to fight the pollution failed to emanate their rich, green color, looking as they had given up the struggle. It was hot and dusty, and the permanent, putrid stench in the air was something else I would have to get used to—this, combined with spewing diesel fumes was enough to make any "fresh" visitor scream bloody murder and flee to the airport. Fortunately, I was already quite seasoned and decided to do the screaming in my head. Despite all that, the locals weren't as bad as their surroundings, and I found them genuinely pleasant; in fact, they were very friendly, much more than in Tel Aviv. Egyptians were definitely used to tourists by now, as they have been coming here for hundreds of years to marvel at the treasures of the pharaohs and their monuments.

Food was incredibly cheap, but dirty. Fruit and vegetables were old, and most of them even moldy. Nothing was fresh, despite the abundance of farms I had seen. Surely, there must be *some* fresh produce… or maybe it was just the heat and the dust that made it appear unappetizing. I did, however, discover the most delicious mango juice at fifty piastres a glass (about twenty cents). Fantastic! I kept drinking and drinking, not getting enough of this elixir. I also discovered a stand selling whole roast chickens for four-fifty (less than two dollars). *They* looked fresh. Right next to the rotating, roasting chickens were the live ones inside their small cages. Tomorrow, they would also be revolving on the spit. Can't get fresher than that! I bought one and devoured it hungrily. Chicken and mango juice was the equivalent of perfection. I loved Cairo—for the moment.

Luckily, I had learned to read Arabic numbers. This is extremely useful in the Middle East. The merchants would strive to rip off any unaware, happy-go-lucky tourist. They tried it with me, but I pointed out the written price and repeated it in their language. They smiled and gave in then, out of respect that a foreigner had made the effort to learn some Arabic. You must haggle over everything here. The traders are only interested in money, and the friendly ones are only friendly if friendship is profitable.

I met my friend Hassan and his Israeli girlfriend at the pre-arranged place. It was good to see each other again, to exchange stories, and catch up on the happenings since my strange disappearance from Moshav Neot several months ago. He and his girlfriend were also going to travel, and she wanted to start with Egypt first.

A fast-food burger place would be nothing special in the rest of the world, but in Cairo, it was the hangout for the more affluent Egyptians—young, fashionable rich kids, and businessmen with suit and tie. The interior design is exactly what one would expect at Wimpy's, but the service was out of this world. The waiters (no waitresses) wore the usual uniforms, but also a bow-tie. They came to the table to take the order, and then brought the burger and fries on a fancy tray. At the end of the meal, the bill also came on a tray—a silver one. I had to laugh, and Hassan, too; having been educated in England, he knew I would find this amusing. Food here cost considerably more than at the usual local eateries, which meant this piece of American culture was out of reach for the ordinary folk—totally unaffordable for them, but for me, still a lot cheaper than in England. It was time to get back to the hotel and agree on the price of a taxi for the next day. We bid our farewells and gave each other a firm embrace, promising to get together in Israel again.

The taxi owner was there on the dot; we negotiated the price, getting the whole deal for eighty Egyptian pounds between the four of us. He was surprisingly good-natured with the haggling and not pushy like other Egyptians who were pining for business. We would have the full use of the taxi tomorrow, and he also insisted taking us somewhere this evening. This was the best way of getting around in this monstrous city, which was bursting with overpopulation—get your own personal taxi, otherwise it would take days to solve the mysteries of local transportation, which I had no patience or desire for. Our driver would take us to the famous Step Pyramid at Saqqara, the Pyramids of Giza, and a visit to a papyrus and carpet factory.

That evening, he drove us to his uncle's perfumery store (One Thousand and One Nights). Refreshments were summoned immediately as soon as we arrived, and I took a dislike to him even before he opened his mouth. His uncle was a sly and cunning character—very rich and with perfume stores all over the world (according to him). I couldn't stand boastful people, and that was exactly how he behaved, also showing us a photograph of himself shaking hands with the famous ex-boxer Muhammad Ali. "He is a very good friend of mine," he continued to boast snugly. I had a feeling that perfume was not his only business, and the bad vibes being emitted from him told me that he was a very dangerous character... not someone you cross.

The numerous array of perfumes beautifully displayed on the shelves were amazing nevertheless. They were of pure, undiluted essence and very intense. Extracts of lotus, opium, and poison were sampled, and by the time we left the store, we reeked like a walking perfumery; embarrassingly, I, too. There was one severe, unsmiling man, whose eyes remained transfixed upon me the whole time while in the store, making me nervous, but suddenly decided to address me—in Hebrew. I made the mistake of answering him back... in Hebrew, too. This caused a commotion and some raised voices amongst the other Egyptian cronies. "I knew you were an Israeli all the time," he eyed me with hatred.

"I'm not Israeli, I'm English," I blurted out in English. Had I been in Israel so long that I now looked like an Israeli? I didn't think so. Surely, I didn't have those "dead fish" eyes, which many people developed after ending their military service.

"So you must be a Jew to speak Hebrew. Only Jews speak Hebrew," he continued in English now, accusing me of this crime.

"So I worked there and I learned the language. How do you know Hebrew then?" I said this in Hebrew now. He didn't answer, but kept staring at me. If, according to these pigeon-brained people, only Jews speak Hebrew, then logically, that Egyptian must be one himself. The uncle barked something to his cronies; it sounded like an admonishment. He seemed upset that his perfume show was now disrupted, and would definitely not get a sale from us. He had been convinced that the Australian girls, being girls, would buy some of his essence. The best thing to do was to leave this place, the perfumery being just a front to whatever else went on behind the scenes. I was sure someone would get a beating tonight. The driver took us back to the hotel.

We met early the next morning at the pre-arranged place and drove to our first stop—the Step Pyramid. Maybe the word "drove" was not the best word to describe this mode of transportation. I had never experienced such driving as in Cairo. There didn't seem to be any driving rules. Cars didn't stay in their own lanes, but meandered between other vehicles where there was a gap, at the same time blaring their horn. Traffic lights were totally ignored—green or red, it was all the same. If it was clear, you went; if it wasn't clear, you went anyway, swerving away from the near collisions, cursing, and all the time with the horn pressed. Pedestrians were completely ignored and were *not* avoided. It was *their* problem how they got across.

Parking was another hair-raising experience and quite entertaining to watch: When there is not enough space to get in between two cars, no problem, a space is very quickly made—you get in backwards at an angle and nudge the car behind you until it moves a few centimeters; you then go forward and do the same to the car in front. You have now created a little more space for squeezing in. At this point, you ram the back car again and repeat the process back and forth until you are wedged in tightly between the vehicles. There is not a millimeter of gap between parked cars—they really *are* squeezed. There is no animosity over destruction of other vehicles because they had to go through the same procedure to get in, too—everybody does it. Getting a squeezed parked car out is the same process—ram the cars in front and back until you can drive out. It didn't matter if they were also squeezed in—the owners would simply have a shorter car next time they park. There is no easy way of walking across the road (without almost getting killed) between parked cars, as there is no leg room between them. You have to climb over the bumpers.

The route took us along a country road through decrepit villages, which straddled one of the channels that bring in water from the Nile to irrigate the sediment-rich farmland, thus providing the local inhabitants a source of survival. Not so far away is modern Cairo, but from this perspective, the view changes dramatically. The panorama before my eyes was from a different era: everywhere, donkeys labored strenuously, carrying enormous bales of hay, or they were pulling carts that were also overfilled; children swam in filthy water while women did their laundry in the same water, leaving the wet clothes to dry on the rocks. These villagers were living in acute poverty. Their homes were constructed out of anything that would support a roof over their heads; nevertheless, they were surprisingly cheerful—smiling and waving. Several times I stopped the driver to enable me to take some pictures. Then I saw it: out of the lush, green vegetation, there in the distance, a pyramid-shaped yellow haze shimmered above the treetops. For the first time I was witnessing this wonder—the Saqqara Step Pyramid—the oldest pyramid dating back to 2700 BCE. Tourists pay a lot of money to fly to Egypt to see this, but these poverty-stricken villagers and their forefathers have woken up to this sight for thousands of years. I wondered if they actually realize what they have here?

We were on our way to see the famous Pyramids of Giza—not along the main road, but an alternate route, where a narrow dirt road meandered through long-established, isolated villages. This was an eye-opener and a once-in-a-lifetime experience. Wide potholes and scrawny animals on the road forced the vehicle to crawl; children came towards the car to stare, and even attempted to stick their heads inside the rolled-down windows. I think we must have been the first foreigners they had ever seen. Surprisingly, we made a stop here. "What are we doing here?" The girls raised their suspicions as the car was suddenly surrounded by curious *baksheesh*-demanding children.

"My uncle lives here," he grinned at us. "We stop to drink coffee." He was still grinning as he led us inside, obviously enjoying our looks of utmost amazement. (These people seem to have relatives everywhere.) The Australians looked tense and somewhat nervous, but I was loving this. He said the magic word—"Coffee," and I didn't need anymore convincing, knowing that delicious Arab cakes would come with the beverage, too. I had been through this procedure many times with the Arabs, and knew there was no reason to be apprehensive about a sudden invitation like this. It was a genuine show of friendliness on their part, and there is never any reason to be anxious over such outcomes. I think it must have been the first for the girls, and they felt uneasy being here, but this was the real Egypt I wanted to see and experience.

We were herded into a spartan room, painted the usual turquoise, and probably the only color of choice in the Middle East, as all Arabic homes I have seen are always painted in that same color inside. I never did find out why. This was the richest and most beautiful house in the village, and this uncle was the village leader. People would approach him with any village problems: disputes, squabbling, and advice over important decisions. He was a respectable and educated man, and his intelligent eyes showed that he had authority. The curious children crowded outside the doorway to peer at the foreign invasion, but they were soon dispersed by the terse command of the village leader. We went into another room, probably reserved for important visitors. A striking and expensive-looking, hand-woven rug covered the floor, and an ornate, glass-topped brass coffee-table pinpointed the center of the room; perfectly positioned, an antique suite, looking more like a showpiece rather than something to be comfortable on, straddled the edge. A photograph of ex-president Nasser hung alone on one of the walls, having the honor of a wall all for himself. As usual, refreshments (and the anticipated Arab cakes) were promptly brought in by the uncle's daughter—a real Arabian beauty... and I couldn't keep my eyes off her.

We said our goodbyes and thank-yous, then continued towards the pyramids. I was still clicking away with my camera when a truckload of camels appeared in the viewfinder. "Follow those Camels," I ordered the driver. This was a mistake: he suddenly swerved at top speed, and I was thrown against the door, which suddenly flew open. Seat belts didn't exist, and having no restraint, I started to fall out, still trying to photograph those camels on the back of the truck. I was three quarters out of the car—arms, head, and body. Somehow, my legs were stuck inside. The driver was still speeding, chasing those damn camels, and with one hand, he was pulling me back into the car without slowing down. The rapidly-passing road was only inches from my face. I could see every stone whizzing by, and the camera was *still* in my hands. It must have been quite a sight for any spectators—this foreign idiot trying to take close-up pictures of the road, and I'm sure the camels were having a good laugh. Suddenly, I felt a sharp tug and was safely back in the car, still in one piece, my nose still there, and only my nerve gone. The Australian girls in the back looked aghast, but the driver was in hysterics.

"The door is broken," he said, still laughing.

"Oh, *really?*" I commented sarcastically. I was somewhat shaken and felt pale and humorless. I almost died there, and that moron was laughing. Later, in the days to come I was actually laughing about the whole incident, too, trying to imagine how I must have looked, almost kissing the road.

I perked up a bit when the Pyramids of Giza materialized, confirming the fact that they truly deserved the title of a Wonder of the World. It was a moment to gawk in silence... with admiration and respect at this sight, and my near death shortly before became history. Luckily, this was low tourist season, and only a few admirers braved the harsh Egyptian sun in the shadeless pyramid area. The horrific part about this was the fact that the Egyptian "tourist botherers" outnumbered the tourists... and made life miserable for all the innocent people who had traveled great distances to see these ancient marvels. This was something you had to absorb slowly, by sitting on a bench and just gazing at these wonders. This would never happen: First of all, there were no benches; secondly, there was this relentless harassment, "My friend, where you from?"

"Nowhere."

"Want camel?" Came the next attack.

Another one came, riding a camel. "Zbecial brice ride camel today."

"Hey… my friend."

"GO AWAY—NO—NO CAMEL," but we were soon outnumbered. The more we protested, the more they persisted. Our anger gave way to strong, abusive language. The girls had their own Australian vocabulary that came out then—words I had not even imagined could exist, but they sounded good, especially in that abrasive dialect. Nothing worked. These nasty camel people were like flies; no… worse… they were bigger… and they could speak—in all languages! The sad part is that tourists here are not considered human, but viewed upon as walking goldmines with dollar signs in their eyes and silver coins pouring out of their palms—touch a tourist and you get rich. We had no choice but to completely ignore them and continue walking. Scabby camels and nasty camel people ganged up from all sides—both human and beast looking quite menacing. Camel riders aggressively whipped their beasts, and the camels glared at us accusingly, as if to make a point that it was our fault that they were getting a beating. We pretended they were invisible, then proceeded to get close to the pyramid. The sheer size was overpowering; the building blocks alone were immense.

The Pyramid of Cheops is the tallest of the pyramids: made up of over two million limestone blocks, each one weighing in a range, from two and a half to fifteen tons. Even with today's technology, to build anything like this would be impossible. The Sphinx sits majestically a few hundred meters further down. It has seen better days, as the nose had long since dropped off, and the lion-pharaoh was being supported with scaffolding with an attempt to prevent it from further deterioration. This scaffolding ruined the view, but I guess it was a necessity in order to preserve this wonderful statue. We would return here tonight to see the sound and light show.

It turned excruciatingly hot and I couldn't stop drinking. Pepsi, at about ten cents a bottle was the best and cheapest cold drink—much, much cheaper than water that cost a dollar. On the way back to Cairo, we stopped to see how papyrus parchment is made: The papyrus reed is peeled, sliced in thick horizontal lengths, and soaked in water for several days until it becomes pliable; while still wet, it is put together, overlapping—a horizontal layer, then a vertical layer. It is then placed inside a press to flatten and remove excess water. This process is repeated over a period of a week until the parchment is dry. It is then ready for writing on and reproducing ancient Egyptian paintings that are a favorite souvenir for the tourists. The Nile is abundant in papyrus, as they are swamp plants, and need the constant supply of water. Mosquitoes are also prone to this area, and yellow fever is prevalent. I was glad I had my vaccinations.

The final stop was the carpet factory. Here, they are hand-woven by very young children, starting as young as from the age of five. It is said that such small knots can only be produced by little hands, hence the use of small children for this work. Their work was remarkably skilled, also by using ancient techniques that were applied to making rugs out of camel hair and silk. A square meter of carpet made from silk takes up to six months to weave. In return, we were told, the children earned the equivalent of about eighty-five cents for a day's work, and they received no other education. Their intricate work was very impressive, but considering that they slaved away for a pittance, they were surprisingly cheerful. I found it, nevertheless, disturbing to witness this child labor while the well-to-do, chunky salesmen, who sit upstairs, profit immensely from this—selling the carpets for a fortune. On the way out, without the owners seeing me, I took a picture and slipped the young girls some Egyptian pounds, which they hid quickly inside their pockets. I was rewarded with smiles. The whole idea of bringing us here was not a simple educational trip into the manufacture of carpets, but the hope that we buy one. Some of these silk carpets cost several thousand dollars. "When a carpet is sold, the person who made the carpet gets a bonus on top of their regular wage," the owner told us. I was wondering what the actual bonus was… an extra dollar?

Back in Cairo in the afternoon, I ate and had a soothing shower, and then we returned to the pyramids once darkness descended upon this ancient land. Our regular taxi driver was made unavailable; instead, we made our journey in a brand new, shiny Mercedes, together with three of the driver's "weird" friends whose bad vibes I picked up like an antenna. It was so obvious to the simplest mind what their game was: These malevolent, slimy Egyptians were here to impress the three girls with their money and charm, and then try to cajole them into *other* forms of entertainment. I was hoping the Australians had more sense than I made out in the beginning, and would notice what was going on, but I had serious doubts, as they seemed to have fallen for their ridiculous smalltalk—the cackling goat proved it. The Egyptians looked upon me as an intruder—a person in the way. Of course, they asked whether I was Jewish. Why did they keep asking me? All the same, I paid for a day's transportation, and therefore I stayed, and on we went to see the sound and light show, viewed from the rooftop of another distant family member that belonged to the driver. Unfortunately, the commentary was in French, but the sound effects and the spectacular illuminations of the pyramids and the sphinx were enough to express the mystical chronicles of these ancient rulers of a vast empire. I was glad not to splash out the ten pounds to see the show in French, whereas, we had an equally wonderful view for free. We did, however, give the owner a little *baksheesh* for the use of his roof.

The Egyptians wanted to take the girls belly dancing, but they were sensible enough to insist being returned to the hotel. I gave them credit for that… and was glad; otherwise, I would have left them to it and found my own way back. The day turned out to be quite extraordinary, and I ended up enjoying it despite the unpleasant company of the three stooges. After another shower, I went back outside and followed my nose to the roasting birds, where I devoured a whole chicken with several glasses of mango juice. Oh, gawd… was *that* delicious!

The days in Cairo were flying by: there was still so much to see and do here, but that would have to wait until another time. The Egyptian Museum (where they kept all the mummies and treasures from the ancient world) was a "must see," but it was closed for restoration. That was a disappointment. First thing in the morning, I bought a train ticket to Aswan —I was dying to get out of this filthy, polluted city. Being in Cairo too long made me giddy and aggressive: constantly pestered by people who wanted something from me. I was so sick and tired of it. Thankfully, the train to Aswan was leaving the following day. The 1000-kilometer train ride cost a mere seven Egyptian pounds—the equivalent of three dollars. That was the price I would normally pay for riding one station in the London underground. The low prices were mindboggling, and with all the money I had earned in Israel, my calculations showed that I'd be able to travel in Egypt for two years—if I survived on chickens and mango juice.

I bid farewell to the Australians, who were not sure what they were doing or where to go, and then to kill the rest of the day, I ventured to the famous Khan-El-Khalili market, which turned out to be a real disappointment. It was extremely touristy, and people hassled me with the now familiar phrase: "My friend, zbecial brice." I certainly did not linger here except to sit down at a local coffee house for refreshments, where I was never bothered, no matter how touristy the area. Maybe it was like an unwritten rule, that nobody is harassed on the owners' premises. This was a very seedy part of Cairo with countless beggars... and mostly everybody in rags. Everyone had their eyes on me. I could sense their resentment from their frowning, menacing faces. Nobody smiled here. This is one of the few places where I had to watch my back, not feeling comfortable at all. I was wandering around alone and made sure my eyes were everywhere. The constant churned up dust from passing vehicles was choking me, and I could not comprehend how everybody tolerated it. On parts of the sidewalk, destitute people simply slept amongst dust and urine, completely oblivious to the world around them; their mouths wide open and collecting dirt.

I returned to the hotel and remained inside for the rest of the day; writing my notes and reading up some facts about the places I was intending to visit in the coming days. This was a wonderful hotel. I was even able to purchase my train ticket to Aswan from them. I was *really* fed up with Cairo, and wondered how the rest of Egypt would compare.

A pleasantly long and uninterrupted sleep was just what I needed. While traveling, one doesn't get much chance to sleep in. When the opportunity arises, make the most of it. Usually, I jump out of bed in a mad rush, dive into the bathroom, and shoot out of the door while getting dressed. But today, I cherished the moment when there was no hurry. I looked out of the streaky, dust-coated window to see the view I had not noticed before, and... oh! Shock! Horror! What an unbelievable sight materialized before my eyes! The rooftop of every single building was drowning in refuse. All kinds of rubble: corrugated metal, oil drums, plastic containers, cardboard, and pieces of wood. Garbage was simply tossed onto the roofs, and then the winds would come and scatter all the paper and plastic containers around the streets of Cairo. Was this the Egyptian garbage disposal system? This was not the worst part: I was even more horror struck when I peered carefully and noticed dwellings had been put up amongst all that garbage... and people were actually living there, and they certainly didn't look like temporary residents, either. Good idea though: when everything else is full, rent out your roof. I wondered what the rent was on that?

I checked out of the hotel, grabbed a coffee, some dusty pita bread from a ragged street vendor, and walked to the train station—Cairo train station. Oh, this was gonna be fun! The first sight upon arrival was the uncoordinated human disarray. Hundreds of lost souls were clumped together inside and outside the train station. There were people of all age groups: some had legs missing; one was walking on his hands, swinging his torso back and forth; some had an arm missing; just about everyone had teeth missing. Hollow, staring eyes found me and remained riveted as I bustled through the crowd. That gave me the creeps, so I made haste to the platform and tried to board the waiting train. Easier said than done: Like a herd of wildebeest, a surge of impetuous passengers threatened to trample me if I didn't move with the flow... so I joined the herd. I didn't know which carriage I was supposed to be in. There was no one I could ask for assistance. The ticket/information booth was being attacked by an angry-looking, confused mob. I decided to board the train from the last carriage and look for my seat that was shown on my ticket. This was the beginning of a 24-hour nightmare and a boarding battle that ensued a barrage of attacks from all sides of the train.

Hundreds of people were clamoring in an attempt to squeeze in through the narrow doors at the same time—pushing, shoving, snorting, and yelling. Some were ploughing their way in with huge overstuffed sacks on their shoulders, at the same time knocking down others with their protruding belongings. Bulky boxes, sacks of grain, pots and pans came on, too. I found out later that a lot of these people come to Cairo to find work, and the ones who are successful, return to their villages by the Nile River with as many goods as they can manage—which, is a lot. A vast number of the villagers don't find work in Cairo, and therefore, end up destitue on the streets of the capital. The only money they had possessed was spent on the train fare to the city. The glamour and get-rich-quick lure of the capital is too irresistible for the villagers.

A brawl broke out in the doorway, but the pushing and shoving continued. Inside one of the carriages I blundered into, I couldn't believe what I was seeing—an entanglement of limbs. Half-naked, ragged, bare-footed people were piled up like animals—anything sittable, they sat on: all seats, arm rests, head rests, the floor, and even the overhead luggage holder contained bodies. There must have been at least a hundred pairs of the largest, dirtiest, most contagious-looking feet I have ever seen—they dangled in mid-air, suspended from the baggage holders. A whimpering sound of an injured dog, and then an exhaled sigh of relief emitted from my larynx when I found out that this was third class, and I was in second. Another carriage I walked into was blocked due to another skirmish. From the hordes pushing me in the doorway, I was lifted off my feet into mid-air together with my backpack, gasping for an inch of space to breathe. This meant war! With full exertion, I forced my way through, purposely making my backpack protrude and hopefully hurting someone. It worked. I broke through, and nobody protested; well, maybe they did in Arabic, but I didn't understand anything anyway, so it didn't count. Women shrieked. Men bellowed. Babies bawled. I muttered and suffered. Miraculously, I located my carriage, and it was the first one! I had gone through all that melee *for nothing!* Astoundingly, there was normality inside this one, and the seat I had reserved the previous day—was there—*empty*—waiting for me—nobody sitting in it! INCREDIBLE!

Punctually at 4.30 P.M., the train departed—exactly on time, to my utter amazement. I was also flabbergasted that the air-conditioning actually worked. Madness was about to commence. Salesmen from all corners of Cairo suddenly infiltrated the train and enthusiastically bombarded passengers with everything they didn't need. They were selling cold drinks —pepsi (bebzi in Arabic, as they can't pronoune the letter "p"), bread, seeds, biscuits, all sorts of unidentifiable green edibilities. They would come along shouting out the description of what they were selling, and at the same time swinging, lugging, and expertly balancing great weights of goods on their heads and shoulders. Huge metal buckets filled with bottles of pepsi and blocks of ice, weighing as much as a sack of potatoes, were swung around as easily as a small bag. I was the only foreigner on the train, feeling very self-conscious and vulnerable suddenly. I thought there would have been other backpackers on board. Everybody stared at me... every move I made, and getting my backpack down from the rack seemed to cause a sensation. Even as I was writing, everybody gawked to see what I was doing. "What strange writing," they were probably thinking. I scratched my nose, blew my nose (must be the air conditioning), picked my nose; during each movement, eyes remained transfixed upon me.

Showtime:

5:30 P.M. —A crazy entertaining salesman enters the stage, selling double-sided combs. He must be very good, making this miserable bunch laugh. I also found myself laughing, even though I didn't understand a word he was saying, then the people who sat around me started to laugh because I was laughing, so I continued to laugh with them. "What strange behaviour," I was thinking. Amazingly, he manages to sell several. The comb salesman is closely pursued by a more serious saucepan salesman, but he doesn't sell anything—he is unable to place a smile on the passengers' grim faces.

6:30 P.M. —I get out of my seat to try and take some pictures of this captivating landscape along the Nile. We are passing the the most beautiful areas one only sees off the beaten trek. Amongst the villages, people are washing clothes, pots and pans, and themselves in the river. None of the windows would open, and they probably haven't seen water since the last rainfall. People would say, "Photo? Window here good," but nowhere was good. They were all too filthy and everything was obscured. What a pity!

The journey continues—the salesmen continue. Now, they are selling tea, beans. and one annoying guy, who reeks as if he had rolled in faecal matter, keeps coming around, hollering, what sounded like, "Al-ha-esh, al-ha-esh," which, I was to learn later, is pita bread with egg, goat's cheese, chillies, fingerprints, and dirt. Tasty as it sounded, I daren't try any of the foods. One look at the hands and black fingernails handling the food was enough to put a damper on one's appetite, but not the Egyptians' though, who ferociously gorged themselves on it, washing it down with *bebzi*. It was too early at the onset of my travels in Egypt to risk that famous stomach explosion known as pharaoh's revenge, especially in a country that doesn't even have toilet rims to cling onto.

7:30 P.M. —The sun is going down. A bright red ball of fire is illuminating the luscious banks of the Nile with its frilly palm trees, papaya, dates, and bananas. Here you can see a perfect example of irrigation as it's been for thousands of years. A cow, attached by rope to a waterwheel, is arduously plodding round and round, moving the waterwheel, which harnesses the Nile water and distributes it into channels, thus irrigating the crops.

9:00 P.M. —The train stops for the umpteenth time. The journey is slow—about 40kph. A scrawny figure with a shock of hair and wild eyes has appeared on the scene—he is selling cigarettes, followed by another lanky hawker with one eye, selling baskets filled with green leaves. What on earth is that? The impatient tea salesman is attempting to wedge through. Now is chaos. More passengers have come on. There is total congestion between passengers and fully-laden salesmen. Arguments break out once again. More shrieking. More bellowing. More bawling. More suffering.

The middle-aged man sitting next to me buys me a pepsi. Being totally ignorant of local customs, I'm not sure what to do in response. Should I return the favour later? Say thank you, or say nothing? Is he after something? I decide to thank him and accept it, grateful for the kind gesture, and feeling guilty about my prejudgement. My mouth is eager to eat the food that I brought along, but my mind says, "No!" Someone has thrown up in the carriage, and the putrid, rancid stink once again ruins my appetite. This is going to be an extremely enduring journey. Now it is dark outside.

10:30 P.M. —Surprisingly, the six hours have gone by pretty quick due to so much entertainment on board. I'm actually starting to relax and enjoy myself. So much commotion. Oh, no! The *al-ha-esh* salesman is back... so is the *bebzi* guy. The soap-allergenic, hydrophobic pepsi salesman looks like a goblin with enormous camel feet, and short, stubby, bow-shaped legs. He's only about four foot tall, grossly dirty, ugly as sin, and stinks so profusely that even a skunk would find it offensive. He resembles some creation out of a horror movie, as he trudges around barefoot on the filthy floor, lugging that never-ending, heavy metal bucket around. His unusually large head wobbles from the constant movements. While handing a drink to someone, he parks himself right beside me, and with his hand inside his *djellabah*, starts feeling himself up... or maybe he is scratching his balls. I was almost sick.

A boy, can't have been more than seven, has just arrived and sits on the floor next to me with a bowl full of nuts, packaging them. He is surveying me. "Are you English?" He suddenly blurts out. A good salesman: he compels me to buy two packs of nuts for five piastres a bag. Nice, pleasant kid; he continues to the next victim. I was watching the people eat their *al-ha-esh,* which was served from a dirty bowl and handled by grimy hands. The *al-ha-esh* salesman has just added a new ingredient— sweat. It is dripping down into the sandwich from his greasy forehead, adding some extra moisture. I seemed to be the only one disturbed by this. My stomach turns upside down. How can basic hygiene be so completely non-existant?

An Egyptian girl, maybe about thirteen, in a canary yellow garment, has sat down oppossite and can't take her eyes off me. I don't think she has ever seen a Westerner, nor anyone with shorts. She's probably from one of the Nile villages. I try to smile at her. She returns the smile, but remains transfixed.

3:00 A.M. —The train has been standing for an hour now. There are bodies sprawled out everywhere, sleeping on the luggage racks, as well as on the nutshell- and seed-hulls-covered floor underneath the seats. Some have mouths open, and saliva is drooling down their cheeks, onto the arm-rests, and on top of other slumbering bodies; some are sleeping and *still* chewing... like camels. I cannot sleep. My legs and back hurt. I feel rotten and I'm sooo tired....

It was almost afternoon when the train stopped in Luxor. After a several-hour lull in commotion, all was full of activity again. Three backpackers boarded my carriage, which perked me up, as I was anticipating making this part of the journey alone. It was always fun meeting other travelers and exchanging stories and giving each other useful tips. Now, I had someone to talk to. Despite this, the train insanity with the relentless salesmen continued until we finally arrived at our destination in Aswan at exactly 4:00 P.M. —as scheduled.

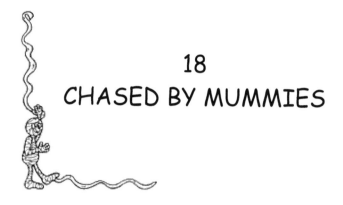

18
CHASED BY MUMMIES

First priority of the day was to find accommodation. It would soon be dark, and I was desperate to shower—to wash off the filth from the train, and get something to eat before darkness finally set in. I was now joined by two Swedish girls and a Dane I had met on the train. We checked into Ramses Hotel—impressively beautiful, airy, and with an extremely friendly proprietor, but the air-conditioning didn't work. With outdoor day temperatures soaring to 45°Celcius, I might have to spend the night in the cold shower.

Aswan is very laid back, resembling a village when compared to Cairo; even the locals are much more relaxed here, especially the very dark Nubians, who walked tall, erect, and with pride. The male population was dressed in the traditional and very comfortable-looking *djellaba*, and when clean, the white cloaks looked majestic against the Nubians' coal-black skin, making them look like royalty. The few women I saw were covered up in *their* traditional dresses—they were walking back from the markets, their baskets filled to the brim with greens, which they expertly balanced on their heads. Sudan is not so far away anymore, and I could feel that this is the gateway to the dark continent—so vast—so mysterious. The town itself is not so visually impressive, but at the same time, it was rather pleasant to take an evening stroll around the colorful markets selling all kinds of wares, fabrics, fruits, and the most amazing array of spices of every shade of brown, ochre, orange, and yellow. The spice shops were a wonder: sacks were filled to the brim, almost overflowing with probably every single spice that exists on planet Earth, and the aroma they emitted, invoked the charm and mystery of the Orient. I was transfixed by the display of colors until the owner came out and started to seduce me with samples. But I was more seduced by the adjacent mango vendor, where I bought a ridiculously large supply (disgustingly cheap), and sat down at one of the numerous coffee/smoke shops devouring them (disgustingly pig-like) with my daily fix of this delicious coffee one finds only in the Middle East. We played *sheshbesh* (backgammon), chatted, and drank more coffee, and ate more mangoes. I felt exhilarated amongst these friendly people. Aswan is a wonderful place to relax for several days without being pushed, dragged, chased by camels, and hawkers thrusting tourist junk into my face. Nobody pestered us, and the *al-ha-esh* salesman and the *bebzi* goblin were history. Now was the time to unwind, enjoy the company, and recover from that ghastly train trip.

The following afternoon, the four of us went in search of a feluca (the small sail boats used on the Nile). That wasn't so difficult: the captains were crying out for tourists. Rather than *choosing* a feluca, we looked for a captain, who did not pounce with desperation, and after sizing them up, we settled for an older, placid Egyptian who quietly sat by his feluca with content and gazed into nothingness. For a very reasonable price, we made a too short two-hour trip around lush, uninhabited small islands, dense vegetation so tightly packed, that palm trees were squeezed off the edge and forced to bow into the Nile. The weather was against us that day: the wind was too strong to continue, and our sailor was having difficulties navigating the boat: it was being blown around from all sides. There was no alternative, but to return to the mainland. Pity, the trip was much too short, but that made us even more determined to undertake a longer feluca trip.

We unanimously decided to look for a different feluca: one that would take us on a longer journey—to Edfu, about 100km north of Aswan. The three-day sailing came complete with a captain and a cook for 100 Egyptian pounds, split between the four of us. It was a definite bargain and a generous earning for the owner. But first, it was mandatory to register with the police, as was required by all foreigners. The boat was reserved for tomorrow, which gave us enough time to book a red-eye taxi (*also* for tomorrow), to drive us towards the Sudanese border to see the famous ruins of Abu Simbel. It was going to be a tough day... with the usual rush and lack of sleep. Why did I inflict such torture upon myself? Traveling was supposed to be relaxing and stress free, but the contrary was the reality. I backtracked to the market again and attacked my second bag of mangoes.

A 4:00 A.M. start was not something I wanted to make a habit of. The driver informed us it was necessary to get there before the fierce afternoon heat hit the 50°Celsius mark. The taxi was late, arriving a half hour behind schedule. The three-hour drive to Abu Simbel was tediously long and boring; nobody spoke: still in dreamland. The driver didn't stop once, but sped ahead, trying to make up for that lost half hour. By 6:30 A.M. it was daylight, and after driving two hours in darkness, I realized that I hadn't missed anything worth looking at. The landscape was totally flat, rocky, and very barren. This was a desert without any colour—just nothingness... and very bleak. We passed some snow-white skeletons lying by the road. "Camel," commented the driver, noticing our attention. Suddenly we were at Abu Simbel, and the monotonous landscape was soon forgotten upon arrival at one of the world's most splendid sights. The four figures are simply enormous, sitting on their thrones and staring out upon the Nile. The sheer size of these figures is a wonder itself, and I felt like an ant in comparison. This being mid-summer, and the temperatures rapidly soaring to over 50°Celcius, kept a lot of tourists away this time of year. Only a few taxis braved this trip—mostly with backpackers who couldn't care less what season it was. Not too far away was the border to Sudan and the border town of Wadi Halfa.

A one-hour stay here was enough. I wanted to remain longer: to gawk at this wonder; to feel it; to stroll around it; to absorb the power and immensity of these giants, but the only thing to absorb was the sickly heat. We had to leave. It was only after nine, and the temperature was intollerable —so hot, I started feeling nauseous and ended up gulping liters of water. It was even hotter than at the Dead Sea in Israel. No wonder the driver wanted a very early start. "We must go before it gets too hot," he urged.

"What? Before it gets too hot?" We stared at him goggle-eyed. What was *this* then if not hot? We gladly clambered into the air-conditioned taxi: myself, the two Swedish girls, and the Dane, and faced the long and boring drive back to Aswan. Some people fly to Abu Simbel and now I understood why.

We drove past the grinning skeleton again, mocking us. If it had thoughts, it would probably be thinking: "This is how you'll end up if you break down." We didn't break down. The taxi just purred along all the way back to Aswan.

The air-conditioning was set on the coldest setting and it was on full; nevertheless, the scorching outside temperature was creeping in, and the windows were red hot. Feeling hot myself, I absentmindedly rolled down the window a little bit and stuck my hand out. It felt like reaching into an oven. "Close the window!" yelled everyone. I did, but that brief fresh air made the temperature in the car jump by ten degrees.

We made a brief stopover at Aswan Dam and the man-made Lake Nasser. There was an entry fee to pay just for seeing the dam, and everywhere there were signs warning not to take pictures. I took out my camera to take a picture, but put it away again when I saw security police with machine guns eyeing me.

"No photo," one of them wagged his finger at me.

"No photo," I agreed.

Back in Aswan we had a couple of hours to shower, eat something, and at four o'clock, we were by the felucas, ready to begin the journey on the Nile. First, it was necessary to buy the provisions we would need for the next days, especially water—lots of water! The captain and the cook tagged along for the shopping expedition and took us to the local market. *They* actually did the shopping, buying whatever foods we needed for the trip—most of the ingredients consisting of fresh produce. We simply paid for whatever they chose. The entire provisions cost a mere few dollars. We all had bags to carry, including a large refreshing watermelon, *and* I made sure that a (very) large bagful of mangoes came along on the trip. All this food was for six people. The water was the heaviest, but it would not last the three days—we would have to stop on the way somewhere.

About 5:30 P.M. we hit the road... er, I mean... the river—and we were off. The wind was good as we left Aswan and sailed north on the Nile. The heat was slightly more tolerable on the water where the gentle breeze gave us some respite. Our captain was a very dark Nubian with the whitest teeth I have seen in Egypt. He wasn't wearing a *djellaba*, but a pair of shorts and a very yellow T-shirt, which made him look like a banana. He was such an expert at sailing, making it look very simple as he manouvered the boat with utmost confidence and expertise, and much better at his job than the guy we had yesterday, who hadn't yet mastered the art of sailing unless the weather conditions were optimal. This captain was the adventurous type and I felt very safe in his hands. After a couple of hours, we made a stop to brew some tea. The other Egyptian was the cook, the tea maker, and the general slave; dressed in a tatty, worn-out and stained white garment that looked more like a bed sheet. He was also a pest, bothering the girls at times, but I couldn't blame him, as the Swedish girls were, well... *very* Swedish! The captain barked at him whenever he buzzed around the girls too much, or he gave him a chore to do. He was a good cook though, as he conjured some very decent food with all that green stuff we had bought, together with a tasty, spicy sauce and rice. Blankets were layed out on the feluca, making it comfortable for us to sit on as we sailed into the sunset, as if in a dream, and when darkness descended, the moon cast silvery light upon the Nile.

It was after midnight when we made a stop at one of the villages, where the captain and cook would spend the night. We four, would sleep on the boat. It was a mystical and beautiful night, heralded by the trillions of stars that were out in full force; it was very warm; all was perfect. It had been a long day, and I dozed off to sleep to the sounds of crackling fire, drums, and laughter coming from the riverside village.

Daylight. There were children at the banks of the river looking into our boat. Nearby, the girls and women folk were doing their early morning laundry and dish washing in the river. They smiled and waved at us when our heads appeared over the edge of the feluca. Pots, pans, plates, clothes, and even rugs were getting a good scrubbing, but *we* were the source of amusement here, getting out of bed Western style and brushing our teeth.

There were people jumping into the river and swimming. I was tempted to join them, but the Nile is one of the most polluted rivers in the world. Swimming in this can cause blindness later on in life, as the parasite bilharzia is prevalent in these waters—and can enter the body through the skin. This parasite is carried by snails, and the second-worst enemy in the country after malaria. Other nasty parasites abound in these waters, and it's not surprising to see so many people with eye diseases and deformities in the Nile villages; even some of the animals were blind or had milky eyes.

The Nile was also the village toilet, which was combined with the dish washing and laundry. We also made stops by river banks for relieving ourselves. Everything would float by, but the locals were oblivious to this. They drank directly out of the Nile, not comprehending the fact that we drank water from a bottle, which we paid money for. For them, that was a waste.

"Drink river... river very good," said one of the villagers with the white glaze already covering his eyes. In a few years he would be totally blind.

"Bottle water clean," I answered, at which he sneered. The cook did use the Nile for cooking with, also for making tea, but I guess the boiling would kill off any parasites in it.

Nearby sits the Temple of Kom Ombo—built by the pharaohs, and still an imposing sight on the banks of the river. This was also the town of Kom Ombo, where we made a stop to buy some more water. We already ran out on our first day. Our throats were permanently parched and we were losing a lot of liquid. The temperatures were in the mid-forties, and we weren't even sweating: any moisture instantly evaporated. We could not keep up with the replenishment.

What a seedy, horrible, and unfriendly place this was. This town reminded me of Rafiah in the Gaza Strip. The ragged people were also wrapped up in bed linen, and followed us around while jeering at the Swedish girls who stuck out like polar bears in a desert. It wasn't possible to buy anything, not even fruit. Prices were suddenly marked up to a ridiculous amount. Once again, we were the center of attention, as gawking, frowning groups of cheats shadowed our every movement. The taxi driver even charged an exhorbitant fare for the one-minute ride than was originally agreed on. This place was a nightmare; surely, it must be the worst place in the world. Finding a place that sold water was an impossible task—nobody sold it. Of course not—no tourists came here, so why should they? These people don't buy water: they are quite happy to drink out of the river. Getting back to the boat was more trouble than I bargained for: the two-kilometer taxi ride should have cost about fifteen piastres (about seven cents), but these antagonizing drivers were determined to slaughter these four cash-cows from the West—five pounds for the return trip. Not yielding to their bilking, we gave them a disgusting look and made a show of walking back to the boat... and strode away. One driver, who stood out from the mob, suddenly came to a snap conclusion as he envisioned his day's earnings walking away: he offered to drive us back for twenty piastres, which was acceptable..., but still a rip-off. Overcome with relief to have escaped hell and back on the boat, we urged the snoozing captain to shake his sea-legs.

On we sailed, without water alas, but after a couple of hours an island appeared on the Nile. Here, we could buy a whole boxful. I could hardly wait. The heat was intense and my tongue was as dry as sandpaper, and the Nile looked *so* delicious. The view from the river was phenomenal —it was the utmost perception of paradise. There was no sign of modern civilization, and the villagers by the river continued to live as they had done since the days when the pharaohs' workforce passed through with giant stones for building their gargantuan temples. This is how I always imagined Egypt—sailing on the peaceful and slow-moving Nile and witnessing the everyday life of the villagers from a distance. From this viewpoint, it made those places look like heaven, but I had no illusions, and knew very well that close up, it was sheer hell—the filth, the stench, and extreme chaos.

The densely-packed vegetation along the banks of the river really did look inviting, and I had a sudden urge to plunge into it. Britta and Anja, the two Swedish girls, felt the same way, as they sprawled out on the boat like caught fish that have given up all struggle—ready to die—they were beyond suffering—such heat. The paradise island with enormous palms was our savior—the place that was well-stocked with boxes of water, and I noticed other felucas with foreigners stopping to buy this life-saving fluid, too. Whoever had the smart idea to open up a stall selling this wonderful drink on an island on the Nile, must have been brilliant—and also rich by now.

We continued sailing and joined up with other felucas heading north. By this time, everybody was racing each other. This was so great! I wished it would never stop... just lazing around on the boat and enjoying the scenery. Captain Banana was having a whale of a time, as he fought with the ropes and sails to make the feluca move faster, skimming along the river, desperately trying to win the race. We all cheered him along. Tomorrow, all this would be over—what a pity.

We sailed on well into the night until the boat stopped at another village. Our captain seemed to be famous here: all the villagers came out to greet him. They clambered onto the boat and started brewing tea, which we also enjoyed, drinking several glasses of it. Our feluca had now become the village gathering point for night entertainment as more people came on board. They all chattered in Arabic, and not a word of English was spoken. The villagers barely took notice of the four Westerners, and didn't make an attempt to involve us in their get-together. It was all men—women did not participate in such gatherings, so the presense of the Swedish girls must have irritated them: infringing upon their very traditional customs. Females had no place in the male circle—no exceptions. The four of us stayed together and had our own gathering and giggling, also ignoring the villagers. We tried to sleep—impossible: the shouting and laughter continued late. I felt annoyed, as I was looking forward to the night sounds of the river and the insects, but now I had to listen to noisy Arabic.

The relentless chatter and tea making went on most of the night until early hours of the morning. I couldn't sleep, and it was hot—roasting —unbearable, without a breath of wind to relieve the oppressive heat, and I was tempted to peel off my skin. Sweat poured off every part of my body, and in the darkness, mosquitoes attacked with vampire-like ferocity. Giving up on sleep, I got up and sat on the deck and gazed at the stars, which shone like trillions of torches. It was no wonder that the ancient Egyptians' lives evolved so much around the heavenly bodies. Above me were tall, frilly, leaning, silhouetted palm trees, completely still in the breezeless night. Some of them lay horizontal, but continued to grow. I relaxed a little bit and then didn't mind the visitors anymore. One of the villagers noticed that I wasn't sleeping.

"You drink tea?" He offered.

"Yes, *shokran*," I responded.

"Egypt beautiful, yes?" He asked hopefully, handing me a glass of tea.

"Yes, Egypt very beautiful," I acknowledged honestly—especially here; this place; this night. I went back to my blanket, suddenly feeling very tired. The Scandinavian trio were already fast asleep.

We didn't leave until late morning after our breakfast of pita bread, goat's cheese, boiled eggs, and olives. The usual sweet black tea (boiled to death) accompanied it. The few hours of sailing took us to our final stop— Edfu. It was another place from hell, and not meant for lingering. We were soon surrounded by the locals trying to coax us into taking the horse and cart the short distance into town. All were quoting different fares, competing with each other and becoming angry, finally falling into a heated exchange amongst themselves We were speechless, ogling with disbelief at this commotion we had caused, and even before we had a chance to say anything. The result was, being cheats and imbeciles, neither of them benefited from the outcome, as any potential business hightailed towards a row of waiting taxis while they were still arguing. We quickly jumped into one that took us all the way to Luxor, putting as much milage as possible behind this awful place.

According to the guide book, it is possible to use the amenities of the big luxury hotels without being a guest. The hotel swimming pool was what we were all craving for. After a wonderfully soothing cold shower, we dived into the pool, spending a good couple of hours soaking up the water like dehydrated crustations. Clean and fresh again, I had to find a hotel for the night. It was already fairly late, so I didn't have time to pick and choose. For about two dollars, I ended up in the sleaziest and dirtiest place I have ever seen. Only after checking in did I realize that this was not the Hilton. I simply dumped my luggage in the room without giving it a second glance, then went out to join my friends at the restaurant. It was time to say goodbye to them. Having already seen Luxor, they were taking the train back to Cairo. I was remaining here for a few days to see the famous temples and ancient burial chambers.

We stayed in the restaurant: eating, laughing, and reliving the feluca journey. Just before midnight, I walked them to the station and saw the Scandinavians hop onto the Cairo-bound train. I strolled back to the seedy hotel. Luxor was drowning in dust. It was flying everywhere, covering my body top to bottom, so even after the earlier shower and swim, I was dirty again. The shower in the hotel didn't work—typical. The toilet didn't flush —typical... and the walls were smeared with secretions. I happened to notice that the only residents in this hotel were Egyptians who were not here to see temples and tombs. So what was this place? I had no idea where I ended up, and I did not feel safe until I double-locked the door, bolted it, and put the back of the chair under the handle, *then* I could sleep in peace... but, the bed stank... bad, so I didn't use any of the supplied blankets (which were still sweaty from previous guests), but stayed on top of my sleeping bag.

I slept like a log, but as soon as my eyes flickered open, I sprang out of bed and made a mad dash for the door to get out of this shit hole. *That* was priority, before even the morning ritual of showering and teeth brushing; there wasn't any water here anyway, but the other guests were not concerned about this little issue—maybe they didn't need water. I found a very nice place called the Sinai Hotel. It was clean, with showers and a friendly manager; it even had a nice cool courtyard with benches and potted plants. My original intention to stay in Luxor for a couple of weeks required a change in agenda. Luxor was hell. I vowed to see the main attractions, then leave. The dust was unbearable, covering everything in sight. Eating outside was impossible, too—every time a car or an animal rode past, a cloud of dust would go up into the air and descend upon the plate of food. It was difficult to breathe: the dirt found its way into the mouth, and deep inside the ears. Two showers a day didn't help. What a filthy little town this was, and not to mention the smell of urine everywhere. All this, combined with temperatures soaring well above 40°Celsius, was not a place to hang around for too long. I soon hunkered down to making taxi arrangements from the hotel lobby—to see the Valley of the Kings. This is what I came for, and the sooner I saw it, the sooner I could flee this city of dust.

Luxor Temple was nearby my hotel; although a ruin, it continued to dwarf the neighborhood houses, and the walls and columns that had tumbled to the ground still retained the ancient artwork. Statues that depicted pharaohs welcomed the visitor at the entrance, followed by the Avenue of Sphinxes, which line up on the left and right as one walks between them to the main part of the temple. I spent several worthwhile hours here, marvelling at the sheer size of this temple with its giant columns; every part of it covered in hieroglyphics from ground to ceiling. This was the best time to tour the grounds, as there were no tourists venturing out in the mid-afternoon heat. I had the place practically to myself, and it was perfect for taking pictures without waiting for anyone to move out of the way.

At 6:00 A.M., the taxi I had arranged the day before, was waiting. A German couple, who also wondered into this hotel, shared the ride and accompanied me on the trip. First, we had to cross the river on one of the barges. On the other side is the location of ancient Thebes, where hundreds of tombs are found in the Valley of the Kings. This is where all the famous mummified pharaohs had been discovered; rooms drowning in all imaginable treasures... or so they should have been: tomb robbers had plundered them first, even before the Romans appeared on the scene.

In Thebes there were large crowds gathering, and I realized that today was market day, and we had wandered into it by chance. The market retained its traditional ambience, but different to the Rafiah market in the Gaza Strip. This one was richer, and mostly fruits and vegetables were being traded. It was void of men. Chador-clad women did the shopping here, some balancing food-filled baskets on their heads like in Africa. But this *was* Africa! The Bedouin women were all covered up in black from head to foot, and where the eyes should have been, was a black netting. Not a millimeter of flesh was exposed anywhere. These women were completely oblivious to our presense and simply ignored us, even when I took out my camera to take some terrific pictures.

It was about ten kilometers to the tombs, so a taxi was necessary to cover all the sites that were sprawled out over an immense area. The heat made it impossible to walk in the valley, which was surrounded on all sides by crumbling, brittle, sun-baked hills, many of which had gaping holes in them. They were amongst the thousands of other caves and shafts that still remained hidden in these hills, still awaiting discovery. In this scorching heat, it was even too far to cover on bicycle, which I was thinking of renting for a day. Upon arrival, we found a lot of the tombs to be closed. One especially worth seeing was the tomb of Seti II, but it was also closed —for renovations: the roof was collapsing after over 3,000 years of being intact. Why today?

The guards, who supposedly guarded the tombs, were a nasty and mean bunch of people, prohibiting any photos to be taken. At some tombs, cameras were not even permitted inside. They had to be left outside on the wall, where the guard would keep an eye on them. Such a pity. The artwork on the walls and ceilings was astounding and amazingly well preserved after eons of time. In the long, narrow passages, the guards used a mirror and silver foil to reflect daylight to illuminate the decorations on the tombs' walls. Photography was forbidden because the cameras' flash would cause discoloration, and in time, destroy the light-sensitive hieroglyphics. I was alone in the tomb with the German couple after the other few tourists had left, when the guard comes inside with our cameras and speaks in a hushed tone. "Pssst... you want bicture?"

"But you said no pictures allowed," I commented.

He grinned, revealing his rotten teeth. "You give me ten bound, you can take bicture."

"Ten pounds?" We all blurted out.

"Ten bound, one bicture," he added, looking back nervously.

"No way!"

"Okay, okay... five bound."

"Three pounds and many pictures," we started to haggle, but approaching voices made the nervous guard rush back outside.

"Bictures forbidden in tomb. Leave camra here blees," we heard him tell the next group of people, but by this time, we were out of the claustrophobic tomb, picked up our cameras from the guard, and continued to the next one—to the tomb of Tutankhamun. Grave robbers had missed this one.

"Bictures forbidden in..." he started, but we interrupted him.

"Yeah, yeah, we know," said the German as we left our cameras with the guard. This is the famous tomb everybody who comes to Luxor makes a point of seeing. From the top, the low, sloping shaft inclines and takes you to the site Carter wandered into back in 1922, making the greatest discovery in Egyptology. Now, all the "wonderful things" are gone—they are in the Cairo museum, but the intricate paintings and hieroglyphics remain on the tombs' walls and ceilings.

One other tomb went down 300 meters, making me feel very nervous; claustrophobic; so deep underground and very spooky. A huge painting of Anubis and Horus were keeping a watchful eye on us and making sure that we didn't disturb anything—or that was the feeling I perceived. It is extremely humid and sticky in these long, deep shafts, and exiting outside again is a shock every time—from the heat and sudden brightness. Most of the shafts are low, so one must stoop while walking. The whole tomb business was making me giddy; it was simply exhausting visiting them, especially for me, as today my stomach put a damper on all the excitement. I think I was coming down with "pharaoh's revenge" — probably from swallowing all the dust in Luxor, which always ended up as seasoning on top of the food. Up and down, up and down; my head was spinning, probably dehydrating, too. Drinking constantly didn't help. The body lost everything immediately and I never needed to pee. So many tombs, and each one of them is different from the previous one—custom made for a specific pharaoh. Some paintings showed a pharaoh's life; some showed the builders at work; another showed a typical village life among ordinary people; so much history, and too much to take in. It was mindboggling.

Our taxi driver had been waiting several hours now. He must have roasted in the car, and he continued to roast as we attempted to see the Valley of the Queens, but a large part of it was closed—restoration in progress. What was left, paled in comparison to the Valley of the Kings. I didn't want to linger here, but went on to see Halmepsut Temple, struggling to walk a mere hundred meters. It must have been well over 50°Celsius— just in the shade, but there *was* no shade anywhere... and I didn't even want to imagine *how* hot it was in the sun. I already looked like a chocolate bar, so even this intense sun didn't give me a sunburn. The Germans, on the other hand, still had their fresh-out-of-Europe skin, and I was sure this must have been torture for them. The guy's face was burnt and looked painful; the girl's nose started to blister; they were both constantly applying sun-cream, but I wasn't sure if it helped. No lotion in the world would prevent burns in temperatures such as this.

Halmepsut Temple was closed (my luck) due to renovation, so we could only view the exterior—we had bought the tickets for nothing! They could have told us at the ticket office that certain places were closed, but no, they wanted our money—anything to extract cash from tourists. Nevertheless, the things we saw here (which were open) were well worth it. Foreign tourists who come here normally have to spend thousands to make this once-in-a-lifetime trip. I was living quite well on about eight dollars a day, including decent accomodation, and all the taxi/train/feluca rides.

We took the barge back across the river and walked back to the hotel, where a wonderful cold shower was waiting. My stomach was feeling pretty bad now. I decided to rest for the remainder of the day and not eat anything. The Germans and I rented bicycles for tomorrow, and I was hoping not to get sick. If I did, this was a fine hotel to suffer in.

There were still many things left to see in Luxor, but this time it was on bicycle. For about a dollar for a day's rental, it was too good to refuse, even in this heat. Cycling in Egypt? In summer? Well, why not. Adventure! So, back across the river we went the next morning, taking the usual barge. My stomach was behaving for the moment, and I took advantage of the situation before it decided to do something else. There were still some tombs and temples I specifically wanted to see on this side of the river; luckily, these were all located nearby, so cycling wasn't too overexerting. In this area, several small villages dot the parched landscape with small, square, ramshackle housing, where the concrete walls have long since crumbled and have been patched up with corrugated iron and cardboard. The gravel road meandered between those villages; it was our route, and where we fell prey to all the children in the neighborhood who came out chasing after us. "Meester, give me *baksheesh*," they demanded aggressively.

When in Egypt, I was told, there is one important word one should know in Arabic, maybe even the only useful one—that is, *Imshi*, which means, get lost or go away. I tried this word out. "IMSHI!" I screamed at them. It worked like a repellant. The childern hesitated then, taken aback and somewhat confused. We rode on into another mob.

"*Baksheesh, baksheesh*," they came after us.

"IMSHI!" Repel. Now others came to us with tourist junk, practically throwing them into our faces and quoting different prices.

"Sbecial brice for you. Cheab."

"Very old... from tomb... cheab money."

"You buy ala... basta spheeenx meester."

"Scarrrab beeetle one bound... you buy... bring luck."

"NO! IMSHI!" Further down the road we were acosted by a group of young girls, all carrying something in their hands. Oh no, what were *they* selling? We had to stop: they were pulling our arms and handlebars, then I saw what they had in their hands—home-made doll mummies. I had to laugh. They looked so funny. I would have bought one just for the sake of it, but I really didn't want to carry anything extra around. Anyway, what was I going to do with a doll mummy? I think the Germans should have bought one, as they were going back to Germany afterwards, and this was something you would never see anywhere again. I felt sorry for the girls, so I didn't use that *imshi* word, but smiled and rode on, leaving the girls looking forlorn.

Everywhere, the children were swarming like flies, the boys being quite aggressive. I just wanted to kick them away as we rode past, and I made sure we were riding as fast as possible. They came to an abrupt stop. We were inside the temple grounds and the guards would not let them through. At least they served one good purpose, but that swarm would be waiting for us with re-enforcements upon exit, and I was not looking forward to that.

At one of the tombs, the path became too steep for the bicycles, and we were forced to leave them at the bottom of the hill. Locks were included in the bike rental and we made sure to use them, so they should be safe enough. There was a village at this spot, and not a good place to leave a bicycle, but we had no choice. As soon as we stopped, a teenage boy suddenly appeared. "I will guard your bicycles," he insisted.

"Go away, we have locks. They don't need guarding," we told him. An older character appeared on the scene and offered to show us around the tomb. "Oh, go away. Not interested." We had a guide book with explanations and a map of the area with more information than this character could imagine. Stubbornly, he followed us around outside, yapping incessantly, not leaving us alone. He then demanded money for giving us a guided tour. We were speechless. Of course, he didn't get a penny. "GO AWAY—IMSHI!" And I think he got the message—cursing and skulking away. Arriving at the tomb opening, the usual guard was sitting there collecting cameras.

"Bictures forbidden in tomb. Leave camra here blees." The same line. We were alone here for the moment.

"We take pictures. How much money? How much *baksheesh*?" We tested him for the fun of it.

"Bictures forbidden. Ten bounds."

"Three pounds for pictures."

"Bictures forbidden," he repeated. "Five bounds." This was quite fun.

"Three pounds," and we showed him three notes. He looked around suspiciously and clasped the three pounds with his grimy hands and black fingernails, whereas he turned his back on us as we proceeded down to the tomb with our cameras. These hieroglyphics and other paintings were not more impressive than the ones outside on temples, and with a flash it would reflect anyway, so I didn't bother with taking any photos. The Germans had to get their money's worth though, and took several. As we exited, the guard was still perched there at the entrance. "Shokran," (thank-you) we said to him. He just lazily raised his hand in a farewell gesture.

Back down the hill by the bicycles a small crowd had gathered. The girls selling doll mummies were there—about a dozen of them, dressed in colorful garments. The boy who offered to guard our bicycles was there, too, and when he saw us, demanded money for looking after the bicycles. "Get lost, we said no," but he hung around. Doll mummies were being thrust into our faces. This was a nightmare. The sooner we were back on our bicycles, the better..., but there was a problem: The German guy's bicycle had a flat tire, and *what* a coincidense that a puncture repairman suddenly showed up out of the blue and offered to mend the tire for a small fee. "GO AWAY!" What a neat trick. They must think everybody is stupid except them. The German said he would rather ride on a flat tire than give money to these beasts.

So we rode off on a flat tire, trying to get as far away from those pests as possible. The dozen girls were running after us with mummies in their hands. I looked back hesitatingly, and in the shimmering heat and scuffed up dirt, saw the mummies chasing after us. The girls were still waving them in the air. "Mummies, mummies, mummies," we heard their squeels diminish as we hastily pedalled away and didn't slow down until the mummies were well behind. We finally took a break at the Memnon Colossi —two gigantic statues that are a remainder of an ancient mortuary temple. The rest had been wiped out by floods centuries ago. It was peaceful here; no mummies; no scarab beetles; no old stutues; nobody harassing us, and we drank litres of water under the fierce, scorching Egyptian sun.

Back in the hotel, I freshened up and cycled off again to see Karnak Temple, which was only three kilometers away. The size of the temple is unbelievable—built for giants and constructed to perfection, not to mention the intricate hieroglyphics which adorned every single column that was a duplicate copy of the other one. The columns are so colossal that they emitted an eerie ambience. Everything was built to precision— probably exact to the millimeter. The sphinxes, pharaoh statues, and other enormous colossi adorned the entrance like in Luxor Temple. The statues and the temple itself made me feel small and insignificant, overpowering me with its austere gigantum, thus the feeling that this was not meant for ordinary human beings, but giants who had ruled the land in ancient times. These architectural wonders will remain for centuries to come, while the hideous modern-day dwellings were already crumbling.

Luxor is not an ideal place to stay if you have seen everything you want to see. The people here are aggressive and quite nasty, preying on tourists in their desperation to devour the contents of their wallets. There is no repect towards foreigners here: as long as you spend your money, you become "my friend," with smiles; otherwise, if you're a cheap-skate, nobody wants to know you. I was the latter, and did not fit into the "my friend" category. I was not sorry to leave Luxor the next morning, taking the first bus out (at 6:00 A.M.) towards Hurghada, the Red Sea resort.

The journey was not at all interesting, just the usual bland, featureless desert landscape. It was a hot and boring journey all the way to the resort until the the dark blue of the Red Sea came into view. I immediately inquired about boats to Sharm-El-Sheikh at the southern point of the Sinai, but there weren't any—not till Sunday, and today was Thursday. I had no choice but to make the journey overland by bus, because on Sunday, the ferry to Greece leaves from Israel, and I wanted to be on it. It was too late to leave Hurghada today, therefore, I checked in at a pleasant hotel for the night. This was not a bad place; extremely pleasant after Luxor, and also quite different from other places I had seen in Egypt. It was more than pleasant—very, very nice, in fact! I liked it. I *really* liked it. It is also worth pointing out that there was an absence of garbage in this town, unlike other towns and cities, where mounds of rubbish is a part of life. There were no beggars here, nobody demanding *baksheesh*, and no doll mummies. This place had the atmosphere of a seaside resort and it had a cozy feel to it. But it was still under construction, destined for mass tourism in the future, like the seaside villages in Turkey. The absence of dust made it especially attractive, and the food could be enjoyed without that extra, unwanted seasoning. My stomach problem was not as bad as the time I had exploded in Turkey, but the discomfort continued for several days.

Again at 6:00 A.M. I was on the bus—to Suez. I was one of the unlucky ones left standing, and then ended up sitting on the filthy floor when my legs were about to give way. It was eight hours to Suez, and I was beginning to have doubts whether I would survive this hell. The bus was packed, and loud Arabic pop music was belching out of the speakers. Egyptian bus drivers had not yet figured out the uses of volume control. Music was either off or turned up to maximum to the most excrutiantingly distorted crescendo—popping eardrums, then working on the explosion of the head. The pounding could also be felt in the vibrations of the teeth, threatening to jump out.

The scenery had now changed, actually becoming interesting and even dramatic with the sudden appearance of mountains. We were approaching the Sinai peninsula, and then, while I was gawking at the fantastic landscape, there was a rude interruption of this paradise when suddenly Suez came into view. I was appalled by the sight of this grotesque city. This intruding abomination was submerged in hideous industrial structures with smoke billowing out of every chimney. It was not the usual grey smoke, but shades of yellow and light orange shot up towards the sky, looking like an erupting volcano. What on earth was burning there? Before entering Suez, I remembered the sky being blue, but inside the city, there was no sky to be seen, and the sun was totally obscured. The air (there was no air) smelled and tasted of sulphur and weighed down heavily upon the lungs, causing a burning sensation after a while. Oil refineries dotted the shores, and flaming oil rigs spewed out their share of pollution in the distance. I was in hell. I could not stay here in this place, but hoped that there was a bus to the Sinai. What if there wasn't one? I would be stuck then.

Bus schedules and travel information were non existant. I was the only foreigner in this sleazy place, made very obvious by the frowning locals giving me menacing looks; the same locals I had seen in the Khan-El-Khalili market in Cairo—I was convinced. The Koran prayers were being recited over the loudspeaker. "Allahu... aqbar... " and the call to prayer went on and on, "woe to the unbelievers...," but the sound I grew to love, felt out of place here. It felt more like a threat instead of the usual inducement of calm and mysticism... and I was far from calm, as I frantically searched for an escape. The bus I arrived on was the only vehicle at the station, and it was continuing onto Cairo after the prayers had ended. As a snap decision, I hopped back on and claimed a seat this time—it would be several more hours driving.

The Cairo I had gotten to know was not the same Cairo I came back to—it was like entering through the pearly gates. After Suez, this was heaven. I immediately proceeded to Tahrir Square to inquire about buses to Israel tomorrow. There was no information—anywhere! —Everything was closed. Time was running... and so was I, desperately looking for a taxi. One came my way and I hailed it down. Naturally, the driver overcharged me, but I didn't care: I was in a mad rush to get to the Sinai Bus Company a few kilometers further. To make it to Haifa by Sunday, it was imperative that I leave tonight... and luck was on my side—there was a bus leaving for Sharm-El-Sheikh at midnight.

With only six hours to wait, I went back out to find some food (chicken and a bag of mangoes), and then it was dark outside suddenly. I walked the streets to find a coffee place—one is never far away, and sure enough, after a few minutes, the familiar sight of tables, chairs, and Egyptians (men only) sucking water pipes, seductively materialized around the next block. "Welcome," and the waiter wiped down my table. I spent a couple of hours in this café, pigging myself on the mangoes and replenishing my loss of caffeine while snacking on my favourite honey-dripping Arab cakes. This was a great place to write up my travel notes. (Someone told me, before coming to Egypt: "You either love Egypt or hate it." I decided to love it. At first, I wasn't so sure, but the longer you stay in Egypt, it grows on you. I vowed to return and see the oases in the Western Desert.) Despite being the only non-Egyptian in this café, I felt very welcome amongst these friendly people. Nobody bothered me, and the waiter made sure I didn't get thirsty. The muezzin was calling the believers to prayer again, but nobody took notice, so I guessed I was amongst the non-believers. I felt content and relaxed.

The bus to the Sinai was impressively modern this time—clean and air-conditioned. Many tourists—foreign and local, were going to spend their holidays at the Red Sea resort of Sharm-El-Sheikh. I was merely flying through all the way to the border. The Egyptians on the bus were not really dressed for the beach *or* the desert, wearing black, flat, and well polished office shoes, pressed trousers, a buttoned shirt and tie. They looked as if they were going to a business conference, rather than spending time on the beach. I was so confused and even asked a couple of them. "Are you going to a business meeting?"

"No, no. We are on holiday. We are staying in Sharm-El-Sheikh. Are you going there, too?"

"No, I'm going to Israel."

"We want to go to Israel some day. I heard it's very beautiful. Maybe next year." Their English was excellent, and they were more than happy to talk to me. I noticed that *all* the Egyptians on the bus were educated and neatly groomed. We, the foreigners, wore shorts, sneakers, and soiled T-shirts. There was also an absense of women amongst the Egyptians—men only.

"Where are the women?" I asked them, genuinely curious. They laughed.

"Egyptian girls cannot go to the beach. They stay at home and wait for their husbands." Obviously, the men were hoping to charm some blonde, Western female out there.

Once again, all night, the music was blaring and my head was pounding—maybe from all the coffee, too. Sometime at dawn, we arrived in Sharm-El-Sheikh, where all the very excited Egyptians clambered off, but I remained on the bus and proceeded to Dahab. From there it was a few more hours to the Israeli border.

Leaving Egypt was easy and straightforward: they even forgot to collect the ten-pound border exit tax, so inefficient they are. Entering Israel was an entirely different procedure. I already knew what to expect, and was ready for the interrogation. Here, the Israelis really make you feel shit with their ridiculous questions and rudeness. They seem to be extra harsh towards anyone who had visited Egypt, convinced that someone there had used a tourist for smuggling terrorist materials, or passing on a letter to some PLO organization.

"Why did you go to Egypt? Who did you speak to? Did anyone give you a letter to send? Who did you meet? Where did you stay? Do you know anybody there? Where did you get that plastic bag from? Do you know why we are asking you this?"

Yes, because you've nothing better to do and you're board to death, I wanted to say, but I simply said, "No."

"Good, you can go," then they attacked the next terrified backpacker.

Back in Israel, I bought a ticket for the midnight bus to Tel Aviv (I am doomed with midnight buses), then spent the day in Eilat. While there, I bumped into my old host family I had worked for at Moshav Sde Avraham, suddenly envisioning mountains of flowers. They were overjoyed to see me again and insisted taking me out to a restaurant. In the evening, I bid this nice, hospitable family farewell and headed to the bus station, still with plenty of time to kill, so I read my book.

I met a Frenchman who was also heading to Greece via Haifa. He happened to know the same people as I did at Momo's hostel in Tel Aviv. We both took the midnight Tel Aviv bus, arriving at dawn. There is nothing worse than the bus arriving at a destination at the same time as birds wake up. The body is still in slumber mode, being deprived of any real sleep; just some dozing here and there, with the usual disturbing awakenings to pick up other passengers at intermittent bus stations. We headed to the beach as everything else was still closed; also, they had real bathrooms where we could clean ourselves up a little. After Egypt, these public bathrooms were a luxury. The Frenchman wanted to visit Momo's hostel for some reason, so I went along with him. He was known there by all, but I was also recognized as the frequent visitor. We stayed there for breakfast and to exchange stories with the people we knew, and catch up on the latest news on who went where.

"Is Germany still here?" I asked, looking around.

"No, he went back to Germany. He lost a lot of weight."

"Oh, what a shame. He was funny."

19
NEW DESTINATIONS

The Greek ferry was making a short stopover in Limassol, Cyprus; enough time to go ashore for some breakfast. I was with the Frenchman. Hoping to find work, he disembarked in Crete the next day while I continued overnight to Athens

I had no plans and no particular destination in mind; even though I was traveling solo, I didn't feel lonely, knowing that before long, another globetrotter would join me in the coming days or weeks ahead. But I *wanted* to be alone for now, to sit in the bar and drink the tasty, ice-cold *Amstel* beer, read my book, and continue writing my travel journal. My mind was at ease, and a feeling of contentment transcended upon me, but also an uncanny feeling that the greatest adventures were about to begin. It had been three and a half years since I first left England, and the Middle East had grown on me during that time—I loved the nature, the desert wilderness, the food, the lifestyle, the history, the temples, the ruins, etc, etc, etc, and oh! —the camels, of course. But it was time to explore new destinations—there were many more I would fall in love with, not to mention the characters I would meet. Traveling had taught me not to get too close to people; simply enjoy their company for a short time: this made parting somewhat less heartbreaking.

Pireaus, the port nearby Athens was the next and final stop. Being a travel hub, it is one of the cheapest places to fly from, and the city is well known for its numerous discount travel agencies that deal with practically every airline in the world. This catered well for travelers on-the-cheap. I would see which destination appealed to me and spontaneously choose a spot on the globe to fly to. South America was not on my priority list anymore—I couldn't explain why.

I left the bar and made myself comfortable on the deck, ready for the dawn arrival. It came sooner than it should have, as the rude awakening of the ship's horn blasted my eardrums once more—they had just recovered from the Egyptian buses. The ship's crew obviously got a kick out of this, and I wondered how many passengers ended up with a heart attack after this wake-up call.

Sea haze and smog enveloped Athens on the horizon. I gazed at the distant port of entry and thought about the first time I had left England several years ago, and how nervous I had been. It was a time when I was awestruck by people who had been traveling for a great length of time. Now I was one of them—a seasoned traveler, dauntlessly venturing into the unknown, in the hands of fate. I knew I could confidently go anywhere in the world now... but where?

I smiled to myself while reminiscing the past few years. The recent trip to Egypt already seemed far away; those girls chasing me with their mummy dolls; the filthy (bebzi) goblin on the hideous train, and that memorable feluca ride on the Nile. I often thought about the old lady I had met in the Troodos Mountains in Cyprus (the name had already faded)— she must be 75 or 76 by now. Was she still on the road? Turkey sprang to my mind; Sally clobbering that wretched demon dog, and the worst diarrhea I ever had—saved by Lomotil tablets. I continued to keep in touch with Sally—she was still in England, but not doing anything special. Tamar also kept in touch with me... excitedly letting me know that she was getting married, having met her future husband while on duty. Funny how things work out! I wondered where all my friends from Crete had ended up? — The beach parties; the noisy crowd in the restaurant with the frowning waiter... and whatever happened to those German hippies? Did they ever reach Goa? I recalled the day when I was walking down the mountain in total darkness and heavy rain, together with the gorgeous Katrina, as we huddled together to keep warm—that was such a perfect day. The Dead Sea area and the panoramic views from Masada were something unforgettable, especially the night I spent on top with my friends—so long ago. Also unforgettable was the hike up to Mt. Sinai, and lounging on the

Red Sea beach with Bedouins while being observed by their camels. Cow #166 sprang to my mind—maybe it had long since been transformed to a steak. Had the treasure hunters from Avdat made any historical discoveries? The wolves on Moshav Faran were probably still prowling for free water by chewing up irrigation pipes. I wondered if Fatma came back to work with the flowers again, or is she now married and has to stay home as a dutiful wife? Jericho would always carry positive memories for me, despite the uprising—the great evening I had spent there in the café with Dirk, playing backgammon. That was quite a journey in that Fiat Uno, which was able to survive the sand storm... and the crazy ostrich! I laughed when I remembered the first camel I had seen in Be'er Sheva, and I wasn't even allowed to take a picture. But my mind went back to the first kibbutz when I was dreading the factory, but it turned out to be fun after all. Was Schlomo still walking around with that spanner and making adjustments? I never did find out what crawled into my mouth that time in the Golan Heights. I laughed when I recalled how I looked with a crooked mouth. The woman on the bus, whose pullover I destroyed, was now a hilarious story. Did she ever forgive me? Most likely not. I couldn't suppress my laughter any longer when I replayed that embarrassing scene in my head— and the mental image of my falling out of the taxi in Egypt while chasing camels... but I *did* get that picture!

All those places will still be there, but not the people who had influenced my life, and I missed them tremendously. The world is a wonderland with adventures awaiting beyond every horizon, and that is what gave me the impulse to continue traveling—to see more—to see the rest of the world. Who will I meet? Where will I be tomorrow? Which country will I end up in next week? I had absoloutely no idea—I was now chasing those horizons, wondering where they would lead.

An announcement in Greek and English informed the passengers to prepare for disembarkation.

ABOUT THE AUTHOR

John Babicz was born in Leeds, England... a country he abandoned for the lust of the world. After spending several years in Israel and backpacking through some amazing places on our beautiful planet, he settled down in Essen, Germany. There, he found his calling as a Language Instructor, where he tortured his students with English and tea. He presently lives, together with his wife and two daughters, in Pennsylvania, USA, and, let it be known, he is no longer stalking camels, but pursuing the completion of his second book.

Made in the USA
Charleston, SC
10 December 2013